WOMAN, MAN, AND GOD IN MODERN ISLAM

Woman, Man, and God in Modern Islam

Theodore Friend

WILLIAM B. EERDMANS PUBLISHING COMPANY
GRAND RAPIDS, MICHIGAN / CAMBRIDGE, U.K.

Published 2012 by
Wm. B. Eerdmans Publishing Co.
2140 Oak Industrial Drive N.E., Grand Rapids, Michigan 49505 /
P.O. Box 163, Cambridge CB3 9PU U.K.

Printed in the United States of America

18 17 16 15 14 13 12   7 6 5 4 3 2 1

Library of Congress Cataloging-in-Publication Data

Friend, Theodore.
Woman, man, and God in modern Islam /
Theodore Friend.
p.   cm.
Includes index.
ISBN 978-0-8028-6673-8 (cloth: alk. paper)
1. Islam — 21st century. 2. Islam and civil society.
3. Islamic countries — Social conditions — 21st century.
4. Islam — Controversial literature.   I. Title.

BP161.3.F75   2012

305.6′97 — dc23

2011032974

www.eerdmans.com

To all the Muslim women
who shared with me
their histories and hopes

Contents

Contents

Foreword

Islam, the world's second largest religion, continues to attract many myths and misstatements in the West, but few as plainly wrong as the idea of a unified, monolithic global faith. In fact, the question "What do Muslims think?" makes about as much sense as an equivalent query about what all Christians believe. The answers differ enormously depending on the historical period and the geographical context, and the only proper response is "Which Muslims? Where and when?" Arguably, over the span of its development, Islam worldwide is quite as diverse as Christianity, and that fact must supply the essential foundation for any attempt to predict the future of "the Muslim world."

That sense of diversity is a central theme of Theodore Friend's wonderfully ambitious and wide-ranging book. However much the Saudis would like to believe so, their ultra-puritanical and authoritarian version of Islam in no sense represents a pristine or uniquely authentic version of the faith, but is rather one among many. It's always useful to be reminded that Islam is anything but synonymous with the Arab world. Of the world's eight largest Muslim countries, only one — Egypt — is Arab in language and culture, and it would not be too far from the mark to see Islam as a religion of South and Southeast Asia. Appropriately, then, of the five studies that make up *Woman, Man, and God in Modern Islam,* Saudi Arabia alone holds up the Arab banner.

Friend's book has so many strengths that it is difficult to know where to start listing them. Above all, we see his generous, all-encompassing interest in other societies. His main theme is women's social role and the impact of feminism within a highly religious and indeed fundamentalist setting. And what topic could be more central to understanding the modern world? Tell me the role and status of women in a given society and I will know all the essential facts about family structure, demography, fertility rates, and (very probably) attitudes to religious authority. All are inextricably intertwined. But it's easy to imagine an academic book struggling to interpret the rival forces of feminism and fundamentalism within Islam, avoiding any temptations to stray into peripheral topics. Not for Theodore Friend, who so comprehensively explores the relationship of gender and religion, but simply finds it impossible to avoid addressing so many other critical topics and stories: political structure and ideology; Islamic, Asian, and Middle Eastern history; scriptural interpretation; education, and so much else. His curiosity is insatiable, and the reader is quickly drawn in. Moreover, our hypothetical academic would probably present the findings in suitably inaccessible academic prose — exactly the opposite of what Friend does in this vivid book, which is firmly rooted in his own personal experiences and encounters. It is above all these numerous and varied conversations that linger in the reader's mind.

I really hope this book finds the widest possible audience, among policy-makers, legislators, and media professionals, who would find it an invaluable corrective to the common myths about Islam and the Islamic world. But the best reason for reading it is that it tells an enthralling story — or rather, many stories. The book is a triumph.

Philip Jenkins
Edwin Erle Sparks Professor of Humanities,
  Pennsylvania State University
Distinguished Senior Fellow,
  Institute for Studies of Religion,
  Baylor University

To Travel

Why did I choose to throw myself into five major Muslim cultures for the sake of this book? There are journalistic answers, such as "to sort out the simultaneous growth of fundamentalism and of feminism." And historical answers, such as "to distinguish, alongside Arab culture, four other major cultures in the Muslim world." Whatever I did, I would be responding as a historical journalist. But the deepest call I was answering was the voice of my late wife, suddenly gone after forty-three years together, saying, "You need a project." She had sometimes endured my long spells away for earlier books. But now I had to learn from absence, without her ever coming back. I began to travel, not yet knowing quite why.

Travel, of course, contains its own suffering. Not just logistical ensnarements, but for one with a thin stomach lining, the danger of disease across all Southern Asia. Above all, the repeated stress of adjusting to very different Muslim cultures. But that was precisely the point: to understand these cultures beyond what I already knew, in a period of new turbulence in the world. To the extent I gave the effort, I knew I would be given understanding, which I could then pass on.

I have sought to write a book that heightens the profile of women in these five cultures. My intent was to talk with women in various professions and callings. And men, too — members of both genders who take religion seriously. I wanted to serve as interlocutor for those forward-thinking persons willing to inform such a program.

My aim required an arc which I covered twice: going halfway around the world to Indonesia, then proceeding to three more cultures westward before concluding in Turkey, halfway back home. Two Southwest Asian cultures were highly resistant to visitors and hostile to researchers — the Kingdom of Saudi Arabia and the Islamic Republic of Iran. Camouflaging my intentions was necessary to entering both these countries. Once inside, I found women of integrity eager to talk.

Before them in that westward arc, I found Pakistan riven by internal strife and aggravated by the foreign policies of the U.S. As an American, I hardly felt welcome. Yet friends and kind strangers made all the difference. There, in fact, I received a blessing from the philosopher Anis Ahmad, who encouraged me in what he called my *jihad* — my moral struggle to understand Islam and Muslim cultures.

Moral purpose is the heart of the matter. I am not the geographer that C. M. Doughty had to be, intrepidly, for *Arabia Deserta* (1888). And certainly not the warrior into which T. E. Lawrence turned himself, sometimes courting insanity, for *Seven Pillars of Wisdom* (1926).

After them came two women who spoke Farsi as well as Arabic — Gertrude Bell (1868-1926) and Freya Stark (1893-1993). The first was multicompetent and fully capable of male imperial errors. The second was a prolific travel writer across forty years.

Any modern traveler in Muslim lands must limit her ambitions and expand her sensibilities. V. S. Naipaul ranged through some of that world (but not Turkey or Saudi Arabia) and produced two books: *Among the Believers* (1981) and *Beyond Belief* (1998). These are rich candies, but sour at their center. What a shame that an Oxonian rationalist should have traveled so widely, observed so elegantly, and understood so little. Why write about Islam if one disdains belief? Why dismiss "converts" as suffering from "neurosis"? This ex-Hindu, post-Enlightenment, neo-cosmopolitan has overcome his rootlessness by grounding himself in his own extensive experience. A reader may trust his eye and his ear, but not his heart. Naipaul's descriptions are arresting, but his compass needle flickers too much. With such an itinerary, a traveler who disbelieves in belief can be at best a connoisseur of oddity.

My own travels were complete when Akbar Ahmed's *Journey into Islam* appeared (2007). This Pakistani diplomat and anthropologist, residing in Washington, D.C., carried with him a young research team. They helped him provide a social science weave to his findings, which are persuasively cast in behalf of international understanding. But my purpose is distinct from his. I undertook solitary travel to consider the roles, rules, and rights of women under Islam. I entered both Saudi Arabia and Iran, where Ahmed chose not to go — the twin peaks, and extremes, of Sunni and Shi'ite society in our time.

I never concealed my own creed, was never required to reveal it, and surely hope that my travels and conversations refined it. In this book, the reader will find respect for Islam conjoined with faith in women, and in their creative and productive potential. I do not arrive there with the reveries of a slowly advancing and returning traveler who dreams at the rail of an ocean liner. I took buses, trains, and planes instead; especially airplanes. Oceans must be leaped across. How otherwise can one study contemporary tides in human affairs, and grasp the thought-waves of over two hundred individuals?

Such a book as mine, these days, must justify itself with regard to carbon emissions. Personal and pension dollars I happily spent in my purpose. But was it worth the global fuel I consumed? I think so. Comprehending the strivings of women in Muslim cultures is valuable not only in deprovincializing the North. Seeing my report, I hope, may marginally re-orient or remotivate some readers in trans-Islamic cultures themselves.

In a crowded world, cross-cultural understanding is not just a requisite for peace, but a tonic for growth. It cannot be fully achieved without going away from home. At its most demanding, such travel vastly transcends tourism. It is above routine and beyond romance. Conducted as a faithful inquiry, travel can be an act of love.

THEODORE FRIEND
June 2011

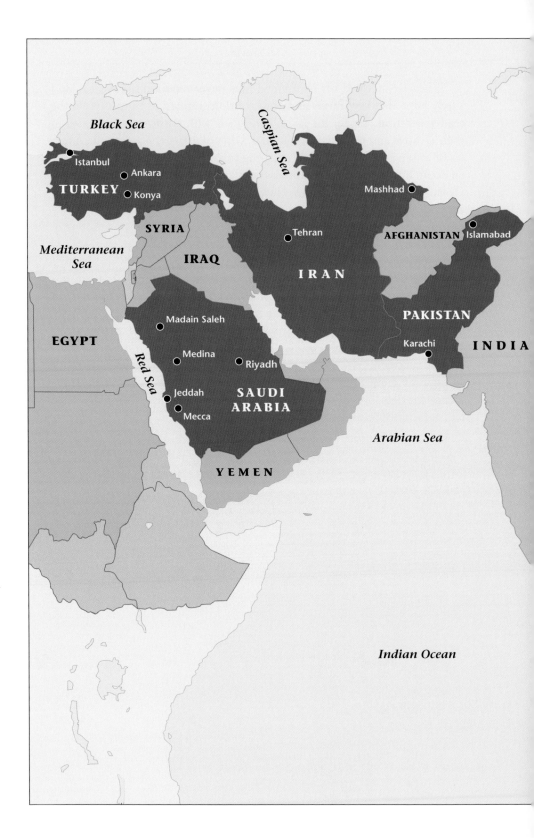

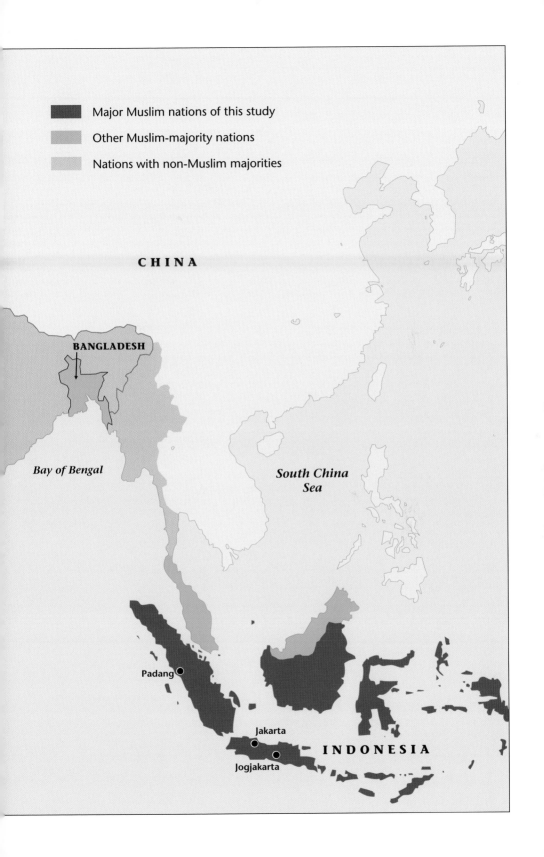

Major Muslim nations of this study

Other Muslim-majority nations

Nations with non-Muslim majorities

CHINA

BANGLADESH

Bay of Bengal

South China Sea

Padang

Jakarta

INDONESIA

Jogjakarta

Weddings in Five Cultures

Saudi Arabia

These two photographs (figs. I.1 and I.2) were taken during the marriage celebrations, in Dharhan, of Khadijah al-Jefri, a medical student. Her mother, an M.D., and her father, an oil company executive, are both Hijazi by birth, but now work in Eastern Saudi Arabia.

Traditional Hijazi weddings might have covered three to seven days. This occasion in 2006, however, was two days and featured the henna night and wedding night. The henna night, pictured here (bride with her two sisters, and drawing veil across her lower face), is all female. As many as seven happily married women may decorate the hands and feet of the bride with henna — or, now, leave it all to a female professional. Hijazi in origin, this custom is similar in many aspects throughout the kingdom.

The wedding night, held in a hotel, rented hall, or home, may include 300 to 500 guests and express family tastes. The bride is likely to wear a white gown, varying by fashion and personal choice, as will her tiara and length of veil. She often holds a bouquet of flowers, as in a Western wedding.

The groom wears a white robe and headdress and an embroidered cloak of cream and gold. His father is distinguished by a cloak of gold and black.

Separate seating for women and men is customary, as at all Saudi public events. Typically the ceremony begins with dancing among the female guests. Men often dance with each other in their section of the wedding. When they merge with the women's section, and some of them join the bridal couple on a raised dais, men also dance in front of the female guests.

Entrance of the bride and groom is announced, accompanied by young bridesmaids. As the genders mesh together, women generally don their veils in a tradition of modesty, because "some of their clothes may be too revealing to be shared except by their other female companions at the celebration."

The mothers of both parties and the sisters of the groom then dance (but the sisters of the bride, unless very young, will not dance before their new brothers-in-law). The couple exchanges rings. The groom presents the bride with a complete set of jewelry. They may or may not dance. They will cut a layered white wedding cake, and will sit with the guests as long as they wish. *Photos, with permission of Khadijah al-Jefri and her family, are by Nimah Ismail Nawwab, who also supplied the cultural data.*

I.1

I.2

Pakistan

Sufia and Shahid Haq wed in Karachi in 1979. The first of their photos (fig. I.3), on the day of the *nikah* (signing of the marriage contract), shows Shahid in white tunic and turban, and Sufia with a bridal garland of roses covering her face. The groom had the same choice, a custom of the Indian subcontinent, but declined to be blinded by flowers.

The second photo (fig. I.4), with groom in a business suit, was taken two days later at *valima,* a celebration following consummation of the marriage. The wedding reception after *nikah* was given by the bride's family; the *valima* reception was given by the groom's family. Each involved dinners for about 500 people.

Some Pakistani families now, regardless of class and despite limits of income, may prolong celebrations for five days. Dancing and singing parties called *dhoiki* may begin at the houses of family and friends as much as a month before the wedding day.

Photos courtesy of Sufia and Shahid Haq

I.3

I.4

I.5 Middle and lower class weddings tend to use public places. Here, a bride and female relatives await a ceremony at Badshahi Mosque in Lahore (2006). The semi-public space enabled the photographer to lean around a pillar and take a shot. *Photo: Elisabeth Braun*

Dana Iswara is Javanese and Dr. Chatib "Dede" Basri is Minangkabau. When they married in 2004, adhering to Dana's family tradition and wishes, they wore Javanese dress in the morning and had the nuptial ceremony performed in a Muslim manner. At that occasion, the President of Indonesia, Susilo Bambang Yudhoyono, to whom Dr. Basri was an advisor, sat at the far end of the table, on the groom's right (fig. I.6). Opposite the president and at the bride's left was former minister Mohammad Sadli (1927-2008), one of the technocrats whose economic discipline had rescued Indonesia from Sukarno's chaos. To the left of Sadli was the *penghulu,* or officiant; and to the further left, the groom's brother.

That evening the reception celebration was held in Minangkabau style. The bride and groom pose for a formal picture in full Minangkabau finery (fig. I.7).

Photos courtesy of the married couple and of Siti Nuraini Jatim

I.6

I.7

I.8 Donny Priambodo and Ita Paramita wed in Central Javanese style: bare-shouldered, wearing *dodotan,* or sarong with ceremonial accoutrements. Such weddings also involve Islamic declarations and registry. They are far more remarkable, however, for the degree to which they manifest regional tradition and culture. *Photo courtesy of the married couple and of Siti Nuraini Jatim*

Iran

I.9 Mass weddings are held in many countries and in many faiths. Here, in Shi'ite Iran in 2001, a just-married couple are posing for a studio photo with a background of starry sky.

I.10 Ephesus, the Cave of the Seven Sleepers, 2005. The bride, wearing white and a head-dress respecting Islamic dress code, prays with her groom at a popular site of pilgrimage.

The legend of the "seven sleepers" concerns seven Christian youth who, in the time of the Roman Emperor Decius, were walled into a cave for their defiance of his pagan observations. They awoke in the reign of the Emperor Theodosius (379-395), a century and a quarter later. Their holiness and miraculous length of life spread their story through Christendom and its literature.

Their tale appears also in the Qur'an, in the Surah called The Cave (18:1-26). In that telling, their sleep is attributed to the peace of surrender to Allah in the face of oppression. Their number is uncertain. Their time asleep has increased to 309 lunar years.

Photo: Abbas/Magnum Photos

Religion, Gender, and Modernity

Women and Modern Social Melee

"Women hold up half the sky." Whether Mao Zedong coined the statement in 1968 or Confucius did so two and a half millennia ago is in dispute.[1] But recent analyses have brought conditions of women to the foreground. They have noted widespread gendericide. They have documented repression of women as inhibiting Arab social development. And they have internationalized, statistically, the study of women's conditions.

A grim figure developed by the Geneva Centre for the Democratic Control of Armed Forces shows that because of abortion, female infanticide, and discriminatory preference for males in allotment of food and essentials of life, between 113 million and 200 million women may be said to be "demographically missing" from our present planet.[2] The largest parts of this absence, of course, are contributed by China and India; but poor parts of the Islamic world also add to it.

A highly focused and controversial study is the fourth in the series of Arab Human Development Reports — the concluding one in 2005, which took in the conditions of women in Arab nations. The net finding, by Arabs about Arabs, is that repression of women in several domains of

---

1. Nicholas D. Kristof and Sheryl WuDunn, *Half the Sky: Turning Oppression into Opportunity for Women Worldwide* (New York, Alfred A. Knopf, 2009).

2. Marie Vlachova and Lee Biason, eds., *Women in an Insecure World: Violence Against Women, Facts, Figures, and Analysis* (Geneva, Centre for the Democratic Control of Armed Forces, 2005), p. vii.

modern life is a major causal factor in the underdevelopment and under-productivity of Arab societies.[3]

A comprehensive study generated by the World Economic Forum, covering 130 nations with regard to fourteen variables in female-to-male ratio, is compacted and annually updated in the Global Gender Gap Report. Its factors may be simplified to four categories: economic participation, educational attainment, health and survival, and political empowerment.[4] Muslim countries appear as pronounced laggards. Four nations of my study are in the bottom decile: Iran, #128, Turkey, #129, Saudi Arabia, #130, and Pakistan, #132, close to Yemen (last at #134). Indonesia rises well above them, but even it has swiftly slipped form the third to the fourth quintile (#68 to #92). Indonesia's relatively good showing, however, raises an important question: How do bilateral family systems in Southeast Asia benefit women? Conversely, the disenabling of females in patrilineal systems must surely be a question for the Middle East Gender Parity Group, created in 2008.

One rejoinder to all this data may be that of the wise man writing on Muslim tradition who declares that "comparison, measurement and calculation — the essential attributes of reason — lose both their importance and their meaning in love."[5] We may, nevertheless, with emotional resolve, take on the forces knotted up in the statistics, and try to unravel them. About contradictions in modern Islam, some of the most astute observers are female. A Pakistani sees, in her country, the energies of modernization contorting themselves into masculinization. A Turkish woman notes such a variety of conflicts — militarism vs. democracy; patriarchal misogyny vs. women's equality; "modern" Islam vs. antique secularism — that one must free oneself from false solemnities with laughter.[6]

Coursing among all global religions, mighty to reckon with, is neo-

---

3. United Nations Development Programme, Regional Bureau for Arab States, *Arab Human Development Report, 2005: Toward the Rise of Women in the Arab World* (UNDP, 2006), pp. 13, 148.

4. World Economic Forum, *Global Gender Gap* (Davos, 2006); esp. framework (p. 307) and rankings (p. 9). *Global Gender Gap Report, 2008*, updated, online.

5. Rusmir Mahmutæehajiæ, *On Love in the Muslim Tradition* (New York, Fordham University Press, 2007), p. 7.

6. These two essays appear in Lahoucine Ouzgane, ed., *Islamic Masculinities* (London/ New York, Zed Books, 2006): Durre S. Ahmed, "Gender and Islamic Spirituality: a psychological view of 'low' fundamentalism," pp. 11-34; and Banu Helvacioglu, "The smile of death and the solemnity of masculinity," pp. 35-56.

fundamentalism.[7] In Islam, Olivier Roy stresses its angry challenge: "Is your behavior consistent with your faith?!" Because human conduct is never consistent with explicit norms, the answer will be tossed on tempests of hope, untruth, and guilt. What is conservative religion attempting to reconstruct? "[I]t is the self itself in some sort of permanent representation and staging of the self."[8] To manifest an individual self is a distinct ambition of our times. Modern as they once were, neither Martin Luther nor Ibn Taymiya, transported to our age, would easily recognize what is going on. But our era is more than pluralistic enough to allow rejoinders to fundamentalism, which was criticized by a multifaith gathering at Georgetown University in 2006 as "the childhood disease of all religions and churches."

Modern political and demographic forces complicate the picture. In Iran, whereas the legal age of marriage for a girl was lowered after the revolution from sixteen years to nine, the average age of marriage climbed in reality during the 1990s to more than twenty-four.[9] In adjoining Iraq, Kavita Ramdas, President and CEO of the Global Fund for Women, notes that Iraq's Family Law Act of 1959 had ensured equal gender rights in personal law. Although Iraq's women, like all Iraqis, suffered from the brutal political repressions of the subsequent Baathist regime and Saddam Hussein, they were actually protected from religious extremism. "The freedom and rights enjoyed by Iraqi women were the envy of women in most other countries of the Middle East," according to Ramdas. After invading Iraq, however, American neo-imperial power elevated leaders mostly allied with Shi'ite clerics, ultraconservative in gender matters. The new Iraqi constitution overturned half a century of women's right to be treated as equal citizens, and installed Islamic law over constitutional principles in personal and family realms. Sectarian conflict predictably made "women's bodies the battlefields on which vendettas and threats are played out." Public executions of women by Shi'ite militias rose, and private executions of Sunni women for reasons of male "honor" flared up to an estimate of thirty a month. Rates of prostitution, human trafficking, and domestic vi-

---

7. Gabriel Almond, R. Scott Appleby, and Emmanuel Sivan, *Strong Religion: The Rise of Fundamentalisms Around the World* (Chicago, University of Chicago Press, 2003); based on Martin E. Marty and R. Scott Appleby, eds., *Fundamentalisms Comprehended* (Chicago, University of Chicago Press, 1995). See also Malise Ruthven, *Fundamentalisms: The Search for Meaning* (Oxford, Oxford University Press, 2004).

8. Olivier Roy, *Globalized Islam: The Search for a New Ummah* (New York, Columbia University Press, 2004), p. 267.

9. Roy, *Globalized Islam*, pp. 140-41.

olence against women all increased.[10] Nor is the Iraq story compensated for in Afghanistan. Initial reversal of Taliban suppression of women was followed by American dilution of force and purpose. The Taliban, re-strengthened, began again to threaten women.

In Kuwait, I met with the "Thursday Morning Group," women there who had made voting their supreme priority among women's needs and issues in their country. Kuwait's constitution, in contrast to the Saudi and Iranian constitutions, gives women all freedom of expression. They have it and use it, the group told me. "The men would be afraid to cut us off." But gender-specific issues, Dr. Rola Dashti said, need votes to carry them. A year and a half later, Kuwaiti women realized their long battle for suffrage, also achieving the right to hold office. In the election of June 2006, one out of every nine candidates was a woman. Not one, however, was elected; nor in the election of 2008. As a wise female commentator said, "This is democracy. You can't force anyone to vote a certain way."[11] In 2009, however, four women finally broke the barrier and were elected to the 50-seat national assembly. One was Rola Dashti.

Force, in sum, cannot ensure democracy; and democracy does not ensure female equality. Sociological trends may not strengthen either religion or selfhood; and neo-fundamentalism, as an attempt to reclaim disoriented souls for old-time religion, will run counter to gender equity.

Religion: 1979 as a Pivotal Year

In 1979, Iranian revolutionaries overthrew the Shah in a flux of events that produced a theocratic constitution and a religiously policed Shi'ite state. Later that same year, Sunni zealots seized the Grand Mosque in Mecca in a move to purify the precincts, challenge Saudi royalty, and reform all Islam — for which effrontery the rebels were beheaded in their native villages. Their challenge not only brought on filters against Western culture, but also led to added wrappings of female dress and further entrapped Arab women in subordinate roles.

This was also the year that Pakistani dictator Zia ul-Haq, playing to his

---

10. Kavita Ramdas, "U.S. Invasion Makes Life Worse for Women of Iraq," Seattle Post-Intelligencer, 2 Jan 07. http://seattlepi.nwsource.com/opinion/297771_women02.html.

11. Author's field notes, Kuwait City, 2 Dec 04; *New York Times*, 30 Jun 06, p. 9; 18 May 09, p. 4.

Islamist constituency, proclaimed the Hudood Ordinances. These perverted the achievements of the Prophet Muhammad regarding the status of women, and imposed tribal-patriarchal standards which had originated in pre-Islamic barbarism. Again in that same year, the Soviet Union invaded Afghanistan, embroiling it in the last ugly dynamics of the Cold War. When the U.S. then funded and armed tribal warriors against the U.S.S.R., these counter-forces strengthened the misogynistic diabolism of the Taliban and provoked to action the global paranoia of Osama bin Laden.

Meanwhile that same year, Jerry Falwell founded the Moral Majority in the United States, renewing a fundamentalist Christianity that included textualized subjection of women. Even if his persuasiveness was largely spent by 2001, he polarized Americans further by his diatribe after 9/11, saying that destruction was not only caused but also deserved by American paganism, feminism, and secularism; and by gays, lesbians, and abortion. Working with Falwell, Pat Robertson, and James Dobson had made young Frank Schaeffer eventually regret helping to turn evangelical Christianity into a political power brokerage. From having been part of its hucksterism and flaky adrenaline-surge, he came to see it as dangerously delusional.[12] But while an open Christianity was just as important as an open Islam, he had to watch political evangelism soar in power, elect George W. Bush in 2000, and then protect Bush's war in 2004. Even now, Franklin Graham stands by his remarks that Islam is evil, and John Hagee speaks of Islam only in belligerent rant.

Amid the backward-looking events of 1979 were others of more promise. In an undertaking little noted at the time, Robert Bellah and his team began research motivated by a fear of "cancerous" American individualism, which eventuated in the influential *Habits of the Heart*. Eleven years after its publication, however, Bellah acknowledged that he had underestimated the degree of erosion in American institutions.[13] Its major cause, a radical individualism, continues today.

12. Frank Schaeffer, *Crazy for God: How I Grew Up as One of the Elect, Helped Found the Religious Right, and Lived to Take All (or Almost All) of It Back* (New York, Carroll & Graf, 2007), pp. 99-100, 116-18, 298-300, 315, 346, 391. Also illuminating is Andrew Himes, *The Sword of the Lord: The Roots of Fundamentalism in an American Family* (2011), which details the separatistic splits of Billy Graham as a "modernist evangelical" from older fundamentalists. There followed the splits of Bob Jones, Jr. on ultra-fundamentalist grounds from Graham, and even from Jerry Falwell.

13. Robert Bellah et al., *Habits of the Heart: Individualism and Commitment in American Life* (New York, Harper & Row, 1985), pp. vii-ix; Bellah's update, 1996, in Almond et al.,

For global perspective: The UN passed in 1979 the Convention on the Elimination of All Forms of Discrimination Against Women (CEDAW). Although 185 states have enacted various forms of adherence to the treaty, the convention has never been ratified by the U.S. government, making the U.S. the only signatory nation not to ratify the treaty. For many cultures, CEDAW is a basic point of traction for advances on behalf of women. For the several Muslim nations endorsing it with heavy legal reservations, it is not.

Dialogues

The present standing of Muslim nations was well expressed from within by Indonesia's President Susilo Bambang Yudhoyono on a trip to Saudi Arabia in 2006. "Islam is all about revelation, about enlightenment, about liberation, about empowerment," he said. "But sadly, while we rejoice in seeing pockets of progress and prosperity throughout the Muslim world, we still see pockets of poverty, deprivation and scarcity among the *umma* worldwide." Of the world's twenty-five biggest economies, he observed, only three are Muslim-majority countries: Turkey, Indonesia, and Saudi Arabia. In ranking for competitiveness, no Muslim country is among the top twenty trading nations. In the human development index, which factors together life expectancy, literacy, and income, none is among the top thirty nations. In seventeen predominantly Muslim countries, primary school education is less than 60 percent. Survival itself is an issue in many such places. Globalization is all around such people, and often in their living rooms, but they don't know what to make of its opportunities.

President Yudhoyono noted that he had come to Saudi Arabia to expand ties with a country enjoying the same size GDP as Indonesia, and one which in 2004 had become Indonesia's largest foreign investor. We must stop blaming ourselves for our problems, he urged; and equally, stop blaming others for our misfortunes. We must realize that the solutions begin with us, the *umma,* the world community of Islam. They require that we embrace technology and modernity (in which we led the world a thousand years ago); that we move at the forefront of globalism (not leaving such leadership to India and China); that we mobilize our resources to help fellow Muslims with conflict resolution and closing of development gaps

---

Strong Religion, p. 231. Christopher Lasch and Robert Putnam have proceeded to give their own strong flavors to the study of radical individualism.

within the Organization of the Islamic Conference (OIC) itself; and that we reach out to non-Muslims and dispel ignorance and disrespect toward Islam.[14]

Yudhoyono ignored the huge cultural differences that separated his own Sufi-inspired nation from the Saudis, whose Hanbali school of law gave them the text-anchored illusion of linguistic ownership of Islam. For the occasion, his Indonesian capacity to blend differences syncretically served Yudhoyono well. He invoked the *umma* in a sympathetic vision, and he tried to yoke the energies of two of its prominent economies in a leadership of productivity and diplomacy. He glided past its largest economy, Turkey, with its history of imperial lordship over fellow Muslims. He tap-danced around the Wahhabi export of petro-propaganda, of an ultra-lineal interpretation of Islam that was indeed creating schools where needed, but also creating divisions in Indonesia that gave off more ideological heat than educational light. He was throwing out a fishing skein woven by his young American-educated speechwriters, and hoping to haul in direct project investment from a nation with ten times the per capita income of Indonesia. A corollary hope was less manifest, but implicit: to voice an Islamic unity of aspiration counter to al-Qaeda violence, while yielding neither to Salafi style in Puritanism nor to Wahhabi mode in literalism. There was lots of room for maneuver to those ends, and Yudhoyono managed it with force and grace. But the Western press, which had been clamoring to hear from "Muslim moderates," did not pick up President Yudhoyono's speech. Their bizarre and self-defeating strategy persisted: editorialize against hatred while reporting chiefly on conflict.

Beyond the wading depth of the media, parity, complementarity, and equality among women and men are debated with intensity. The example is invoked of Umm al-Darda, a jurist of seventh-century Damascus, who taught in the mosque, and whose students included the caliph of Damascus. She prayed shoulder-to-shoulder with men, and issued a *fatwa* in defense of that practice. Indeed, the scholar Muhammad Akram Nadwi, of the Oxford Center for Islamic Studies, has found 8,000 notable female scholars in the 1,400 years of Islam.[15] Their waning in number after the sixteenth century arguably shows ossification in Islam, rather than certifi-

---

14. Speech at the Islamic University of Imam Muhammad bin Sa'ud, 26 Apr 06; forwarded by The American-Indonesian Chamber of Commerce, New York City.

15. Carla Powers, "A Secret History of Feminist Scholars of Islam," *New York Times* Sunday Magazine, 25 Feb 07.

cation against women. What are serious young Muslim women with scholarly talent to do now? Go to Cairo's Al Azhar University and credit themselves in *fiqh* for years among male jurisprudes? Or go out in the wider modern world to equip themselves with knowledge of women's needs, inspired by such wisdoms, female and male, as they may find? Both are tough courses. Each may be argued for. Certainly women are needed in Muslim law and the righting of the dynamics of Islam. If something caused Islamic theology to undergo an early crib death, there is still every reason to try to spare Muslim girls and women from social suffocation.[16]

The media remained preoccupied with bombings — everywhere, including European cities such as London and Madrid, and as attempted in New York City. So relatively few of the Europeans who had stopped attending church, or of the Americans who still filled their churches, realized that a peaceful religious and cultural initiative had been underway and elaborating since 2007 — the initially Muslim outreach known as "A Common Word." Provoked by an ill-conceived speech by Pope Benedict XVI in his home city of Regensburg in Germany, a number of Muslim leaders led by Prince Ghazi bin Muhammad of Jordan gathered together and made theological overtures to Christian and Jewish counterparts.

A "clash of civilizations" was obviously a dangerous idea. Even if the reality was better described as a collision of ignorances, it remained perilous. Across the next few years the Muslim leaders and their welcoming respondents, numerous religious figures in the United States, put together a sequence of conferences in which were highlighted moral teachings shared by Islam, Christianity, and Judaism. Fundamentally: to love the Lord thy God, and thy neighbor as thyself. That is the Common Word.[17] It is simple, and it is shared among the three monotheisms. Using that as a starting point, the interlocutors among the faiths charged up a momentum that might enable anyone aware of it to see that instead of the lightning and thunder of angry ignorance, the relationships among the faiths could be developed as a mesh of understandings. And while disagreements would persist, because contradictions were inescapable, all of them could be treated in a sunlight of good will. Even where clouds might form, their fallout could be a gentle rain of mercy.

16. Occasional footnotes in later chapters will suggest more women thinking hard about this problem.

17. Miroslav Volf, Ghazi bin Muhammad, and Melissa Yarrington, eds., *A Common Word: Muslims and Christians on Loving God and Neighbor* (Grand Rapids, Eerdmans, 2010), *passim.*

As interfaith dialogue accelerated under the stimulus of "A Common Word," intragender discussions were intensifying among Muslim women, aiming to review the scriptural and social bases of subjection that they had experienced for centuries, and were still undergoing. Dating the subjection, like most everything else in a rich religious history, was arguable. Had the Prophet Muhammad not spoken of the equal dignity and special rights of women, and encouraged their education? Yes, but what happened after he died? And when, and how, and why did those things happen?[18] In any case, the world was now not what it ought to be, for modern women in a thoughtful Islam that traced its roots to the revelations of the Prophet.

A series of conferences across several years meanwhile gave impetus to one in Kuala Lumpur in February 2009, with hundreds of women and scores of men attending. Their meeting and their cause — equality and justice in the family — carried the name *Musawah*, which is the Arabic word for *equality*. That goal was to be sought in every relevant dimension, including the tackling of shari'a and *fiqh*. As a Pakistani jurist saw it, shari'a make up the laws as found in the Qur'an and in the hadith, the recorded sayings of the Prophet which help explain the Qur'an. The holy book itself creates a context of flexibility by stating the importance of accepted practice, or a community's recognition of fairness. Through such coping, one arrives at *fiqh:* the human effort to understand the Qur'anic revelation and to apply its injunctions. Layers of meaning become inescapably thicker for the interpreter of *fiqh*, because he or she must reckon with fairness not only as seen in original texts, but also as assessed by subsequent commentators. After weighing and allowing for interim changes of emphasis or nuance, the interpreter then speaks as objectively as possible from his or her own time and culture and normative values.

Women's rights can clearly be rescued from centuries of suffocation and reestablished in consonance with the vision of the Prophet.[19] Islamists, however — as dogmatic or rigidly conservative Muslims — may oppose such efforts and findings on two grounds: an internal argument that appeals to the inviolability of the text, and an external argument that objects to certain reinterpretations as flawed by cultural relativism.

18. Homayra Ziad sees al-Shâfi'i (d. 820) as powerfully representative of those male jurists who gave canonical authority to modes of resolution devised by scholars who were comfortable with non-egalitarian gender norms. "Women and Islam," ch. 12 in Roger Allen and Shawkat Toorawa, eds., *Islam: A Short Guide to the Faith* (Grand Rapids, Eerdmans, 2011). Ziad also writes of undue weight having been given to misogynist *hadiths* of the eleventh century.

19. 2009 Global Meeting; see www.musawah.org.

Advocates of the rights of women may, in addition to contending over the sacred texts, take recourse to the CEDAW. This "bill of rights for women" became thirty years old in 2009. It had 186 national signatures subscribing to the principle of equality of men and women in their legal systems, and abolishing all forms of discrimination against women. Signatories agreed to set up tribunals to protect women and to outlaw all discriminatory acts against them by persons, organizations, or enterprises in all relevant areas, including health, education, employment, marriage, and family life.[20]

CEDAW by now contains a powerful corpus of examples and body of precedents. But its use in some countries, signatory or not, is likely to prompt the sophisticated dismissal that anyone appealing to it is calling on "UN shari'a" — which is to belittle CEDAW as a secular international consensus with no status in Islamic divine law.

Secular and Islamic Feminisms

As Muslim nations, now long sovereign, seek to escape the economic and cultural overlordship of Western powers, Muslim women seek to rise from the overlordship of Muslim men, and to function not in a subjugated parity but as an autonomous affinity. They risk the criticism of being over-affected by social influence from former imperial powers. To this their replies are many. But basically their schools are two: secular feminists and Islamic feminists.

The total momentum of both schools for liberation of women was marked, over a century ago, by two men — an Indian and an Egyptian. Mumtaz Ali, in Delhi, published *Rights of Women* in 1898. Basing himself in his own reading of Islamic law, he tackled girls' education, marriage, divorce, polygamy, inheritance, and women's seclusion. And Qasim Amin, in Cairo, published *The Liberation of Women* in 1899, taking up in his own way the same controversial issues, and then overloading the case for his other points by attacks on veiling — which linked him too closely with European critics and therefore with "Westernization" and "colonialism." Similar criticisms would arise over a century later against the annual Arab Human Development Reports of 2002-5, culminating especially in the one on

---

20. Continuing reporting, deliberation, and action under CEDAW since 2008 takes place in the office of the UN High Commissioner for Human Rights: www2.ohchr.org/English/bodies/cedaw/cedaws43.htm.

the conditions of women and their empowerment.[21] The authors, who were Arabs, both female and male, knew that was coming; still, they offer their research with rigor and state their discoveries with tenacity.

In such sensitive discourse, naturally, the tone is the music. Margot Badran, who has studied these subjects across time and culture for decades, notes that female pioneers in such subjects before Amin produced "a dispersed and scattered discourse" that was often fed by an oral feminist energy, which took shape in debate in women's salons, sometimes essays in women's journals, and occasionally also in men's papers and journals. Badran lingers on tone: "In speaking to each other, women were gentle and compassionate." While they could confidently express a forceful agenda for change, they also commanded the essential vortex of feeling from which that agenda proceeded — a discourse of suffering — to let other women know they were not alone, and to register upon men the impact of their neglect and negativity. Badran allows herself to say that Amin often exaggerated depictions of women's backwardness, apparently to goad men to act. She contrasts the understatement by women, and their "gentility and affection," with Amin's habit of sometimes falling into a tone which "could be crude, sententious, and haranguing."[22]

Secular feminists, in any case, have been at work since the late nineteenth century, trying to craft a modern life in consonance with educational advances. Then in the late twentieth century, electronic technology helped to spur Islamic feminist thinking both locally and globally. No longer could the state preempt feminism, as Atatürk may be said to have done in Turkey. And no longer could maledom monopolize interpretation of the Qur'an. Against gender-reactionary Islamists, women were now interpreting the Qur'an for themselves. As a result, feminisms, secular and Islamic, now radiate from many points, and do not gauge themselves by the West. The homes of the present feminists in Islam are their own heartlands and whatever radii bring back reinforcement.

From the final years of the twentieth century into the present, secular feminism, while continuing to do good works, has needed the impetus of a new ideology. Islamic feminism provided this new cutting edge and the new burst of energy. While secular feminism had insisted on the full equal-

21. Isobel Coleman, *Paradise Beneath Her Feet: How Women Are Transforming the Middle East* (New York, Random House, 2010), pp. 29-30, 44-48.

22. Margot Badran, *Feminism in Islam: Secular and Religious Convergences* (Oxford, Oneworld Publications, 2009), pp. 55-63; quotations, pp. 56, 57.

ity of women and men in the public sphere, in the private sphere it had accepted a model of different and complementary functions, even to the point of yielding to male authority within the family, and to hierarchical gender roles. The new energy from Islamic feminism derived from its full gender equality — full in both the public and private spheres. To achieve this was a socio-political struggle and, at the same time, an intellectual-spiritual struggle. The modern Islamic feminist was thus dedicated to gender *jihad* in a way that had nothing to do with erroneous Western notions of militant violence, but to *ijtihad* (from the same Arabic root), or interpretation of sacred texts liberated from patriarchal domination of those exercises.[23]

An ambitious and determinedly secular variant on these themes comes from Isobel Coleman, in her *Paradise Beneath Her Feet*. Her book represents extensive travel, earnest thinking, and careful reporting. With her husband or her son, she has entered countries not easy for Western women — Saudi Arabia and Iran — and out of her prime orientation to American foreign policy she has gone to Iraq, Afghanistan, and Pakistan. With other and collateral travel, but with these nations in prime focus, she aims to depict present conditions and future probabilities: "The stability of our world as we know it will likely be determined in this volatile part of the globe. The future of women's rights within each will be central to determining the future of these societies." Certainly such thoughts may supply a cutting edge for American readers. But one may be wary of the blade she is employing.[24] She was persuaded by the then-president of the Council on Foreign Relations (New York City) to undertake gender studies of the Middle East. She discovered that the struggle for women's justice is "central to many of the most pressing [American] foreign policy concerns: alleviating poverty, promoting economic development, improving global health, building civil society, strengthening weak and failing states, assisting democratization, tempering extremism."[25] The declaration is candid and welcome. But it may also generate hesitation about the liberal secular agenda that she advances in her own voice, resonating with her employer's aims, and natural reservations about the capacity and the rightness of American foreign policy when it is motivated by transforming mission.

23. Badran, *Feminism in Islam*, chs. 9 and 13; esp. pp. 306-311.

24. The title page of Coleman's *Paradise Beneath Her Feet* contains the statement "A Council on Foreign Relations Book." In a spirit of disclosure, I should say that I have been a non-resident member of that council for over twenty years.

25. Coleman, *Paradise Beneath Her Feet*, p. xvii.

Coleman never ventures into former President George W. Bush's vaingloriously stated policy framework of democratizing the Middle East. But neither does she transcend the inspiration supplied by Les Gelb to see gender as a lens for U.S. foreign policy.

For a modern Muslim female, gender is not about anybody's foreign policy as much as it is an essential context in which to consider and to live her religion.[26] Among several deeply percipient recent female commentators on the subject is Kecia Ali. Her studies of the texts move her to confront the ever-present tension in the Qur'an between egalitarianism and hierarchy. Eventually she concludes that the Qur'an is thoroughly androcentric, but not misogynist. In her honesty she concedes "the strength of some scriptural interpretations positing a privileged role for males in family and society." But this does not daunt her from noting "equally compelling feminist interpretations of the text when historical context is considered and when critical principles of justice, kindness, and love are taken seriously."[27]

26. In www.contestations.net, 28 May 10, Hania Sholkamy's blog complains thoughtfully about "the persistent need to package, simplify , and deliver development at any cost." While differing from her in nuance, Margot Badran in response also opposes such instrumentalization of religion.

27. Kecia Ali, *Sexual Ethics & Islam: Feminist Reflections on Qur'an, Hadith, and Jurisprudence* (Oxford, Oneworld, 2006), esp. pp. 112, 115-16, 131-32; quotation on p. 133.

Among recent textual commentators was Fatima Mernissi, who was groundbreaking with *The Veil and the Male Elite* (New York, Basic Books, 1991; 1st French ed., 1987) and *Scheherezade Goes West: Different Cultures, Different Harems* (New York, Washington Square Press, 2001). Jane Damman McAuliffe, ed., *The Cambridge Companion to the Qur'an* (Cambridge, Cambridge University Press, 2000) contains excellent grounding essays.

Leila Ahmed, *Women and Gender in Islam* (New Haven, Yale University Press, 1992), is consistently disciplined in its invocation of histories and cultures, and in *A Quiet Revolution: The Veil's Resurgence from the Middle East to America* (New Haven, Yale University Press, 2011), Ahmed stresses that the veil, once an emblem of patriarchy, since her earlier book has become a symbol of individuality, justice, and women's rights. Barbara Stowasser, *Women in the Qur'an, Traditions, and Interpretations* (Oxford, Oxford University Press, 1984), is exacting in its command of texts; and Sachiko Murata, *The Tao of Islam* (Albany, State University of New York Press, 1992), demonstrates ways that "polarity expresses unity."

More recent commentators prominently include: Asma Barlas, *Believing Women in Islam: Unreading Patriarchal Interpretations of the Qur'an* (Austin, University of Texas Press, 2004); Amina Wadud, *Qur'an and Woman: Rereading the Sacred Text from a Woman's Perspective* (Oxford, Oxford University Press, 1999), and *Inside the Gender Jihad: Women's Reform in Islam* (Oxford, Oneworld, 2006).

Valuable collections: of women's eloquence, Elizabeth Warnock Fernea and Basima Qattan Bezirgan, eds., *Middle Eastern Women Speak* (Austin, University of Texas Press, 1977);

Religion and Secularism: Osmosis

Amid these contrasts, in their swirls of change, I lay out the book that follows. It undertakes an arc from eastern Indonesia to western Turkey, traveling through Pakistan, Iran, and Saudi Arabia. I have tried to embrace the most Sufi-influenced nation (Indonesia); the one most secular by convention, but containing a newly energetic Islam (Turkey); the classical Sunni state (Saudi Arabia), whose monarchy still plays to its ultra-literalist Wahhabi lords of text; the revolutionary Shi'ite state (Iran), whose mullahs sit on the aftershocks of violence and hope that social writhings beneath them do not portend another eruption; and the most India-affected state (Pakistan), whose basic anarchy emboldens extremists to outdo each other in the name of valorous Islam. In this way, I hope I capture some chief national variants of modern Islam without pretending to distill an elixir from among them. I leave out Iraq and Afghanistan as over-complicated by the presence of American troops. I presume Indonesia will convey many (of course not nearly all) of the phenomena of Malaysia; and Pakistan likewise for Bangladesh. The Maghreb, sub-Saharan Africa, and Egypt each have their own dynamisms; but they are too much for me to try to include without diluting my findings about women in Islam, which would be as serious a misstep as essentializing them. On the pent-up Arab protests of 2011, I offer summary reflections in an epilogue.

I hope to have avoided two kinds of anti-historical errors. One of them says of religion, "it's all over," as a strong secular narrative did, blinded by social science for several decades after World War II. It's not over, but has restarted itself, as signified not only by Islam, treated here, but also by enduring convictions in the U.S., evangelical storms in Latin America and Africa, and the vigor of religious renewal in China — Taoist,

---

on modern social dynamics, Valentine M. Moghadan, ed., *From Patriarchy to Empowerment: Women's Participation, Movements, and Rights in the Middle East, North Africa, and South Asia* (Syracuse, Syracuse University Press, 2007).

Laleh Bakhtiar's revised edition of *The Sublime Quran* (www.sublimequran.org, 2009; 1st ed., 2007) provides the first translation by an American woman. In her preface (p. xv) she observes, "Clearly the intention of the Quran is to see man and woman as complements of one another, not as superior-inferior." Among men sensitive to women's dimensions in theology, but only briefly articulate about it, are two with Iranian heritage: Hamid Dabashi, *Islamic Liberation Theology: Resisting the Empire* (Abingdon/New York, Routledge, 2008); and Abbas Amanat, *Apocalyptic Islam and Iranian Shi'ism* (London/New York, I. B. Tauris, 2009).

Buddhist, and Christian — despite decades of policy suppression under a one-party government.[28]

Ian Buruma has written a thoughtful book entitled *Taming the Gods*, in which he argues that religious faith will not go away. Danger, as he sees it, lies chiefly in quasi-religious political movements such as Nazism and Stalinism, not to mention emperor worship in Japan before 1945, or cultic veneration of the dictator Mao Zedong. Buruma comes out of what he calls the "liberal pillar" of a Dutch society that was once vertically segmented by religious ideology. This apparently leaves him skeptical about faith, but most of all concerned with "how to stop irrational passions from turning violent."[29] I cannot see that giving fuller measure to the growth of women as individuals and opportunity for their social expression would accomplish that noble goal, or that anything in the current laboratory of humanity will reliably ensure it. Equality for women, however, may be argued on the simple grounds of economic productivity, and must be advanced on the basis of principle.

Despite the growths of religious intensity in the last thirty years, it's not "all over" with secularism, either. Europe demonstrates secularism's triumph, if it be that, with the poignant emptiness of its churches. And the U.S. does so in its own dramatic style, with its peculiar mixture of consumer cultism, collusive anarchism, and Jeffersonian dogma. Radical individualism continues to penetrate the membranes of American society.

Religion and secularism will go on struggling in American life, without fundamentalism ever coming close to prevailing. It finds it must always compromise, even if yielding on one front manifests a sterner stand on another. So the Southern Baptist Convention in 2000 apologized for its past racism while announcing subordination of wife to husband in marriage and dependency of women in general and confirming a male-only pastorate.[30] In such tactics, fundamentalism will flail but not prevail. Meanwhile, compunctious secularity is unlikely ever to be able to rule souls in the way that a confessed faith may do. After all, what soul satisfaction is there in the "Powers of the Secular Modern" as articulated, with tragic sensibility, by Talal Asad? However the "modern" expresses itself, in

28. On China, I am especially grateful to Prof. Nathan Sivin, who is the only foreign-born certified practitioner of Taoist religious rituals, as well as an abundantly published expert on Chinese science.

29. Ian Buruma, *Taming the Gods: Religion and Democracy on Three Continents* (Princeton, Princeton University Press, 2010), p. 10.

30. Almond et al., *Strong Religion*, p. 227.

the Middle Eastern state or the Western state and their subordinate forms, there is a tendency to premature closure implied in "modernity." Asad's agonized progressivism would move conceptually between Islamic tradition and Western modernity to weave something new.[31]

A "secular modern" seems to be granted extraordinary power by Isobel Coleman when she writes, "I suspect that over the long term, Islamic feminism, like other reform movements that preceded it, will end up unapologetically secular. Only then will never-ending debates over religious interpretations be removed from politics." Does Coleman actually mean that all Islamic reform movements end up secular? If so, some examples, please. Or does she mean that all feminist reform movements end up secular? If she means the latter, she might with more acuity observe that reform for women in Islam began as secular over a century ago, and has recently tended to become religious — even, in order to prevail in the present environment, grounded in sacred text.

What does "unapologetically secular" mean? In the Upper East Side of New York City, where Coleman and colleagues are professionally located, secular-speak is the prevailing language. To be, in that locale, unapologetically religious would be the rare case. But Coleman apparently wishes a future not religious at all, in order for "never-ending debates over religious interpretation" to "be removed from politics."[32]

The real point about never-ending debates, I think, is that they never end. What happens when they are removed from politics? When the structures of power absorb spiritual prerogatives as well as temporal, we then see Nazi Germany, Stalinist Russia, Maoist China, and Imperial Japan. The costs in these modern cases included relentless persecutions and arbitrary executions, and Coleman is clearly far too humane to wish for those. But her concluding logic might carelessly lead in such directions. She does not realize, as Buruma quietly makes clear, that a blur of powers with ambiguity about realms is a corollary of the most tenacious modern democracies. In such polities there is never a "firewall" between church and state, but there nevertheless must be definable membranes separating them. Membranes, however, are sensitive tissue, and they permit osmosis. Interpretive debates are a sign of vitality in a democracy. Ms. Coleman is a sincere and hard-working advocate for women's rights in Islamic worlds, but her pre-

---

31. David Scott and Charles Hirschkind, eds., *Powers of the Secular Modern: Talad Asad and His Interlocutors* (Palo Alto, Stanford University Press, 2006), *passim*.

32. Quotations, Coleman, *Paradise Beneath Her Feet*, pp. 274-75.

mature epistemic closure on religion would not allow those societies, or any society, to flourish long-term in humane ways.

Popular attitudes nevertheless persist in Muslim countries, vivid in proverbs which project "an attitude akin to that which led to the burying of girls alive." Denial of education and religious authority to women recalls *al jahiliya,* says Akram Nadwi, evoking the ignorance and barbaric practices of pre-Islamic Arabia.[33] But a counter-momentum is gathering. The UN, in 2006, published a "Study of the Secretary-General" entitled *Ending Violence Against Women: From Words to Action.*[34] The catalogue of violences is thick, but this small book cuts through and condemns the tangle. My own travel and observations take only an Islamic path, but I certainly do not ascribe to that faith a unique obstinacy. Hypertextual fundamentalism in the U.S. and in Christian and Jewish communities elsewhere can be heavily obscurantist and suffocating to women. By saying so, I am by no means trying to be a surreptitious deicide. On the contrary: I believe that reflective religion, Abrahamic and other, can give integrity to human lives and sublimity to human purpose.

In self-critique, I may observe that a truly bizarre phenomenon is a Christian male undertaking the task of reporting on and appraising the rights, roles, and rules affecting women in Islam. But I nonetheless make the attempt, fully conscious of what Margot Badran observes, that liberal discourse by males will not save women in Islam, nor will conservative discourse by males doom women in Islam. What follows intends to be open and exploratory discourse by an outsider, lacking non-Western languages other than Indonesian, but one who, in English or with aid of interpreters, has generated over 200 interviews to help him understand what he sees.

From Arabia to Java, as a word for pedigree, there exists the term *silsila.* It can mean, roughly, a genealogical tree, but when used in religious context it has the ambition of meaning a course of learning traceable back to the Prophet. For Sufis especially the word is valuable, implying or denoting a spiritual genealogy for centuries, by the disciplines passed on

---

33. Nadwi cited in Powers, ". . . Feminist Scholars . . ."

34. The study was mandated by General Assembly resolution 58/185, and prepared by the Division for the Advancement of Women of the Department of Economic and Social Affairs of the United Nations Secretariat.

through specific illustrious teachers. A *silsila* identifies and legitimates the Sufi seeker. In a more practical context, Badran uses it to mean the acknowledged transmission of inspiration and tactics among feminists in Islam. I, of course, have neither longitudinal connections in Islamic *silsila* nor lateral radius in feminist *silsila*. But I humbly presume to enter both realms of discourse, hoping that my credentials might be my genuine interest and my ability to learn.

Joining the conversation, I would wish to engage in it in ways signified by my title: *Woman, Man, and God in Modern Islam.* I don't conceive of women apart from men, and don't conceive of either apart from God. Lacking *silsila,* I can only bring to bear those chains of influence that significantly affect my life: a church which may be called progressive Calvinist; an interfaith discussion group which in an average gathering of fifteen people may contain six world religions; and the Metanexus Institute, where as a board member for a decade I have identified with its mission of generating dialogue between religion and science.

My central belief regarding the dynamics I discuss is simple: that women and men are equal in the eye of God, and should be equal in human law. I know that each of those statements is intensely debatable, but I do not wish to weaken the declaration here by over-definition. In my pages themselves the reader may find occasions to differ. For discussions and correction I am available online: doriefriend@prodigy.net.

My approach carries convictions with it: that Christianity and all religions should be open to faithful inquiry and critical dialogue, and that the best of Islam, as in Rumi and Hafiz, has always been open and remains so. In Islamabad, Professor Anis Ahmad wished me well in my *jihad,* and his welcoming spirit is with me still. As for understanding women, indeed in understanding both genders, I would wish to rise to the sublime perception of Maulana 'Abdur Rahman Jami, five hundred years ago, writing about the eighth-century saint Rabi'a of Basra:

> If all women were like [this] one,
> Then women would be preferred to men.

> For the feminine gender is no shame for the sun,
> Nor is the masculine gender an honor for the moon.[35]

35. Annemarie Schimmel, *My Soul Is a Woman: The Feminine in Islam* (New York, Continuum, 2003; 1st German ed., 1995), pp. 78, 181.

1.1-2 Communist (1965) and anti-Communist (1966) demonstrations. In front of the U.S. Embassy, mid-September 1965 (top), large, organized demonstration makes clear its anti-American and pro-Sukarno energies. Tension from numerous such rallies climaxed in the attempted coup of 30 September, and exploded in violence for many months.

By September 1966, a year later, killings of Communists had largely ended. As the country sorted out its political sentiments under General Suharto, marches remained frequent. In another part of the demonstrations pictured (bottom), banners labeled the Communist party "traitors to the people."

In these two images, female headgear is important. The young women in straw hat and cap (top) signify their secularism or atheism. Those in white headscarves (bottom) manifest religiosity. From their drums hang pennants for a Muslim madrasa.

Photos: Beryl Bernay

1.3 Pilgrim women in Ulukan, Central Sumatra, 1989. They are praying at the tomb of
Sheikh Burhanuddin, a Minangkabau scholar-leader and Sufi who made this small town
a seventeenth-century center for propagation of Islam. Veneration of saints is strictly forbidden in orthodox Islam, but comes naturally to Indonesians. *Photo: Abbas/Magnum*

1.4 Muhammadiyah school in Gresik, East Java, 1989. Founded in 1912 as a Sunni social and educational organization, Muhammadiyah now claims 30 million members, and schools approaching 6,000 in number. The *jilbab* (Arabic: *hijab*) is mandatory for girls' dress. Here, obviously, boys may study in the same room, but genders are clearly divided by an aisle.   *Photo: Abbas/Magnum*

1.5 Biology class for female students in a Muhammadiyah boarding school — the Assalam pesantren in Solo, Central Java, 2004. *Photo: Abbas/Magnum*

1.6 Celebration of Maulud, birthday of the Prophet, Yogyakarta, 1989. This religious procession features men wearing sarong and a ceremonial umbrella, in festive traditions elaborated through the palace of the Sultan.   *Photo: Abbas/Magnum*

1.7 Javanese pilgrims to the shrine of Sultan Agung (Imogiri, Central Java, 1989) are obviously at ease in mixed gender with bare shoulders — unimaginable in puritanical desert Islam. Sultan Agung, a military-administrative figure in the early seventeenth century, has become a figure of devotion in Central Java. Strict Islam, however, considers even veneration of the Prophet to be dangerous deviance from absolute monotheism.

Photo: Abbas/Magnum

1.8 Islam in Sulawesi culture: this wedding in Gorontalo, 1989, shows the groom taking symbolic possession of the bride. *Photo: Abbas/Magnum*

1.9 Four women, Sulawesi: two of them are wearing their sarong as chador. Of the bare-armed pair, one is wearing a simple blouse, and the other a t-shirt.

Photo: Abbas/Magnum

1.10 Choice of cultures, Surabaya, East Java, 2004. Three women wearing Islamic head covering pass window displays for Western female underwear and hairstyle.

Photo: Abbas/Magnum

1.11 "Faith and Gender." Some of the participants in a dialogue (Jakarta, 2004) hosted by Siti Nuraini Jatim (center) for the author (to her right), and reported by NOOR, a monthly for Muslim women. Juni Djamaloeddin, in light blue, is on the left, and on the right are the editorial and business leaders of NOOR, Sri Artaria and Ria Alisjabahana.

Photo: Gita Wirasti

Chapter 1

INDONESIA

Indonesia suffered more adversely from the Asian financial crisis of 1997 than any other nation. Yet after a period of quasi-anarchy that followed dethroning the dictator Suharto, its new leaders and a galvanized electorate did more to restructure their country than any other in the post-crisis years. If Russia failed at both restructuring its economy and providing freedom of expression, and if China has achieved restructuring while not daring to liberate opinion, Indonesia may be said to have achieved significant gains in both dimensions. A decade after the crisis that ripped economies in East and Southeast Asia, Indonesia was presenting itself to the world as the country where democracy, modernity, and Islam were walking hand in hand.[1]

Islam in Oceania

The progress of Islam in the islands now called Indonesia was slow and largely peaceful. From around 1000 C.E., traders from Arabia, India, and China increasingly lingered and settled in Indonesian ports, bringing with them influences from the new international circuit of Islam. By the late thirteenth century, homegrown Islamic communities had been generated,

---

1. On the meltdown, see Theodore Friend, *Indonesian Destinies* (Cambridge, Harvard University Press, 2003), pp. 292-98; on recovery a decade later, see Dewi Fortuna Anwar, "United States and Indonesia: Bilateral Relations and External Factors," USINDO conference keynote speech at Johns Hopkins, SAIS, Washington, D.C., 19 Apr 07.

Sufi in temperament. From these entrepots Islam slowly moved into the interiors, where it confronted Hindu and Buddhist kingdoms that survived until the sixteenth century. Against Indianesque rajas, Islamic sultans eventually prevailed.[2] And the hierarchic received religion gave way to universal and egalitarian Islam, a faith that contained the ability to communicate directly to God without an intervening agency, with dimensions of social responsibility and adaptability to Indonesia's rich layers of cultural tradition — Hindu, Buddhist, and animist.

Indonesia presented a cultural easel on which to paint Islam wholly different from the Arabian backdrop. Its islands, across the Southwest Pacific and the Southeast Indian Oceans, offer a vastly different atmosphere. Indonesians exist at 80 to 95°F (Arabs may be much hotter by day, much colder by night). They live at 80 to 95 percent humidity (Arabs conduct a dry life, generally, except in Jeddah and coastal areas). Sun, rainfall, and vegetation establish a world in contrast to Arab sun, sand, and aridity. Indonesians naturally dress so as to maximize evaporation. The Qur'an does not address such problems, because the Angel Gabriel spoke to the Prophet Muhammad in a dry climate. Who shall criticize the Arabs for having developed the *abaya,* a long black robe for women, and the *thobe,* a loose-fitting, ankle-length robe, most often white, for men? One must keep the sun off one's body and prevent wind from driving sands against one's skin. Variances of style are marginal to these essential protections.

Extremes, however, arise from theology. The *burqa,* a woman's garment that reveals only the eyes, and may cover those with a mesh, is a function of religious-political teaching. No climate requires it, nor does the Qur'an. But the Taliban prescribed it during their years of rule in Afghanistan, along with much else that limited women's vision, education, presence, and opportunities.

Indonesian costumes are flexible and vary by region. Javanese women have traditionally worn *kebaya* and *sarong* — a blouse that falls below the waist and a sheath-skirt that covers the ankles. But unless one was working in the sun, no head covering. Modern concessions began, however, with the Islamic revival, which began to smolder in the 1970s, and for arbitrary precision can be said to have ignited in 1979.

The Iranian revolution made itself felt in Indonesia, even though its native context was Shi'ite and its consequence was a theocratic state. The

---

2. Jean Gelman Taylor, *Indonesia: Peoples and Histories* (New Haven, Yale University Press, 2003), pp. 59-67, 72-75.

ripple effect of resurgent Islam across the miles and over the waters reached Indonesia as simple assertiveness of Muslims affirming their religion for the sake of personal identities, and against two forces: the culture and the presidency. Indonesia had been a multi-confessional state since founding, in its own revolution of 1945-49. The Sukarno-Hatta duumvirate that led the nation for its early decades eliminated from its draft constitution a phrase that would have required all Muslims to obey shari'a law. The consequences of the seven words that they struck would have meant, they feared, secessionism in provinces where Christian minorities were pronounced, and resentment among Hindus, mostly on Bali, and Buddhists, mostly descended from Chinese immigrants. Indonesia, therefore, began hospitably to major world religions.

The five principles, "Pancasila," voiced by Sukarno to clinch the constitution and inspire the populace, are easily understandable in the North: nationalism, democracy, social justice, humanitarianism, and belief in a Supreme Being. Suharto, who deposed Sukarno in the violence of 1965-66, and suffocated him politically, took the fifth of the principles and made it the first. Atheistic communists were allegedly the chief provocateurs of the violence — for which half a million of them, and their sympathizers, paid with their lives. A major test of loyal citizenship then became belief in a Supreme Being. Atheism was communism, diabolically subversive. Theism was all-Indonesian. The nature of your god and liturgy mattered less than simply having them.

In the calm following the mass killings, Suharto increased his presidential power and intensified the claims of Pancasila upon the public. He eventually made Pancasila the "sole basis" of all organizations, public and private. On the road toward this ideological strait-jacketing, many Muslims demurred. A clash with police and army in 1984, in the poor port area of northern Jakarta called Tanjung Priok, led to hundreds of deaths, responsibility for which is still being sorted out a quarter-century later.

There is no question in my mind, having later talked with his military chief of staff at the time, that the source of the order to shoot was Suharto. But having driven home his Pancasila ideology, Suharto began to wake up to world Islamic resurgence. By 1991 he made his first hajj and had established ICMI, the Indonesian Muslim Intellectuals Association, to give him leverage on religio-political dynamics.

But while laboring-class men protested violently in Tanjung Priok, Indonesian women of all classes were feeling new Muslim dynamics in their own ways.

Islamic Revival, Poverty, and Disaster

I first encountered Indonesian Islamic revival in the form of women's dress. Late in 1982, I made a research trip to Indonesia after a lapse of a dozen years, to complete work on a book that I'd suspended to become a college president.[3] The first thing that struck me was the number of Indonesian women wearing headscarves. In the late 1960s, very few or almost none had done so. Now many did so. Polls in Indonesia were still scarce, and could not tell me a percentage of scarved women. "Many," I could say, but certainly far from "most."

Wardah Hafidz remembers the new seizures of women's consciousness at that time. Of slight build, serious mien, and determination, she obtained her doctorate in Indiana, in social policy. She came there knowing only Hollywood images, and thinking well of the U.S. She was unprepared for what she experienced in Muncie. There she heard some Americans hooting at others, "Hey, nigger." She began to understand the Ku Klux Klan with its grotesque garble of allegedly biblical teachings. Now she saw a more complex America.

Back in Indonesia in the early 1980s, she found new splits affecting women. Initiatives for equal opportunity had been making some progress, despite Suharto's ultra-patriarchal mode of governance. But now, instead of pressing onward for equal opportunity, some women were coiling back and staying at home, dedicated to being good Muslim housewives. Others, she found, "secular like myself," were told to stay home in Muslim respect, despite their counter-convictions. To deepen the confusion, some Muslim women, applying for jobs and wearing the *jilbab* (an Indonesian term used rather than the Arab *hijab*) were turned down for that very factor — clothing that appeared anti-secular, anti-social, even anti-Suharto, or just implicitly argumentative.

"With some friends . . . dissenting, we introduced feminist critical thinking to Indonesia. We created controversy," she later recalled. She began to quote Fatima Mernissi (later published in Indonesian), the eloquent Moroccan who was challenging male Arabic scholars on the meaning of texts. Likewise the Pakistani Riffat Hassan, who later served in Musharraf's government.

Wardah stayed on these issues for several years until her article in

---

3. *The Blue-Eyed Enemy: Japan against the West in Java and Luzon, 1942-1945* (Princeton, Princeton University Press, 1988).

Ulumul Qur'an, entitled "Misogyny in Islam," provoked a critical attack in a ten-page article from the Dewan Dakwah. This major Indonesian council for the propagation of Islamic faith castigated her for behaving like a dog with "her howling and barking." They categorized Wardah as a *kafir* — as infidel, unbeliever, heathen. A modern Indonesian-English dictionary[4] elaborates a dozen kinds of subdescription of infidel. Wardah didn't say which kind, or kinds, they called her. The dogmatists showed their canine teeth by circulation of their attack to *mushollas,* places of worship in residential areas and office buildings.

Then the Dewan Dakwah invited Wardah to appear on a panel. Her friends warned her it would be conducted as a public trial. She consulted Nurcholish Madjid about the matter. Madjid's career beliefs, devoted to Islam and objecting to Islamic political parties, affected a whole generation. He had launched a new Muslim university in Jakarta, whose curriculum was rich in social science and natural science, leading Paul Wolfowitz, then American ambassador, to believe that it would someday be Indonesia's equivalent of a Georgetown or Brandeis University. Madjid was highly influential among Indonesia's small but growing middle class.

Madjid and the leader of Nahdlatul Ulama (NU), Abdurrahman Wahid, had both grown up in Jombang, East Java, and had attended liberal *pesantrens* led by their fathers. (*Pesantrens* is an Indonesian term for traditional Islamic boarding schools — distinct from what the English-speaking world has taught itself to call *madrasas,* which in Indonesia are Islamic day schools.) Their fathers' schools were open to frontiers of learning, as the best of Islam had been a millennium before. The national standing of the two men was contained in their universal nicknames: Madjid as "Cak Nur" and Wahid as "Gus Dur." Wahid brought to rural Islam an openness correspondent to that which Madjid brought to urban Islam. Gus Dur was elected president, post-Suharto, in 1999, but was impeached and unseated a year and a half later, his Sufi anarchism having worn poorly in high office.[5] Cak Nur's own attempt at the presidency failed in 2004.

In consulting Madjid concerning her problem with the Dewan Dakwah, Wardah Hafidz was reaching out to an intellectually flexible reformer. "Ignore them," he told her. Instead of letting herself be tried by the council, she

---

4. Alan M. Stevens and A. Ed. Schmidgall-Tellings, *A Comprehensive Indonesian-English Dictionary* (Athens, Ohio University Press, 2004).

5. I published a critical celebration of Gus Dur upon his death, "Abdurrahman Wahid, The Indonesian Republic, and Dynamics of Islam," Foreign Policy Research Institute (Philadelphia), E-Notes, Jan 2010.

sent them a further article. They attacked it vituperatively. Many people were now telling Wardah's parents, with sympathetic alarm, that she was *"kafir."* Her parents asked her to explain what was going on. She recalls chiefly that "I feel bad [that] I gave trouble to my family." She changed her field.

Wardah felt there were now plenty of people in the women's movement, but she was tiring of the jealousies within it. Very few at that time were working on urban poverty — on advocacy of the rights of the millions of poor in Jakarta, many of whom were being evicted from their homes or seeing them burned down by the army. That was the "main reason" she shifted her focus.

Islam, of course, does not cause poverty. But neither UNDP nor World Bank national tables of income suggest that it alleviates poverty. Wardah is now tackling that poverty, one of her country's major problems. Some women in other Muslim nations are doing likewise, in rural as well as urban areas.

Wardah immersed herself in Jelembar Baru, a kampong in West Jakarta which flooded even without rain, because of tides rolling in and out. She found three noxious influences there. It was adjacent, first of all, to a red-light area. Many of the women who lived there were sex workers, and many of the men were security guards to sex establishments. Boys got into sex at twelve, eleven, ten years of age, and contracted sexually transmitted diseases early in life. A second debilitating influence in the kampong economy was the prevalence of gambling. And the third, who failed to be an influence counter to these factors, was the *ustad,* the male religious teacher who owned the biggest *pesantren* in the area and held, profitable to himself, grand study conferences each month. He made people who didn't pray five times a day and didn't fast during Ramadan feel like bad Muslims. Behind her glasses, Wardah furrowed her brow at the guilt contributions he sought; very poor people have no time for praying when they are hunting for jobs and for food. And, if they are hungry anyway, more physical harm than spiritual good may come from fasting.

Wardah shook her head. "Islam in Indonesia requires rituals, and people feel good practicing them. . . . But the society is corrupt, manipulative, murderous. In Islamic terms, it is *munafik,* hypocritical. . . . You see many men in religious attire, who beat their wives and keep concubines."

At that point I observed that hypocrisy cuts into all religions. Wardah agreed. Yet she pursued her point that religion in Indonesia doesn't relieve poverty: "If you give two and half percent [of your wealth, annually, as prescribed by the Qur'an], while you are stealing 50 percent from the people, what are you doing? Many give this tithe, expecting your good image as Muslim gets you two and a half hectares of land in heaven. . . . Question is, how much they steal?!"

What is the income, I asked Wardah, of the poorest of the urban poor? A family of five, she reckoned, might scrape together 150,000 rupiah per month. Divided among five, I calculated, that is 1,000 rupiah a day. Or, at then-current exchange rates, *twelve cents a day*, on which the poorest of the poor must survive. Wardah nodded, and added that most of them are squatters.

The CD-ROMs of Wardah's Urban Poverty Coalition (UPC) show the impact of Jakarta's frequent floods and forced evictions by police and army.[6] Squatters don't have ID cards, and so they are marginalized with regard to government programs to alleviate poverty. World Bank subsidies, when channeled by the government, are blocked by corruption before reaching the very poor. Water and electricity are being privatized for profit, and "beautification" of cities often means eviction by land grabbers.

If you take the UN standards of poverty, a dollar or two a day, Wardah went on, in Indonesia about 40 percent of the population are included, which means about 90 million poor. What about the "poorest of the poor"? I asked. She said they are 20 or 30 percent of the total. That means 18 to 27 million people living on less than one dollar a day. Wardah illustrated such plights by telling me the recent story of a mother with two children, one with brain cancer, who had no means to put the child in a hospital. She burned herself and her two children to death, leaving a devastated husband behind.

I asked about scavengers. Wardah implied that they did not need my utmost sympathy: "They are in the middle layer of the poor." They can earn two and a half to five dollars a day, which is better than fruit-sellers or female laundresses.

Wardah asked me about violence in Karachi, of which she had heard (see Chapter Two). "Here," she said, "much more greenery, much more smiling." But state violence is high. The poor are pitted against each other. Local elites and interest groups work through the police and military, which hire jobless males as enforcers. The mayor of Jakarta ordered an attack on Wardah's Urban Poverty Coalition in 2002, and managed to get himself reelected despite that assault, or perhaps because of it.

---

6. See especially "Kota Dalam Baskom," "State Violence," and "Asian People's Dialog," produced by *Konsortium Kemiskinan Kota* (Urban Poverty Coalition), Jakarta.

She relayed a conversation from her meeting with *becak* (pedicab) drivers, who were complaining about their mistreatment by security guards.

Becak driver A: "Why don't we kidnap one of them?"

Wardah: "Where do they live?"

Several drivers: "They are our neighbors. Our houses are the same as theirs inside, except for their uniforms."

Wardah (provocatively, and perhaps still smoldering from the attack on her UPC headquarters): "Why not kidnap the mayor?"

Several drivers: "That's too tough a job."

Driver B: "I can get an *orang pintar* (literally, a clever person; by implication the kind of *dukun* who is skilled in sorcery) from my village to cast a spell on the mayor."

Wardah: "But he has many *dukuns* to protect him, doesn't he?"

Upshot: the drivers assembled could not decide on collective action. Driver B was later reported as leaving Jakarta and going back to his village to live.

I asked Wardah why the suffering does not deter, nor the hypocrisy defeat her. "To be cynical," she answered, "is to admit defeat. You must keep going, keep struggling, keep optimistic, finding a way to break through. . . .

"I learned a good lesson from the urban poor . . . under a railroad bridge. . . . I got news this community was going to be evicted. Our UPC was in panic, but the people were not. They had been living there twenty years, always under threat." Once they were burned down; another time force-sprayed with ditchwater. A third time their houses were demolished with bars cantilevered from a passing train. "Why should we be in panic?" they said. "Why should we even be angry? We will plan, and we will survive."

"The poor can be very resilient, very strong," said Wardah, obviously inspired by this community. After it was burned again, they were ready, and rebuilt their houses in several hours.

She added an example of a boy who had been on the streets since age eight, and three times arrested by age twelve. Once his mother bailed him out by selling his sister's earring. With no such resources left, the next time he had to figure his own way out. He found a hole down in the prison latrine and swam his way through the sewage, out into an open field.[7]

7. Wardah Hafidz, interview, Yogyakarta, 18 Dec 04.

Wardah's next phase of career was in Aceh. She moved there for UPC shortly after the tsunami at the end of 2004. That cataclysm took an estimated 163,000 lives in Aceh alone, and up to a quarter of a million around the rim of the Indian Ocean — more than the atomic bombs on Hiroshima and Nagasaki combined, and about the same number as the Haiti earthquake of 2010. The destruction of communities and dislocation of families persuaded her to relocate herself from Jakarta, leaving others of her UPC in charge for the capital city.

Acehnese rebels in this province nearest to Mecca had been fighting off and on since 1976 for independence. Perhaps 12,000 had died in the quarter century of struggle for Acehneseness, which includes strong Muslim elements. The central government put in an estimated 40,000 troops in 2003 to try to end the fight, but it was not ending. Then on a sunny Sunday morning the waves crashed in, and the humanitarian crisis eventually brought about a truce.

"The water was as high as coconut trees — twenty meters," Wardah recounted from survivors. Women were at home, but if they had time to try to run for the hills, carrying or pulling children with them, the water might catch them in full Islamic dress. Sodden clothes pulled them under. Even if the water threw them to higher ground, many had swallowed "deadly stuff" on the way and died later.

Wardah chose as her base an area a quarter of an hour's drive from the drowned provincial capital, Banda Aceh. She introduced herself, for the UPC, to a cluster of twenty-four communities trying to rebuild their villages, two hundred meters to two kilometers from the ocean. Only 10 percent of their population had survived. And most of those, nearly 90 percent, were men, saved by strength and mobility, by being well out at sea, or by being without skirts. But what kinds of communities would they make, with so few women and children? Some men suggested that someone should "ship hundreds of women here." But who would send them, from where? Would they be good Muslims? Above all, who would come?

Aceh's history includes notable high points of activist women. In the late sixteenth century, the era of Elizabeth I of England, the female admiral Malahayati commanded a fleet numbered by a British observer at a hundred galleons. This most effective naval force in the Malacca Strait included the Armada Inong Bale, made up of 2,000 women, mostly widows like Malahayati herself. In the court of the Sultan she added functions of a foreign minister, as appropriate to the prizes of trade that were then the crux of regional wealth. In the mid- and late seventeenth century, four successive queens ruled Aceh, three of them with high effectiveness.[8] Female warriors Cut Nya Din and Cut Meuthia were prominent among those opposing the Dutch in the late nineteenth and early twentieth centuries. And during the recent rebellion, a number of Acehnese widows and young unmarried women took up arms for a brigade called, for historic reasons, "Inong Bale."

These examples, however, were not pivotal for the poor fisher folk Wardah was trying to assist. Both men and women were rendered helpless by the tsunami. The village men, who had conducted all public gatherings, now had to confront new realities. Collecting and burying bodies en masse was a necessity; strangers were washed ashore and had to be buried among beloved neighbors. Only then could they get to salvaging belongings and erecting temporary structures. UPC was there, in the person of Wardah, to work with them on rebuilding. A *woman?* A woman *from Jakarta?*

"I preside, I coordinate," Wardah says. She worked with twenty-four elected village leaders. "All *men.* . . . Some are very *macho.* Some are okay. . . . All are very Muslim in public life. Their way is to *domesticate* women."

How, then, do they get along with someone like Wardah? I imagine her, thin, serious, worried, regarding two dozen village leaders through her spectacles, and confronting them with her experience in organization. She wouldn't pull her Ph.D. on them. But she would use her urban logic and her street smarts, adjust it to local conditions, and speak in streamlined sentences, implacably, on what is necessary and most practical. "They have to accept me because they see that I am capable. When they see [that] . . . they don't mind. They call me '*Ibu*' (Mother). . . . They are more democratic than the Javanese. They *elect* their leaders. And those who don't work get thrown out."

Was it possible, I asked, to have a public discussion of gender questions? "Maybe," was Wardah's answer. After the Special Autonomy Law of 2001 for Aceh, and accelerated recognition of shari‛a, a woman who went without a veil had her hair sheared as punishment, and tight clothing was scissored apart to require more modest dress. Some, including a powerful *ulama,* even said that the tsunami occurred because women were behaving badly.

But the UPC insisted on including women in discussion of building

8. Jennifer Dudley, "Of Warrior Women, Emancipist Princesses, 'Hidden Queens,' and Managerial Mothers," www.staff.murdoch.edu.au/~jdudley/Malahayati.

houses. The men were irritated. More women, nonetheless, flowed to meetings, and the men came to "accept." Wardah recalls that "women were very silent at first. . . . Then they started to speak, to *squeak,* really. Now they are talking, especially when their own lives are affected."

Householder names are a big issue. "What if only a woman survives? What of man/wife? Some men say head of family is man. What if one brother, two sisters survive? Do all three own equally? Basically men agree to a new equality, fearing that if they don't, UPC won't build a house for them."

Wardah freely acknowledges the power of UPC's organization and the leverage of its resources, but the corollary is implicit: after the job is done — rebuilding 3,000 houses — old cultural patterns will reassert themselves. "I was hoping gender imbalance would change things for the better for the women. And so far it has not."

The hugely skewed numbers of men in relation to women had its personal effect on Wardah. One night she was in her Acehnese secretariat, in a room shared with others, asleep in her bed, under its mosquito net. She suddenly awoke to find arms around her. She shouted, awakening all in the room. They surrounded the intruder, who was still in the room. He helplessly explained, "I didn't know who was in the mosquito net."

Wardah, in shock, returned to Jakarta for several days. She felt it was "like an earthquake," even though she understood the instance as arising from "the gender imbalance problem." I did not press any of the questions that occurred to me. Could he truly be imagined as intending rape in a crowded dorm room? Or did he simply, mindlessly, even tenderly, wish to embrace nurturant power?

On her return to Aceh, she told her story to "the elders." They cried, were ashamed, discussed it with all the villagers. She asked that there be no violence against the man; she just didn't want to see him ever again. They obliged by asking him to go back to Malaysia where he had once worked, and had relatives. He went.

"I was traumatized," Wardah recalls. "I lost my . . . trust in men. . . . But there was no way of lingering in [that] feeling." The fortitude that had served her against the moral abuse of the Dewan Dakwah, and political/ police assaults of the mayor of Jakarta, rose anew in this decimated provincial environment. "I had to go back and to coordinate all the engineers."[9] I remarked on her courage. She accepted the observation with a faint, reflective "Okay." Never vain, never defeated, she bends but does not break.

Two years later I was invited to a UPC celebration of its completed work: 3331 houses rebuilt, along with community centers, village roads, drainage, water and sanitation systems, and the reintroduction of eco-farming and small-scale industry. Ownership and participation were the most highly motivating factors in rebuilding social cohesion.[10]

At the time of the disaster, I had said to a prominent neuroscientist from Toronto that the mass of suddenly dead in Aceh probably were radiating a barely imaginable concentration of grief. The overwhelming instant, the unsparing force of nature, with calamity after calamity in family after family — all this in one coastal sector of one long island must lead, for some, to unmanageable emotions. Loss compounded by loss, with no feedback but loss.

How would you treat that? I asked him.

His answer was to ship to Aceh huge quantities of antidepressant pills. Fortunately that was not attempted. But Aceh did get peace — an agreement fostered and levered by the directly and enthusiastically elected president, Susilo Bambang Yudhoyono. Aceh also got more international donations of money, time, and expertise than Pakistan got for its terrible earthquake less than a year later.

But grief cannot be easily dispelled. What role did religion play? I asked Wardah. She rummaged for a reply, as if my question were a phenomenon of a strange order. She is not an observant Muslim, wears no *jilbab,* and is not easily led to such speculation. "They try to cope by being active." There was plenty to do. "But in evening together they talk about it. They say it is 'God's will.' They say it is a 'test from Allah.' They have to accept it as it is." They invoked the concept of *nasib:* fate. "Religion gives them psychological strength."

Antidepressants would have been a huge distraction, leading to maladministration, over-individualized therapy, and possible addictions. "Hard physical work addressed the deep trauma," as Wardah saw it. Con-

9. Wardah Hafidz, interview, Jakarta, 30 Jun 05.
10. Wardah Hafidz to the author, 14 Mar 07.

trary to the secular narrative of much of twentieth-century Western social science, the most profound resource of the Acehnese in extremity was their religion. That was proved not by a controlled experiment, but by the tsunami as a sudden, terrible, lethal test.

Matriliny against Wahhabi Zeal

My good friend Nuraini, an agnostic, was a poet in her youth, and remains one. She listens acutely. She has a good heart. She was going to volunteer in Aceh. But peace bubbled up there, through the mud and debris. Indonesia turned to others of its problems. Nuraini has four children and her grandchildren to think about, along with a wide radius of other relatives.

She comes originally from a part of Sumatra adjacent to Aceh, but a province not so affected by the great waves. Hers is an inland people, many of them highlanders: the Minangkabau (Minang, for short). Of this tribe, with its rich history, about four million live in West Sumatra, which number approaches the population of the Irish Republic or Singapore. The total number of Minangs throughout Indonesia and elsewhere exceeds seven million, roughly equal to the population of Israel.

The Minangs are of great interest to Northern anthropologists and feminists because they are the largest matrilineal (and uxorilocal) society in the world. Not "matriarchal," which would mean female dominance of decision-making processes, or the obverse of "patriarchal" — a well-known term for a complex phenomenon. Matrilineal denotes, first of all, tracing one's descent through one's maternal forebears. Among the Minang, this means that property is conveyed from mother to daughters. Sons, in consequence, go elsewhere "to seek their fortune," in old-fashioned Western terms. *Merantau* is the specific Minang verb (noun: *perantau*) for the time of life when a male empowers himself elsewhere — Java, Jeddah, a Western megalopolis. Having proved himself worthy, he may come home to wed a woman who wishes him in marriage, and so signals to senior relatives in such a way that a negotiation may be conducted. Marriage is not about romance, a senior Minang woman said once to me, contemptuous of flimsy Western arrangements; "Marriage is a *business*." But it does not exclude love, she added. "Love comes from caring, don't you think?"

So: instead of contemporary "cosmopolitan" archetypes of sex/maybe love/maybe marriage/maybe children, the established proper Minang sequence is arranged marriage/sex/children/probably love. It usually works, Minangs assure me. They speak of matrilineality as a social security system for women, which grants daughters the traditional family lands, and in modern times, liquid assets, while requiring sons to fend for themselves, driven and ennobled by the requirement of *perantau*. A high percentage of the first generation of leaders of the modern Indonesian nation were Minang, and they are still over-represented in leadership positions relative to the 3 percent that Minangs constitute of the overall population.

A system that protects women while it motivates men contains genius of forethought. No one can ascertain by written records how it began, but a state myth of the Minangkabau crystallized around historical events of the sixteenth century in which Minang kingdoms contended against neighboring Acehnese power. Islam is already recognized in the tale, but *adat* — traditional law and customs of the Minang — prevails. The indisputable source and focus of power is Bundo Kanduang (Real Mother), the original queen who "stood by herself, created together with the universe." She has no husband, but after longing for the tongue of the crocodile and drinking from the ivory coconut, she became pregnant with "the Substitute of Allah in the world, a living sacred man, the king to whom homage is due morning and afternoon." Her sons contend among neighboring powers for advantages in marriage and influence. The tale unfolds with magic, lies and intrigue, visionary dreams, bluster, honor, and great stakes in small deeds — which may seem to a Western reader not dissimilar to myths of King Arthur, except for the queenly radiance that prevails throughout.

Codes of conduct, in the Minang myth, are illustrated by human actions that fulfill them or betray them. Both *adat* (wise tradition, preexisting, from the divine soul) and *sarak* (Islamic law) are necessary for appropriateness and prosperity within the social order. Correct behavior and supporting consensus keep the tangible world in concert with the cosmos. The result may sound tautological, but for Minangs it has the satisfactory quality of truth swallowing itself: "*Adat* is based on *sarak*, and *sarak* is based on *adat*."

In the state myth, then, we have a kind of matrilineal constitutional theory, a social guidebook, and a synthesis of primordial Minang history with Islamic penetration long prior to Vasco da Gama. God is expressed not through "creations," but through emanations, starting with Bundo Kanduang, which become increasingly human, decreasingly divine, with passing generations. The myth overcomes the contradictions between *adat* and Islam, and gives a mythic sanction to the social model that it voices.[11]

But the moral entropy implicit in the God-story, expressed through the free-standing queen and then through her increasingly free-falling descendants, came to an actual and bloody phase of reckoning in the so-called Padri War of 1821-38. Minang men on religious *perantau* in Arabia began picking up the puritanical Wahhabia that had crystallized there in the mid-eighteenth century, and which has for most of the two and a half centuries since bonded a peculiar theology and its elite bearers with a special royal family, the Saud.

What happened in Sumatra when influences from a divine kingdom encountered a cosmic queendom? Prolonged conflict. Men dressed in long Arabian white clothing and turbans fought with men dressed in multicolored Minang garb woven with threads of silver and gold. The matter previously reconciled in myth — Islamic law with Minang *adat* — was torn open by the absoluteness and exclusiveness of Wahhabia. Differences could only be resolved by might.

The Wahhabi-Saudi combine had seized control of Mecca in 1803, imposing strict Qur'anic regulation on Arab conduct, and that regime would inspire Minang pilgrims returning home to West Sumatra. Religious teachers, outside the Minang royal hierarchy of mosques and patronage, had formed their own base in villages and farms, which raised export crops including coffee and pepper. Their network included rural schools for boys, with advanced students as boarders, and young men traveling as *perantau* by land and sea in the wider world of Islam. Now, with Wahhabi impact, they returned. Minang reformers first denounced male excesses as un-Islamic: cockfights, gambling, alcohol, opium. With their zeal gathering momentum, they then attacked Minang traditions specifically advantageous to women: customs on marriage, dowry, and residence. And, as ever in emanations from Arabia, there were new injunctions about attire — rejection of colorful Minang patterns in both men's and women's clothing in favor of simple white or blue, in volumes that concealed the shape of the body. Women covered all but eyes and nose. Men grew beards.

The puritanical reformers were called Padris. Perhaps Padria was a corruption of "padre," and conveyed contempt for a priestly zealot. Maybe it denoted a man who embarked for Arabia through Pedir, a major port in

---

11. Quotations from Taufik Abdullah, "Some Notes on the Kaba Tjindua Mato: An Example of Minangkabau Traditional Literature," *INDONESIA* 9 (Apr 1970), pp. 1-22.

Aceh, and whose orientation to authority radiated back inside. In any case, the Padris advanced from denunciations to organized attacks, and in 1815 they murdered Minangkabau's royal family. Against violent Padri reforms, traditionalists gathered in mining areas, preserving Javanese connections and Minang *adat,* and looked to support from the Dutch. Zealous reformers were led by Imam Bondjol, a Minang who had founded his own small state, subjugating communities through armed bands, imposing Qur'anic law and collection of taxes. In 1832 Imam Bondjol learned from his delegated *haji* that in Mecca the Wahhabi had fallen, and that Islamic laws as conveyed to him were invalid.[12] In an epiphany of remorse he apologized to the traditionalists and sought truce with the Dutch. Imperial misdeeds, however, launched him on a new phase of war in 1833, with Minangkabau society now unified against Dutch occupation.

The Dutch inclined strongly to royalty rather than "reform," to familiar structures of power rather than convulsions of puritan Muslim enthusiasm. They could not win in Minang mountains and forests against Padri fighters, who were allied with neighboring Bataks and hoisted enemy heads on their spears. By blockading Minang ports, however, the Dutch finally broke Padri power in 1837, exiled Imam Bondjol, and restored authority to the clan chiefs who had ceded them sovereignty in return for promised security sixteen years before.[13]

In Minang regional culture, a new compromise between shari'a and *adat* was reached. Shari'a was based on the Qur'an and purified by Islam, while the matrilineal system was preserved. Resolving trilateral tensions of argument among Minang traditionalists, Islamic reformers, and colonial administrators actually appears to have strengthened Minangkabau culture over time, and helps account for its continuing modern strength.[14] Today Minangs can proclaim to the world that matriliny is consistent with orthodox Islam, and fellow Indonesians at least, conceding their cultural charisma, will not usually contest the point.

Dutch suspicion of Islamic intensity and reform organizations none-

12. Jeffrey Hadler, *Muslims and Matriarchs: Cultural Resilience in Indonesia through Jihad and Colonialism* (Ithaca, Cornell University Press, 2008), pp. 21-30. Astonishingly slow transmission of news: actually, Wahhabi Mecca had been routed by the Egyptians in 1818, who occupied it until 1840. Alexei Vassiliev, *The History of Saudi Arabia* (London, Saqi Books, 2000), chs. 5 and 6.

13. Jean Gelman Taylor, *Indonesia's Peoples and Histories* (New Haven, Yale University Press, 2003), pp. 254-56.

14. Hadler, *Muslims and Matriarchs, passim.*

theless continued for more than a century. The war against the Padri was only one of several bloody struggles, most of them prolonged, by which the Dutch cobbled together their empire across three thousand miles of islands. The Netherlands East Indies, an extractive, exploitive corporate enterprise, supplied Indonesians with only one great resource — an enemy against which to unify. But that was enough to induce birth for a modern nation, in which flourish many regional cultures.[15] Indonesians are never just "Muslim" or "Christian" or "Hindu," but they live, with deep layers of meaning, as Acehnese, Minang, Batak, Javanese, Balinese, Buginese, and other.

The Padri-initiated war continues to echo in history with its hyper-monotheistic reforming zeal, its ravishing of local custom, its implacable and often brutal belligerence. The same thought waves that moved eastward from Arabian sands thousands of miles into Sumatra could ripple westward as well. In 1996, an absolutist reformer issued a *fatwa* against a wholly different and more complex foreign culture. Five years later, his followers, in a stunning act of low-tech judo against a high-tech system, hijacked and crashed passenger jet planes as missiles against the towers of the World Trade Center in New York City. Osama bin Laden's motives, just as surely as Imam Bondjol's, were religious. His politico-military means were far more cunning and sophisticated, and the scale of his ambitions much vaster. But the culture war declared by Osama resonates with the Padri reformers and warriors among the Minangkabau even if he had never heard of them.

The destruction of the twin towers by suicidal Wahhabi in 2001 has been linked to many modern events and factors. But in historic terms, its first predecessor moment is violent Wahhabi conquest of Mecca in 1803. And insofar as global al-Qaedism is fated to be a cause of prolonged and bloody hostilities, its first far-traveling precedent is the Padri war in Minangkabau, almost two hundred years ago. As the Padri warriors stormed against women owning houses and lands, modern Wahhabi rise against women driving cars in Riyadh. This hyper-puritanism perceives matrilineality as blasphemous, and anything matrifocal as irreligious. In the eighteenth century, Mohammad ibn Abdul Wahhab rivaled Jonathan Edwards of Connecticut in hellfire exhortations. In the twenty-first century, Osama exceeded even Pat Robertson in categorical condemnations. But the reassuring dimension of evoking the war initiated by the Padris is

15. Friend, *Indonesian Destinies,* pp. 17-23.

that the uxorilocal, matrilineal culture of the Minangs survived it and continues today. Native Indonesian pluralism has prevailed over foreign puritanism for nearly two centuries, and will continue to do so, if necessary, by adding another layer without eroding the strata below it. So may other local cultures, and regional pluralisms, take heart for their own forms of resilience.

The Qur'an and Women's Clothing

Nuraini remembers the Islamic boarding school to which she was sent in Central Java: far from her Minang homeland, with strictest of disciplines. On weekends she was allowed to visit family friends in Jogjakarta. A son of the house picked her up on his motorcycle, which she rode sidesaddle, stripping off her *jilbab* and gown at traffic stops so she might arrive, content and comfortable, in her normal clothing underneath.

Across the length of her life she shed many layers of Islamic teachings as well, to reach what she found as her more essential self — a Minang mother, a poet alive to the beauties of several cultures and peoples, and to fundamental things: tensions in society, trouble in the family, the loves of her children, unpredictable grandchildren.

She took an interest in my inquiries about women and the Qur'an, and assembled for discussion in Jakarta the leaders of a style magazine for Muslim women: *NOOR*. Its title means "light." From its monthly covers shine the smiles of radiant young women. *NOOR's* women, of course, do not let their tresses dangle. They cover up, containing their locks in ways that accentuate the curves of forehead and temples and convey the labyrinthine suggestions of ears. Their eyes are not downcast, but friendly to the camera.

Nuraini's initiative with the editorial women of *NOOR* gathered a crowd of seventeen, including six men, of which I was one. Of the eleven women, only four were wearing *jilbabs*. But the "Discussion of Faith and Gender," as Nuraini had billed the event, brought out strong convictions of many kinds.

Ibu Ria Alisjahbana, founder and publisher of *NOOR*, had come from an "*ulama* family" but was not taught Islam at home. She characterized her father, a famous literary figure, as an *ulama*, by which she meant not a cleric but a broadly educated person, religious in instinct but not robe-wearing. (This grammar and usage would surprise an Arab, for whom *ulama* is the plural of the singular, *alim*, meaning specifically a religious

36

scholar.) Ria went to medical school, but faced a crisis in her second year when "dissecting carcasses gave me nightmares of the face of my cadaver." She left and went on *hijra*. She found peacefulness in Islam — "far more than as 'religion'" — as a lifestyle encompassing everything.[16]

Early on in the four hours of discussion, a male facilitator of Qur'anic study at an urban foundation flung out two verses on clothing:

"Children of Adam, we have given you garments to cover your nakedness and as adornment for you; the garment of God-consciousness is the best of all garments. . . . Children of Adam, do not let Satan seduce you, as he did your parents, causing them to leave the Garden, stripping them of their garments to expose their nakedness to them" (7:26).[17] And then, getting down to female specifics: "Tell your wives, your daughters, and women believers to make their outer garments hang low over them so as to be recognized and not insulted" (33:59).

Ria picked up these themes. Her poetic take on the matter was that the "raiment of righteousness" is the best of all garments. And that the best guide in life is *takwa*, total obedience to whatever God wants you to do, which became the dominating concept of the discussion. But on raiment, views differed. The commentator explained the verse on dress in Arabic as meaning to "screen your private parts"; but he allowed that ways of obeying this directive might depend on culture.

The two most senior women present had long nationalist heritages, with prominent husbands and their own personal distinctions in leadership. Ibu Saparinah Sadli spoke for herself and for Ibu Herawati Diah, neither of whom wore a head covering. Ibu Sap remembered the revolutionary women, fifty and sixty years before, like Sukarno's first wife, Fatmawati. They wore at most a *kerudung* — a shawl that could be put over the head quickly for the requirements of a mosque. Why the *jilbab* now? Why something that fits tightly around the head, covers the shoulders and chest, and must be worn all day? Maybe it's important for us, she said with all the dignity of her doubt, to understand *why*?

"Trendy!" exclaimed Ina Samadikun. To her it did not matter where mere fashion came from. It would go away. "But my relation to God has nothing to do with my hair."

16. Conversational summaries and quotations that follow are from my notebook of 16 Dec 04, of the gathering hosted by Siti Nuraini Jatim.

17. For this quotation and all subsequent citations from the Qur'an, unless otherwise specified, I use M. A. S. Abdel Haleem, *The Qur'an: a New Translation,* Oxford World's Classics (New York, Oxford University Press, 2004).

The Qur'anic commentator shot back into action to remind the group of the greatness of the vision conveyed to the Prophet by the Angel Gabriel in 49:13 — "All mankind, men and women, we have made you into tribes and nations. . . ." which verse I recognized well enough to complete with my own emphasis, ". . . so that you may *enjoy* each other." Having the American join in on a high note seemed to give pleasure around the room.

The group fell into scoffing at Saudi women who, as international airplane passengers, hasten to get out of *abaya* and veil. And at Indonesian women in malls who wear a *kerudung* on top and body-tight clothes from there down. A man, still angry from a moment on hajj with his mother, told of being struck with sticks by religious policemen crying *haram!* What was forbidden? Holding her hand. "*Ummi!*" he replied, with one of the few Arabic words that he knew — "My mother!" He was shocked to have to justify holding the hand of her who gave him birth.

The commentator popped up again, expatiating on 4:33-36, which he asserted conveys no difference in gender, no discrimination of any kind, no slavery. Islam means submission to God. All that matters, therefore, is being humble before the Lord, being truthful in speech and deeds, and men and women guarding their chastity from illegal sexual acts. All of this sounded fine. But later, reading the passage, I found in verse 34 instructions which would take much historical sociology to explain to me, and even after that would remain offensive-sounding: "If you fear high-handedness from your wives, remind them [of the teachings of God], then ignore them when you go to bed, then hit them." Even the translator's footnote on hitting does not appease my own conviction that marital discord should be resolved without physical force: "This signifies a single blow."[18] But, I reply, a single blow signifies the failure of reason, understanding, forbearance, and the possibility of just compromise.

Two men present spoke to me aside before they left. One, with a Harvard MBA, said that Indonesian men don't have strong opinions about *jilbab,* veils, semi-veils, et cetera. They agree with many women that what matters most is not what's on the head, but what's in the heart. For men, the major issues are slavery and polygamy. They are glad that the Prophet outlawed the first and defined limits to the second. Even if they have only one wife, they cherish the "right" to have as many as four if, as the Prophet says, they are able to deal with all of them justly.

The other man had read widely in Judaism, in Christianity, and espe-

---

18. *The Qur'an,* Haleem trans., p. 54, note 6.

cially in Vedic traditions. He was tested by his own son, age twelve, who'd been taught in school that Christians go to hell. But the boy's best school friend was a Christian. "Is it true?" The father had answered by referring his son to the texts, to make up his own mind.

"And now, at your own current age of wisdom," I asked, "how would you answer your son?"

He hesitated only briefly. "I would answer 'no.'"

Juni Djamaloeddin had been a major energizer of the *NOOR* event. She wore bright blue from head to toe, only face and hands revealed, a mode she'd adopted in middle age. Her friends say that she still dances, in full Muslim dress. Her eyes shone with proprietary interest in the talk; she wanted to write me about the issues. Another organizer explained why: some of the women felt that the men had preempted too much of the discussion.

Juni's essay to me in Indonesian arrived about a month later. She cited two dozen Qur'anic texts, among them Surah 3:133-34 three times — a vital guidance to humankind, which she read as ordaining the giving of charity in fair weather and foul, restraining anger, forgiving the trespasses of others, and doing good deeds without stint of affection. Her overview caused me to wonder if I had taken my own Christian searchings as thoroughly into account in all expressions of my life.

I wrote Juni back that I found her statements of principle clear, and comfortable to understand — particularly so on matters of dress, where she ventured that the injunctions of the Qur'an might be shaped by the individual woman and the culture in which she lives. To drive her point home, she insisted that no single culture has a priority or prerogative in applying the Qur'an.[19] This latter I took as clear resistance to those Saudi authorities who would judge for all Islam.

Juni made clear her conviction that the Qur'an contains a rich understanding of womanhood, and is a wholly reliable companion and guide to a woman's personal safety and lifelong growth. It leaves to her own Qur'anically inspired heart of hearts a choice of modest clothing, unthreatened in her personal conscience and her national culture.

Around the daily question of what to wear, then, spin two questions of

19. Juni Djamaloeddin, "Islam, Perempuan, dan Jilbab," 4 Jan 05; reply by Theodore Friend, 9 Feb 05.

international import: *Arabisme,* as the Indonesians call dictates of mean- ing and style from that peninsula; and *ijtihad,* understood worldwide by Muslims as the problem of who shall interpret the Qur'an, and how.

Meutia Hatta is the daughter of the great Minang moral and political leader Mohammad Hatta, who was Indonesia's vice-president from the revolution until his open split with Sukarno in late 1956. Hatta had made a youthful vow not to marry until Indonesia was free. His daughter, Meutia, was one issue of the marriage that her father contracted at age forty-three, with the nineteen-year-old who became her mother. Meutia holds a doc- torate in anthropology and has lectured at the University of Indonesia. In- donesia's first directly elected president, former General Susilo Bambang Yudhoyono, chose her as his Minister of Women's Empowerment.

Outside her office — she would allow, as it happened, an overrun of my appointment to an hour and a half — I studied portraits of ten histori- cal Indonesian heroines, and five ministers of this very department. Only three of the heroines wore *jilbab,* and only two of the ministers. Meutia herself, I discovered, did not cover her head, and was articulate and em- phatic about the matter. "I do not cover my hair, my neck, my feet and an- kles. . . . For all it is decent, this way [not to do so]." She saw it as one major focus of her job not to let anyone "destroy [the] idea of decency that Indo- nesian[s] have from the past." It is not necessary, she insisted, to dress like an Arab to be a good Muslim or a good Indonesian.

Convictions flowed from the Minister in a hospitable glow. Her job, she stressed, was not only to see that women be empowered, but that they empower themselves. Her grandmother and her mother were examples to her. When the Japanese invaders closed all Dutch institutions, her mother had not finished high school. But she educated herself in Dutch, English, and German. And, as young wife of the vice-president, she added French. Inspired by such standards, Dr. Meutia was quietly proud to be a high offi- cer of government. As a girl, she said, "my only problem was I could not dance. [In that way] I was very timid."

All religious texts, she asserted, require cultural interpretations. Women must not just listen to men's understandings of the Qur'an, the Bi- ble, or the Veda. Even male experts in gender studies don't see the impor- tance of Mary, the Mother of Jesus: "She has *gaib,* invisible, supernatural power, because God gives her a child without need of a man."

As Maryam in the Qur'an, she receives more attention than in the Bible. Here the Minister interrupted herself, attesting her credentials for understanding Christianity by reciting the "Hail Mary" in Bahasa Indonesian. "Priests are always men, why not women?" (I inserted the fact that many modern Protestant churches have ordained females.) "Women can make a deal," she rolled on, "not in bloodshed. There are some fierce fools in history, women who made blood, but as for women in general, they may be more gifted as priests than men."

There are good Qur'anic verses on being a woman; but men have suppressed these verses for their own advantage. Having four wives is hadith, yes. Some people need more than one for their own reasons, or for the woman's reasons. The Prophet married only widows, because they were neglected, seven times, except Ayesha, who was young. "Ayesha had the ability to self-empower. . . . She tried to catch information, and was the extension of her husband's activities. With access to his teaching, she became [a] teacher.

"The Prophet did not marry for desire, but to protect. You have to be fair to all wives. . . . But nobody can be fair to four wives. This is my opinion, and the opinion of many Indonesian women. You can give all your wives movie tickets. But they each have emotional needs, abilities, and limitations. . . . So fairness is impossible. . . . Not possible even for two wives." I inserted, without rejoinder from the Minister, that it is difficult to be fair always to one wife, and she to her husband.

Meutia went on to questions of modesty. She saw Arab environment, culture, and patriarchy as driving interpretations of the matter. "The *back*, even, is only for the husband to see. But in Bali, and among the Dani, we allow breasts to be seen as functional. They are *tools*, as nourishment for a baby. In our climate, a shoulder-revealing *kebaya* is natural. But Arab tradition makes woman cover hair, eyebrows even, as *aurat*, improper to be seen. The *eye* is even too tempting. . . . Heavy dress, it is torture for the women, with heavy sanction. I feel so much pity. . . . Now Aceh and West Sumatra they even *jilbab*. They have lost traditional hairdo. . . . But seventeenth-century Acehnese woman admiral Malahayati had uncovered hair. . . . You can't be an admiral, or any kind of fighter, with covered eyes!

"Protecting women against raping, all this about the eye, is all Arab culture. . . . Meat consumption makes them more sexually driven." She smiled. "Too bad there are no vegetables in the sand.

"Ecology, biology, culture go together. . . . Saudi Arabian weather requires them to wear some kinds of protective clothes. . . . But we don't worry so much about sunburn, or desire, or food, or segregation, which is needed more there than here. . . .

"We must not destroy our own culture because of imitation of Arab fashion. Many women with *jilbab* are asked by their Muslim husbands to wear it. Others think [mistakenly] it is the Muslim way.

"My secretary, her *jilbab* made her sweat, need deodorant, so I give it to her. But her sister said not to use it because it contains alcohol. . . . But *alcohol*," she drove her point home with an exhale that contained some exasperation, "there is nothing in the Qur'an about external uses. Only swallowing."

We had reached a comical extreme. Mentally I formulated a rule: "Wallow but don't swallow." Meutia came back to her historical overview, responding to a story I had heard about a Minister of Agriculture from the newly successful (Islamist) Party of Justice and Prosperity. He had allegedly refused to shake the hand of the Minister of Trade. Was it because — in rapidly expanding order of likelihood — she was Chinese, Christian, or female?

If true, the Minister said ("But *I* have shaken the hand of the Minister of Agriculture"), it is not good for cabinet integrity. . . . Not the way my parents taught me. . . . Not the way it was with Bung Karno.

"Mutualism in our pluralistic society," she stressed, "was taught by our founding fathers, even before independence. We are united by national culture, which is multicultural. That is the way to become children of this one country, citizens of this one nation."

Bhinneka tunggal ika is the Sanskrit motto for the Republic of Indonesia. It means "Unity in Diversity," and it makes me think of American coins stamped with the last official Latin in American life: *E Pluribus Unum*. The republic's crest, with the motto, hung large on a wall of her office. Pointing to the motto, and with the Indonesian smile that belies its content, Meutia said that the Party of Justice and Prosperity "will destroy this!"

But lest I think the enemies of Indonesia were only internal, she riffed on dangers from foreign business elements. "This country can be eaten by multinational corporations. . . . They have no *jiwa* (spirit), but *we* have *jiwa* here." She pointed again to the republican crest and its motto, adopted and sworn to by the anti-colonial generation of her father and Sukarno.[20]

20. Minister Meutia Hatta, interview, 15 Dec 04.

Ijtihad: Interpretation

As the principal advisor on foreign policy to President B. H. Habibie, the successor to Suharto for a year and a half, Dewi Fortuna Anwar commanded more national attention than Meutia Hatta, by virtue of her office, could do. She too was Minangkabau. Her late mother, in West Sumatra, described to me Dewi's training at home in Islam, her living with a great-uncle for several years to learn Minang *adat,* the family's residence in London, her doctorate in Melbourne, and her Congressional Fellowship in the U.S. with Congresswoman Pat Schroeder (D-Colorado) and Senator Kent Conrad (D-North Dakota). The result, in a proud maternal eye, was an English accent not so round as the British, nor so sharp as the Australian, nor as flat as the American. Not only that, her mother said, but she was 100 percent Muslim, 100 percent Minang, and 100 percent woman. Some Muslims might not appreciate her "feminism," but it was all of a piece with her own modernity and seriously borne Minang tradition.

Her advice on foreign affairs included trying to ease Indonesia of a policy burden in 1999 by conducting a referendum in East Timor, whose forcible annexation had never been recognized by the United Nations. The results of the referendum were four-to-one for independence. The surprised Indonesian military, then led by the power-hungry General Wiranto, clicked into play or allowed others to launch a plan for scorched-earth retreat, which destruction through their militia cost perhaps two thousand lives.[21]

Dr. Anwar felt the international outrage at the time. And after leaving office she also paid a retaliatory price at the hands of Jakarta thugs, presumably funded by still-offended military. They stormed the Habibie Center, her think tank. Days later she received me in a boarded-up building with police protection, and she ordered lunch in rather than go out to the restaurant I'd proposed.

In a subsequent talk on Islam and culture, however, Dewi was calm and reflective.[22] She clarified what *tauhid* means to Indonesian Muslims: strict differentiation between vertical relations with God and horizontal relations with humans. Aberrance from *tauhid* is *syirik* (Indonesian spell-

---

21. The full story is told in Geoffrey Robinson, *"If You Leave Us Here, We Will Die": How Genocide was Stopped in East Timor* (Princeton, Princeton University Press, 2009).

22. The preceding and following observations contain elements of conversations with Dr. Dewi Fortuna Anwar dating back to 1997, and culminating in an interview of 15 Dec 04.

ing): the sin of giving divine qualities and powers to beings other than God. She invoked Imam Bondjol, the nineteenth-century Minang Wahhabi, who got rid of cockfighting, alcohol, ancestral funerals, and practices of grave- and saint-worship.

To illustrate Arab policing of *tauhid*, Dewi told of her experience on hajj, when at the tomb of Muhammad a group of Iranian Shi'ites began, in their own pious sincerity, to cry and weep in chorus. The *laskars* (religious police) began whipping them, crying *Syirik! Syirik!* And *Haram! Haram!* (Forbidden!). Wahhabi tradition says that wailing, or prolonged mourning, is wrong, which latter interdiction would certainly bring into question elaborate ceremonies for grieving in Java, seven to a thousand days in length. All forms of great distress over death are a manifestation of lack of faith in the sovereign will and sovereign power of God. Who are we to decry God's will? And on hajj, furthermore, we are in vertical obedience to God, not in horizontal veneration of his messenger, the Prophet.

"*Syirik* includes 'partnering God' — praying to or through others than God himself. For Muslim orthodoxy, Catholics sin in a bizarre way by praying to saints. . . . [So] Calvin and Knox have a lot in common with Wahhab."

Unprompted, Dewi swept into her own survey of Muslim cultures. "Most of the outside Islamic world thinks that the Kingdom of Saudi Arabia is practicing Arab culture, or even Bedouin culture. There, men had to protect themselves against sun and sand, and women had to be guarded like cattle or goats.

"If you look at Egypt, Persia/Iran, or Iraq, countries with thousands of years of civilization, they had developed *different* societies" — different from the Saudi kingdom, and often notable for the prominence of their women. "Women have much more freedom [in those countries] . . . as in Syria and Jordan. There they look down on those from Arabia not only as those who killed Hashemites, but as uncouth Bedouins." Women's freedom in those countries is *not* due to "Westernization." Egypt, after all, was ruled by great queens.

"A great innovation of Islam was to liberate women . . . whereas in India and China, and even in Greece, daughters were killed or regrettably drowned, as a drain on resources. . . . And how were Western industrial societies constructed? If one looks at Europe, you find it less developed than many Islamic societies until recent times. Even in the nineteenth century, in some European countries, women could not inherit property."

I returned to the question of what caused the relative decline of Islamic nations in modern times. Dr. Anwar's answer was unvarying. "Regression suffered by Islam? When the House of Saud, in alliance with Wahhab, became the power that controlled Mecca."

If one locates that moment in the mid-eighteenth century, I thought, it may have some explanatory power about development indices in the twentieth century. But, I thought to myself, the Saudi kingdom has never had a large empire, and until philanthropic and political export of its oil monies in the last thirty-five years, Wahhabia has not been in many places a controlling mode of influence. But we hadn't time to pursue that line of thought.

Dewi returned to Southeast Asia, with its bounties of nature, with gender-shared farming — men doing the hoeing and heavy work and women the planting, seeding, harvesting, and marketing. Such sedentary societies are constructed very differently from nomadic warrior societies. She smilingly offered the example of Malaysia, where women are especially powerful in Kelantan, and cartoons by Lat in *Malaysian Life* are highly popular. "His women are big, burly chain-smokers sitting atop goods in the market, with a tiny man in a skullcap skulking in the corner."

The Padri war had been a great trial for her Minang society, but its eventual peace and compromise between matrilineal *adat* and Wahhabi doctrine were rule-of-thumb, practical, and enduring. Anything not explicitly forbidden in Islam, but traditional practice in Minang, is okay. And because the Qur'an and hadith in no place and in no way prohibit matrilineal transmission of property, Minang life goes on with its fundamental basis undisturbed. If Wahhab had ever heard about Minangkabau *adat,* he probably would have prohibited it. But the vigor of that tradition is evident today even in Jakarta city-dwellers, who are among the three million Minangs who live away from their native province. One such is Dewi's sister, Desi, who was a television anchor at the time I came back from West Sumatra. Her first and eager question to me was: "Did you see my *lands?*"

Dewi Fortuna Anwar and I ended upon a question in the new government that was then a preoccupation of Jakarta gossip: the matter of shaking hands. She had gone to a recent diplomatic corps dinner for the new chairman of an Islamist political party, at which no man of that party had offered a hand to shake. She contrasted the behavior of the massive sociopolitical organizations, Nahdlatul Ulama and Muhammadiyah, who allege forty and thirty million members respectively. "They shake hands, but PKS [the Islamist party] and MMI [the Indonesian Islamic Warriors'

Council] *don't* shake hands." She cracked up in laughter, in which I joined her, over the discovery that puritans and terrorists don't do handshakes.

The Universitas Islam Negeri in Jakarta became, in 2002, Indonesia's first State Islamic University. Its rector from 1998 to 2006, Dr. Azyumardi Azra, is a man of gentle demeanor and fierce working schedule. His numerous publications in Indonesian, Arabic, and English establish Indonesia's place in the international network of Muslim scholars that existed in the seventeenth and eighteenth centuries, and they imply flexible normative positions on many present problems. His institution-building gives Indonesian higher education an Islamic flagship. That flag snaps noisily in the crosswinds of contemporary debate in religion and politics. Azra's colleague in Yogyakarta, Dr. Amin Abdullah, before his retirement in 2010, brought the largest state educational institution in that city along in the same Islamic direction, by the curricular steps required to fashion a modern university with international standing.

Azra and Abdullah are patient, dedicated men. They are deeply versed in Islam. They know the society in which they live. Azra, when I asked him to describe for me the current spectrum of political and social views in Indonesian Islam, easily arrayed sixteen different institutions and orientations, from ultra-rigid (including violent) to hyper-flaccid (impotent), with every discrimination of nerve and muscle in between. He did so without hesitation and without recourse to notes.

The views and momentum of these men and others may be seen as part both of Indonesia being more religious than it was fifty years ago and — contrary to any stereotype of rigid Islam — of Indonesia's remaining largely flexible in the nature of its religious profession and practice.[23]

From 1979 on, of course, Indonesia has registered its own part of a global religious intensity that has affected Muslims and Hindus, Jews and Sikhs, Buddhists and Christians, and others. To call this "fundamentalism" would be ascribing to very different religions a term that arose a century ago from intense debate between Protestant Christians of liberal perspective and those clinging to traditional beliefs ("the Fundamentals").[24] But

23. Interviews, Rektor Azyumardi Azra, Jakarta, 28 Nov 03, 1 Jul 05; Rektor Amin Abdullah, Yogyakarta, 4 Dec 03.

24. Martin G. Marty and R. Scott Appleby, eds., *Fundamentalisms Comprehended* (Chi-

whatever may not be distinguished by that term, its rough aggregation of many behaviors is helpful. We must *redeem.* Shall we restore, reform, or renounce? Or do all these and more at once? Vital showdowns are involved as different peoples from different traditions respond to hyper-materialistic and bourgeois sensate forms of modern culture. Something real and enduring must be relied on against the commercial power of what is popular, accessible, media-easy — culture so radically and mindlessly subversive of the spirit that it requires both defense and counterattack. Religious fundamentals are a common answer, and everywhere a pronounced part of that reply is textually based tradition as interpreted by male authorities.

Patriarchalism, however, is not the necessary answer to the threat of spiritual deracination. Dramatically different modes of feeling and thinking exist in the worldstream of modern being. Many of them manifested themselves in the Convention on Elimination of Discrimination Against Women (CEDAW), adopted by the UN's General Assembly in 1979. It entered into force in 1981, while the Iranian revolution and its wave effect were still at high intensity.

The Indonesian government ratified CEDAW in 1984, without the damaging reservations that some Muslim countries adopted in passing it. That fact, in retrospect, seems astounding. Despite Suharto's presidential power being at its height, and his Dharma Wanita (an organization of government employees' wives that prescribed the duties of women in a comprehensive Javanese patriarchal way) in full career, the major Indonesian "Women's Affairs" ministry changed its name to "Women's Empowerment." Suharto himself, trying to strengthen his Javanism with decorous Islamism, would go on his first hajj in 1991. But his attempt at employing Islam in his political favor was in the long run neither savory nor successful.

In Indonesian universities, and in many other social institutions, communication has remained constant on CEDAW principles. Networks of centers of women's studies arose at that time, a decade and a half after they appeared in the United States. Many observers would agree that CEDAW represented a culmination of the nineteenth-century movement for women's rights, abetted by economic growth.

But challenges remain for forward-thinking Islam in Indonesia, as elsewhere in religious worlds. Holy texts are cited toward subordination of

cago, University of Chicago Press, 1995), pp. 13-14 and *passim;* Malise Ruthven, *Fundamentalism: The Search for Meaning* (New York, Oxford University Press, 2005), pp. 1-21 and *passim.*

47

women. A prominent teacher at UIN Jakarta said to me, "Here at the university we try not to deny the verses, but seek to use the courts, the legislature, and authorities" as pivot-points for arguing change. *Fikh,* Islamic jurisprudence, is strong even in Indonesia (stronger yet in republics and kingdoms defined as Islamic), so other modes of thinking must be used to contest with tradition. Analogy works; so does "consensus"; and appeals to the public good may also cut open a path.[25]

These modes of thinking and behavior, however, brought about an attack by a critic, Hartono Achmad Jaiz, in a book entitled *Permurtadan di UIN* ("Apostasy at UIN"). He charged that this university was trying to take students away from Islam and to Westernize/Christianize them. UIN faculty are accustomed to reply to such theopomorphic religiosity, in which the will of God is everything. They simply assert an anthropomorphic, or human need, to learn other than by rote memory and to behave other than by "just doing it." Anthropology, sociology, and political science all help in understanding human dynamics. "We never use the word 'secular,' but we study human needs within our religion," as the teacher put it. Critics like Hartono reply that Islam is perfect as it is. But UIN sends young Islamic scholars who know *fiqh* to the West to learn social science, in order to teach religion more richly and to achieve *pengarus utamaan gender* — gender mainstreaming — one of Minister Hatta's chief goals, and one continued by her successor.

The battle over *ijtihad,* interpretation, took classic and furious form in a public debate at UIN under student sponsorship. They matched "perfect Islam" against "liberal interpretation" in a head-to-head exchange between Hartono and Ulil Abshar Abdallah, a young leader of Jaringan Islam Liberal (JIL — "Liberal Islamic Network"). The event had a strange and unclear outcome.

Ulil is tall for an Indonesian, rangy in build, with a loose-jointed fluency in motion. His head is large and elongated with a broad mouth and prominent chin. His face is a genetic tan, almost unlined. Bright eyes shine behind large spectacles. The effect of talking with Ulil is of being in touch with a friendly thinking machine.[26]

He grew up in the town of Pati, on the northern coast of Central Java, in a "traditional, conservative" Muslim family. Both of his grandfathers

---

25. Quotations and summaries regarding action and debate at UIN are from my field notes of conversation with Dr. Amany Lubis and Dr. Fuad Jabali on that campus, 2 Jul 05.
26. The following notes are from interview with Ulil Abshar Abdallah, 1 Jul 05.

were *mursyid* — Sufi masters, religious guides. Religion surfaced in politics even then, but a cultural life burdened by politicized religion did not exist then as it does now. He sees serious cases of a shrinking exercise of freedom. Against such happenings, Ulil stated his conviction that "to be a good Muslim is to maintain individual liberty." Knowing that his stress on the last word, and calling his movement the "Liberal Islamic Network," had aroused criticism, I questioned his semantics in his own cause. Ulil readily supplied alternatives for his key word: "progressive," "moderate," "flexible," "transformative." I argued for one or two of them as valid in Indonesian context without being irritating. But Ulil stuck to his guns: "I chose 'liberal' . . . to show that we lack liberty."

Nuraini, who had arranged our dinner of three, queried Ulil's stress on individual liberty, and asked if Islam were not a collective idea. "Every religion is about forging collective consciousness," he answered. "The danger comes when collectivism goes into politics." The Sudan, he observed, has been more and more Islamic the last twenty years, but at a proposal to make Khartoum "an Islamic city," the Sufis spoke out, objecting.

"Sufis are liberal people," he observed with approval, as part of his preferred social recipe. But something more was needed: "Secularism — which has saved millions of people from religious persecution." Yet while that is a vital ingredient, "In excess, secularism leads to emptiness in the spiritual dimension." Still, Ulil concluded, smiling with approval at a formula suggested by a friend at Emory University, "We need secularism, human rights, *and* religion."

I only later heard the scurrilous objection from some riled-up orthodox Muslims who deride such a point of view with Indonesian verbal play against secularism, pluralism, and liberalism. They may be combined in acronym as a *sipilis,* which in English means "syphilis." Such scorn, coming from those who believe in comprehensive, pious submission to an absolutely unitary God, does not ennoble their view. But against a fear of a threatening God, one might well remain aware of what the late Philip Rieff called "that far greater horror: the absolute authority of man."[27]

Ulil's point of view is mystical in the classical sense of seeking unity with God. But he stresses that "In my stream [of thought], Sufi practice should be kept as personal experience. . . . If you expose it, you endanger your spiritual life." He likes Rumi, and recognizes that for some recent

---

27. Philip Rieff, *Charisma: The Gift of Grace and How It Has Been Taken Away from Us* (New York, Pantheon, 2007), p. 212.

years the thirteenth-century mystic has been the best-selling poet in the U.S. But he follows more closely the teachings of Ibn Arabi, who lived just before Rumi, in particular his guidance that "you must distinguish between your ideas of God, and God himself or herself."

My query of the feminine pronoun led Ulil to an animated series of thoughts on patriarchism, *Arabisme,* and reform in Islam. Allah in Arabic is male-gendered,[28] he says. That has led modern Islamic feminists to object, and to re-invoke the Sufi concept, more feminine, of Allah as lover.

Nuraini then recounted the story of the death in Melbourne of an eighteen-year-old Malaysian woman. The sheikh presiding at her funeral service said to her spirit, "You have been so exemplary that when you go to heaven you will look through the window of paradise." Nuraini had turned angrily to a friend and whispered that even in the Muslim afterlife, a woman is second class — she can't go through the door; "she can only look through the window." She elaborated her reaction now — "If men are promised 72 *houris* in paradise, then women deserve 72 *torreros!*"

Ulil took the discourse back to the Qur'an. There, he said, the bliss of heaven is described as wine, women, and young boys. Pedophilia is a sexual deviation in the West, but in Arab Muslim society an affair with a young boy is not deranged, and indeed may occur normally because of excessively strong segregation of women from men. The Qur'an reflects this cultural life, and its descriptions of paradise project the fantasies of desert Arabs.

"I don't want to be portrayed as hating Arabs," Ulil interjected. "I admire the language, the literature, the calligraphy. My point is the over-association now of being a good Muslim with taking on Arabic symbols of dress and language." That was becoming more than a mere fashion in Indonesia; "there is a serious Arabic mood in religion here." There is no single big Arabist voice, but there are many politicians who use Islam in slick ways to recruit and to polarize. He mentioned Din Syamsuddin, elected leader of the thirty million-member Muhammadiyah, who has ambitions for all of the Republic of Indonesia. In my own meeting with Din I found him an aggressive textualist concerned with building his reputation.[29]

Despite a recent increase in Arab patriarchalism, I observed, the Indo-

28. No, Roger Allen says to me by e-mail, 28 Mar 11 — the word is gender-neutral. Allen is chair of the Department of Near Eastern languages and Civilizations, University of Pennsylvania, and past president (2010-11) of the Middle East Studies Association of North America. The research of Dr. Carolyn Baugh (sent to the author, 29 Mar 11) on balance supports his view.

29. Interview with Dr. Din, 29 Nov 03.

nesian cultural setting remains friendly to women. The social setting gives them many roles not found in other Islamic countries, such as having women recite the Qur'an during opening ceremonies of important gatherings.[30] Mingling of genders is natural, and the Saudi practice of the PKS, not to shake hands, seems odd to most. Veiling, Ulil stressed, may protect the face or skin, but it is not a religious requirement. Grow a beard if you will, but now it is an arbitrary Arabic promotion. Arabic culture is okay if you like (or American culture, or French). But veiling is only natural in Arabia, Pashtun, Yemen, Nejd. In North Africa, Ulil added, the *males* of the twelfth-century Moravid Dynasty veiled their faces against sun and sands, which proves the matter a geocultural one and not a gender requirement of religion.

Islam *itself,* not its trappings, is what matters. It is now going through a process similar to that which Christianity experienced in the sixteenth century. Obscurantist reactions naturally rise against change. But Ulil is "happy" to see many young intellectuals emerge who are equivalent to "Protestant reformers." He sees Gus Dur and Cak Nur as his intellectual "fathers." Azyumardi Azra and Amin Abdullah are his intellectual "brothers." And already he sees his own "sons" devoted to making this "become a democratic country that practices Islam in a reasonable way."

Reform can take a hyper-religious cast, as in the authoritarian revolution of Shi'ite Iran in 1979, or in restoration of democracy in the Catholic Philippines in 1986. There, I interjected, Cardinal Sin brought down the dictator Marcos and oversaw the installation of his own candidate as president, the widow Cory Aquino. His actions defied both Pope John Paul II and Philippine constitutional doctrine, received from America, which had separated church from state. Ulil nodded. But Indonesian political reform from 1997 onward, he concluded firmly, was driven by secular and democratic people, "while Suharto was trying to use Islam as a status quo maintaining force."

Now that Indonesian democratic reform is accomplished, women's issues are at the core of the needs of modern Islam. In Indonesia, two strands of feminism exist. The weaker one works from a Western concept of secular feminism, which tries to impose itself on an Indonesian cultural setting. The stronger form attempts to work out change from within Indonesian Islam, in a new gender discourse.

---

30. Dr. Nikolaos van Dam, Ambassador of the Netherlands to Indonesia (and, earlier, to Iraq, Egypt, Turkey, and Germany), considers such cultural matters globally in his speech at the graduation ceremony of The Institute for Qur'anic Studies, Jakarta, 29 Apr 09. www .nikolaosvandam.com/pdf/speech2009.pdf (English); id.pdf (Indonesian).

Ulil smiled with a radiant flexibility. Only the next day did I learn that from the point of view of UIN progressives, Ulil's TV image is too uncompromising. He comes through as a "rationalist fundamentalist." Sometimes harsh criticism accompanies his exposition, "just the way that literalists do." He doesn't allow that he himself might be wrong, they felt, and does not assume the good faith of the other. The on-stage debate arranged at UIN, of Ulil with Hartono, was very difficult to moderate, and neither one developed sympathy with the large crowd assembled. Ulil made the audience so angry that he left the stage by the back door.

But his smile? I asked. "They don't hear his smile. They hear his tone and thoughts." Ulil, said the UIN faculty members, shows lack of respect for previous *ulamas*. In 2008 he was declared apostate by a group of *kiai* in Bandung. They are not the only group that speaks for Islam in Indonesia, but their edict made him "subject to death." However, the professors said, "This is not an Islamic republic." The impact of the *fatwa* is therefore not an order to execute him, but it has a powerful effect in excoriating him.[31]

In March 2011, bombs in mailed packages arrived at four sites in Jakarta. A policeman was seriously injured in defusing them. One of the addressees was Ulil Abshar Abdallah, now in politics with the Democratic Party of President Yudhoyono. The others were advocates of pluralism like him, or figures representing diversity. Who sent the bombs? Members of Jemaah Islamiyah, which has renamed itself Tanzim Al Qoidah Jihad? Even as prosecutors proceeded against its co-founder, Abu Bakar Ba'asyir, for funding a terrorist training group in Aceh, acts of violence hit Christians in Central Java and Ahmadiyah in West Java in early 2011, indicating more diffuse initiative in radical Indonesian Islam than could be attributed to one leader. Indeed, deaths among such militants in the last decade have exceeded fifty, and arrests six hundred, testifying to the insecurity they can generate. The recently merged umbrella group of militants, Indonesian Islamic Forum, has implied that by his tolerance of the Ahmadiyah, President Yudhoyono himself has breached the 1965 law on blasphemy.[32]

31. The leader of the group issuing the *fatwa* later claimed it was based on a questionnaire to 700 faithful, some of whom thought Ulil "ought to hang." He alleged that its motive was to obtain police restraint of Ulil, who was causing "restlessness." Among Ulil's liberal and controversial positions is defense of Ahmadi religious freedom — a group born in Qadian, India, persecuted as heretical in Pakistan, and growing but threatened in Indonesia.
32. For data on deaths and arrests, see Rajaratnam School of International Studies 45 (2011), www.rsis.edu.sg/publications/Perspective/RSIS0452011.pdf.

"What Happened to the Smiling Face of Indonesian Islam?"

The forced resignation of President Suharto in 1998 immediately brought new lines of gender expression into Indonesia. In his later years he had reinforced Javanese patriarchism with Muslim orthodoxy, which converged against equal status for women. But modern catalysts that tend to differentiate rather than obliterate individual rights, as well as to promote rather than suppress gender equity, rose sharply for and after Suharto's removal. Equality advanced in the three brief presidencies that followed: of Habibie, who surprisingly promoted democratic institutions; of Wahid, a social liberal; and of Megawati, a female. They continued to make way under the stable presidency of Susilo Bambang Yudhoyono, directly chosen in 2004 by a number of votes that surpassed those for George W. Bush in the same year, and reelected in 2009 with more votes than Barack Obama had received the year before.

Against political flexibility, social progressivism, and feminist principle, however, there remained formidable opposition. An intensified Indonesian Islam could not be merely dismissed as *"Arabiste."* In Java, the densely populated major island (with as many people as Bangladesh, and more than Russia), a prevailing cultural conservatism argued on behalf of father-as-leader, family, and community. In Java, unlike Minang and Batak areas of Sumatra, received moral hierarchies tended to discount individualism. Islamic teachers might play on Javanese strings at the same time as they drummed on Qur'anic texts.

Amid growing numbers in hard-edged Islamic piety have been bombings — of thirty-eight Christian churches on Christmas Eve 2000, and the world-renowned attack in Bali in October 2002 that killed over two hundred people. Such factors are collected by the Dutch expert Martin Van Bruinessen in a formidably apprehensive essay entitled "What Happened to the Smiling Face of Indonesian Islam?"[33]

How much lament, however, should go into the disappearance from the scene of Nurcholish Madjid, with his glowing, dignified, good-humored manner, and Abdurrahman Wahid, the irreverent Sufi wit, fond of puns and tactical surprises? Van Bruinessen himself concedes that many

33. Martin Van Bruinessen, "What Happened to the Smiling Face of Indonesian Islam? Muslim Intellectualism and the Conservative Turn in Post-Suharto Indonesia," Rajaratnam School of International Studies, Working Paper 222, 6 Jan 11 (45 pp.), www.rsis.edu.sg/publications/workingpapers/wp222.pdf.

Indonesians are now drawn to Sufi-inspired devotional movements, led by popular preachers in cathartic chanting toward altered consciousness. I may share his preference for clarity in theological groundwork.

Yet in recent years women's empowerment has taken new, ingenious, and courageous forms. Special local schools that teach reading, writing, and reproductive health also teach income generation and gender awareness. And practical subjects such as processing virgin coconut oil are available along with courses implying vision, such as human rights and English language.

Indeed, language itself was growing more sensitive in all areas touched by sex. "Gender activists" had adopted their new self-descriptive term in the late Suharto years, as more relational than "feminist" and more likely to include and persuade men. But Javanese men, insofar as willing to talk about rebalancing gender roles, were likely to ask with anxiety, "How far will it go?" They feared, as did many women, that emancipation would bring in a sexual freedom undermining marriage and family with Western, especially American, values. The TV-fed image of a career woman *(wanita karier)* was usually of a white-collar family breaker, ignoring the already potent prevalence of Indonesian women as stall- and shop-owners and small-business managers.

Such fears had led, by early 2007, to more than two dozen regencies passing shari'a-inspired laws restricting women's mobility and mandating their dress. High fashion, which had opportunely embraced Muslim codes years before, now displayed them in full and long-sleeved batik silk blouses with long, flowing chiffon skirts. The buyers and wearers were increasingly likely to advance quasi-Islamic social reasoning in their behalf: "Have you ever heard of a woman wearing a veil being raped?"

On gender matters the Indonesian government was hard to predict. The parliament, aroused by the first locally published issues of *Playboy*, weighed and eventually passed a tough ban on pornography. Meanwhile the administration was contemplating the widening of a ban on polygamy, extending it from civil servants to legislators and soldiers and other government employees.

Perhaps the distinctive nature of Indonesian womanhood in changing world Islamic cultures was captured by Maria Ulfah, a sonorous musical reciter of the Qur'an, which ordinarily male art had been taught by her father, himself a distinguished cantor. As her fame grew and the crowds attending her swelled, Ulfah spoke wonderingly of herself and proudly for Indonesia. She remarked that she could recite the Qur'an freely in free circumstances, when in the Middle East the female voice may not be heard in public at all.[34]

Meanwhile comprehensive reform views were advanced by an Indonesian woman, engaging critics without jeopardizing her safety. Siti Musdah Mulia was born in South Sulawesi in 1948. Her grandfather was a noted *ulama*. If she hung out with an ethnic Chinese friend, or a Christian, her parents ordered her to shower afterward. Only when she traveled did she find that "Islam had many faces." Musdah was the first woman to obtain a Ph.D. in Islamic political thinking, and its top doctoral candidate at Syahid Institute of Religious Studies in Jakarta. She entered the political scene to find out if it was as "slick, dirty, and masculine" as commonly said (and found it not so), and to learn if Islam is in conflict with modernity (not at all, she realized, but containing within it undeveloped principles of reform).

A mother of three and author of multiple books, she wears a *hijab* and an accommodating smile. As director of religious research and social affairs at the Ministry of Religious Affairs, she was given the task of updating the compilation of articles under Islamic law that Suharto, in his reinvention of himself as Muslim, had issued by decree in 1991, in order to guide judges of religious courts. But, as Siti Musdah observes, the decree provided no stipulations at all regarding illegitimate children, and contained no helpful references regarding domestic violence. In two other key matters, she seeks change. On polygamy she finds the Turkish and Tunisian cases instructive: both governments had made it *illegal,* on the grounds that it produced serious social inequities. On interfaith marriage, she sees realism necessary, and articulation of principles that thoughtfully accommodate it, because globalization makes it inevitable. *Jilbab?* In comparison with the foregoing matters, a relatively trivial issue: a fashion statement. There is no single directive requiring or forbidding it, so wearing or not wearing it becomes a matter of choice, and doesn't concern other people.

She wholly accepts the five pillars of Islam and the six pillars of faith, but "The rest can be negotiated." Noisy modern global commotion has to be managed so that Muslims may hold true to the core of their faith while unhampered from "appreciating other religions, from accepting

---

34. The state of social discussion in Java is from Clarissa Adamson, "Gendered Anxieties: Islam, Women's Rights, and Moral Hierarchy in Java," *Anthropological Quarterly* 80:1, 2007. Other phenomena are as reported in Jakarta *Post,* 11 Dec 06; *South China Morning Post,* 11 Dec 06; Reuters, Jakarta, 28 Nov 06; *Los Angeles Times,* 17 Dec 06; and *TEMPO* 22, vii, 30 Jan 05–Feb 07. For these sources I am indebted to the late Gordon Bishop.

another religious righteousness, and from interacting with other religious followers."[35]

Mulia, however, is seen by some *ulamas* as a kind of acrobat in *jilbab*, doing satanic gyrations with the Qur'an and hadith that they cannot accept. The patriarchal undertones and overlay of Indonesian politics remain such that the Minister of Religion annulled the new draft of Indonesia's Islamic law after it was made public early in 2005. Among the many voices of ensuing protest were those of the National Council on Violence against Women, which asserted "the public's right to discuss new ideas" and denounced the denial of citizens' rights to hold differing opinions.

But the draft is still out there, in the current world, for Indonesian women and others to consider. It provides a refreshed context for unofficial debate, in which values are examined, and without edict, slowly evolve. Because women's issues are at the core of reform of modern Islam, Siti Musda Muliah's systematic legal effort to reconcile Islamic law and tradition with modern dynamics is globally important. Its very modesty, however, leaves it in the shadow of provocative statements such as those by the Pakistani from Canada, Irshad Manji, and the actions of the American exegete of the Qur'an, Amina Wadud, who held the first mixed-gender prayer service led by a woman. For many, Manji's voice of intelligent protest in *The Trouble with Islam Today* is compromised by her simultaneous assertions of her lesbianism. For others, Wadud's courageous example may be complicated by her preoccupation with negritude in the United States.

Siti Musdah Muliah comes through more simply. She says, I am a Muslim, a wife and mother, and a reformer. Her scholarship is deep and extensive. She grounds herself in the principles of the Arab philosopher Al-Ghazali, from almost a millennium ago. Yet she writes unreservedly about "the relativity of Muslim law" and the importance of applying "thematic commentary" — which themes include gender equity and justice, pluralism, nationality (with no second-class citizens), human rights, and democracy.[36] On deep foundations she erects a hospitable modern struc-

35. *Jakarta Post,* 10 July 04, "Gender Expert Musdah Speaks Within Reason," and Editorial 12 Mar 05, "The Woman's Voice." Many of Siti Musdah's writings have been gathered in *Muslimah Reformis: Perempuan Pembaru Keagamaan* (Female Muslim Reformers: Women Renewing Religion) (Jakarta, Mizan, 2005).

36. Among her articles, Siti Musdah Mulia had these two sent to me: "*Metologi Pembaruan Hukum Islam*" (Methodology for the Renewal of Muslim Law), presented to the postgraduate program of IAIN Alauddin Makasar, 24 Mar 05, which piece appears to be the kernel for a more fully developed and annotated 20-page essay "*Rekonstruksi Pemikiran Is-*

ture of Islam. That enables her to handle modern Islamic squabbles over family teachings with a smile: "The whole marital law is man-made; none of it is a fax from heaven. Why be afraid? God won't get mad. He's very wise."[37]

One may then answer with a challenge to the question which doubts the smiling face of Indonesian Islam: compare it with the changing expressions on the Islamic face of Turkey, with the hyper-orthodox frowns in Wahhabi Arabia and post-revolutionary Shi'ite Iran, or with the murderous angers abounding in Pakistan. Indonesian Islam remains comparatively benign — and at times smiles radiantly.

lam Tentang Perempuan: Prospek dan Tantangannya Bagi Penerapan Syariah Islam di Aceh" (Reconstructing Islamic Thought about Women: The Prospect and Challenge of Assembling Islamic Law in Aceh), presented to the international conference on Islamic Syariah and the Challenge of the Global World, Aceh, 19-21 Jul 07.

37. Women Living under Muslim Law (www.wluml.org), citing interview with Hera Diani, *Jakarta Post,* 3 Oct 04.

2.1 Pilgrim girls camp among tombstones, shrine of Sheikh Bahauddin Zakaria in Multan, 1988. The photographer's caption declares, "Contrary to orthodox Muslim tradition, Pakistanis regularly conduct pilgrimages to shrines of revered saint."

Photo: Abbas/Magnum

2.2 Darul Uloom Madrasah, Karachi, 2004. One of the largest and oldest of Deobandi centers of education, this major campus had a fresh architectural appearance, and much new building underway. *Author's photo*

2.3 Midday prayer, Darul Uloom, 2004. Students and faculty stride to the mosque, slide out of their shoes, and kneel to pray. *Author's photo*

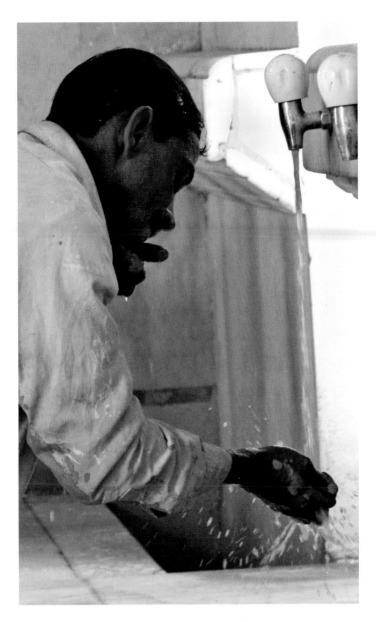

2.4 Ablution before prayer. The man ritually washing himself at the Badshahi Mosque, Lahore, 2006, with a smile gave permission to the photographer. *Photo: Elisabeth Braun*

2.5 At a Sufi shrine. Old man, girl, and boy in Kasur, Pakistan, 2006. *Photo: Elisabeth Braun*

2.6 "Blasphemous caricatures" of the Prophet generate a "million march," called by the six-party religious alliance, MMA, and joined by other opposition parties. This demonstration on 5 March 2006 jammed Jinnah Road in Karachi as far as the eye could see.

Photo: Hamid Hussain, published in the Daily Times, courtesy of Sufia Shahid

2.7 "Hate Denmark . . . Crush America." A female contingent of the giant protest, 5 March 2006, makes clear its priorities.

Daily Times, Karachi, 6 March 06

2.8 Opposing the Hudood Ordinance. It took a full generation to overcome General Zia's retrogressive edicts of 1979, which grossly diminished women's standing in law and society. Among the campaigners who finally succeeded in partial repeal, 2006, was this young reporter for GEO, Aliyah Salahuddin. *Author's photo*

2.9 Shi'a are perhaps 15 percent of Pakistan's population, a proportion much less than Iran or Iraq, about the same as in Turkey, and greater than in Saudi Arabia. Their embattled minority status in Pakistan, combined with their martyrology, comes to an annual peak in the season called Ashura. Here, in Karachi, 1988, commemoration of the killing of Imam Hussein by Sunnis takes the form of Shi'ites flailing their backs with blades attached to chains, and using swords to lacerate their scalps.   *Photo: Abbas/Magnum*

2.10 Benazir Bhutto served twice as Pakistan's prime minister, 1988-90 and 1993-96. These photos by Abbas (Magnum) show her differently in the two electoral campaigns that proved victorious. The sensual poster of her (Faysalabad, 1988) was erected by the left-centrist party she chaired, the Pakistan People's Party. *Photo: Abbas/Magnum Photos*

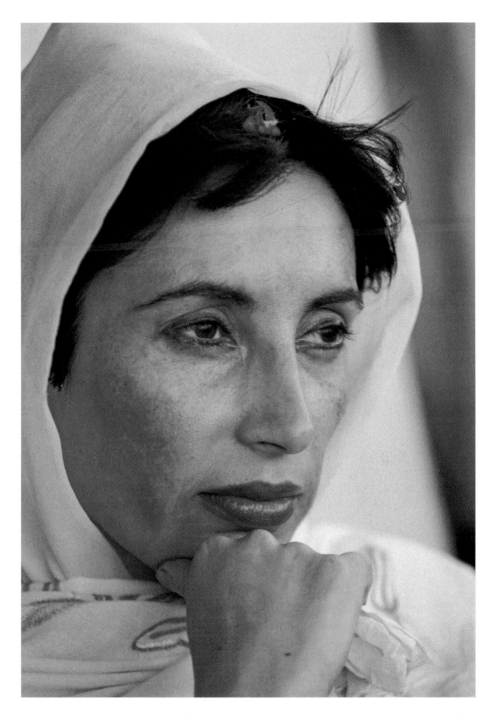

2.11 The portrait captured by Abbas as she campaigned in Punjab Province (September 1993) conveys a reflective woman, just forty years old. She has been the world's first female Islamic prime minister, made her own mistakes, and been dismissed from office. She will go through that whole cycle once more, plus exile — followed by return, her fourth campaign, and assassination in December 2007. *Photo: Abbas/Magnum Photos*

2.12 Sufia and Shahid Haq. They were married in 1979 (see figs. 3 and 4, Introduction). This scene at their home in Islamabad, 2006, suggests their Islamic blend of love, laughter, and progressive attitudes. *Author's photo*

Chapter 2

PAKISTAN

Benazir Bhutto's father said to her, "You are my jewel. You always have been." Zulfikar Ali Bhutto spoke these words in his death cell, the night before his scheduled execution by hanging. He had been prime minister from 1970 to 1977, until overthrown by a coup. His successor, General Mohammed Zia ul-Haq, had the legal system impose a death sentence on him, and let it be known that he would entertain a plea for clemency only from Bhutto himself or his immediate family. Benazir recalled that her father forbade it. They interred him in Garhi Kudha Bakhsh, the burial place of Bhuttos for generations. Her father had taken her there before she left for Harvard in 1969, saying, "Whatever happens to you, you will ultimately return here . . . your roots are here. . . . And it is here that you will be buried."[1]

A generation later, she lies there. From prison and exile after her father's death, she returned to Pakistan in 1986, when martial law was lifted. After Zia's unexplained death — his airplane crashing after takeoff — she was twice elected prime minister (1988-90, 1993-96), exchanging majorities with Nawaz Sharif. After eight more years of exile, she was allowed back to lead her father's party and her own in elections scheduled for early January 2008. After surviving suicide blasts that killed 179 members of her party, she continued her open campaigning, accusing the government of failure to supply adequate protection, and certain leaders of the Inter-Services Intelligence of animus against her. A second attack killed her. With her in the

---

1. Benazir Bhutto, *Daughter of Destiny: An Autobiography* (New York, Simon and Schuster, 1989), quotations pp. 21, 27, 29.

59

large mausoleum she built for her father lie her two brothers, one of whom died in Cannes of poisoning, the other in Karachi by a storm of police gunfire.

Benazir Bhutto was the Muslim world's first female elected prime minister. As she often said, you cannot jail or hang an idea. She stood for democracy. She stood against Islamist terrorism. But understanding how Pakistan's democracy was encumbered, and the consequences of her challenging Islamic extremists, requires looking into the historical bases of Pakistan.

Whispers to the Newborn Nation

Pakistan, created by split from India, split once again within a quarter-century of its birth, when civil war gave off Bangladesh. Now, Pakistan still remains torn inside. Its army is sapped by battles to the west along the Afghan border and the struggle it prefers on its east in Kashmir. Under such tensions, the ideals of Mohammed Ali Jinnah, Pakistan's founder, are largely forgotten: "Women's rights, human rights, minority rights, upholding the constitution and the rule of law."[2]

To help explain Pakistan's tortured national condition, there floats a charming story of two *azans* among its literati. Traditional practice requires that the father, or a senior male, whisper in a baby's ear the *azan*, the prayer call. What is heard by megaphone from the minarets would not be comprehended by a newborn, but a whisper from paternal authority will go straight to its soul to begin its formation.

But what if the babe that is Pakistan had whispered to it contradictory *azans* of its national destiny? The first gave it a standard formula for a nation-state — geographical boundaries, flag, and anthem. Yet the second added the expectations of an Islamic republic, organized to realize the religion revealed to the Prophet, and to instill in its citizens right lives. The story of the two *azans* implies that Pakistan will never escape their contradictory demands; must always seek to answer both; is not doomed to de-

2. Akbar S. Ahmed, *Jinnah, Pakistan and Islamic Identity* (London/New York, Routledge, 1997), p. xx; Asma Jahangir, "Human Rights in Pakistan: A System in the Making," in Samantha Power and Graham Allison, eds., *Realizing Human Rights: Moving from Inspiration to Impact* (New York, St. Martin's Press, 2000), pp. 167-93, esp. p. 169.

feat, but is destined to division; and when wracked with trouble must be respected for its struggling with the impossible.

With ordinary Pakistanis, other notions are even more popular. One is the idea of the "Orphan Nation," which focuses on Jinnah, the Shi'ite who struggled for the birth of Pakistan from out of the British Empire, free-standing from Hindu India. He had the vision and courage to realize it in depth. But a fatal series of infections took his life within a year of independence, and even his devoted sister Fatima could not save him. So the weaknesses of Pakistan, this grieving and unforgiving version has it, are Jinnah's fault — for dying too soon.

Still more dangerous is the theory of the "Heroless Nation." For whatever reasons — the early death of Jinnah without time to form institutions, the weakness of its educational system, the stinging failures and scorching ends of its presidencies — Pakistan is a nation without heroes. Therefore it should make a hero of any reasonable candidate.

The frailty of the idea of Pakistan may be illustrated in the careers of two very different men. Sahabzada Yaqub Khan represents the first prayer call, to a Westphalian nation-state in whose every generation are new fathers and mothers to give Pakistan rebirth. Abdul Qadeer Khan stands for the second call, to Islamic and heroic power, regardless of all else.

Sahabzada Yaqub Khan and the Modern Nation-State

Sahabzada Yaqub Khan: the first particle of his name is a hereditary title from the ruling family of Rampur, a Muslim princely state of British India. Aristocratic birth, military education, athletic discipline (he was an international polo player), and intellectual passion: these should be enough to equip a man for a life of leadership, and to overcome the possible handicap of extreme good looks. Yaqub's wife Tuba emanates beauty, wit, and hospitable instinct, with a tart tongue. Together they have made a team that could hold its own in any company. In addition to the English and Urdu which were Yaqub Khan's by birth and early education, he added elements of Arabic and Bengali. As a German prisoner of war (1942-45), he enhanced his French and acquired German, Italian, and Russian, and grappled with Nietzsche and Tolstoy. Later he broadened his poetic-philosophical background in the writings of Ghalib and Iqbal to include Zen Buddhism. From this East/West conceptual grounding Yaqub pursued understanding of developments in international science and, as Chairman of the Board of Aga Khan University (1985-2001),[3] he was immersed in the cultural problems of his age.

The young Sahabzada Khan, a commander of the bodyguard to Jinnah, rose in the military to be the commander in East Pakistan in 1971 at the time of its insurrection under Bengalese nationalists. He strongly advised his president against military action. When his recommendation to attempt a political solution was declined, he resigned as lieutenant general so as not to be involved in the ruin of his army and the destruction of his country. What followed, in the words of a long-time military associate, was the vainglory of a fourth-class army being forced to its knees by a third-class adversary — India.[4]

As witness to or actor in all four of Pakistan's wars with India — over Kashmir in 1947 and 1965, over Bangladesh in 1971, and over Kargil in 1999 — and of forty-three national disputes with India since independence (only Israel-Egypt and China-Japan rivalries have produced more),[5] Sahabzada Khan knows the limits of force. He also grew acquainted with the limits of persuasion by serving as Ambassador to France (twice), Russia, and the U.S., while Pakistan's military expenditure was increasing at 19 percent per year in order to challenge India. For nine years (1982-91) he became Pakistan's Minister for Foreign Affairs — at a time when Pakistan was secretly intensifying its attempt to develop nuclear fighting capacity.

Rife with foolhardiness as these decades may have been, Yaqub Khan's behavior appears to have remained level-headed. He proceeded from philosophical premises: the brain of the human child grows faster than his motor functions, and makes him conscious of his inadequacies. The frustrations of infancy, if not alleviated in time by due success, may result in an inferiority complex. When the same phenomena are played out at a national level, Khan thought, a collective and dangerous complex may form. He did not need to invoke Russia vis-à-vis NATO, or China vis-à-vis Japan; or to mention Pakistan face to face, always, with India. He held on to an ideal of the heart catching light and begetting love, even while acknowledging the "acute conflict between emotional behavior and the neocortex,

---

3. Basic biographical information from Anwar Dil, ed., *Strategy, Diplomacy, Humanity, Life and Work of Sahabzada Yaqub-Khan* (San Diego, Intercultural Forum, 2005). Personal impressions from interview, Sahabzada Yaqub Khan, 9 Mar 06.

4. Abdul Quyyum, "Sahabzada and I," in Dil, ed., *Strategy, Diplomacy, Humanity,* pp. 306-24, esp. p. 317.

5. T. V. Paul, ed., *The India-Pakistan Conflict: An Enduring Rivalry* (Cambridge, Cambridge University Press, 2005), pp. 42-43.

which is the source of language, logic, and symbolic thought." Humans in general are a "mentally unbalanced species" through whom burns a passionate irrationality, producing the holocausts of past and recent history.

Pakistan, under Presidents Bhutto and Zia, manifested its irrationality in a rancorous jumble of legislation, much of it aimed at the Ahmadis. This large minority assert themselves as fully Muslim, but follow a successor prophet of British imperial times, Ghulam Ahmadi, who preached "continuous divine guidance," including a conviction that Muhammad bestowed the possibility of prophetic perfection upon his followers, enabling Islam to be a living faith while Judaism, Christianity, and Hinduism were dying or dead. The parliament in 1972 passed constitutional articles 260.3 and 106.3, and then at the urging of zealous *ulamas* and politicos, a blasphemy law instituting life imprisonment for anyone "defiling the Holy Qur'an" (1982), and death for "derogatory remarks" regarding the Holy Prophet (1986).[6] By then, Article 20 of the constitution was highly compromised, which promises every citizen the right to profess and propagate his religion, and also provides protection to every religious denomination and sect.

Sahabzada Khan, accustomed as he was to deal with the mighty and the mad, gave little sign to me that he cared about minority religions in Pakistan. Although comprehending high mysticism which can see into the core of Hinduism, he appeared indifferent to folk and vernacular Islam, and to popular Sufi Islam. Also to Saudi money flowing into Pakistan, which would suffocate all but the rigidly literal Islam that connects easily to its rabidly radical forms.

At the age of 78, Khan was called by his country to go on a special mission to the U.S.: to persuade Americans in government and media that Pakistan's latest coup, which put General Pervez Musharraf in power, 1999, was a good and necessary thing, and of course temporary. He made the case to William Safire that General Musharraf had promised to return Pakistan to an electoral process as soon as possible. "We've heard this same song about a necessary quick fix four times in fifty years," Safire replied. "Is there something endemic in Pakistan that corrupts government, subverts civil society and makes a coup necessary almost every decade?" Khan answered, "Is it part of our culture? Frankly, I have no answer to that. So far,

6. Yohanah Friedmann, *Prophecy Continuous: Aspects of Ahmadi Religious Thought and Its Medieval Background* (New Delhi, Oxford University Press, 2003; 1st ed., Berkeley, University of California Press, 1989), pp. 42, 186, and *passim*.

as you suggest, each of our attempts to cure ourselves has failed. But we must continue to try, and it is in your interest as a democracy to help us succeed."[7]

Pakistan went on to generate a fifth crisis in 2007, the one that sparked the assassination of Benazir Bhutto. Its entropic drift contrasted with the path of Turkey, which had also generated four military coups in the late twentieth century, but with some gains in social remediation. And when, with Pakistan, it also produced a fifth crisis in 2007, Turkey resolved it without bloodshed or coup.

When I met Sahabzada Khan, Pakistani-American relations remained in a painfully impacted state. I was eager for my allotted hour with the retired foreign secretary and lieutenant general described by his friends as punctual and peremptory, fastidious and elegant, decorous and formal, disciplined and decent, rationally intense and sustainedly brilliant. We spent nearly three hours together.

He took on the two-*azan* theory by calling the first one, the nation-state, a tangible "quiddity" that everyone understands. The second one, that of the Islamic republic, is a *"noumenon"* which takes different forms in individual minds. The two are in conflict. The quiddity is vivid but superficial. The *noumenon* is vague but deep. Individuals shift from one to the other without being aware of it. Emotional passion is invested in both. When concrete sympathy for Palestinians, Chechens, Moros, and others far away springs from the second *azan*, Westerners may complain that Pakistan is "undercutting its own national interest." They don't realize the massive irrational energy invested there, which could suddenly behave like Iran's did in 1979. Forces resembling the dark matter of the universe come into cohesion and, like anti-gravity, repel what the West considers forces of light.

Pakistani Muslims, in things of the soul, in poetry, music, architecture, have dreamed of Tashkent, of Bukhara, of the blossoms of Kandahar,[8] not

---

7. For Khan's political views and quotations, see Dil, ed., *Strategy, Diplomacy, Humanity*, pp. 29-30, 305-6; 34-35, 290-92, 324-25.

8. Tashkent, Samarkand, and Bukhara are all in what present political geography calls Uzbekistan. For purposes of visualizing this Islamic area, largely outside of Pakistan, Tashkent may be imagined as the apex of a roughly isosceles triangle, of which the base is established by a line drawn from Islamabad to Mashhad in northeastern Iran.

to mention Mecca and Medina. All their symbolism is *non-Indian.* Qawwali, for example, is *not* Indian classical music. It is dervish, Mevlana, Sufi, a music of mystical longing. The recently deceased Nusrat Fateh Ali Khan poured out his longing to Mecca and Medina. Sahabzada compared him to Meister Eckhardt, the fourteenth-century German philosopher and mystic.[9] Eckhardt, whose years overlapped the lives of both Rumi and Hafez, never knew either one, but partook with them of lucid beauty, timelessness, welcome to trial, submission to grace.

Jinnah did what was needed, said Sahabzada, returning to politics. For Muslims, partition from India meant that "After years of dreaming, here is our citadel." So strong was this conviction that it initially obscured the importance of the thousand-mile difference between West and East Pakistan, or Bengali culture, or looks and languages — which eventually produced bloody repetition of partition, and Bangladesh.

Zulfikar Ali Bhutto (president, 1971-77) adopted Islam late, when his populist, secular, socialist policies were failing, and he needed legitimization and support. Muhammad Zia ul-Haq (1977-88), a son of an *imam* and himself a fundamentalist, was a "second-*azan*" president from the beginning. He thought all he had to do was to summon up the energies of Islam. His impact through legislation continues to be felt in impingement of religious freedom against Ahmadis, Christians, Hindus, and others, not only in legal proceedings but in vigilante killings for apostasy.[10]

The two-*azan* problem is peculiar to Pakistan, Khan said, with the exception perhaps of Israel, which has both an international definition and a religious definition as part of its identity. Saudi Arabia he mentioned only in power-political terms, with regard to its east, where both oil and Shi'ism are concentrated. Indonesia he mentioned not at all. He spoke dismissively of Turkey, as if its spiritual *azan* were not the highest, calling it a nation "pickled in Kemalism." He heated up on Iran, which has both a national

9. An excellent brief selection is provided by Ursala Fleming, ed., *Meister Eckhardt: The Man From Whom God Nothing Hid* (London, Fount, 1988; Springfield, Ill., Templegate, 1990).

10. Gordon Fraser, *Cosmic Anger: Abdus Salam — The First Muslim Nobel Scientist* (Oxford, Oxford University Press, 2000), p. 264 and *passim;* http://nobelprize.org/nobel...prizes/physics/laureate/salam-speech.html; editorial, Lahore *Daily Times,* 22 Nov 06. On the close connection of women's rights and rights of religious minorities, see Jahangir, "Human Rights in Pakistan," pp. 180-82. U.S. Department of State, International Religious Freedom Report, Pakistan, 2007, appears comprehensive, with the brunt of its evidence arising from cases involving Ahmadis: paragraphs 2-18, 23-35, 40-83, 90, 94, 122-31, 149, 158, 162, *inter alia.*

tradition and a strong Shi'ite instinct for a "greater Iran," including Iraq. But limits are being thus far set by Iraqi Shi'ite leaders more loyal to the national idea of Iraq than to a "greater Iran or a greater Iraq."

Sahabzada moved on to differences in civilizations. We are dealing, he said, with two systems of thought, deductive and inductive. The West itself had been in a millennium of Aristotelian slumber while Islam was on the cutting edge in sciences through the twelfth century. (Only later did I learn of, and inform him about, the "Maragha Revolution," in which astronomers, from their observatory in Iran in the thirteenth through the sixteenth centuries, shifted away from Aristotelian cosmology to empirical physics and mathematical astronomy, later used by Copernicus.) When Europe gained momentum in the Renaissance and Reformation, it shattered the claustrophobic dome of the Church's deductive thinking. Francis Bacon represents the sixteenth-century breakthrough with his creative reasoning by induction. "This is the Revolution of Modernism, to which Islam is a stranger. We still posit truths and draw deductions."

The Qur'an itself invites reflection on cosmology, on the tides and the stars, and on the rise and fall of cultures and nations. "But somehow," Khan said sadly, "that truth hasn't reached many Muslim scientists." On this questing note I left Sahabzada Yaqub Khan, at age 85, plumbing the depths of culture, and longing for the thinker, both Muslim and Baconian, who will synthesize science and religion for a new phase of glory in Islam.

A. Q. Khan and the Islamic Bomb

What has Abdul Quadeer Khan in common with Osama bin Laden? Both lived most of the present century in seclusion — bin Laden in a cave on the Afghan border and then in a compound in Abbotobad, and Khan under house arrest in Islamabad. Each was certain that his native government had dealt with him unfairly — Saudi Arabia by shunning bin Laden, Pakistan by silencing Khan — while both were certain that the threat to civilization from Anglo-American pride and greed is so great that no hubris need be imagined in any form of Islamic resistance to it. As early as 1979, Khan criticized the American-British double standard and moral bullying with regard to nuclear weapons. "Are these bastards the appointed guardians of the world, [stockpiling] hundreds of thousands of nuclear warheads . . . ?"

In that same year, Abdus Salam became the first self-declared Muslim and still the only Pakistani to be awarded a Nobel Prize in science. He accepted his honor in physics with allusion to the need for encouragement of Third World countries deficient in resources and opportunity. And he paraphrased the Qur'an as containing "the faith of all physicists; the deeper we seek, the more is our wonder excited, the more is the dazzlement for our gaze." But his religious reverence and stress on equal opportunity for all were not accepted by some Islamic elements in Pakistan. Because Dr. Salam was a member of the Ahmadi minority, the word "Muslim" has been erased by hammer and chisel from his gravestone.[11]

The need for a national hero, however, has propelled A. Q. Khan into a limelight not merely of publicity, but of near worship. An able but not brilliant metallurgist, he finally achieved his Ph.D. at age 36. A careful note-taker, he capitalized on casual access to data about European centrifuges. A super-motivated shopper, he assembled the components of Pakistan's atomic bomb from numberless sources around the world, an accomplishment he rates as greater than his theft of plans. He then allowed himself to become a bloated and overly decorated hero and a black-market profiteer in instruments of death.

In the year 1998, when it detonated its first fission explosions, Pakistan ranked 159th out of 200 measured entities in per capita income. What means, and above all what motivations, account for this feat in such circumstances? Pakistan's struggles with its larger neighbor, India, are paramount. The two countries' adjacent land masses are proportionate to New Zealand and Australia, between which neighbors there is no possibility of war. Religion, however, adds lethal elements far beyond the annoyances of mere proximity. Zulfikar Ali Bhutto, as a young foreign minister in the 1960s, famously said that Pakistanis would eat grass, but they would have their bomb. One month after Pakistan's surrender of Bangladesh in 1971, Bhutto, as new prime minister, held secret meetings of about seventy Pakistani scientists and asked them for a nuclear bomb. India then detonated its own Hiroshima-sized fission device in 1974.

Bhutto quotably described what he called Christian, Jewish, Hindu, and communist bombs, which implied the need for an "Islamic bomb." When the more zealously Muslim General Zia ul-Haq, overthrew him in 1977, he proved to be just as committed to a nuclear bomb as Bhutto. So Abdul Quadeer Khan flourished. His lab complexes elaborated into biomedical and geometric engineering. His role in developing a nuclear bomb became public. He picked up six honorary degrees, three gold crowns, and

11. Fraser, *Cosmic Anger*, p. 264.

forty-five gold medals, and twice was granted the highest Pakistani civilian award. He was giving money to hospitals, mosques, and schools. He was buying houses and luxury cars. His appetite for fame became insatiable, with no limits applied to it by the political elite of a "degenerated feudal culture," as one observer put it, "who also did whatever they wished whenever they wanted."[12]

Then in May 1998, India, breaking a quiet of two dozen years, tested five atomic bombs, one a fusion device with three times the power of the bomb that flattened Hiroshima. Despite pleas from Bill Clinton and Tony Blair to take the high moral ground, Pakistan let popular appetite and army logic prevail. That same month it replied by testing six bombs of its own. One up, for the moment. World emissaries finally succeeded in calming the two South Asian powers.

After 9/11, the international political climate went through an irreversible spasm of transformation. The U.S. put sudden intense pressure on Pakistan with regard to the Taliban government that was host to bin Laden and al-Qaeda. Musharraf relayed Pakistan's choice to his people as formulated by Bush on the phone: "Do we want bombs falling on us, or bombs falling on Afghanistan?"[13]

The American government also now pressured Pakistan regarding A. Q. Khan. But it was too late; the nuclear cats were long out of their bags. Khan had been justifying his sales of nuclear plans and materials to rogue nations on grounds that "all powers are created equal." The Pakistani government carefully moved Khan out of his lab in 2001, but not his associates; it claimed to restrict Khan's travel, but in fact did not do so.

The whole matter broke open with the interception, in October 2003, of a freighter carrying centrifuge parts and other Khan products made in Malaysia and bound for Libya.[14] Now the U.S., followed by the International Atomic Energy Agency with its own amplifying information, laid out its comprehensive case against Khan as a nuclear black marketeer, directing an international syndicate selling abroad. Khan had used the same people and the same channels for government activities and for freelance profiteering. As the former assistant secretary of state for non-proliferation told me,

---

12. William Langewiesche, "The Wrath of Khan," *The Atlantic Monthly,* Nov 05, pp. 62-85, and *The Atomic Bazaar: The Rise of the Nuclear Poor* (New York, Farrar, Straus and Giroux, 2007), pp. 150-56.

13. This is the popular characterization of his message, given to me by several Pakistanis.

14. "As Nuclear Secrets Emerge in Khan Investigation, More are Suspected," *New York Times,* 26 Dec 04, pp. 1, 18.

"we were in their computers, in their bank accounts, in their networks." The U.S. had been telling the government of Pakistan since 2001 it "had a problem." False reassurances had come back. Now Khaddafi, in early 2004, made the matter irrefutable, telling what he had bought for Libya, and from whom. The Bush government presented Musharraf's government with a "blinding light" of facts. The details of the Khan syndicate became world-wide front-page news.[15]

Why had Musharraf only "fired" Khan in 2001, when his mercenary sales were already perhaps fifteen years old? Why did he call Khan "my hero" when in 2004 he required him to make a public apology before pardoning him? Both the apology and the pardon were palpably spurious statecraft, designed so that neither Khan nor Musharraf needed to tell more of the ugly truth. But in late 2009, with Musharraf out of office, Benazir Bhutto and her defense minister dead, and the UN and concerted powers applying pressure on Iran, the rules on information changed. Khan himself went on TV to summarize his patriotic nuclear career before being suppressed again. A British journalist he had befriended leaked Khan's secret letter to his wife, which ends, "They might try to get rid of me to cover up all the things they got done by me." The things done included: providing China with enough enriched uranium for two nuclear bombs in the summer of 2002; giving Iran a set of drawings, some components, and the names and addresses of suppliers, on the advice of Benazir Bhutto's defense minister, to neutralize Israel's power and to build a regional Muslim bloc strong enough to counter international pressure; providing drawings and machines to North Korea through a retired general in return for $3.3 million; and assisting Libya in like manner.[16]

Dr. Khan's cooperation with the two Bhuttos and with Zia gave him an accumulated power that sharply compromised Musharraf's presidency. First, he was a national hero, grander in popular imagination than the coup leader at the top of the country. Second, he had become an independent center of power — of technological and scientific initiative, with corollary finances and influences — in a state whose porous nature had bred within itself statelets of many varieties. Third, he had supporters within the military; how many, with how much power, with what intentions, and

15. John Wolf, Assistant Secretary of State for Non-Proliferation (2001-4), interview, 12 Apr 06.

16. Open Source Center: Pakistan: Dr. Abdul Qadeer Khan Discusses Nuclear Program. TV Talk Show: Karachi, Aaj News Television in Urdu . . . 31 Aug 09; timesonline.co.uk/tollnews/world/asia/article6839044.ece [re Simon Henderson, 20 Sep 09].

precisely who, even Musharraf could not know in full detail. The president, to mollify America, had to act to contain Khan without arousing more enmity than he could handle in his own fraternity, which already contained, in the Inter-Services Intelligence and elsewhere, Islamists who made his own Muslim faith (whiskey-drinking, with Pekingese lapdogs) look humdrum. So he cut down Dr. Khan very slowly.

What damage had already been done when the U.S., with its own documentation, forced Musharraf to act in 2004? The quantities of materiel detected to have been exported suggest that still another nation — Saudi Arabia and Syria are the most likely candidates — might have received Pakistan's proliferating generosity. The tentacles of Khan's operations, beyond his original thefts in the Netherlands, included Malaysia, which bought aluminum from Singapore for centrifuge parts and shipped them to Dubai as an assembly and distribution point for Libya. Other suppliers and middlemen came from Switzerland, Turkey, Germany, Morocco, South Africa, Britain, Spain, and Italy. Dr. Khan's recent travels had included at least fourteen other countries of Southwest Asia, the Middle East, and Africa, plus Kazakhstan.[17]

One Pakistani general, cooperating with American and international authorities, consulted with his president during the showdown. Musharraf asked him if his own revelations about and requirements of Khan had gone too far. No, Mr. President, was his reply; you didn't go far enough. To me, this general spoke of Khan with disgust: "This man had possession, in trust, of the crown jewels. And he *sold* them, for *baser motives*."[18] A pivotal American official expressed his own judgments: "The man was . . . diabolically evil. . . . And Pakistan, on its own national security, was derelict and duplicitous. How can it be in the national interest of Pakistan to allow nuclear information to Iran? But nobody stopped it. . . . In history, [Khan] will be seen as one of the real villains of the twentieth century."[19] That concept of villainy, of course, is premised on the concept of a world that should not destroy itself by mindless accretion of nuclear weapons, leading to tinderbox accidents or terrorist carnivals. In such a framework, Khan's activities have more clearly advanced the probability of global disaster than Osama bin Laden's.

17. *New York Times,* 26 Dec 2004.
18. Conversation with Maj. Gen. (ret.) Mahmud Ali Durrani, 9 Mar 06. Durrani is the author of *India and Pakistan: The Cost of Conflict; the Benefits of Peace* (Washington, D.C., Johns Hopkins University Foreign Policy Institute, SAIS, 2000).
19. Wolf, conversation 31 Mar 06; interview, 12 Apr 06.

70

But that is a comparison of paired odium. Better to reflect on the contributions of Abdus Salam to physics, through theorizing the massless neutrino and "electroweak" interactions in electromagnetism. The productivity of his long and avid research life was amplified by his founding, in Trieste, of an International Centre for Theoretical Physics, which emphasized updraft of talent from lesser developed countries. In practice that was his nearest realization of a noble ambition to reengage Islam and science in mutual dynamism. Despite his Nobel acceptance speech, which reverently quoted the Qur'an, his grave has been desecrated by the anti-Ahmadi prejudice which runs high in Pakistan. It is sad that Salam should be overshadowed, in the warp of his nation's values, by the braggart and profiteer A. Q. Khan, who volunteered to Zulfikar Ali Bhutto his nuclear shoplifting talent to make an Islamic Bomb.

Poverty and Misogyny

My eyes told me that Pakistan was poor, beyond the degrees in which Indonesia is poor. But poverty itself needs explaining. What was going on beneath levels of investment in the military and its nuclear bomb?

Shahnaz Wazir Ali, Prime Minister Benazir Bhutto's special assistant for the social sector, headed the Pakistani delegation to the World Conference on Women in Beijing in 1995. Later, leading reforms in the fiscal and legal frameworks for NGOs in Pakistan, she was one of a small group of independent sector leaders chosen to meet with President Bush on his quick visit in 2006. Ms. Wazir Ali is not tall but, even seated, conveys an imposing presence. Her firm mouth, penetrating eyes, and level voice convey a flow of conviction. She opened up to me about what's amiss in Pakistan, and what needs to be done.

Reality here, she said, is not grounded in religion, but in the economics of poverty and in a rigid class structure. Women feel these realities much more than men. The vast majority are poor, marginalized, undernourished, and disenfranchised. Thirty to 40 percent struggle for a daily living. They don't have *time* to worship. "Religion is a good thing for middle classes," she said, "and an opium for the poor."

Many women spend their whole lives in a little cluster of hamlets. "They marry at age thirteen, and they look sixty years old at the age of thirty." Three-quarters of all births are at home. How to pray five times a day? Where to get enough water for ablutions before prayer? These women can't read the Qur'an, or maybe anything at all. They pray by rote. They know that they are Muslim, which means they must maintain chastity, cover the head, observe Ramadan, and serve the man as master. The state provides them virtually no windows of change or opportunity.

Into this initial and explosive description I injected a simple question about the state: "Why?"

"Lack of will," she answered, with an emphatic snap just short of intemperate. The will to deliver justice, education, health, or *anything* effectively. The state is not without resources. It is simply responsible for its *failure of management*. Of whatever it pledges — way too little — utilization may be only 50 or 60 percent. External donors are frustrated by a like impact on grants and loans.

The educational departments often don't have roads to go places, vehicles to travel the roads, or petrol for the vehicles. (Nobody volunteered me facts on literacy rates, perhaps because they are so discouraging: the most optimistic figure for adult literacy in Pakistan in 2006 was below 50 percent. Women's literacy was less than two-thirds of men's. More than half of grown Pakistanis were illiterate.) Shahnaz dramatized her recital with maternal mortality: so high that 48 percent or less of the population is women.

What are the solutions? Economic growth alone cannot decrease poverty, Shahnaz insisted, skipping over the common developmental premise that growth is a precondition for improvement. She wished to query distribution of income and asset ownership: How do they change? "Pakistan has learned that things *don't trickle down*. Poverty was only 26 percent just eight years ago."

I did not interrupt her to ask what standard she was applying. UN data published in 2004 showed that 13 percent of Pakistanis lived on less than one dollar a day, and a staggering *66 percent* lived on less than two dollars a day — and this at a time when economic gains were markedly reducing both categories throughout the world. Using a combined index of human poverty (life expectancy, illiteracy, deficient water sources, underweight children, and income), Pakistan ranked seventy-first out of ninety-five developing countries. The other Islamic countries I traveled in were doing much better: Turkey was at nineteen, Saudi Arabia at thirty, Iran was thirty-first, and Indonesia came in at thirty-fifth. Pakistan's performance put it below Haiti and Yemen.[20]

20. UNDP, Human Development Report, 2004. After construction of the "Multi-

"Issues of Islam are subsumed by struggle for survival." Out of dire need and desperation, families send boy children to *madrasas* for food and education. They provide a service the state cannot provide. Middle-class Pakistanis contribute to them, as does the Pakistani diaspora; and so have Saudi Arabia, Iraq, and Iran, for public relations motives, and to aid religious political parties.

So the boy goes to a *madrasa*. What does the girl do? Ms. Shahnaz asked the rhetorical question with a special bite. "The girl can't do anything but stay at home."

The combination of factors, of poverty enhanced by government mismanagement and intensified for women by religious and traditional values, was overwhelming me. I interjected a question on extraordinary solutions: What chance was there of revolution? Of a secular progressive reformer like Atatürk? Of a new Prophet? Shahnaz did not address prophetic transformation. Of revolution she said there was "very little chance." Regarding leadership, she mused briefly on Mahathir's achievements for Malaysia.

The poor, admittedly, do not throw up the necessary leaders, she continued. Pakistan was 88 percent rural when it was created, and is still two-thirds rural. People coming into the cities could, theoretically, propel change. There are now more Pathans (also called Pashtuns) in Karachi than in Peshawar. But migrants from the country just add to slum settlements and demands for urban services, and serve as vote banks for the big parties. The government and its would-be leaders choose to address only what they want to address.

Shahnaz Wazir Ali now wove religion back into her dire narrative. The poor that strive to become middle class and succeed *then begin* to take religious positioning. Only in the middle classes do you see the *burqa*. Its international emergence is a phenomenon of the need for Islamic identity. Among the poor there is no time or means for that. But with means and time, dress is the most obvious way to convey a message. And that message is expressed chiefly as codes of behavior in relation to men.

"The middle-class woman in a congested area is a symbol of her husband's honor." When his wife was sweeping the street, so what? But in a good third-floor apartment, with a need to go to the grocery, to send a

___

dimensional Poverty Index," the 2010 UNDP Human Development Report showed Pakistan to be 125th out of 169 countries, immediately above Congo. Fifty-one percent of Pakistanis were multidimensionally poor, and 60 percent lived on less than two dollars a day.

daughter to school, to receive visits from relatives, *there* the male becomes possessive. These are *his women.* Keep them covered, modest, and at home.

President Zia's insistence on the *chaar diwari* was a symbol of lower-middle-class status. The term translates as "four-wall *chador*" and conveys two rules about women at once: cover fully and stay in the house. As resources improve, in the professional upper-middle class, the dominance of the man differs. A woman may then be seen as having a need to study or drive a car. Some of this combination of means and motive produces strong and powerful professional women (one way Pakistan differs from Saudi Arabia). In other families, means and motives will be expressed more religiously. Women will "go *hijab.*" Either by the husband's wish or their own, they will cover themselves, while considering the socially self-exculpatory question, "Are we less intelligent and progressive, have we less potential, by covering our heads?" They answer that question, "No."

These dynamics date largely from the first influence of Zia, who among other things made media women cover themselves, in the late 1970s and early 1980s. Zia's promoting retrogressive steps to his political ends "prodded us to start up a women's rights movement" and to define "deliberate anti-stereotyping" in our own way, Shahnaz said. At the same time others, such as Dr. Ferhat Hashmi, out of an opposite conviction, went to conservative covering and founded hostels for girls in that spirit, which movement was rapidly spread in the mid-1990s by Saudi funding.

I asked, "What are the ways out and up from women's travail in Pakistan as you describe it?" Shahnaz Wazir Ali did not hesitate. First, make the schools *functional.* Second, pass strong measures of land reform and distribution, allowing women ready ownership, access to credit, and the financial means to help their own children. She knew where she stood. Her convictions were so vivid that I only realized later that I should have asked how much Benazir Bhutto, her boss as female prime minister, had achieved in these directions. Given the polite fury of what Shahnaz conveyed to me, I assumed it was far from enough.

Dr. Farzana Bari was a founding member of the Islamabad chapter of Women's Action Forum, which had been launched by Shahnaz Wazir Ali and others in 1979 to resist President Zia's actions against women. Now she is head of gender studies at her university. Study and action are integrated in her life, however fragmented they may be in Pakistan as a whole.

She recognizes Simone de Beauvoir in the 1950s, Betty Freidan in the 1960s, and Germaine Greer in the 1970s as groundbreaking advocates in women's affairs, all of whom remain relevant. But many feminisms evolved, and much scientific scholarship has arisen, which together construct a discipline. Women in Pakistan were struggling for equal pay, job rights, and child support in the 1960s and 1970s, and they made a lot of gains. To some degree satisfied in the public arena, and supported by cooperation with Western democracies, the movement's "angry commitment ebbed." On the theoretical front, however, thinkers like Chandra Mohanty are still generating momentum. Dr. Bari then mentioned ten other women, two of them Western and eight from South Asia. I found that the two Westerners but none of the eight South Asians appear in Mohanty's compendious bibliography, which suggests that even the most ambitious theorist can't read everybody, or that South Asia's problems are intensely special, or both. In any event, the most fertile recent essays seem to me those that cut beneath allegedly universal declarations which rely on the agency of the nation-state. Instead they argue for "gender justice" as outlined in the Qur'an, and manifested in education that reconstructs interpretation of Islam toward social justice for all.[21]

Such justice was imagined in Social Action Programs (SAP) prepared for 1993-98, and again in 1999-2003. They sought World Bank and multinational consortia help to renovate Pakistan's health, education, and water sanitation systems. A woman involved, expert in ways to attract more women to provide midlevel health services in rural areas, judged both

---

21. Chandra Talpade Mohanty, *Feminism Without Borders: Decolonizing Theory, Practicing Solidarity* (Durham and London, Duke University Press, 2003), is conceptually copious and strong. It appears to sharpen arguments that date back to Zillah Eisenstein, ed., *Capitalist Patriarchy and the Case for Social Feminism* (New York, Monthly Review Press, 1978). In Jane Flax, another writer recommended by Dr. Bari, I find "the laugh of Medusa," release of "suppressed discourses," and "polyphonic conversation": *Thinking Fragments: Psychoanalysis, Feminism, and Postmodernism in the Contemporary West* (Berkeley, University of California Press, 1990). More recent publications of guiding value to me have been: Gisela Webb, ed., *Windows of Faith: Muslim Women Scholar-Activists in North America* (Syracuse, Syracuse University Press, 2000); Ghazi-Walid Falah and Caroline Nagel, eds., *Geographies of Muslim Women: Gender, Religion, and Space* (New York, The Guilford Press, 2005); and Fawzia Afzad-Khan, ed., *Shattering the Stereotypes: Muslim Women Speak Out* (Northampton, Mass., Olive Branch Press, 2005). For systematic range in theology, see Amina Wadud's *Inside the Gender Jihad: Women's Reform in Islam* (Oxford, Oneworld, 2006); and for essays on advancing states of play, see Margot Badran, *Feminism in Islam: Secular and Religious Convergences* (Oxford, Oneworld, 2009).

SAPs as "dismal failures." She saw them marked by empty, locked-up health centers, "ghost schools," diehard planners, and die-fast plans that sought money rather than solutions. Ignorance and arrogance reinforced each other in mumbled mantras and stagnant muddle.[22]

The possibilities still remain vast, says Farzana Bari, as do untapped energies. Everyone votes. Everyone is different in her interests. Islam has never stopped women from working. The hypocrisies are *cultural*, Dr. Bari stressed, with an overdeveloped division between public and private domains. "The problem is not with women. . . . It is with men. We are doing all we can. But they don't give us due respect for our work."

In the rural areas of Pakistan, there exist no schools or health services for women. At this point I mentioned a conversation I had had with an accomplished Pakistani man, whose early career had been as a public health psychiatrist in rural areas. I had told him of the remark of a Harvard administrator and psychiatrist, who said that 20 percent of entering freshmen were on antidepressant pills, a figure since rising toward 25 percent. Why? "Too many choices." My Pakistani friend reflected a moment on the American luxury of options. Then he spoke of rural women in his nation: "They have *no* choices." The astounding prevalence of clinical depression among rural women remained with him — along with traumatic impressions of his two weeks of later service in the mountains after the great earthquake of 2005. Falling mountains and collapsing women seemed too readily symbolic of the fault lines of Pakistan's polity and society.

Yes, Dr. Bari nodded. "Headaches you cannot explain. Strange fits. And so forth. These are manifestations of frustration and depression," especially pronounced in a country which is heavily rural, with increasing poverty and enduring gender bias. Where Farzana Bari works, women are not only suffering from "inferior sexism," but from malnutrition. In addition, men are under increasing pressure to leave in search of work, shifting the burden to women to be heads of family in the full sense — not only vegetable-growing and cotton-picking, but somehow ensuring the survival of the whole family. "'Oppositional consciousness' arises. [A woman] *knows it's not right*. She doesn't have to be a feminist to feel that." She wants fair treatment, more dignity, and more opportunity.

I supplied a quote from Mary Ellen Lease, the Populist leader in Kansas of the 1890s: "Raise less corn and more hell." Dr. Bari shook her head.

---

22. Samia Altaf, "Pakistan Picaresque," *The Wilson Quarterly* 22:1, Winter 08, pp. 14-21.

"Social movements here have not reached rural Pakistan. . . . Women are suffering alone. . . . The structural problems are huge." If an organization came to them, women would enlist. But "we must take the blame," she said, because Pakistani movements for women's rights have not sufficiently connected with farm women or with female urban factory workers.

She went on to name significant exceptions: the Sindhi Women's Movement, which has organized at the provincial level; a women's movement in Kaghan Valley where poor villagers organize to protect trees on common land against contract cutting; a movement centered in the city of Okara which helps women farmers fight to protect their land.

Then came what I recognized in various countries as the "9/11 sigh." Dr. Bari's tone changed to take account of what has happened since that day. Religion is now a bigger force for women to cope with, pushing them toward more conservatism, with negative impacts for women in general — such varied reactions as "don't go to dances" and "don't go to female doctors." In her view, America's handling of the attack and its sequels has been very short-sighted. Its governmental attitude and invasions have intensified Islamic intolerance, with negative effects upon women generally.

To alleviate the wretched conditions of Pakistan's poor, the parliament took action in the year following the assassination of Benazir Bhutto. The Benazir Income Support Program was initiated in 2008-9. In 2009-10 it intended to distribute cash benefits to almost 10 percent of the population. Initial design suggested that payments be made only to adult females. A cutoff sum would be determined in 2010 by a "Poverty Scorecard" survey. The program had the potential of being the largest and most sophisticated poverty-reduction effort in Asia. At last, in memory of the murdered prime minister, Pakistan had the prospect of alleviating its most grievous social problem.

Madrasas and Social Dysfunction

In the Qur'an, about two hundred verses command believers to pray, but three times as many exhort them to reflect on the wonders of Allah in nature and the cosmos. Whatever proportions of attention teachers might give them, there was no question about the centrality of the holy book to

Muslim learning. The places of learning, the *madrasas,* seminaries for Islamic knowledge, were from 1000 to 1500 C.E. the central institutions of society. One who proceeded effectively through their requirements was not credentialed in any way analogous to Western universities, but was linked through his sheikh, or religious scholar, by "a chain of transmission reaching back through time to the moment of revelation itself."[23]

Then modernity struck, with superior Western projections of strategic power. The stricken, who analyzed it over decades and generations, detected a "secret wisdom" that had best be initiated, lest they be annihilated. Centrally directed governmental reforms, notably those of Muhammad Ali in Egypt and Mustafa Kemal in Turkey, undertook Western study of war and administration, and sought to remediate sluggard culture with a more general education, which included what the ultra-orthodox considered dangerous "worldly subjects."[24]

Among the most learned, adventurous, and morally inspired of Islamic thinkers in this period was Shah Wali Allah (1703-62). He tried to cope with those problems as a macro-sociologist in ways that long preceded efforts of Comte and Marx and Weber to be similarly comprehensive.[25] He presented the injunctions of Islam on premises of their compatibility with human nature. But two and a half centuries later, this comprehensive approach, shared by a twentieth-century disciple, led to frustration: "If we cannot explain it [the Qur'an] to the Muslims among the college students in the way in which we can successfully explain it in the madrasas, how then would we ever be able to teach the Qur'an to those who are not even Muslims?"[26]

That question might reverberate through Pakistan today were it not overpowered by calamitous institutional failure. In the aftermath of 9/11, President Pervez Musharraf undertook a third wave of *madrasa* reform. Beyond previous efforts of the early 1960s and late 1970s, he was directly intent on bringing *madrasas* under government regulation. The gargan-

23. Robert W. Hefner, "Introduction: The Culture, Politics, and Future of Muslim Education," in Robert W. Hefner and M. Q. Zaman, eds., *Schooling Islam: The Culture and Politics of Modern Muslim Education* (Princeton, Princeton University Press, 2007), pp 1-39; quotation, p. 9.

24. Hefner, "Introduction," pp. 14-17.

25. Muhammad al-Ghazali, *The Socio-Political Thought of Shah Wali Allah* (Islamabad, International Institute of Islamic Thought, 2001), pp. 10-11, 35-36; *passim.*

26. Muhammad Qasim Zaman, "Tradition and Authority in Deobandi Madrasas of South Asia," in Hefner and Zaman, *Schooling Islam,* pp. 61-86; quotation, p. 69.

tuan shape of the problem and his own impatience were implicit in his public question: "I ask these seminaries how many mosques . . . there [are] in the country to accommodate all these one million students as imams."[27]

Guarding culture and morality and other bases of "identity formation" is always, of course, the first mission of education. Musharraf could also have been answered: There are many social roles beyond and beside imam contemplated in modern madrasa schooling.[28] Or: There are plenty of defects in "worldly knowledge." Lost mission and confused purpose generate in some Western, and particularly American, education a grotesque funhouse distortion.

Whatever the vectors of argument, public education in Pakistan is demonically stunted with regard to funding of government schools — 1.8 percent of GDP.[29] And if one turns to the *madrasas* for ethical gravity, one finds them explosively increased in numbers of institutions and students precisely because public education has failed so badly. *Madrasas* are dedicated to shaping Islamic souls, as distinct from Pakistani citizens. But they have lost the vision of global intellect held in India's advanced *madrasas* from the time of Akbar, the sixteenth-century Mughal emperor, until the last of his successors was deposed in 1858.

Islamic scholars in India, losing political-cultural confidence and reacting against a failed elite, went back to Qur'anic basics in the late nineteenth century. Stripping out European and Hindu learning from their curriculum, they founded a blinkered *madrasa* at Deoband, north of Delhi, which bore analogy to Wahhabi teaching, and which has radiated a puritanical influence in North India and Pakistan ever since.[30] In its broadest reforming reach, Deobandi energy consciously included women. The influential volume *Bihishti Zawar*, written in Urdu at the turn of the twentieth century, was a primer for girls' literacy and a guide to social and ritual norms, intended to make the female reader the equivalent "of a middling 'alim."[31]

27. Quotation in Zaman, "Tradition and Authority in Deobandi Madrasas of South Asia," p. 61.

28. Barbara Metcalf, "Madrasas and Minorities in Secular India," in Hefner and Zaman, *Schooling Islam*, pp. 87-106, esp. pp. 103-4.

29. William Dalrymple, "Inside the Madrasas," *The New York Review of Books*, 1 Dec 05, pp. 16-20; datum, p. 16.

30. Dalrymple, "Inside the Madrasas," *passim*; Alexander Evans, "Understanding Madrasahs: How Threatening Are They?" *Foreign Affairs* 85:1, Jan/Feb 06, pp. 9-16, esp. pp. 10-13.

31. Barbara D. Metcalf and Thomas R. Metcalf, *A Concise History of India* (Cambridge, Cambridge University Press, 2002), p. 146.

Woman as mediocre cleric, or commonplace religious scholar? A demeaning idea, a century later. The point, however, was not to render her impotent in scholarship, but to avoid distracting her from something holy — the essence of the female, as it was then considered.

The present-day *madrasa* in Pakistan, in any case, is an all-male institution. There were 245 such religious schools at the time of independence. In 2001 they numbered, by government count, 6,870, with enrollment rising perhaps toward 1 million. A more recent census, as part of an effort to identify and control extremism, yielded 13,000 *madrasas*, of which 9,461 had allegedly been registered by early 2006, as part of the government's requirement to have audit reports from each of them. My informant, Maj. Gen. (ret.) Jamshed Ayaz Khan, President of the Institute of Regional Studies, Islamabad, said that they now must declare that they will not teach hatred, and will teach "worldly subjects" like English, math, physics, chemistry, and Pakistan studies. The government intended to establish a "super-board" over the five different boards then running the *madrasas,* so that it would govern the "biggest NGO in Pakistan," with responsibility for an estimated 1.3 million students. General Khan made the proud point that no assailants of the president or prime minister had yet come from these *madrasas.* That assertion, combined with his statistics, was not reassuring to me. Three years after we spoke, a general who had been Musharraf's education minister summarized matters simply: "The madrasa reform project failed."[32]

Can Pakistan untie its loose but real links among poverty, education, political violence, and terrorism? Sustained and determined reform of all education would be needed. Many more public schools are required, with modernized curricula. The *madrasas* certainly require broadened curricula, and injections of temperance against "their common hatred of the Westernized Pakistani elite, India, America, and Israel."[33] Empowering priorities on major participation by girls and women are vital in the totality of reform.[34] To state these aims is to hope grandly. To wait without action would be to fail.

As American cabinet officers, both Donald Rumsfeld and Colin Powell contributed to the media fallacy of picturing *madrasas* as "schools for ter-

32. Quoted by Sabrina Tavernisi, *New York Times,* 4 May 09, p. A6.

33. Quotation from Hassan Abbas, *Pakistan's Drift into Extremism: Allah, the Army, and America's War on Terror* (Armonk, M. E. Sharpe, 2005), p. 239.

34. Mariam Abou Zahab, "Sectarian Violence in Pakistan: Local Roots and Global Connections," in Institute of Regional Studies, *Global Terrorism: Genesis, Implications, Remedial and Countermeasures* (Islamabad, 2006), pp. 383-96.

ror." A fuller context for assessment of *madrasas* might include West Bank
yeshivas with a reputation for violence against Palestinians, and Serbian
monasteries that sheltered war criminals. Very few *madrasas* are said actually to give covert military training. A likely upper estimate of Pakistani
madrasas simply teaching violent *jihad* may be 15 percent. Not a comfort-
ing figure, because that could mean nearly 200,000 students being indoc-
trinated in such a way.[35] Some say that *madrasas* are filling a void in Pakistan's education, with their free education, room, and board. But what are
they filling it with? Educational emptiness as part of the total condition of
Pakistan prompted the grim humor in the general who remarked to me,
"We think God is on casualty leave."

The *madrasa* movement is a thousand years old, but its Deobandi stream is
not yet aged a century and a half. I visited Darul Uloom in Karachi, in December 2004, accompanied by a retired naval commander. I'd been in-
trigued to learn that they had recently introduced computing and a limited
amount of English-language study.

Mufti Muhammad Taqi Usmani made himself generously available in
the *madrasa* founded by his father, the late Grand Mufti of Pakistan.
Usmani is the author of, among other books, the eleven-volume *Discourses
on the Islamic Way of Life,* and for twenty years was a member of the
Shari‘a Supreme Court.[36] His campus manifests itself as a walled, gated,
and guarded campus with much green lawn inside, and several new buildings under construction. The Mufti is a man of slight stature and powerful
spectacles. His dark eyebrows contrast with his goatee dyed with henna,
which was recommended by some hadith and may even have been used by
the Prophet. When Usmani removed his brocaded white cap to mop his
brow, the dye color of his thinned hair looked orange. His upper front
teeth protrude where not actually missing. An impish, even eerie, appearance yields to authority as he talks. When he gathers momentum on controversial issues — *shirk* and roles of women — I feel his capacity to be
aroused with anger. Taqi Usmani's website does not shy from argument; it

---

35. Dalrymple, "Inside the Madrasas," p. 17, is the source of the percentage estimate, to
which I have applied reasoning from estimated present enrollments.

36. Fuller information on Taqi Usmani: Zaman, in Hefner and Zaman, "Tradition and
Authority in Deobandi Madrasas of South Asia," pp. 65, 75, 79-81.

contends that "Western banking and financing is based on oppression and the Islamic financing system is based on justice and compassion. World Bank does not possess the treasures of the universe. Allah is the possessor of all treasures."

The Mufti, in conversation, interprets "Islamic Republic" to mean that Pakistan is duty-bound to convert all laws to shari'a. But this is difficult. Pakistan's rulers for two centuries have been educated and trained in British law inherited from India. Now many issues need to be defined and resolved, such as the concept of corporate entities. What Islamic principles should govern declaration of dividends, sales of shares, mergers?

"In the light sent us (from the seventh century, C.E.) . . . we have to exercise *ijtihad* regarding the constitutions of 1956, 1962, and 1973." In 1979 another institution was established by Article 203, the federal Shari'a Court — a judicial body which any citizen can approach if he finds something repugnant to Islam, in order to learn the standpoint of government and obtain a hearing. If conditions are found contrary to shari'a, the government must bring itself into conformity by a certain date. This "judicial review" is not mere recommendation, but requires action — which can be appealed to the shari'a appellate court, where the final say resides.

In a wide-ranging discussion, I asked about the aim of Usmani's own *madrasa.* "We try to make our students practicing Muslims, with a deep knowledge of sources of shari'a, and the circumstances around us." To determine likely viewpoints regarding Shi'ites, I cited the Qur'an, 6:159: "As for those who have divided their religion and broken up into factions, have nothing to do with them. Their case rests with God; in time He will tell them about their deeds." The Mufti's take on this verse was that "a difference of opinion is not to be condemned. . . . But schism or hostile interpretation of the Holy Qur'an and Sunna is [condemnable]. . . . On the basis of such differences, we excommunicate or fight."

Pursuing the matter, I cast Muhammad Ibn Abd al-Wahhab as a divisive extremist. Usmani answered, "You are right to some extent. . . . His insistence on *tawhid* [the unicity of God] went to such an extreme that I do not agree with him. He exaggerated some minor issues and made them *shirk.* . . . Yet (he put new stress in his voice here, as if to recover ground perhaps unnecessarily given away) I respect Wahhab very much because in so many respects he contributed to the *umma.*"

He then inquired into intended themes of my book. Still early in my project, I made the mistake of voicing a merely alliterative thought, "the veil and the vote." Usmani immediately remonstrated against Islam having

82

been misinterpreted as "behind the veil." "The foremost beliefs of Islam are *tawhid*, the teachings of the Prophet, and belief in the hereafter. . . . The veil is only mentioned in one verse, and that one is open to interpretation. . . . Islam is a package of different social, economic, religious, and political instructions, of which the veil is only one part of the social. . . . To identify Islam with the veil is mistaken and unjust."

Properly forewarned, I assured the Mufti of my faithful intention to plumb deeper meanings. His prayer time having arrived, we parted cordially. He invited further questions by e-mail.

The commander and I drove back to central Karachi in a car without effective air-conditioning, through the omnipresent dust and smog, across dry gorges that would roar with water in other seasons. We breathed in particulates of industrial, animal, and human exhaust. I marveled at the diversity of vehicles on the road: giant trucks, including drinking water trucks, capable of crushing us; buses veering from lane to lane, overloaded with passengers, festively painted in arabesque, with floral and celestial motifs; grimy private vehicles like our own; bicycles navigating the flow; tractors lugging wagons with produce from the farm; donkey carts; and even a few camel-drawn carts, pulled by beasts holding their heads high above the honking tumult as if to say, "I am descended from creatures who bore the Prophet; who are *you?*"

My thoughts went back within the walls of the Darul Uloom *madrasa*, and I asked my sponsor and guide, "Riazullah, why, in an educational institution, are there armed guards at the gates?" He thought only briefly about it. "Maybe it is to protect the mufti. Stop somebody try to shoot him." I pursued the question: "Why would anyone want to kill the mufti?" Riazullah did not answer. In retirement, one of his several businesses is a security service, and he had a uniformed commando officer driving us, a fit, taut, taciturn man, adroit at the wheel. Motives did not seem to waken Riazullah's interest. His business is security, whose demands are practical.

Dr. Abdul Bari Khan is a heart surgeon. His wife, Dr. Farrah Khan, is an emergency obstetrician-gynecologist. Their children, two boys and a girl, all wish to become doctors like their parents. Bari and Farrah had an arranged/consent betrothal, followed by four years of being affianced while they studied medicine. Their wedding was a four-day affair, of which they showed me the photo albums. Seven hundred guests attended ("That's not so many. At a politician's wedding there can be five thousand people"), including their 108 first cousins. The first day was marked by henna and yellow dress for the bride; the second day, by legal papers and red dress. The third day, for the ceremony itself, the bride wore a heavy red, blue, and green embroidered *dopatta*, which at certain points was dropped over her forehead and eyes, so that two attendants had to lead her (Bari, as groom, declined to be blinded by a male garland of roses). The fourth day brought ceremonies in which the bride left her home in Peshawar to join her husband's family in Karachi.

The facial demeanor of the bride, December 1991, included eyes modestly downcast. Yet now, say Bari and Farrah, brides not only eye the camera, but flare smiles at it. *What next?* they worry. Their children may be tempted to ask for independent marriages. "But we are teaching them the tradition, in the hope they will not embarrass us." They smile on their children, who smile back.

The wedding days were followed by two weeks of dinners given by relatives, at each of which the bride wore a new gift dress. For their first anniversary, three more days of celebration were fully photographed. The point is family bonding. Farrah and Bari said to me, "We wanted to show you Pakistan!" The photos generously made their point.

A few shots of each other suggest the honeymoon. Farrah walking at sunset on a Karachi beach in a multicolored dress to her ankles. Bari at water's edge, in a faded blue dungaree suit, his jutting beard and bold stance making him look like a seaside cowboy with giant horn-rimmed glasses.

Bari can perform a heart valve operation for $2,000, which in the U.S. costs $30,000. He showed me his institute, with diagnostic lab, pharmaceutical center, and blood bank. Then the modern operating room with an up-to-date heart/lung machine. In rooms recuperating from operations were two women and four men, one of whom had walked from Afghanistan, drawn by word of mouth to Bari's prowess. Patients come in and out on a five-day cycle.

As a medical student in 1981, Bari helped lead his colleagues in breaking a strike of professional blood donors, then the main, and insecure, source for transfusions. They wanted more money per pint. (This was just before AIDS was first diagnosed in the U.S.) The medical students increased their own blood donations — Bari for a long while gave four times a year — and they broke the professionals' presumptive hold on the lifeline. So infuriated were the strikers that the medical students, to avoid attack, traveled only in groups for months afterward.

Bari now gives free surgery. Some of his operating days last from 5 a.m. to midnight. To support his heart institute, he relies on donors who follow the Islamic injunction to give one-fortieth of their wealth every year. How many do so? "Maybe 50 percent." Then 1.25 percent of all wealth in Pakistan is available for charity every year? "Yes. And it is necessary. Because Qur'anic law does not allow us the kind of endowment that draws interest, like you have in America."

Working in this system, Bari built a following of donors to help him establish a new hospital, which opened in the second half of 2006. Situated in a catchment of Karachi with a population of two and a half million people, it aims to give primary through tertiary care to 150 bedded patients. Bari's study of hospital management and business organization in the U.S. convinced him that a mission statement must be broadly cast and must drive progress by its reinterpretation. So he defined it for his hospital this way: "Provide excellence-driven comprehensive healthcare free of cost to the creatures of Allah." The economic dimension interested me. Won't poverty be alleviated in time? I asked. No: Bari doesn't see Pakistan shaking free of the control of poverty in the next 50 or 100 years. And, anyway, in the U.S. there are some free hospitals, like those of the Shriners. The key words in his definition are "comprehensive" and "free of cost." They will stimulate review and progress. He smiles. Now he had to complete the funding by expanding his corps of donors. He smiles again.

Of Bari's six brothers and four sisters, only one brother, Muhammad Jamil, went to a *madrasa*. Seven years older than Bari, he observed the wish of his father, a prayerful businessman, that he become a religious scholar. He was the only member of a well-to-do family to choose this course of life, including his 108 first cousins. The family often discussed the tensions between *madrasa* education ("overdrawn") and secular education ("too much worldliness"). Summing up his own convictions, Bari says, "Man-made rules are not perfect. . . . If you are a true believer, the only thing that can stop you from sin is your religious law. Even so, in Pakistan, perhaps 20 percent of people *drink* against this law." His family defined a balance in education between religious ethics and science, and Muhammad Jamil, inspired by these discussions, set out to realize them in practice. He founded Iqra (from Allah's first message to the Prophet, "Read!") — first in the late 1980s at the primary level, and advancing to tertiary education. Now there are 35,000 students in the system; cumulatively, 100,000 have been educated there.

A basic aim of Iqra education is first to make each student a *hafiz* — one who has learned the Qur'an by heart. The majority do so by age nine, and some even earlier. Bari himself did not become a *hafiz,* but the kind of guarded education he received did not permit him to go to the movies until Class 10 (roughly a sophomore in high school). "Then I was so busy, no time for it." He saw his first movie, in order to accompany Farrah, at age thirty-five. He sometimes watches movies with her now on TV, but has still seen only two of them in theaters.

"A child who learns the Qur'an by heart can learn anything," says Bari. By Class 10 they compete with "worldly schools" in "worldly subjects" like math, science, geography, and English. But they have a strong previous base in ethics. Very few Iqra students choose to teach in *madrasas.* They become doctors and engineers, or enter the bureaucracy, "where understanding the impact of right and wrong is needed."

Muhammad Jamil expanded Iqra's programs nationally while also writing an ethics column for a major newspaper. He organized and led groups to Mecca in Ramadan, as well as in formal hajj season. He also led and raised funds for the International Society for the Protection of Accomplished Prophecy. He was devoted to belief in one God and in angels, and to the conviction that the Prophet Muhammad's message was unshakably complete, with no allowable sequel. Over this last tenet, in his student days, he had gone to jail after a campus battle between the orthodox and the Ahmadis, believers in the prophet who had insisted that he was a Muslim inspired by the Prophet of the Qur'an.

Late in the year 2004, on a weekend in the full flowering of his work, Mohammad Jamil was in Lahore, where he met Maulana Asad Madani, an *alim* prominent in India's public life, whom he invited to Karachi. But a Pakistani visa permits a visitor from India an itinerary of only one city. Muhammad Jamil, without even word to his family, came back to Karachi on a Saturday to contact government officials on behalf of Madani to enable his further travel. After consultations in the bureaucracy, he asked a friend to bring him his car. He drove home, as a surprise to his family, at 5:45 p.m. He blew the horn and his youngest son ran out to greet him.

The boy abruptly ran back inside the house crying, "Someone has shot father!" The unknown assailant, who had followed him home, fled after firing. His family immediately rushed Muhammad Jamil to the hospital. But he did not survive.

The family decided not to lodge a case. At the murder of a nonviolent and creative man, I was puzzled and deeply dismayed. Why not press for an investigation? Bari observed, "When the president or prime minister is attacked, they get the man at once, or in hours. But when you know there is not going to be a result, you don't try."

I was still shocked. Why not *try?* Because, he answered, there has been killing of religious leaders in the last few years. No one is caught. The government is suspected.

I said, "I can't understand the *motive*."

Bari: "I can't, either. . . . Shi'a against Sunni, as now in Iraq, again? No, not here." (Actually, 4,000 sectarian killings occurred in Pakistan in the two decades before 2006.)[37] Bari's limited but insistent perspective is that "All the ones killed have been Deobandi leaders in Karachi who could *mobilize people*." He ruminated: the trend is traceable to Iran's attempt to export its revolution of 1979, followed by Saudi Arabia's counter-pressures. (Inside Pakistan, these high international tensions have bred sectarian militant groups, such as the Sunni SSP, "Soldiers of the Prophet's Companions," four of whose leaders were killed between 1990 and 2003.[38]) He ruminated that it could be like Kemal Atatürk's getting rid of leaders for their ideas. This further astonished me. "Atatürk? Assassinations?"

"Yes, he did lots of them."

I accepted what Bari said as a Pakistani impression of Atatürk. His best biographer, however, sees the matter differently. In response to an assassination plot against him, the Turkish leader in 1926 launched a "measured terror" against his most powerful opponents, which included political trials that in four cases concluded with "judicial murder."[39]

The real question Bari and I were alluding to in this conversation was the nature of Musharraf, who often remarked that he admires Atatürk. Bari observed that Musharraf wants to maintain his position, has no other ambition, and would do anything to keep power. I persisted in maintaining that Muhammad Jamil's charismatic popularity need not endanger a

---

37. *The Economist,* 4-10 Mar 06, pp. 22-25.

38. Zaigham Khan, "Religious Militancy and Sectarian Violence in Pakistan" (Islamabad, The Network for Consumer Protection, 2004), esp. pp. 18-23. Stephen Philip Cohen's comprehensive *The Idea of Pakistan* (Washington, The Brookings Institution, 2004) acknowledges the rise of violence in Karachi since 1999 (p. 210), "where each year between 400 and 600 political murders occur" (p. 208).

39. Andrew Mango, *Atatürk* (Woodstock/New York, Overlook Press, 1999), ch. 23, esp. p. 451.

dictator. I was slow to see the mercurial mutability of religion and politics in Pakistan, where "What *kind* of Islam?" is a life-or-death question. Bari asserted that his brother "had been a most *non*-controversial religious leader. He was a force of bringing people together. He had no political motive. He had no personal needs."

Then, I asked, could there be, among the Ahmadis, those who resented his pressure against them on behalf of Accomplished Prophecy? Bari considered but dismissed the thought. He came back to "a killer who doesn't know who or why he is killing."

Who hired him? The fact exists, I said, that only some few in the bureaucracy knew where his brother was on that afternoon.

Bari replied with the words of Muhammad Jamil himself. Because Deobandi leaders A, B, and C had been killed, maybe he was "D."[40] The others had been shot in Karachi. So his family and friends persuaded him to be careful there and active elsewhere.

I: "Couldn't a family member — you? — go to the visa officials and ask questions to pin down communications on that afternoon?"

Bari: "All that was needed was one tracker, who tells the hired killer he [Jamil] has left Lahore for Karachi."

I: "But even if the killer is vanished, those who knew where your brother was late on that Saturday were very few. They can be investigated."

Bari shook his head. "The destiny of everyone is fixed. That [knowledge] gives us our basic support."

I: "But how frustrating and agonizing for the family to conclude to every question, 'We don't know, and we can't find out.'"

Bari was on an Eisenhower Fellowship in the United States at the time of the killing. His first emotional reaction was to leave and go back to his family. The concept of destiny, however, took over. He realized that his brother's job was done. Now he had to do his own job, which meant that for now he needed to stay in the U.S. in order to do it better back in Pakistan. "When my time will come" — he was speaking now about his own appointment with death — "I will go."

When he did return home, people came to see him "to condole." They

---

40. Zaman, in Hefner and Zaman, *Schooling Islam*, identifies three prominent leaders of the Jami'at al'Ulum al-Islamiyya, assassinated in Karachi 1997, 2000, and 2004 — "all presumably by Shi'i militants" (p. 73). Their dogmatic background and institutional history yield "of all the Pakistani madrasas . . . [a] reputation for militant activism . . . surely the best deserved" (p. 74). Muhammad Jamil Khan, however, although educated at this *madrasa*, was leading his own institution for years before his death.

said it was a great loss. He answered, "No, it isn't. The greatest loss would have been the death of the Prophet. But the Prophet said his death would not matter. He had only twenty-three years to do his job, but he organized it, and he did it."

Mohammad Jamil had nineteen years, in which years, Bari said, other institutes arose with the same ideology and similar names. He gave away his syllabus to them. He shared always, to multiply the effect of religious and ethical and scientific education among the well-to-do. With a quiet pride, he said of his brother's work: "It is not finished. It is moving, it is flourishing. That is the beauty of an institute."

Beneath that beauty, and the pride and pain of Bari's family, I glimpsed the explosive wiring of public issues in Pakistan, which can resemble dynamite tentacles around a nuclear bomb. To be a volunteer sapper is suicidal; something will go off before the device is defused. The crisis of occupation of the Red Mosque in Islamabad in mid-2007 is illuminating. It began with a deceptively mild initial incident: activists from the Women's College attached to the Red Mosque occupied an adjacent children's library in protest against government moves to demolish mosques illegally constructed. Escalation showed combustible tensions within the so-called "mullah-military complex," as well as Jama'at-i-Islami Party opportunism, and Abdul Rashid Ghazi's willingness to die in memory of his father, whom he alleged had been murdered by the ISI in 1998. Musharraf, irresolute, finally ordered a crushing government "operation" which resulted in "one hundred" official — or several hundred actual — deaths.[41] The Red Mosque massacre not only stripped away voters from Musharraf's PML-Q party, but allegedly motivated the eventual killers of Benazir Bhutto, who had decried its occurrence.

Disaster and Decorum

Not all Pakistani troubles are self-inflicted. In the mountains, with an epicenter 65 miles north-northeast of Islamabad near the capital of Pakistani Kashmir, an earthquake struck on October 8, 2005. Mountain passes, roads, and paths were obliterated; whole villages were swallowed up or tumbled down. At one point an estimated 3.3 million people were homeless, with

41. Numerous sources, including Anatol Lieven, "Pakistan, the Red Mosque Phenomenon," http://intellibriefs.blogspot.com/2007/06/pakistan-red-mosque-phenomenon.html.

winter soon to come. The government's official death toll came to 74,500; international estimates reached 86,000. Even so, Pakistan's dead numbered only half those killed by tsunami on the Indonesian island of Aceh alone, which was the greatest part of an eventually stabilized count of 230,000 dead and missing rogue-wave victims throughout the Indian Ocean. The international community nonetheless pledged aid of $5.8 billion to Pakistan in less than six weeks, compared to $7 billion to those nations affected by the tsunami. Between these two Asian mega-events, Hurricane Katrina hit the U.S. Gulf Coast, causing at least 1,800 deaths and the greatest property losses in American history. But the dead were only one-fortieth of those in Pakistan, and one-ninetieth of those in Indonesia.[42]

In Indonesia, the newly elected government of President Susilo Bambang Yudhoyono put a rigorous and honest administrator in charge of relief in Aceh, and arrived at a cease-fire there in August 2005, which has since held. Far less impressive performance by Pakistan's government and military was among the causes of that nation's being ranked ninth in the world in a failed-state index, between Haiti (marginally worse) and Afghanistan (marginally better).[43]

On my first trip to Islamabad, I took an elevator up several floors of what I later learned was a twelve-story building — part of the luxury apartment complex called the Margalla Towers. The Hyder family was my host for a discussion of wearing *hijab*. Their style of furnishings reminded me of my paternal grandmother's. With Aila Hyder were her daughter, Maleeha, a young family friend named Amina Sajaad, and the Hyders' son, Fahad, chaperone for the occasion. The mood was cheerfully polite. It was my first experience of women who would not, out of religious conviction, shake hands. I pulled back my offending hand and waited for a teacup around which to wrap it. Even in Saudi Arabia, the women I had met were either of a professional class that did offer a shake, or were so clearly traditional that the gesture did not occur to me. The Hyder family group put me at ease with eager discussion of their values.

42. "Tsunami," Wikipedia, 1 Apr 06; "Pakistan earthquake," Wikipedia, 5 Apr 06; "Hurricane Katrina," Wikipedia, 25 Apr 06; all three disaster entries as updated 23 Apr 07.

43. "The Failed States Index," *Foreign Policy* and the Fund for Peace, *Foreign Policy,* May/Jun 06, pp. 50-58. Also on the list of sixty nations were Indonesia at 32, Russia at 43, Iran at 52, and China at 57.

Aila Hyder (mother): No, I did not always wear *hijab*. Only after I began to study religion in a group of seven or eight persons. . . . I find a group gives you a lot of support.

Maleeha Hyder: In my teenage years, Allah allowed me to meet a couple of friends with *hijab,* age 15 or 16, whose conversation I liked better than [that of] my non-*hijab* friends. . . . When I did what the Qur'an and Sunna say, I felt better than when I didn't. . . . [My reasons now are]: (1) Why should a woman consider her beauty so cheap that she displays it to everybody? And (2) "I am gift-wrapped for my husband." When you give flowers, you want them fresh, in a wrapping. . . .

Amina Sajjad: The most precious of God's creations is a woman. . . .

Aila Hyder: . . . and the most exploited of God's gifts is the woman.

Mother and daughter then differed on frequency of wearing. The mother said that she took it up gradually, and felt that her daughter had rushed into it. "You don't have to make it obvious . . . or appear overpious." Maleeha responded, "You do it your way, I'll do it mine."

I asked, Why does God/Allah create us so capable of division and schism and contest?

The women answered: Because God also created us capable of unity and concord.

Fahad (brother): Allah gives us free will and messengers to tell us the difference between a glass half-full and one half-empty.

Maleeha and her brother, working on a metaphor together: Life requires the use of a blender. But it comes with instructions. God gave us a user's manual, which is the Qur'an.

Amina Sajjad: "I've been preaching in Bangladesh . . . and have also represented Islam in a debate on the BBC. Back then I used to take the *niqab* [which covers nose and mouth] . . . not easy to do . . . takes courage. . . . But the face is a very important part of communication, and I'm a teacher [so now she wears only a hair-covering and face-framing veil]. . . . Islam does not mean to have us mass-produced, but allows us to express our culture. And covering is a matter of personal identity."

When the evening ended, Amina Sajjad accompanied me down in the elevator. Before she proceeded to an adjoining tower, I gave her my card, and she wrote her telephone number and e-mail address in my notebook.

Ten months later, when the earthquake hit, Islamabad shook. The two adjoining towers remained standing, but the Margalla Tower in which we had talked came down. Steel reinforcement bars (rebar) should link and overlap vertical with horizontal beams, to transmit horizontal seismic stresses down to the ground. Poor rebar means bad deflection of stress. Poor cement means no adherent integrity. If both are absent, a building can shake apart.

The central Margalla Tower had "pancaked" in the early morning of October 8, 2005, killing eighty-one people, with many more injured. Maleeha Hyder and her brother were not in the apartment at the time. The body of the father of the family, Mehboob, could not be found for a week. Mother Alia fell eight floors onto a pile of rubble, breaking both arms and her left leg. She slowly recovered, reciting the Qur'anic verse *innalillahe wa inna illaihe rajioon*, "We all belong to Allah and to him we will return."

Amina Sajjad, living in the next tower, was protected by sufficient rebar and adequately mixed cement. Photographs show the snapped struts, bent supports, and jagged puzzle-edges of the standing towers adjacent to the empty space where the central tower had stood.[44]

Through a close friend I inquired into the recovery of Mrs. Hyder and the well-being of the family. I tried to reach Amina Sajjad three times by e-mail across the next half-year, and by telephone on my next trip to Islamabad. No replies. I knew she was physically unhurt, but I discovered on the web that she was feeling a moral injury from other causes. She had been invited to do a special program named "A Tale of Two Women" for CNN, in which an American housewife named Lisa Pinto would come and live in "her shoes" for a week, and then Amina would travel to New York and spend a week in "Lisa's shoes." When the producers arrived days before the program was to go on, however, Amina found out that Lisa was a lawyer and a Republican Party strategist. The American ambassador would be involved in the program; also, a handicapped child in Peshawar, whose parents the Taliban had murdered before his eyes; and a female activist aiding women abused by husbands and in-laws. "Lisa would not be living with me nor me with her. Nor were we allowed to contact each other at all, except for interaction during the program." For Lisa's security, a "family friend" would accompany her — one who worked for the U.S. government.

Amina asked what has all this to do with living in "MY SHOES" for a week? The producer, upset, said that spice and variety were needed for viewers, and she needed to be flexible. Amina asked why couldn't they also meet a family that had benefited from the Taliban, to balance the story? Lisa and the camera crew were now in town, but Amina felt repelled by

---

44. Flickr, "Margalla Tower taken on 23rd October," uploaded by Talhah, 1 Nov 05.

"the stench of their deception." Lisa and a friend wooed her with gifts and dinner and arguments. Having prayed to God, however, Amina said she had received "a clear sign to back off." Before leaving Pakistan, Lisa called to tell Amina how she had wasted her time, and how shameful it was to have allowed her to leave her children behind for nothing.[45]

Amina's own account does not acknowledge the degree to which she tied up people and dollars in a fallible romantic hope of helping Americans understand Pakistan and Islam. She might have cut away quickly rather than prolonging uncertainty and expense. She correctly discerned, however, that the project was not about living in other shoes, but about reinforcing extant American images.

The larger point demonstrated by Amina Sajjad's experience had much earlier been captured by Akbar Ahmed: "Nothing in history has threatened Muslims like the Western media; neither gunpowder in the Middle Ages . . . nor trains and the telephone, which helped colonize them in the last century, nor even planes which they mastered for their national airlines earlier this century. The Western media are . . . ubiquitous; never resting and never allowing respite. They probe and attack ceaselessly, showing no mercy for weakness or frailty."[46]

My second trip to Karachi, early in March 2006, plunged me into the cartoon controversy, then burning out in many countries, but still aflame in Pakistan. "Blasphemous sketches" was the local term of choice for a project begun when the editor of the *Jyllands Posten* initiated a cartoon competition as a publicity exercise to help a Danish writer find an illustrator for a children's book she wished to produce on the Prophet Muhammad. Among the entries, in a spirit of outrageous fun, was one of the Prophet wearing a black turban shaped like a bomb, with a lit fuse sticking out of it. That was the cartoon later described around the world. In places indifferent to blasphemy, it was published with pious declarations of freedom of the press — which would be better described, in this case, as freedom for incendiary imagery.

A timely hearing by the Danish prime minister, sympathetic to felt reli-

45. Khusro Mumtaz, online, The News/Jang Group, 7 Feb 05.

46. Akbar S. Ahmed, *Postmodernism and Islam: Predicament and Promise* (London and New York, Routledge, 1992), p. 223.

gious insult yet firm in delineation of Danish law, might have prevented much of what followed. Instead, stonewalling built resentment, exaggeration, and misinformation. In December 2005 and January 2006, the European Committee for Honoring the Prophet, an umbrella group of twenty-seven organizations, visited the Middle East carrying a 43-page dossier with the offending cartoons and others not published in Denmark. In one the Prophet was depicted with a swinish face, and in another as having sexual congress with beasts. Meetings in Mecca, Cairo, and elsewhere led to a swell of critical sentiment. On January 10, 2006, a Christian newspaper in Norway reprinted the cartoons; in the next month, news media in at least fourteen countries reprinted them. Of thousands of newspapers in the U.S., only four did so, of which the *Philadelphia Inquirer* had by far the largest circulation. The prevalence of reprinting in Europe brought accusations of hypocrisy, based on the fact that several countries had laws making denial of the Holocaust a crime. You can't offend Jews, but you must offend Muslims?

Saudi Arabia kept its cool and simply pulled Danish products off supermarket shelves. But Danish missions were burned in Beirut, firebombed in Damascus, and attacked in Tehran with fire and stones. Iran and Syria, of course, had governments already locked in contention with the Northern powers, and could cultivate their own domestic support by unleashing violence. But other nations, in less antagonistic relations with NATO countries, also underwent violent protests. Cities as diverse as Cairo, Amman, Islamabad, Lahore, Karachi, Dacca, Colombo, Jakarta, and Manila flared up, and renewals of old Christian/Muslim tensions rocked Nigeria. In Shrinagar, India, a group of veiled women invaded stationery stores and destroyed Valentine cards as representing Northern sensual-commercial values. That was a kitschy demonstration, perhaps, but in many places anger was grimly serious. Before the tumults subsided, six newspapers had been closed, and three foreign ministers and a prime minister were forced to resign. At least 45 people died around the world in protests over the cartoons;[47] if all associated clashes are included, that number might exceed 240.[48]

47. Foregoing and ensuing details are from the *New York Times* and *Philadelphia Inquirer,* from late Jan through 9 Feb 06; the *Arab News,* 10-23 Feb 06; *Dawn* and other Pakistani newspapers, 2-12 Mar 06. Among numerous fertile opinion essays: Ronald Dworkin, "The Right to Ridicule," *The New York Times Review of Books,* 23 Mar 06; and "The Cartoon Crisis: a need for multicultural understanding," *Postscript* (The Habibie Center, Jakarta), 3, 3 Mar 06.

48. Jytte Klausen, *The Cartoons that Shook the World* (New Haven, Yale University Press, 2009), table 2, p. 107.

In early February, perhaps two months too late for preventing down-ward spirals into violence,[49] the Danish prime minister finally expressed "deep sadness and disbelief." But the rage in summoned mobs was already beyond reason. Muslim wise men such as Iraq's Ayatollah Sistani knew that rioting was misguided, and said that destruction would win no friends. In-ternational gatherings of the OIC, and of Europeans seeking calm and co-operation, glided toward statements of mutual religious respect.

Deep differences remained, though, partly because "the cartoons were surrogates for a push back against Western pressure to promote democrati-zation in the Middle East."[50] In any case, considering the Trans-Islamic and the North Atlantic worlds, textures of worship are dramatically dissimilar, as are modes of reasoning and manners of protest. Thermostats of anger slide on different scales. Those in the same political room feel different tem-peratures, and cannot begin to agree on even micro-adjustments. A North-erner may want to express Voltaire's willingness to defend to the death a Southerner's right to express a belief he does not share. But he is not obliged to do so if that belief has coiled within it a spring trigger for his own death.

Arriving in an aroused Pakistan, early March 2006, I had to find a bed for the night. I had reserved a room at the Marriott in Karachi, but I real-ized that I had already eaten or slept in two Asian Marriotts that had been attacked. So I changed my reservation to the Pearl Continental. I could do nothing about George W. Bush having suddenly been scheduled to arrive in Pakistan while I was there. I flew in and settled at the Pearl. Out my win-dow, a quarter of a mile away, I could see my third injured Marriott — with windows blasted hours before. As a greeting to President Bush, a sui-cide bomber, deflected away from the American consulate, had swerved into the first diplomatic limo he saw arriving for the morning, killing the American officers within and three Pakistani nationals. (Two years later, a massive bombing of the Islamabad Marriott killed more than fifty, mostly employees, but resolute Pakistani ownership repaired the hotel in three months.) Pakistani friends called to tell me to stay inside my hotel for forty-eight hours. For the first time in my life, I obeyed such advice. The opposition had focused on the next day for a general strike ("lockdown and wheeljam") and the following as a "Black Day" to protest the pub-lished blasphemies and the presence of Bush. So I was in a triple vortex: anti-cartoon, anti-Bush, and anti-Musharraf.

49. Klausen, *Cartoons that Shook the World*, esp. pp. 73-75.
50. Klausen, *Cartoons that Shook the World*, p. 179.

I reflected on why Northern journalism sees free speech as comfortably including blasphemy. That moved me, a month later, to travel to New York to voice a question. Amanda Bennett, chief editor of the *Philadelphia Inquirer,* was on a panel at the Asia Society.[51] I told her that I thought her newspaper had suffered a lapse of taste and judgment in republishing the cartoon, and I asked, "Do you believe in an *absolute* right of freedom of the press, unlimited by concerns about blasphemy and hate speech?" Ms. Bennett's answer bobbed in a foam of narrative, context, and intention. But it did include the phrase "*nearly* absolute freedom of the press."

My thoughts turned to the words of an unlikely mental ally, Nicolas Sarkozy, then the French Minister of the Interior, later President of the Republic. In this crisis he had declared a preference for extremes of caricature over extremes of censorship. Okay — if we must deal in extremes.

Violence against Women

No clinical term can suggest how deeply rooted subordination of the female may be in some tribal cultures. Or worse: definitions of the female as disposable chattel and, all too often, despicable. These are, of course, male definitions. When their holders are challenged, they may invoke the Qur'an, Sunna, and hadith to ends far removed from the aims of that figure of exquisite justice, the Prophet Muhammad.

Against such historical slovenliness stand the definitions of Professor Riffat Hassan, an experienced Pakistani administrator. Her essay, "Human Rights in the Qur'anic Perspective," lays out a dozen general and particular rights, all grounded in the Qur'an and its vision of humans freed of their own bondages, seeking a destiny proclaimed as "Towards Allah is thy limit" (Qur'an 53:42).[52]

New illumination and vast social momentum are certainly required against bondages in Pakistan. Discrimination may begin in son-preference as a norm, and feeding a girl less and poorer food. The main expressions of violence against women in Pakistan, however, are not measured in attitudes

51. That excellent summary discussion, "Not a Laughing Matter: Behind the Danish Cartoon Controversy," 22 Mar 06, featured Torben Getterman, Consul General, Denmark; Mahmood Mamdani, Herbert Lehman Professor of Government, Columbia University; and Amanda Bennett, Editor and Executive Vice President, *The Philadelphia Inquirer.*

52. Published as Appendix A, pp. 241-48, to Gisela Webb, ed., *Windows of Faith: Muslim Women Scholar-Activists in North America* (Syracuse, Syracuse University Press, 2000).

and teaspoons. They are wife-beating, bride-burning, acid-throwing, rape, and murder.

Wife-beating occurs in all cultures to some degree. Its relative burden, weighed against psychological cruelty of wife to husband, is worthy of worldwide study. But such finesse of inquiry is not necessary in a nation where, for instance, 211 women were murdered by their kin in just four months of the year 2003. Husbands committed 37 of these acts, brothers 23, fathers 10, and sons 5; in-laws 16, paternal uncles 7, and various other male relatives, 113. Murders of men by female kin were not tallied.

Burning reveals a stark sociological snapshot of Pakistan. Because of the prominence of kerosene stoves in lower-middle-class and lower-class families, all of the cases, including those that survive to hospitalization, can be reported as accidents. Seven out of eight of the women victims were aged 16 to 25 years; more than nine out of ten were married. Only one out of five could be recognized as having husbands employed above various laborer levels: salaried workers (8 percent of the total), shopkeepers (5 percent), overseas workers (3 percent), and landowners (3 percent). The leading "reasons" for killing the bride were disputes over dowry, husband's cruelty, suspicion of wife's fidelity, and forcing of perverse sexual acts disliked by the wife.

Only about 10 percent of victims surviving foul play agree to testify (Where will they go afterward? Can they take their children?). Less than 5 percent of those burned to death received postmortems. Police broker deals and collect rakeoffs for their management of investigations.

A group of Pakistani legislators moved a bill in 2004 to shift the burden of proof in these cases to the husband of the victim, or the eldest male relative resident in the household. That is a toehold toward state-level acknowledgment that "stove deaths are actually dowry murders." Attempts to go further through limiting dowries by law have had no impact on popular psychology.

Honor killing is common in Pakistan. The popular term for it, *karo kari*, "blackened man and woman," reveals some of the dynamics affecting women in tribal societies. Male heads of family "own" their women, no less than they own their cattle. But women are more than belongings. They represent the "honor" of the man through the life sequence of virginity and fidelity, and with that, of course, the power to dishonor him — an utterly basic offense in Pakistani tribal territory, punishable by death.[53] Not

---

53. The foregoing and following summary, including all data, is drawn largely from the

only there, but in the literate, hyper-affluent royal family of Saudi Arabia: In Jeddah in 1977, Princess Mishaal bint Fahd bin Mohamed and her lover, Khalid Muhallal, nephew of a man who later became information minister, were apprehended in their flouting of her family's will. Both were executed, extra-judicially.[54]

"Kari" refers to the "blackened" woman who has caused her husband dishonor. *"Karo"* is the term for the offending male, complicit in the dishonoring, which amounts to the symbolic emasculation of the husband. To *karo kari* becomes a verb for achieving vengeance, which in theory relieves the husband of anguish by ending the lives of his torturers.

Other terms than *karo kari,* which is Sindhi, are used in different parts of Pakistan, but all of them refer to the same phenomenon. The classic case begins with a male suspicion of a female family member having illicit relations with another man. She is butchered and dishonorably buried, and he, if not immediately murdered (or later hunted and killed), may present himself to the feudal lord *(wadero)* of his area to buy his way out with cash or family women to the *kari's* family and a service charge to the *wadero.* If a case proceeds beyond such extra-judicial settlement (which happens only rarely) and it enters a court, "tainted evidence and touted witnesses" will come into play to prove that the killer acted under "grave and sudden provocation," which is lightly punished by the penal code.

In the tribal scheme of values the one whose honor is defiled may kill the defiler or allow him to pay two of his women in compensation, one to replace the *kari* and a second as price to spare the *karo's* life. The *kari* is only the object of dispute. The husband's status inheres in her behavior, protected by the good, sullied by the bad. Women, without independent status, can only be a source of honor or dishonor to their male owners.

Recognizing this value scheme is also necessary to understand a certain kind of rape. In a classic type, common also in Northern cultures, a woman is a target of infatuation, or of anger, or of raw opportunity to an entranced, or incensed, or predatory lusting man. But in a type more specific to Pakistan, the rapist acts symbolically to degrade, or to take revenge on behalf of males of his family. This latter type of violent crime rose "phe-

excellent booklet by Tahir Mehdi, "Women on Trial: Gender Violence in Pakistan" (Islamabad, The Network for Consumer Protection, 2004); quotation on stove deaths, p. 10; evaluation of Dowry and Bridal Gifts (Pakistani) Act of 1976, p. 12.

54. Geraldine Brooks gives two versions of the story in *Nine Parts of Desire: The Hidden World of Islamic Women* (New York, Anchor Books, 1994), pp. 50-51.

nomenally" after the Hudood Ordinance and Islamic laws of evidence were introduced by President Zia in 1979.

What has been the effect upon women? If she is not killed by the culprit trying to hide his act (in the first type of rape), the woman is subject to a lifelong stigma. She is disqualified by shame from married family life. She may commit suicide. She may be stripped naked and paraded in public — of which shame-upon-shame treatment forty cases were reported in the *State of Human Rights in Pakistan, 2003*.[55]

Akbar Ahmed generalizes about traditional agricultural societies in all of South Asia, where rape "is a double burden. It violates the woman and it also alienates her from her own society as she is considered 'impure.' Honour, modesty and motherhood are all deemed to be violated. . . . Rape is thus deliberately employed by ethnic neighbors who are fully aware of its expression as political power and cultural assertion to humiliate the internal other."[56]

Rape as an instrument of vendetta is dramatically illustrated in the case of Mukhtar Mai. Then known as Mukhtaran Bibi, she was a woman in her late twenties of the Tatla tribe, living in Meerwalla, a village in southern Punjab without telephones, thirteen kilometers from a police station. The Tatla live close to the stronger Mastoi tribe, with whom disputes existed. On June 22, 2002, three Mastoi men abducted Mukhtaran's boy brother Shakoor, accusing him of raping a girl of their clan, Salma. No evidence ever substantiated that claim. But to the counterclaim, that Shakoor was then sodomized, a doctor testified subsequently in court. Both clans assembled in outdoor gatherings in the late afternoon. The Mastoi, numbering 200 or 250, were holding Shakoor, and released him to the police on sex crime charges.

An inter-clan negotiation then took place upon Mastoi demands. The Tatla agreed to settle by having twelve-year-old Shakoor marry twenty-six-year-old Salma; by also having his elder sister, Mukhtaran, marry a Mastoi man; and — if Shakoor were formally found guilty — by some Tatla land being given to the Mastoi. This proposal was found acceptable by a Mastoi chief. But two of Salma's family, joined by other men, demanded revenge of *zina* for *zina*: rape for rape.

Those two of Salma's family went to Mukhtaran and her family and demanded an apology to their gathering, now diminished to about seventy. She went with her father and maternal uncle to comply. As twilight

55. Mehdi, "Women on Trial: Gender Violence in Pakistan," quotations, pp. 14, 19, 20.
56. Ahmed, *Jinnah, Pakistan and Islamic Identity*, p. 161.

proceeded toward darkness, in an area with no electricity, Salma's brother, Abdul Khaliq, armed with a .30 caliber pistol, forcibly took Mukhtaran inside a dark room with a dirt floor, while other Mastoi males restrained her father and uncle outside. Abdul Khaliq and three other Mastoi men then raped Mukhtaran and threw her back to her father and uncle clad only in a torn *kameez* shirt.

A woman in a nearby village, raped just previously, had solved her problem of disutility and permanent dishonor by swallowing a bottle of insecticide. Mukhtaran considered that she herself had three options: suicide, silent suffering, or complaint. The local *imam* preached against the rape the following Friday, and brought a local journalist to Mukhtaran's father, who persuaded the family to file charges. Mukhtaran, recovering from voiceless despair, substantiated the complaint nine days after the rape, with a full medical examination which found internal abrasions and traces of semen.

The story hit Pakistani headlines and international news. The case was given to an "anti-terrorist court." By its flexible standards of evidence, six of the Mastoi were swiftly found guilty of mass intimidation and sentenced to death. Nearly three years later, however, on March 3, 2005, the appeals court in Lahore, highest court in the Punjab, acquitted five of the six men. Mukhtaran, pale, with eyes downcast and voice breaking, allowed her lawyer to appeal to the Supreme Court of Pakistan, and said, "My case is in the court of God." To the media she pleaded, "Please keep my case alive. . . . Me and my whole family are in danger. They [the accused] are a constant threat to us." The Supreme Court subsequently agreed to retry all fourteen men originally tried, both the six convicted and the eight acquitted. Farzana Bari translated Mukhtaran's mother tongue, Saraiki, into Urdu and English. "I will stay and fight for the rights of the women and men of my village and will continue to run my school [created with an $8,300 award from the government] to spread the light of education."[57]

On a trip to the United States, Mukhtaran was asked by *Islamica* mag-

57. Nicholas Kristof in his *New York Times* op-ed column brought American readers early, vivid, and continuing accounts of Mukhtaran's trauma and case. Wikipedia appears to contain an abbreviated and balanced account to date, including references to transcripts of the initial trial. Her own story, Mukhtar Mai, *In the Name of Honor* (New York, Atria Books, 2006), is appealingly modest. Pervez Musharraf, *In the Line of Fire* (New York, Free Press, 2006), is elusive and mendacious.

azine how to get rid of tribalism and feudalism at the highest levels of Pakistani government. She replied simply.

Mukhtaran: Well, I can only tell you about Meerwalla. . . . Now people go to the police when they have an issue. And when there are domestic disputes [Mukhtaran Bibi smiles], the women tell their husbands, "I'm going to Mukhtaran Bibi!"

Islamica: So tribalism will end because of Mukhtaran Bibi?

Mukhtaran: It will not end because of me, but it will end if these girls and boys who are getting an education (in the schools we've set up) will grow up to be people who will act with more sensitivity.[58]

The highly politicized case languished in the Supreme Court from 2005 until 2011. Then a three-man panel decided, by a two-to-one margin, to reject the prosecution's version of events, stressing the "presumed innocence" of the defendants. Only one prison sentence was upheld.[59]

The area of law in which Mukhtaran Bibi dared to tread was fraught with traps and spikes that might impale her. Prior to the eleven-year presidency of Zia ul-Haq, Pakistan's laws were not oppressive, but merely "patronizing toward women." The Supreme Court in that era, on the basis of religious law, had even reached a landmark decision that allowed women the right to dissolve their marriage on the grounds of incompatibility.

But Zia in 1979, by edict, promulgated a hyper-Islamized series of four laws known collectively as the Hudood Ordinances. They also applied to non-Muslims in Pakistan. *Hadd,* with its plural, *Hudood,* means Islamic punishment, including stoning to death, whipping, and amputation of hands and feet. Zia felt he had little to gain from alliance with highly educated Pakistanis; enormously greater vote potential lured him to proclaim affinity with Muslim masses. So he set into law a series of principles that might make a sinner shudder, but could allow a believer to imagine that the president was at last achieving a Muslim state.

But what if the believer is "she," rather than "he"? And what if she is

58. Islamica-online, No. 15, Winter 06.

59. Pamela Constable, "A Test of Women's Rights in Pakistan," *Washington Post,* 26 Apr 11. A secret diplomatic document of 2006 later released by Wikileaks conveyed the consternation of six Pakistani NGOs over what had become the undue influence of Mai's brother and herself over the local village council; http://www.dnaindia.com/world/report_gang -rape-victim-mukhtaran-mai-abused-her-power-wikileaks_1554614 (13 June 11).

not the perpetrator of a crime, but its victim? After Zia's ordinances, the legal condition of women in the area combining adultery and rape may be summarized as follows:

1. *Zina* (adultery) and *Zina-bil-jabr* (rape) are treated together with equal *hadd,* as ordained by Qur'an and Sunna, and with the same requirements of proof of crime: four adult male witnesses.
2. The Qur'an's requirement of four witnesses to *zina,* however, had been totally different in motivation. It was meant, rather, to discourage slander of women. Anyone who could not produce four witnesses to his statement that a woman had been adulterous was subject to be struck with 80 lashes.
3. A victim of rape, nonetheless, under Zia's Hudood, finds this requirement turned against her. If she cannot supply four witnesses to the crime, she accepts under oath that she has had sex with a man who is not her husband. The victim of rape bears the burden, in effect, of proving her innocence. If she initiates a case, she can be tried for adultery and if found guilty, severely punished — although such extreme punishment as stoning to death is not mentioned anywhere in the Qur'an.
4. Because of the Hudood Ordinances, adultery moves from personal immorality to become an offense against the state. This leads to bribe-seeking harassment by police who, when they spot a man and a woman alone, can ask for "proof of marriage."
5. The Hudood Ordinances speak only of male witnesses. Women, in any number, are not acceptable as witnesses to such crimes.
6. If falsely charged and after trial acquitted, a woman must file a separate case against the accuser, who does not stand automatically implicated by the earlier decision in her favor.
7. Because of these extreme definitions and procedural weightings against women, many husbands, brothers, and fathers file false cases of *zina* out of revenge against a spouse, or coveting the wife's property; or in order to take another wife, or out of mere disapproval of a sibling's or a child's marriage.[60]

The net effect of these laws upon Mukhtaran Bibi, in retrospect, must have seemed formidably daunting. She needed four male witnesses to her

---

60. Aliya Salahuddin, interview, 6 Mar 06. The seven salients I describe are distilled from her email to me of 7 Mar.

rape. But inside the dark hut were only the four gang-rapists themselves. She was in theoretical jeopardy of admitting to multiple sex acts with men not her husband, and therefore becoming legally judged a multiple adulterer — subject to being stoned to death in a public place.[61]

It was perversely fortunate that the Mastoi men, in their neighborhood terrorism, generated so many bystanders knowledgeable of their acts against Mukhtaran Bibi — a thrust of hate, lust, and indifference to opinion other than that of their own tribal line. Were their actions compounded by blood feud? That is not ascertainable by a reader of a condensed account based on trial transcripts. Neither can we know whether the twelve-year-old boy Shakoor allowed himself a more than friendly glance, or any glance at all, at Salma. She was determined by doctors to be about twenty-seven years old and to have been sexually active for almost three years, during which time she had had a miscarriage. But some undocumented initial cause, reopening an ugly inter-tribal history, aroused the Mastoi one afternoon and early evening to gang-sodomize a boy and, with a .30-caliber pistol as guarantor, to gang-rape his older sister. Vendetta rapes continue in Pakistan, with uncertain justice, and many of them continue to go unreported.[62]

Asma Jahangir, daughter of a much-jailed lawyer who had protested against military dictators, herself became a lawyer and rose to positions as a UN Special Rapporteur, first on Extrajudicial Executions, and then in 2004 on Freedom of Religion or Belief. (In late 2007 she was put briefly under house arrest by Musharraf's regime during that constitutional crisis.) She and Benazir Bhutto both instance the case of Safia Bibi in the mid-1980s — a blind servant girl who bore a child after rape by her employer and his son. Because she could not produce four male witnesses, she was sentenced to be stoned to death. This injustice brought women out on the streets of Pakistan for the first time, mobilizing what until then had been silent public opinion. Their protests forced ultimate acquittal.[63] The Hudood laws with their "horrific . . . brutalizing" impact, Jahangir says, reflect an almost obsessive hatred of women. "One can only specu-

61. Ordinance VII of 1979, ch. 1, 5 (1, 2).

62. "Vendetta rapes . . . ," *New York Times*, 14 Oct 06, p. A6; "How Many Rapes per Day in Karachi?" in *All Things Pakistan*, 16 Sep 08.

63. Asma Jahangir, "Human Rights in Pakistan: A System in the Making," in Samantha Power and Graham Allison, eds., *Realizing Human Rights: Moving from Inspiration to Impact* (New York, St. Martin's Press, 2000), pp. 167-93; esp. pp. 177-78; Bhutto, *Daughter of Destiny*, pp. 315-16.

late what would have happened if Zia ul-Haq had ruled any longer. Orthodoxy and a very twisted view of women and Islam had begun to permeate every institution."[64]

Aliya Salahuddin, a reporter, worked steadily for repeal of the Hudood Ordinances. She interviewed a fifty-year-old woman with eight children whose husband got her jailed on *zina* with a creditor of his, so he wouldn't have to pay. He then remarried. "The rich," says Aliyah, "do *zina* all the time, but don't get prosecuted." She asked the poor jailed woman if she might take a photo of her, acknowledging that it was against custom. "Hide my face?" the victim asked. "Why? No, *show* my face." Such increments of assertiveness perhaps have done more than three federal commissions which recommended repeal of the Hudood Ordinances. Aliyah published results of her interviews with twenty-five mullahs, of whom twenty stated that there is no Islamic basis for requiring four male witnesses to a rape.

"This nation is so frightened of its women," Aliyah said to me, "that they live in paranoid fear of what happens if we let these creatures free." But finally, late in 2006, the parliament carried a reform act that took rape and adultery cases away from shari'a law and assigned them to civil courts. Much reform still remained unachieved. But Zia's misogynist views had at last been confronted and defeated, if only because the Islamist parties did not attend the vote.

Democracy and Murder

I was invited to lecture on "The West and Islam: Problems of Mutual Understanding." I fretted about the occasion at the International Islamic University in Islamabad, for the crisis over the blasphemous cartoons was not yet dispelled. Two women had voiced wishes to attend, but family needs, or the burden of appearing in public on such a theme, prevented them from coming. The audience, twenty faculty and graduate students gathered around a large rectangular seminar table, was entirely male.

I began, "Brothers in the love of God and the love of understanding. . . ." Everything seemed natural after that. My proposed recipe for the next twenty-five years focused on an expanded cultural curriculum in Northern education, especially where America was limiting itself through

---

64. Jahangir, "Human Rights in Pakistan," pp 179-80.

its own provinciality; and the resacralization of Northern values, with recognition that freedom of religion was at least as important as freedom of the press. Outside Islam, I said, self-restraint is required regarding depiction of the Prophet. Within Islam, I said, there should have been moral force exercised to prevent the Taliban from destroying with artillery and dynamite, in 2001, the ancient statues of the Buddha in the Bamiyan Valley. Islamic voices must arise in the future in respect for other faiths and their symbols.

Regarding the South, I articulated a wish for a new gender balance. Such a balance, in Pakistan, would certainly mean reform of the Hudood Ordinances (an achievement since begun). The cultures within Islam, I suggested, need accelerated scientific consciousness, using Baconian inductive method rather than Aristotelian-style deductive logic. I understand the Qur'an as hospitable to reflection on the rise and fall of nations and cultures (social science), and on the behavior of the stars and the tides, and of fauna and flora (natural science).

The best question was from a graduate student who asked if encouragement of Baconian reasoning would not elevate in Muslim minds the global father of desacralization. I acknowledged that might happen, while stressing my conviction that science, insuperable in analysis of the "what and how" of nature, is incapable of answering the "whys" of meaning for human life. That is best done in religion.

I left the International Islamic University a happy man, invited to return. Then I joined my friend Shahid Haq for Friday midday prayer at the Faisaleyah Mosque, the nearby beautiful gift of a late Saudi king, and a landmark at the foot of the mountains. Shahid advised me to wait outside while he prayed. I sat against a wall in marbled shade, and sank into reflection, including about why I was not invited inside.

When thousands of men streamed out of the mosque, I saw half a dozen flowing toward me. They had discovered their recent lecturer under the call of the *azan*. Several graduate students, led by the challenger of Francis Bacon, engaged me in renewed talk. I was glad to feel again how universal ideas may be shared in Pakistan, and cordially disputed.

My special good fortune was twice to spend several days with Sufia and Shahid Haq at their home in Rawalpindi. The surrounding compound may have a hundred families or more, and includes a small market, a laundry, and, of course, a mosque. A number of military families live there, and not far away is one of the many A. Q. Khan laboratory facilities. Inside the gate of the Haq family is just room enough for two parked cars. Both father and mother are often in motion: Shahid as executive vice president of marketing for Pakistan Long Distance Telephone, and Sufia in an equivalent public relations position for the Hashoo Group, a wide-reaching conglomerate.

Sufia's express and generous wish was that I see "how a progressive Muslim family lives." Their home for me (they gave me their son's room, who was away at college) was a model of relaxed kindness. I was made to feel that I became a happy habit with them, and was missed when I was gone, to the point that Sufia, or their daughter Sana, or Neelam the Christian serving girl (not live-in, but in walking distance from her work) would forgetfully set a dinner plate in my absence.

But even Sufia, early in my first visit, allowed herself to say about American foreign policy, "You corner us, and we become ferocious. . . . You destroy a whole nation [Afghanistan] to get one man? We have been inspired by your knowledge. . . . We cried with America over 9/11. . . . Now we rage against it." That theme could arise eventually in any conversation — and climaxed a public event organized by Sufia for a group of eleven Urdu comic poets. Seated cross-legged on stage, they took turns at the microphone for three hours before 375 people. They got laughter, applause, and occasional repartee from people lolling on the floor against red plush cushions, or resting on an elbow. I seldom knew what the laughter was about. In my ignorance, the rhymes felt to me exotic, as if matching unlikely ideas like "stork, torque," or "badger, cadger." It seemed as if stress hung on solitary words that sounded like "sorghum, lessee, catarrh, Islam, benefice." After early husband/wife jokes and doctor/nurse jokes, summarized for me, the skits went political. The audience delighted in portrayals of Mush-Bush, the former sycophantic to the latter, and in ridicule of their president's failure to keep his promise to take off his military uniform. Then I caught a lot of "Amer-*ik*-a." The last performer, Anwar Mahmoud, engaging in tones, facial expressions, and body language, had grown up in poverty and made a reputation for himself as a serious poet in addition to being a comic one. One of his better lines, an air marshal was pleased to tell me afterward, was apropos 9/11: "Just step on a monkey's tail, and all hell breaks loose."

In a genuine democracy, one may educate oneself out of poverty. Real advances for women and the marginalized in Pakistan are achieved by concerted efforts of ordinary people in that direction. Aliya Salahuddin's mother, Sadiqa, among many other Pakistani women, is active in trying to change social dynamics among the less educated and uneducated. She is a member of a "Beijing Plus Ten" informal group, which did reviews in twelve areas of concern for women. Each country established priorities for itself. In Pakistan, violence against women emerged *at the top of the list.* Likewise in India, Bangladesh, and Nepal, where such violence prevails and was also prioritized. Similar results in all these South Asian countries, whether Muslim, Hindu, or Buddhist in majority, Sadiqa says, prove that the dynamics of such violence "have *nothing to do* with religion." The causes are poverty, illiteracy, and feudal social structure.

She illustrates all three factors converging in rural Sindh, where her Indus Resource Center (IRC) coordinates the work of tiny NGOs. In one village she was consulted because a girl in Class 9 had run away with a boy classmate. The village decided the solution was not to send their girls to school anymore. What was wrong with the school? Sadiqa asked. Nothing much. She asked the elders for permission to talk separately with the girls present. Among about two dozen, aged seven to fifteen, she asked, "How many of you are married, engaged, or promised?" Every girl there raised her hand. Her report to the elders carried a question for them to ponder: if you don't listen to your daughters, and they have no choice in a mate, what may happen?

Sadiqa illustrated for me the impact of child marriage combined with "exchange marriage" (double marriages, across gender, in two families, e.g., brother A/sister B and brother B/sister A). "Girls are a commodity, exchanged for another commodity." A good "deal" obviously doesn't necessarily mean a good match. She illustrated with a three-and-a-half-year-old girl, recently "divorced." Her uncle had married at a time when his family had no other girl to "give." So her father signed a marriage document in her behalf, while she stayed home as "an investment" of her husband's family to be claimed at puberty. But her uncle didn't like his new wife, and divorced her. When exchange marriages don't work, double divorce may be necessary, and then there are two stigmatized women. The three-and-a-half-year-old girl may eventually "remarry," but she will not get a good match. She has not yet lost her virginity, but she has lost her "value."

This treatment of women as commodity occurs not only among the poor, but among the rich, too, directed by landlords and feudal bosses. I asked, "How do you stop it?" Sadiqa answered sharply, "Stopping it is a *big dream.* . . . We educate women to be informed, and talk to the state about enforcing the law that says a boy can't get married before he's 21, and a girl, 18. This is a pre-CEDAW law. Thirty years ago this country was much more liberal. But everything got worse after the Afghan crisis. The Russians invaded, the Taliban arose, refugees flocked here, Zia's laws took hold." And, Sadiqa says, the Americans not only helped the Taliban then, but helped Zia too, for their own reasons of state — in a spasm of mega-power competition oblivious to the social impact of their behavior.

Sadiqa and her IRC are proud of their own schools, which have a total of 154 female teachers and 4,100 students, of which 3,700 are girls. They also provide adult literacy for men. Included in the curriculum are women's rights and environmental issues. "We don't make long speeches. That would be counterproductive."

I carried the tenor of this conversation forward with Shagufta Alizai, a prominent sociologist, married, who works now from her house, and Nuzhat Ahmad, an economist, single, who is Director of the Applied Economics Research Center of the University of Karachi. The two are very different in style, but close in friendship, and eloquent from long experience of the issues. We dined at a crowded Northwest Frontier restaurant called BarBQ Tonight, with roaring fires outside and menus inside which included soup and pasta and ground beef. Late in the evening I asked them, "If you could do one thing for women in Pakistan tomorrow, what would it be?"

Shagufta: "I'd give them *the right of choice.* An empowering blanket. . . . In most homes, choices are made *for* them, not *by* them. Even if it is the right choice, it is not *theirs*." Once, thirty years ago, working in an office was the "worst thing you could do." But Shagufta had dared to do it, as a journalist. Now, for their children, the issues are different.

I asked them both, "What should the world know about Pakistan that it doesn't yet understand?"

Nuzhat: "I would like them to know that you can be a very staunch Muslim and still have modern ideas. . . . You can blend Western values and Islamic values, and work in both places."

Both women pray five times a day. Shagufta has done hajj; Nuzhat, not yet, maybe never, because she is reluctant to go alone to Saudi Arabia as a single woman. They agree that religion is not an obstacle to them, but a basic way of life within feudal and tribal ways of life that need challenging.

When I ask about role models, they name Mukhtaran Bibi and Fatima Jinnah. The choice of a rape victim and a ruling figure interested me, but they hastened to say that publicity alone does not make a role model. There are many other kinds of women in Pakistan, pushing out envelopes, breaking through barriers, and setting new standards every day, in every segment of life, as examples to other women of creative lives in troubled times. They see themselves as such examples. So do I.

Benazir Bhutto was once the hope of Pakistani women and the hope for democracy in Pakistan. At age thirty-five she became the Muslim world's first female prime minister. But her two stretches in office (1988-90, 1993-96), totaling nearly five years, did not greatly advance conditions for women. There were some gains in rights and education, but fewer than reasonably hoped.[65] Even after she went into exile again — bright, beautiful, compromised, frustrated, angry — she remained for many an icon of Pakistani democracy. Her two successors, Nawaz Sharif and Pervez Musharraf, a semi-Islamist businessman and a military pragmatist, did little to advance society or nation.

Pakistan had once appeared to have a capacity to become a middle-income democratic state. But contradictory visions of its destiny, paucity of leadership, misapplication of resources, and grossly stunted social investment all fouled it up. Dramatic overinvestment in the military throttled the potential of its human capital, especially untapped energies in its women. What promise was contained in Benazir, on return late in 2007, to remedy these conditions?

Among the opportunistically hopeful regarding Ms. Bhutto were American officials. They saw Musharraf swiftly losing control in consequences of deaths at the Red Mosque, suspension of the constitution, and confrontations with Pakistani lawyers. They helped persuade Musharraf to let Bhutto return — a privilege that the banished Nawaz Sharif accorded himself, only to be bounced back abroad.

Granted the paucity of talent and alternatives, one may nonetheless ask if the American negotiators were fully aware of some tarnishments in Bhutto's record. For governing power in 1993, firstly, her PPP included in its coalition the JUI, party of Deobandi zealots and sponsor of their ideological product, the Taliban — which after taking power in Kabul in 1995

---

65. Cohen, *Idea of Pakistan,* looks at gender matters in a context of Pakistan's "problematic liberalism," pp. 147-48.

turned over its training camps to the JUI.[66] Second, many of her friends sadly concluded that power had made her vindictive, arrogant, and corrupt.[67] Even if the $1.5 billion total accusation against herself, family, and political forces was intended as a legal barrier to her return, withdrawing the charges could not erase the grandeur (4.3 million pounds) of the Bhutto estate bought in the U.K., or airbrush away the money-laundering case launched in the Swiss government.[68] Third, there remains the astonishing fact that Benazir Bhutto, given the honor of speaking before a joint session of the U.S. Congress in June 1989, had lied to that body. She told it that Pakistan neither possessed nor intended to assemble a nuclear bomb. Even if she were not fully in the loop of her own generals and the ISI, she had been given a detailed briefing on her own country's weapons program by the director of the CIA on the previous day.[69] Did she expect beauty and bright youth to overcome barefaced and brazen untruth?

Yet eighteen years after Ms. Bhutto's lie to Congress, American officials sought to deploy her democratic buoyancy to keep Musharraf in power. This while he was, in his way, double-crossing the U.S. — promising to root out al-Qaeda and the Taliban while striking peace deals on his Afghan frontier. In fact, the combination of rugged mountain ranges, Pushtun warrior culture, and easily detonated Islam gave the Pakistani government little leeway in its northwest, while its army favored attention to the Indian army in Kashmir to the east. American diplomats had to settle for a Musharraf who at last took off his uniform, and a Bhutto cloaked in pseudo-democracy.

On return in October 2007, she summoned masses to ensure eventual swells of votes. Against government security advice she laid out a triumphal return from the airport to the mausoleum of Jinnah. "I must confess I felt safe in the enormous sea of love and support that surrounded me" — three million people was the figure she alleged, exceeding the one million that greeted her in Lahore on return from exile in 1986.[70] Two bombs went

---

66. Mahmood Mamdani, *Good Muslim, Bad Muslim: America, the Cold War, and the Roots of Terror* (New York, Doubleday, 2005), p. 150.

67. Mary Anne Weaver, *Pakistan In the Shadow of Jihad and Afghanistan* (New York, Farrar, Strauss, and Giroux, 2002; 2nd ed., 2003); *passim*; corruption charges, pp. 211-12.

68. Huffington blog and Wikipedia.

69. Weaver, *Pakistan*, pp. 206-7.

70. "I felt safe . . . ," Benazir Bhutto, *Reconciliation: Islam, Democracy, and the West* (New York, HarperCollins, 2008), p. 10; "179 martyrs," p. 19. For welcoming crowd sizes, p. 7; see also Bhutto, *Daughter of Destiny*, p. 325, and — a lesser figure — p. 392.

off, rocking her armored truck and killing 179 people in the human shield around her. She nevertheless continued to insist on what Hindus call *bhakti:* "the mutual intense emotional attachment and love of a devotee toward a personal god, and of a god for the devotee."[71] On December 27, after a speech in Rawalpindi, she kept visible through the sunroof of her van to ensure that emotional attachment. Gunshots and a bomb blast went off. Twenty followers died, as did Benazir herself.

Benazir's Shi'ite mother had chosen a Shi'a for Benazir's husband. A cultivated martyrdom also comes through in Benazir's outlook: endorsing a Shi'ite folk belief that in every generation there is a Karbala. Although the tragedy that wiped out the grandson of the Prophet and his family in 640 C.E. now was seen to embrace the Bhuttos, she declares that "our resolve never faltered."[72] Benazir herself now dead, crowds of PPP followers chant, "How many Bhuttos can you kill?" Volatile anger and mortal quarrel, however, are poor building materials for democratic growth. Pakistan requires leaders capable of formulating and executing policy in socially equitable, including gender-fair, terms. In the words of one of its own philosophers, "The Muslim community cannot live indefinitely in frenzy and be kept in trance."[73]

In 1993 Benazir Bhutto had been clear on her aims: "As a daughter of the East I want other women, born into this tradition, this environment, where they're forced to submit to those societal pressures and those fates which have been written for them, to see how I fight — as a politician, as a woman, as a mother — and how I survive. I want to show them that they can rise above these pressures, too, and that they can demand to make their own choices, and not have others — fathers, husbands, or brothers — make their choices for them."[74] In her second autobiography, completed just days before her death, she faithfully developed the theme of women's equality — with additional stress on education and science, within Islamic democracy — all buttressed with five dozen citations from the Qur'an. She quoted Fazlur Rahman (the late Pakistani modernist scholar who exiled himself under fundamentalist pressure to the University of Chicago) on consultation, consensus, and independent judgment, and the Pakistani poet-philosopher Iqbal on "spiritual democracy." She invoked two Indo-

71. Online Encyclopedia Brittanica, "Bhakti."

72. "Karbala . . . ," *Daughter of Destiny,* pp. 303-4; *Reconciliation,* p. 53.

73. S. M. A. Sayeed, *The Myth of Authenticity: A Study in Islamic Fundamentalism* (Karachi, Royal Book Company, 1995), p. 337. See also pp. vii-xv and *passim.*

74. Weaver, *Pakistan,* p. 210.

nesians: the university founder and TV pundit, Nurcholish Madjid, on how *ijtihad* builds a stronger *umma,* and the presidential Sufi, Abdurrahman Wahid, on the fertile generosities of unfettered pluralism. Convinced that gender equality produces flexible societies, economically viable and democratically stable, she endorsed Amina Wadud's idea of Women of the *Umma* — to consolidate women's rights groups in order to challenge dictators and extremists, and to serve as lynchpins of civil societies everywhere, which ought to be linked in a Civil Society International.[75]

Several more linked visions ("somewhat out of the box," she proudly declared[76]) rely in the end on "the Gulf states to jump-start economic and intellectual development in the rest of the Islamic world," and a Marshall Plan for the Muslim world from North Americans, Europeans, Chinese, and Japanese, to advance tangible moral and economic goals, with pragmatic political impact for peace.[77] But motivating the Islamic world with other people's money is unlikely to happen. The greatest act of international generosity, after the Second World War, was also a deeply prudent one. America did not "jump-start" Europe, but put money into the rehabilitation and recovery of developed societies which remembered how a complex economy works. Benazir's last vision was nonetheless exuberant, Qur'anically sound, and socially progressive. Out of the box — excellent. One may wish that she had remained, in Rawalpindi, inside the van.

Electing Barack Obama gave the U.S. at least the possibility of a serious approach to the Afghan-Pakistan tangle of problems and theater of operations. But what could be achieved through American statecraft and military power? Purchasing policy alignment in Pakistan had always proved to be like buying a black hole. Fractious Islamism, endemic anarchy, and absence of education continued to minimize traction for social advances. The losers were gender balance, rural hope, and social equity.

In 2011 thirty thousand people were reported to have died in the previous four years from terrorism, sectarian murder, and army attacks on various militants and separatists. Dramatically revealing were the assassinations of the governor of Punjab and the national minister for minorities,

75. Bhutto, *Reconciliation,* pp. 276-84; pp. 288-94.

76. Bhutto, *Reconciliation,* pp. 317-18.

77. Bhutto, *Reconciliation,* pp. 295-315; quotation, p. 295.

who had stood for repeal of the blasphemy law that facilitates oppression of minorities in Pakistan.[78]

Against such phenomena may be argued the expansion of the overall economic growth rate, as well as an asserted capacity for Pakistan to follow Indonesia in overcoming its natural disasters (earthquake, 2005; floods, 2010). Can Pakistan, like Indonesia, also heal itself by amending its constitution, and by the examples, in the last decade, of surmounting separatisms, acts of terror, and civil-military suspicion?

Pessimistic riposte springs from the fact that 60 percent of Pakistan's budget is reserved for paying foreign debt and building military expansion. The military itself, in its obsession with India, uses national security to throttle national development.[79] Murder, suicide, and rape are key social indices, and such acts of violence affecting women are rising — in a threatening correlation with increased fundamentalist extremism as well as export of deeds of terror.[80]

78. *The Economist*, 2 Apr 11, pp. 36-39.

79. Stephen Coll, "Flood Tides," *The New Yorker*, 6 Sep 10, pp. 19-20.

80. Ahmed Rashid, "The Anarchic Republic of Pakistan," *The National Interest*, Sep-Oct 2010, www.nationalinterest.org/article/anarchic-republic-pakistan-3917.

Camels and Wheels
3.1 Saudi Arabia's modern wealth in oil has changed its ways of work and sport. Racing with boy jockeys is a popular sporting use of the camel.

Photo: Fahd Al-Safh

3.2 A motorcycle gang: motorcycling businessmen on a weekend fill-up at a gasoline station in the western central desert, 2004. *Author's photo*

3.3 Cars on sand and people on the horizon illustrate the pastime of dune driving.

Photo: Fahd Al-Safh

3.4 The Springs of Ali. North of Medina, not far from Khaybar, is the ghost town of Bishr: a tumbledown castle and mudbrick houses with rotting wooden doors. It contained until recently a site where the Prophet's son-in-law, Ali, had allegedly struck the ground with his sword, and water sprang forth. Shi'ite pilgrims for fourteen centuries made their way there to drink from the holy source. *Photo: Fahd Al-Safh*

3.5 In the early twenty-first century, Wahhabi officials, insisting on their super-Sunni version of history, obliterated the site of the springs. This photo shows it in 2006, covered with earth and stone. *Author's photo*

3.6 Al Ula lies halfway between Medina and the border of Jordan. The structures of the present city, mostly white, are backed by wind-eroded red hills. In the foreground are mudbrick houses, many hundreds of years old, recently abandoned. *Author's photo*

3.7 Medain Saleh in architectural and cultural style is closely akin to the more famous Petra, 320 kilometers further north. Both settlements marked trade sites of the Nabatean Kingdom, which declined after the first century C.E. Before one of the hundred-plus tombs carved in red sandstone, the author braces himself against a February wind.

Author's collection

3.8 Mount Rahma. A pilgrim reads his Qur'an on the "Mount of Mercy" while his friend rests [Abbas/Magnum, 1991]. Popular Muslim belief holds that Adam and Eve were reunited here after leaving Eden, and sought forgiveness for their sins. For some this site is the acme of the hajj, because prayers from here are especially powerful.

3.9 The Ka'aba and pilgrims in reverent circumambulation. According to the Qur'an, Abraham and his son Ishmael built the Ka'aba (Q 2:125-127). The Prophet Muhammad later rid its surroundings of the Arabian tribal gods of his era. The black silk curtain with gold calligraphy, the *kiswah,* is replaced yearly. Its weave contains the *Shahadah,* or Islamic declaration of faith.

Photo: Fahd Al-Safh

3.10 Sunset prayer, Mecca, during hajj 2003. Although the great Haram Mosque had been recently expanded, it could not contain the faithful, who here overflow outside it. The Kaʿaba is the black cube in the upper center. *Photo: Abbas/Magnum*

3.11 Soad Al-Dabbagh in her tent. Some modern Saudis, like this anthropologically sensitive designer, maintain traditional settings within the grounds of an otherwise gated urban residence. *Author's photo, taken in the presence of Al-Dabbagh's son, Achmed*

3.12 Thursday morning group, Kuwait 2004. One of the group was this scarf-wearing woman, Safia Al-Saleh, struggling with the others for female rights to be voters, candidates, and office-holders. The vote was achieved in 2005, but no woman was elected to parliament until 2009. One of the four chosen then was Dr. Rola Dashti of this group, an economist also active in assisting refugees and in democratic reform. The Qur'anic verses on the wall ask for protection from evil. *Author's photo*

Chapter 3

SAUDI ARABIA

Of major modern Muslim nations, the two most skeptical of "civil society" are Saudi Arabia and Iran. The belief of Saudi leaders that they are evolving the classical Sunni state often puts them on collision course with their Persian neighbors, who believe they are fashioning the essential Shi'ite state. Royal Wahhabis and revolutionary Shi'ites, however, share a conviction that under-monitoring is the highway to hell. Both consider "civil society" a subversive concept, stinking of errant Western social values.

Modernists elsewhere would argue to the contrary: that an independent and discerning civil society contributes to more social options, to more occupations and variety of labor, to more individual and artistic imagination, and to more tolerant values that enable international coexistence. Understanding why such an angle of vision is suspect in Saudi Arabia requires a look back in its history.

Puritans Compared

Muhammad Ibn 'Abd al-Wahhab and Jonathan Edwards were contemporaries. These puritan evangelists were unaware of each other. If either had been required to refute the other, he would have obliged with zeal, but the eighteenth century of the Common Era did not format such clashes.

The Crusades — Catholic wars against Muslims (1095-1221) — were long over. The European Wars of Religion — Catholic and Protestant wars with each other (1517-1648) — had ended before the failed siege of Vienna (1683) showed Ottoman power ebbing. Europe would lapse into the state of national wars, combined with intellectual self-congratulation, that came to be called the Enlightenment. Benjamin Franklin, in his secular generosity, would speak for that era, and for Philadelphia, when he said, "Even if the mufti of Constantinople . . . were to send somebody here to preach Muhammad to us, we should be tolerant, we should listen, and we should offer a pulpit."[1]

Muhammad Ibn 'Abd al-Wahhab (1703-91) was born just before and died just after Ben Franklin (1706-90). He lived the length of that century without taking note in writing what was happening to the north and west of him, in the Mediterranean and beyond. Jonathan Edwards, born early in the same year, died much sooner (1703-58). He fought the moral battles of his time as they were waged in the American colonies from Massachusetts to New Jersey, just as 'Abd al-Wahhab did between Riyadh and Mecca. Those provinces were to the Arabian and the American theologians wholly sufficient domains for their furious thinking and copious writing. They shared a monotheistic tradition which we now call Abrahamic, but they were driven by different texts and arrived at discernments containing unsharable terms.

'Abd al-Wahhab, says a careful modern commentator, "made it clear that men and women were equal in terms of their responsibilities toward God."[2] This simple association clears him of the misogyny found in many modern male interpreters of the Qur'an. And although he could not, and did not try to, escape the patriarchal cast of Arabic family customs, he, like the Prophet Muhammad, conceived within those customs the possibility of gender balance: "He dedicated . . . space, time, and evidence to the protection of women, seeking to avoid their debasement through licentious practices and upholding the limitation of sexual relations to marriage so that women could not be exploited." He prohibited concubinage, sexual relations with slaves, and rape. He granted women the right to stipulate favorable conditions in marriage contracts. He recognized their right to be educated, to be considered business partners, and to share access to public space, as in wedding feasts. Women's God-given rights, as found in the Qur'an and hadith, were for him the means to "empower and reempower women," in the tradition of the Prophet, in the context of his own times,

---

1. In Walter Isaacson, "Value-based Leadership in a Changing World," *International House of Japan Bulletin* 24:1 (Spring 04), pp. 20-26; quotation, p. 25.

2. Natana J. Delong-Bas, *Wahhabi Islam: From Revival and Reform to Global Jihad* (New York, Oxford University Press, 2004), p. 127.

and he effectively provided "a possible springboard for reform in the twenty-first century."[3]

Jonathan Edwards lived a very different life. Even though Mark Twain saw him as "a resplendent intellect gone mad," Edwards continues, a century after Twain, to be "a kind of white whale of American religious history." The early twentieth century tried to fix him to one sermon, "Sinners in the Hands of an Angry God," but his embrace of the universe went far beyond that. A recent evaluation finds his "post-Newtonian statement of classic Augustinian themes" to be "breathtaking." If God created a universe in which sin is permitted, he must have done so to communicate love to his creatures. A glimpse of that love, in Jesus, will draw humans away from a self-centered universe, and will open to them the redemptive love of Christ as the true center of reality, of beauty, and of God's loving creation.[4]

Edwards saw creation as "a system of powers to communicate." His published works — twenty-five volumes thus far — do not contain a special volume on marriage, as does the work of his Arabian counterpart, but in the man's life itself may be caught the inflection of his beliefs. In Northampton, Massachusetts, Edwards guided his parish through the "Awakenings" of 1734-35 and still more intensely, 1740-42. Most gratifying and most humbling to him were the religious visions of his own wife, Sarah, across a period of more than two weeks in 1742. Her transports and swoons, her overcomings by God and swallowings up in grace, her readiness to postpone the joys of heaven and to endure "a thousand years in horror, if it be God's will" constitute a rare exaltation. The plentiful evidence of Sarah's prolonged ecstasy was met by her husband's joy in her experience. Such joy we cannot even imagine in the record of his contemporary, 'Abd al-Wahhab. Islam is not without its female saints and mystics, but his appreciation of those saints is not evident, and his deprecation of mystics is clear.

Sarah and Jonathan partook of the patriarchy of their time. They both believed in duty of wife to husband as ordained, without regard to equivalent duty of husband to wife. Submission of both to God would yield, as it had for Sarah, sublime visions of God's acceptance. Jonathan, just the same, could see some persons tranced and dizzied in ways of which "Satan took the advantage." The dark forces were always there, as a Calvinist

---

3. Delong-Bas, *Wahhabi Islam*, pp. 190-91.

4. George M. Marsden, *Jonathan Edwards: A Life* (New Haven, Yale University Press, 2003), pp. 504-5; quotations of Twain and Joseph Conforti, p. 500.

would know. Yet sufficient compensation for all woe was the power of transport beyond it such as Sarah Edwards enjoyed.[5]

Fornication tests any theological system, and Edwards's ministry was no exception. Within two years of the great awakenings in Northampton and his wife's own celestial visions, he found himself doubting the experience of his community as a kind of false spring. A long ordeal, initially caused by minor expressions of illicit sexuality, brought Edwards down to earth.

A few young men had discovered books on sex and midwifery. Out of their ignorance, inexperience, and repression, they were taunting young women of the town with crude allusions to menstrual functions, and other raw gaucherie. Our later century might see all this as a primitive but socially corrigible form of sexual harassment. For Edwards, however, laxity in what men said to women signified weak theological grounding, and he set about to rebuild moral foundations. Looking on a woman's nakedness, even in imagination, was a sin. The biblical demands (e.g. Romans 14:13, Colossians 3:8) were unmistakable. Lascivious use of literature was of a piece with tavern-haunting, excessive drinking, late-night frolicking and dancing, not to mention bundling, and an alarming increase in premarital pregnancies readily tracked in early postmarital births.

Edwards's campaign in this instance found family culture, youth culture, and tavern culture all against him. Edwards fought them, at best, to a standoff. Some fights weaken the support of a public advocate, and here, not for the first time or the last, Edwards proved himself an incomplete politician. His finger-pointing aroused doubts about him in the three cultures with which he contended, and laid the groundwork for the time, several years later, when he would be voted out of town. His own congregation, only males voting, would go ten to one against him.

All of this occurred in an era during which Northampton court records show only one person, male, convicted of fornication. The historical evidence suggests innumerable offenses, little social compunction, far less juridical or canonical action, and an enormous amount of tongue-lashing. Edwards was spitting against the tides. In getting offenders to court he was ineffective, no matter how sure he was that they were prancing themselves to hell.[6]

5. Marsden, *Jonathan Edwards*, pp. 240-49.
6. Marsden, *Jonathan Edwards*, pp. 291-305.

Edwards and 'Abd al-Wahhab shared one point of historical reference, Aristotle, but chiefly to refute him. Edwards was Augustinian in emotion and Newtonian in science. 'Abd al-Wahhab rejected Aristotelian theories of logic, and followed the great antirationalist teacher, Ibn Taymiya (1263-1328). In addition to a famous polemic against Christian theology, Ibn Taymiya is remembered for opposition to "self-evident propositions intuitively apprehended." He found them suspect, chiefly because of the vast discontinuity between alleged universals in the mind and infinite particulars in reality. Relating back to Ibn Taymiya meant overwhelming dependence on the Qur'an and the hadith as interpreted by the "pious ancestors," especially the Companions of the Prophet.[7]

'Abd al-Wahhab was addressing a provincial culture very unlike that of New England. It too was patriarchal and patrimonial, but far more so. Tribal, in a highly mobile way: Bedouin space, at that time nomadic within roughly predictable wide areas, bore no ecological resemblance to New England culture. There was obviously no central village green. There was no town meeting hall. Governance came out of male leaders, sheikhs, confabulating under a tent.

In his own manner, 'Abd al-Wahhab addressed sex and gender problems, consistent with his principle that marriage was the only permissible context for sexual relations. As for the Qur'anic likening of women to "tillable soil" (Q2:223), he denied a common male understanding of this verse to mean possessive belittlement, and instead interpreted it as honoring women's reproductive capacities. He never broached what may be likened to a medieval Catholic view that sexual relations were for reproductive purposes mainly or solely, and he took a realistic view of arousal and desire in both genders. Men, 'Abd al-Wahhab said, may not have sexual relations with their slaves (which would, because of their purchasability, amount to prostitution); but they may free a female slave to marry her and do loving justice with her among the shari'a legal maximum of four wives. He recognized the existence of homosexuality by observing that men with effeminate behavior or with bisexual tendencies may be invited to wedding

---

7. I rely here on John L. Esposito, ed., *The Oxford History of Islam* (Oxford, Oxford University Press, 1999), esp. ch. 6, "Philosophy and Theology from the Eighth Century c.e. to the Present" by Majid Fakhry, and ch. 7, "Islam and Christendom: Historical, Cultural, and Religious Interaction from the Seventh to the Fifteenth Centuries," by Jane I. Smith.

feasts, as long as they control themselves and avoid sin in fulfilling community responsibilities.

Normality, however, preoccupied him. The allure of a woman could drive a man to a state of deranged temptation *(fitnah)*. He held *man* responsible for avoiding any such situation, and therefore "forbade the man from looking at a beautiful woman to whom he is neither related nor married, thus providing a mechanism enabling men to control their sexual desires and impulses." Nonetheless, both genders must "control their own carnal desires." From that command flows 'Abd al-Wahhab's "practical advice to women to dress modestly for their own protection." Because visual contact can result in lust, and because both parties may initiate a quest to satisfy desire, both are enjoined against excessive viewing of the other. In general the two hands and palms and the two feet are proper for viewing; among family and friends "he denied face veiling as a requirement for women." Hair? Not to be seen except by family, or a man considering marriage with the woman in question. All these positions were supported by citations from Qur'an and hadith.[8]

Cultures and *zeitgeists* contrast and change. Modern Muslim interpretations of gender matters vary. They puzzle foreigners, young Americans in particular — so much so that a famous professor of Arabic literature at the University of Pennsylvania, Roger Allen, invites into his classes an Iranian colleague to demonstrate "Twenty Uses of the Chador." Iranians are apt to dismiss the invention of covering as an early Arab defense against sand and sun, and to extol their own subtle adaptations of what became an Islamic religious injunction. One use of the *chador*, or *hijab*, of course, may be to intrigue. I confess to the impact that a Muslim woman had on me after a day of public discussions when, in a brief private conversation on the same matters, she threw back her head covering to reveal long, wavy, dark brunette hair.

One Muslim man summarized the rules of modesty to me as "cover your charms." This clearly interdicts present-day exhibitionism among some Western women, whose erotico-commercial company moves me to think, "To cover is to charm." Recovery of modesty in the West means winning back a vast amount of yielded cultural ground.

One sin against which 'Abd al-Wahhab, like Edwards, contended a quarter of a millennium ago was fornication. Calling humans to account

---

8. Delong-Bas, *Wahhabi Islam*, pp. 153-71; quotations, pp. 155, 156, 158; effeminacy, pp. 165-66.

for sexual encounters with the other gender in an unmarried state is fiercely difficult, as the lone conviction in Edwards's Northampton attests. We do not know, or have not yet found, records in 'Abd al-Wahhab's Arabia that are precisely comparable. But we do know what he advocated as sanction against any man, Muslim or non-Muslim, who fornicated with a Muslim woman. The penalty was death by stoning.[9]

Unlike the Prophet Muhammad, 'Abd al-Wahhab did not prescribe the same punishment for the woman as for the man. Here, perhaps, is a central datum, surprising as it may seem to Northerners, for considering 'Abd al-Wahhab "enlightened." He was advanced for his time and his culture in protecting female vulnerability against male sexual desire, and in making errant males suffer greater punishment.

'Abd al-Wahhab took pains to persuade; he did not wish to get himself thrown out of town more often than necessary. His wholly uncompromising doctrine of *tawhid,* however, by its nature identified secular enemies and attracted religious critics; and not until his pact with Ibn Saud gave him armed princely sponsorship did he find security for his preaching of an utterly absolute monotheism.[10]

Those whom his teachings could alienate may be arranged in an ascending scale of presumptive orthodox power. Sufis were not to be trusted, because mysticism was not a sure guide to understanding. Shi'i were to be distrusted, because their imams did not possess, as they pretended, secrets that yield infallible utterances. *Ashraf,* descendants of the Prophet, deserved respect on that account, but no special heeding; they carried no hidden knowledge, because all was revealed in the Qur'an and elaborated in the hadith. Many *ulama* resisted him because they clung to memorization as a route of instruction — a method that, once an innovation, had long become ossified. In the lifetime of the Prophet, however, and in the era of the Rightly Guided Caliphs, scripture was understood through historical context as a matter of common sense. And such contextualization was the key to 'Abd al-Wahhab's own method.[11]

Wahhabi reform doctrine, nonetheless, did not criticize groups of

9. Delong-Bas, *Wahhabi Islam,* pp. 129-30.
10. Delong-Bas, *Wahhabi Islam,* p. 19.
11. Delong-Bas, *Wahhabi Islam,* p. 43.

people so much as actions that violated the principle of absolute monotheism. Worship of a ruler was as loathsomely wrong as in the time of Pharaoh. Worship of trees and *jinn* was forbidden as harking back to pre-Islamic paganism and animism. Worship of prophets was wrong because they were human, even if radiantly so, as in the cases of Moses and Jesus. Worship of saints and tombs was misapplied specificity that distracted from God, errors common to both Shi'ism and Sufism, especially in their popular forms.[12]

All of these practices violate *tawhid*, devoted adherence to the single God in thought, word, and deed. Each such practice leads to *shirk*, the sin of association of any person or thing with God or his attributes. *Shirk*, according to the Qur'an, is the one unforgivable sin. As such, and as the opposite of *tawhid*, 'Abd al-Wahhab allowed it absolutely no room. He who commits *shirk* will be condemned to hell in the afterlife. *Shirk* was evident even in the imitation of past juridical rulings, which behavior elevates human knowledge over God's sovereignty and power as revealed in the Qur'an and hadith. 'Abd al-Wahhab's doctrines entailed natural costs in sharp contest with other teachings, and in the rigidity of some of 'Abd al-Wahhab's own eminent followers of succeeding centuries. Sheikh Abdul Aziz Bin Baz, the blind Grand Mufti of Saudi Arabia in the late twentieth century, owned a view of the Qur'an and a holy indifference to science which led him to believe that the earth is flat and that the sun revolves around the earth — a view he only moderated by talking with a royal pupil who became an engineer on the *Discovery* space shuttle.[13]

Vivid and repeated descriptions by 'Abd al-Wahhab of *shirk*, or "polytheism," or associationism, or the dilution and hence the demeaning of God had the effect of distancing Islam from other Peoples of the Book, even though he was careful to respect the Prophet's example of recognition of Christians and Jews. Unlike the Prophet, the twentieth-century ideologue Sayyid Qutb argued for holy war against Christians and Jews as a permanent state of necessity, and as a continuing revolution to prevent Muslims from being led astray. Despite his association with Wahhabi doctrine, Osama bin Laden owed far more to Sayyid Qutb than to 'Abd al-Wahhab.[14]

12. Delong-Bas, *Wahhabi Islam*, p. 61.

13. Antoine Basbous, *L'Arabie Saoudite en Guerre* (Paris, Perrin, 2004), pp. 128, 132. For appealing open-mindedness in Bin Baz, see Robert Lacey, *Inside the Kingdom* (New York, Viking, 2009), pp. 87-90, esp. p. 88n.

14. On Sayyid Qutb, see Delong-Bas, *Wahhabi Islam*, pp. 256-65, esp. pp. 260-62; on Osama bin Laden, pp. 266-79, esp. p. 274.

If association-with-God as distinct from devotion to God was a supremely damning sin for 'Abd al-Wahhab, Christ had to be stripped of divinity. For Jonathan Edwards, however, Christ was the very manifestation of God on earth, and the only sure route to salvation. Edwards, in dealing with the doctrine of original sin, resolved it as a matter of *inherent propensity* to sin. If, however, there was a sin likely to tilt toward the unforgivable, that one sin would be pride.[15] Christ was no mere associate of God, but his redeeming presence on earth. To refuse him was the sin "most difficultly rooted out, and . . . the most hidden, secret, and deceitful of all lusts." A different danger, a different salvation, a different universe than that of Islam, lay in his injunction "that pride is the worst viper that is in the heart, the greatest disturber of the soul's peace and sweet communion with Christ; it was the first sin that ever was, and lies lowest on the foundation of Satan's whole building."[16]

Once Edwards had overcome his own youthful resentment of the total sovereignty of God, he found a way to trust God with a sense of glory and rapture in his redeeming love. Ordinary parishioners, however, required from him a verbal picture of hell — they needed to hear "the shrieks and cries of the damned," in their infinite pain and infinite terror for infinite time. Although God wishes to share his love, our universe is in a state of war because of Satan's rebellion against God. In raging counterattack to the awakening of 1735, Satan caused a craze of suicides, against which power stood only God's restraining grace. Although the unrepentant may suffer hideously in this life, their pain is nothing compared to the wrath of God that will be felt in the next, which can be compared to an infinity of being eaten by worms.[17]

Severer visions yet occurred to Edwards, in a category of standard "awakening" sermons founded on the New Englander conviction that hell was as real as China. One that he delivered at Enfield, Connecticut, on a midsummer morning in 1741 remains welded to his name. His vivid imagination and resonant voice conveyed his meaning without the need of gestures. He reached his congregation with image after image, until they began to shriek with apprehension and appeals for salvation. He took them

15. Marsden, *Jonathan Edwards*, pp. 450-58.
16. Marsden, *Jonathan Edwards*, p. 225.
17. Marsden, *Jonathan Edwards*, pp. 136-87, 161, 167-69.

from the comforts of their hearthfires to show themselves as the unconscious minions of Satan. He terrified them with the hellfires that await; for a just God must condemn those who hate the good.

God holds you lovingly in his hand, Edwards reassured his congregation, to keep you from falling by the sheer weight of your sins into the fires of hell. But, he told his now moaning audience, hypnotized by his intensity, "The God that holds you over the pit of hell, much as one holds a spider, or some loathsome insect, over the fire, abhors you, and is dreadfully provoked; his wrath towards you burns like fire; he looks upon you as worthy of nothing else, but to be cast into the fire; he is of purer eyes than to bear to have you in his sight; you are ten thousand times so abominable in his eyes as the most hateful venomous serpent is in ours. . . . Oh sinner! Consider the fearful danger you are in."

Edwards probably did not reach much beyond this point. The audience was in hysterics. He probably was not able, that morning, to sound the note of hope he intended, of "a day wherein Christ has flung the door of mercy wide open . . . crying with a loud voice to poor sinners . . . washed . . . from their sins in his own blood, and rejoicing in hope of the glory of God."[18] A modern rhetorician might disdain that sermon as a catenation of devices to extort the undereducated. But it remains a certain kind of peak in American homiletics.

At about the same time, 'Abd al-Wahhab denounced sexual immorality so strongly that a group organized to attack him under the cover of night, intending to kill him.[19] He escaped, and flourished. But 'Abd al-Wahhab later found himself compelled to invoke the ultimate Qur'anic penalty against a woman who repeatedly confessed to him, of *zina* — sexual intercourse outside of marriage. "After several discussions, two inquiries into the woman's circumstances, and three opportunities to change her ways," 'Abd al-Wahhab gave in to the local *ulama* and reluctantly agreed that she be stoned to death,[20] according to one American-based academic. A scholar published in Riyadh, however, stresses that the great

---

18. Marsden, *Jonathan Edwards*, pp. 223-24.

19. Delong-Bas, *Wahhabi Islam*, p. 23, suggests that other motives existed, but that particular one prevailed.

20. Marsden, *Jonathan Edwards*, pp. 27-28; p. 297n53-56. Puritan law in the seventeenth century made adultery a capital offense (as does Leviticus 20:10). But wearing of the letter A and/or whipping or branding usually sufficed as punishment. The story of Jesus and the woman accused of adultery (John 7:53, 8:1-11) conveys wisdom and compassion interceding against bloodthirsty legalism.

man "made sure that the woman was not insane, was not raped, and that she was making the confession of her own free will." Only then, Jamal Al-Din Zarabozo says, did 'Abd al-Wahhab order the stoning in consonance with the woman's desire for purification, and in total and proper accord with Islamic law. This once-renowned case, the commentator adds, with fastidious contempt, is becoming famous again today "among those who believe in 'freedom and licentiousness.'"[21] Hellfire preaching may have become diluted in the U.S. since the days of Edwards, but Zarabozo's argument reflects a Wahhabiya newly strong in Saudi Arabia and subsidized for export to other Muslim regions.

Arab Tribes at War

Muhammad ibn 'Abd al-Wahhab, burning to purge the Arab world of paganisms, preached absolute monotheism with such rigor that he was forced out of the town of his birth, and later driven from Basra. (Even Edwards, when voted out of his pulpit in Northampton, was given time to depart.) But 'Abd al-Wahhab returned home and married the aunt of a local Najdi ruler, which alliance foreshadowed a later friendship with the wife of Muhammad ibn Saud, and a pact with Saud himself signed in Diriya, 1744. The two men swore a mutual oath with an imam pronouncing the hadith, "Blood for blood, and destruction for destruction." Ibn Saud was to be responsible for political and military matters and 'Abd al-Wahhab for the religious. The potentate dedicated himself to promoting *tawhid* and eradicating *shirk,* and the advocate, realizing that the political leader takes risks for religion without expecting earthly rewards, pronounced assurance that Allah would grant him rule over Najd and its people.[22] Conquest and consecration were joined like two hands washing. So power and piety remain inseparable in Saudi Arabia today.

The oath by itself did not guarantee the first Saudi state, let alone untroubled succession to the present. Ibn Saud struggled for twenty-seven years to conquer Riyadh. After that was achieved, 'Abd al-Wahhab actually

---

21. Jamal Al-Din M. Zarabozo, *The Life, Teachings, and Influence of Muhammad Ibn Abdul-Wahhaab* (Riyadh, Ministry of Islamic Affairs and Endowment, 2005), pp. 33-34, 121-22. I am grateful to Tanya Hsu for providing me this book in PDF format.

22. Delong-Bas, *Wahhabi Islam*, pp. 34-35; Basbous, *L'Arabie Saoudite*, pp. 51-56; Alexei Vassiliev, *The History of Saudi Arabia* (London, Saqi Books, 2nd ed., 2000), pp. 80-82.

resigned his role as imam in 1773, and withdrew from political economic life until he died in his nineties.

The modern reputation of "Wahhabism" began to be fashioned, not from the founder's teachings per se, but from the approach of Mohammad Ibn Saud's son and successor to his rule. That involved an approach of "convert or die," and an expansive propensity for acquisition of property and wealth. Popular hysteria about the "Wahhabis" was fanned by the Turks, who coined the term as one of reactive alarm. The Ottoman Sultan had claimed the Hejaz since 1517, and had assumed the title of "Protector of the Two Holy Sanctuaries" in Mecca and Medina, ruling there through Arab *sherifs*. Ibn Saud's successor now contested, and on Wahhabi principles criticized that rule — for lack of security and justice, extensive brigandage, corruption, treachery and fraud; for infidelity to Islam, unlawful commerce with women, and failure to control pilgrims polluting the holy cities with lust and debauchery; not to mention ostentation, decoration, smoking tobacco, and the kissing of hands of imams and sultans, all Ottomanesque cultural depravities not part of the example of the Prophet.[23] The list of sins foreshadows that issued by the armed puritans who would seize the Grand Mosque in 1979. Saudi-Wahhabi zeal conquered the Hejaz and took Mecca in 1803, but the fervor of that power exceeded its stability.

The loss of Mecca provoked the Turks, through the son of their Egyptian proxy, Muhammad Ali, to respond in force. After a decade of fighting, they defeated the Najdi warriors and drove them back to Diriya, at the center of the Arabian peninsula. There the House of Saud retained its holy alliance with the descendants of ʿAbd al-Wahhab, referred to collectively as "Al al-Sheikh" ("family of the sheikh"). They built back a second, smaller, Saudi state, but it fell to a different tribal leader, Muhammad ibn Rashid, supported by the Ottoman Empire, in 1884. A young scion of the Sauds, Abdul Aziz, in exile in Kuwait, pondered the lessons of family disunity and the art of balancing imperial claims of Ottomans and the British. In January 1902, with a band of forty men, he took the fort in Diriya with a brief hand-to-hand battle at dawn.[24] Thus ended the chance of the giant penin-

---

23. Delong-Bas, *Wahhabi Islam*, pp. 245-47.

24. Vassiliev, *History of Saudi Arabia*, pp. 211-14. Rachel Bronson, *Thicker than Oil: America's Uneasy Partnership with Saudi Arabia* (New York, Oxford University Press 2006), p. 29, speaks of Abdul Aziz's force as being "sixty-three in total." I use Vassiliev's figure of "only forty men" (p. 211) because he appears to be closer to the Arabic sources.

sula becoming Rashidi Arabia. Abdul Aziz Ibn Saud formed the third Saudi state, which endures.

The Ottoman Empire lasted a little longer than the Spanish. In 1898, Spain was shorn of its last colonies, Cuba and the Philippines, by the U.S. But Turkey's empire was not overseas; it was all contiguous to itself. And its shearers were Great Britain and France.

In retrospect it is surprising to discover how little the British truly knew about the Arabic-speaking peoples they sought as allies against the Turks. Far less did they understand with accuracy what was needed for making policies that might last. Oxford and Cambridge men, confident of their class and their Latinate education, drew grand designs of imperial imagination. One of them privately acknowledged, in Latin grammatical terms, that they expressed their ambitions, not in the imperative mood, but in the optative, which was reserved for wishes and even for whimsy. When competitive appetites and fragile trust were fashioned into secret pacts, such as the (British-French) Sykes-Picot agreement of 1916, they did not define results so much as describe intentions. Mutual misgivings and Arab suspicion forced that pact into the open not long after. There it joined other wartime correspondence in lasting disregard, such as the Balfour Declaration and the McMahon-Hussein correspondence. Those documents made Palestine a twice-promised land — both promised as a "national home for the Jewish people," and also dangled as an inducement to Arabs to struggle for their independence from the Turks.[25]

The Arab leader most prominently in discussion with the British, Sharif Hussein of Mecca, was doing some disingenuous dangling of his own. To make the British salivate for an agreement against the Ottomans from within that empire, he offered the prospect of an "Arab revolt." He and the Arab secret societies at various times boasted ability to rally ten or hundreds of thousands of Arab troops against the Turks. But Hussein had no army, and the secret societies had no following. Their pretensions to military capacity would come down to guerrillas of unimpressive quality. His son Feisal, excluding ex-Ottoman prisoners of war, commanded about 1,000 Bedouins. And whatever they mustered in action would eventually face British inten-

25. David Fromkin, *A Peace to End All Peace* (New York, Henry Holt, 1989; 2001), pp. 179, 183-87, 297.

tions to govern wherever they could, directly or indirectly, throughout the Middle East, linked to empire in India and in Pacific Asia. The First World War and the settlements that followed it would add in all to the British Empire nearly one million square miles.[26] But it would not change Arab mistrust of European projects, or tribal memories of war among themselves.

In wartime Cairo, British officials packed gold sovereigns into cartridge cases and loaded them onto camels to journey with T. E. Lawrence into the desert. Feisal was the key figure on their payroll. From his subsidies, he complained that he had to spend 12,000 pounds a month just to defend against attacks from Ibn Saud, who was himself receiving 5,000 pounds monthly. The British, in effect, were gold-plating two tins of kerosene and waving a torch above them.

In all, the British investment in Hussein's "revolt" would eventually come to eleven million pounds sterling, or far more than half a billion dollars in early twenty-first-century terms.[27] It was a massive investment; but what Gertrude Bell observed of Lawrence was true for all of Great Britain: he bet on the wrong horse. In the tribal struggle for power, Ibn Saud would prove to have more stamina, ingenuity, and bloody motivation than the Hashemites, the Rashids, or even the Sha'lans, whose ferocity was real but whose location was so far north that the Allies chewed up all their territory at the peace table.

The major common enemy was Ottoman, but the Arabian tribal divisions were at critical junctures more important. Ibn Saud added momentum through a Wahhabi religious revival that had begun in 1912, and whose force had become known as the Ikhwan — the Brethren. He found it easy to put himself at the head of it. Surrounded as he was by Ottoman possessions and by hostile Turks and their vassals, he needed to maximize all his local assets, of which puritan fervor was a major one.

Some Wahhabi brethren were gathering together to live more sedentary lives in order to reinforce each other in strict Islam. Such a movement incidentally diminished separations between tribes and authority in other tribal leaders. Ibn Saud naturally encouraged that, and promoted the Bedouin selling of possessions to settle into cooperative agricultural communities for living strictly by Wahhabi standards.[28] All this fostered his own supra-tribal power.

26. Fromkin, *Peace*, pp. 186, 223, 312, 401.
27. Fromkin, *Peace*, pp. 223, 311-12, 395, 424.
28. Vassiliev, *History of Saudi Arabia*, pp. 223, 227-31.

Peace in Paris did not mean calm in Arabia. The self-proclaimed Caliph, Hussein, found the Wahhabi puritanical surge moving near him in the Hejaz and sent Hashemite expeditions to stop it. The last one, May 1919, led by his son Abdullah, was a trained Hejazi army of 5,000 with modern British equipment. But an advance force of Ikhwan, armed with antique rifles, swords, and spears, struck them at night so badly that the British sent airplanes to the Hejaz and warnings to Ibn Saud.[29] In choosing the Hashemites, the British clearly had backed a lesser force in their financing of Arab revolt. Ibn Saud overthrew remnants of the Ottoman-linked House of Rashid at the end of 1921. In 1922 his Ikhwan, in a party of three to four thousand raiders, came within an hour's camel ride of Amman before the British crushed them to protect Abdullah, whom they had made king of Jordan. In 1924, Ibn Saud's men captured all the Hejaz and drove Hussein into exile.[30]

Abdul Aziz, "Ibn Saud," was the first effective Arab player of international politics in the twentieth century. But still he had to contain the Ikhwan. When they were not his chosen spearhead, they were a thorn in his side. Their raiding style, of purity and plunder, seemed to him an unsuitable agency for his intended modern kingship. In 1929, with brothers on either side of him, he defeated the Ikhwan at Sibila after an hour of hand-to-hand combat. In conquering deviant puritan ferocity, Ibn Saud solidified the long-standing pact between the House of Saud and the House of Ibn 'Abd al-Wahhab. He declared his now massive territories to be "the Kingdom of Saudi Arabia" in 1932, having agglomerated the most stable all-Arabian power in the peninsula since the time of the Prophet. He had also established a preeminence against whatever he declared to be errant extremists; and in that he could count on most *ulama* and many tribes and townsmen.[31] But not everyone.

Radiations around charismatic fanatics twice have disturbed the seemingly reliable links depended on by royalty. First was the seizure of the Grand Mosque of Mecca in 1979 by hundreds of gunmen led by an Ikhwan descendant, Juhayman Al-Otaybi. Then the bombings and gunnings in Riyadh, Jeddah, and oil facilities in the East since 2003, inspired by Ikhwan-like motives and a sophisticated Al-Qaedaesque ideology. Public beheadings finished Juhayman and his miscreants of 1979. The Grand Council of Ulama, summoned by a fearful king, described them as rene-

29. Fromkin, *Peace*, p. 425.
30. Bronson, *Thicker than Oil*, p. 31; Fromkin, *Peace*, pp. 513-14.
31. Vassiliev, *History of Saudi Arabia*, pp. 32-33.

gades. But the Sheikh Bin Baz, in return for support of the royal house, required counter-reforms against female freedoms, employment of women, and sales of alcohol. He refused to brand the rebels as apostates, for he had several disciples among them.[32]

The recent troubles in Saudi Arabia erupted less than two years after 9/11, and from similar causes. Three compounds housing Westerners in Riyadh were attacked by coordinated truck and car suicide bombers, causing heavy loss of life. Roundups and imprisonings, with reeducation and cooptation of the misguided, have been accompanied by public calm. But the dynasty may well feel that it is sitting on dynamite. Sweeping arrests were made of 136 of a "deviant group" in 2006 and 172 more in 2007. In continuing roundups, 113 were apprehended in early 2010 and 149 later that same year. All attest to continuing ferment, and to energetic surveillance of plots to blow up oil installations, attack officials and military posts, storm prisons to free comrades, and damage the financial system and/or relations with the U.S.[33] Beneath the outbursts in 1979 and since 2003 lie relentless echoes of the blood pact of 1744: modern wealth and power provide grander chambers to play out its variations, but the players always include doctrinal purists and violent activists convinced of extreme literalism, and of betrayal by the Al-Saud of the holy covenant.

Two other major factors entered the life of Saudi Arabia long before the death of Abdul Aziz: oil and Israel. The king gave American oil a first concession in 1933. He steadily favored their interests because, unlike British colonialists, they were not bent on restructuring Saudi domestic politics. The well that "blew" in Damman in 1938 made the company later called Aramco more influential by far than the Department of State in dealing with Riyadh.

The shape of international politics following the Second World War contained a new powerful positive in Saudi-American relations, and a new powerful negative. The kings of Arabia — Feisal was even more religious than his father Abdul Aziz — were willing to spend millions against "godless communism," as expressed by Soviet influence in Egypt and elsewhere. In the bipolar world of the Cold War, the Saudi entity was a strong American ally.

---

32. For narrative conviction, see Yaroslav Trofimov, *The Siege of Mecca* (New York, Doubleday, 2007), *passim*. For intellectual continuities, see Gilles Kepel, *The War for Muslim Minds* (Cambridge, Harvard University Press, 2004), esp. ch. 5.

33. *New York Times*, 28 Apr 07, p. A1; 27 Nov 10, p. A9.

But that alliance had to heal a stress fracture caused by the resettlement of Jews in Palestine. Ibn Saud thought they belonged in Europe, where their problems had arisen: "the Heavens will split, the earth will be rent asunder, and the mountains will tremble at what the Jews claim in Palestine, both materially and spiritually." In and after their epic meeting of early 1945, on a U.S. cruiser near the Suez Canal, President Franklin D. Roosevelt promised King Ibn Saud that the U.S. government would not change its policy on Palestine without full prior consultation with Jews and Arabs. And he would never do anything hostile to the Arabs. A week before he died, he confirmed his pledge in writing. Three years after that death, President Truman recognized Israel. Helping to rebuild a Judean state, as had an ancient Persian king, touched Truman's historical fancy. "I am Cyrus!" he crowed. King Ibn Saud, until he died, believed that Truman had betrayed Roosevelt's promise to him[34] — which, of course, he had. But dead presidents do not control live ones. Anguished as the Saudi monarch was at Truman's hubris, he kept his focus on his first priority — the security and development of his kingdom.

Volatile negotiation, charismatic generosity, and grievous betrayals — nearly a century ago, all these rose up in T. E. Lawrence's life among Arabs, still a revealing life to recount. His grasp of Arabic language and mastery of sublime English made him the ultimate expositor of the "Arab revolt," and the trusted advisor of Hussein's son Prince Feisal at the Paris Peace Conference, whose own hopes were dashed by the subsequent meltdown of promises into protectorates. Lawrence's idealism need not be doubted, nor his courage either, in recognizing that he had chiefly made things happen by carrying camel-loads of gold sovereigns to the key Arabian princes to win them further from the Ottomans, and to allay their own ambiguities. In a later American idiom, he was the bag man for British empire.

But "the money," Lawrence wrote, "was a confirmation; mortar, not building stone. To have bought men would have put our movement on the basis of interest; whereas our followers must be ready to go all the way

34. Bronson., *Thicker than Oil,* pp. 36-54, quotation of Ibn Saud, p. 41; Thomas W. Lippman, *Inside the Mirage: America's Fragile Partnership with Saudi Arabia* (Boulder, Westview Press, 2004), pp. 273-74, 276. Quotation of Truman, Robert Kagan review of Michael B. Oren, *Power, Faith, and Fantasy: America in the Middle East, 1776 to the Present* (New York, Norton, 2007), in the *Washington Post,* 21 Jan 07.

without other mixture in their motives than human frailty. Even I, the stranger, the godless fraud inspiring an alien nationality, felt a delivery from the hatred and eternal questioning of myself in my imitation of their bondage to the idea. . . ."[35]

The noble idea, of course, was an Arab nation independent of the Ottoman Empire. Lawrence would eventually learn of the McMahon letters and the Sykes-Picot Agreement and the Balfour Declaration, all of which cross-striped everything he achieved with livid contradictions. He wryly summarized: "to show us that it could give as many promises as there were parties, the British finally countered Document A to the Sherif, B to their Allies, [and] C to the Arab Committee [in Cairo], by Document D to Lord Rothschild, a new power, whose race was promised something equivocal in Palestine."[36]

Lawrence had a vision of the Arab flag standing for a "pan-Islamic supra-national state,"[37] which aim Feisal, hungering to be Caliph, voiced in his own way. Lawrence's personal map of "Arabia" suggests the difficulty of realizing the vision. On the vast rough parallelogram south of Turkey and west of Persia, he drew four dotted entities with much empty space between them. The dottings were tribal, and were labeled with names of individual leaders. From the Red Sea and Mecca-Medina to mid-Arabia was "Sherif" (Hussein, later Feisal). From the Persian Gulf and Riyadh to mid-Arabia, abutting, or nearly bumping the other big tribal blob, was "Ibn Saud." To the north of them both was "Ibn Rashid." And a still more northerly blob, drawn so that its western boundary was a long section of the Hejaz Railway arriving in Damascus, was labeled "Nuri es Sha'lan."[38] Hashemites, Rashids, and Saudis the present world has heard of. But why not Sha'lanis? The space of "Nuri es Sha'lan" was eventually digested in four different post-Versailles political tracts, now known as Iraq, Syria, Jordan, and Saudi Arabia. Lawrence, as connoisseur of "the precarious princes of the desert,"[39] saw Nuri as a kingly exemplar of "nomadism, that most deep and biting social discipline." The connoisseur, however, had little contact with any Saud or Rashid. He was chiefly an ally of the Hashemites: Sherif Hussein of Mecca, and his sons Feisal, who would be

---

35. T. E. Lawrence, *Seven Pillars of Wisdom* (Garden City, New York, Doubleday, Doran, 1935), p. 548.

36. Lawrence, *Seven Pillars*, p. 555.

37. Lawrence, *Seven Pillars*, p. 53.

38. Lawrence, *Seven Pillars*, map, p. 32.

39. Quotations, Lawrence, *Seven Pillars*, pp. 37, 173.

made King of Syria (until driven out by the French) and crowned King of Iraq (more lastingly); and Abdullah, made Emir of Jordan, whose monarchical line continues there in the early twenty-first century.

Of Nuri, Lawrence provides a brilliant description: thirty years a leader, he had gained the headship of the Anazeh tribesmen, including the Rualla, by killing two of his own brothers. In all the realm from Jauf through Wadi Sirhan, a chain of oases and waterholes, to the edges of the Turkish-held city of Damascus, "his word was absolute law. He had none of the wheedling diplomacy of the ordinary sheikh; a word, and there was an end of opposition, or of his opponent." Lawrence remained amazed that Nuri Sha'lan, without demanding a price, had joined their Young Arab Movement, "for he was very old; livid, and worn, with a gray sorrow and remorse about him and a bitter smile the only mobility of his face. Upon his coarse eyelashes the eyelids sagged down in tired folds, through which, from the overhead sun, a red light glittered into his eye sockets and made them look like fiery pits in which the man was slowly burning. Only the dead black of his dyed hair, only the dead skin of his face, with its net of lines, betrayed his seventy years."[40]

The Emir Sha'lan early brought contradictory British documents to Lawrence, asking which to believe. Foreseeing the future day when they would be "dead paper," Lawrence answered in an agony of duplicity that he should trust the latest in date. Shamed by his "dishonourable half-bargain" with Nuri, and in revenge against his circumstances and his superiors, Lawrence silently vowed to make the "Arab revolt" justify itself by success. As they pressed toward Damascus, Nuri came back to him with an expanded file of documents, asking again which he might believe. Lawrence, as before, glibly answered, "the most recent." Nuri accepted that in humor. "Ever after he did his best for our joint cause, only warning me, when he failed in a promise, that it had been superseded by a later intention!"[41]

After they entered and won Damascus at the beginning of October 1918, Lawrence tells the reader that he was "tired to death of these Arabs." They had defeated the Turks. But what had the "Arab revolt" availed? Even at the moment in Damascus, it relied on the Rualla revolt, which was not joined by the Rashids, far less the Saudi-Wahhabis, who opposed and would later overcome the Hashemites, whose leader would cut an elegant figure at Versailles while being undercut by interallied agreements.

40. Quotations, Lawrence, *Seven Pillars,* pp. 174, 546.
41. Lawrence, *Seven Pillars,* pp. 435, 545, 546, 547, 555.

Somewhere, something also went wrong with Lawrence's link to Nuri Shaʿlan — an angering moment that is remembered to this day in oral tradition by one of his mature descendants. Nuri allegedly felt he had cause to "give the standard Arab warning of three days. Meaning I shall be decent enough to give you a three day headstart to get out of here, and if I catch you I warned you."[42] That story, as told, is fixed regarding the "1915-1916 Sykes-Picot era." All the narrative cooperation of Lawrence with Nuri in *Seven Pillars of Wisdom,* however, takes place after that era, and in mutual sophistic comprehension of the cynical British-French document. If Lawrence offended Nuri, either he overcame the threatening mistrust of the warning and never mentioned it, or the moment actually arose sometime after victory at Damascus; or even after the demonic peace. It is also possible that retrospective memory of Allied belittlement of Arabs and their carving up of Shaʿlan territory may have become negatively focused in tribal memory on "Lawrence of Arabia" as the betrayer. Such an Arab explanation would be unfair to Lawrence, who felt close to insanity trying to be true to them, or what he imagined to be their best interests. But his own postures nourished his jeopardies. Allowing himself to grow into a myth may have eventually magnetized negative feelings around his figure, and given rise to anti-myths in which Arab memory figuratively cuts Lawrence down to size by threatening him with death.

Perhaps, as Lawrence's keenest biographer suggests, he demanded heroic achievement from himself to relieve an unconscious sense of worthlessness which arose out of being illegitimate in birth.[43] Whatever the case, Lawrence's medieval sense of the epic prevails in subtitling his *Seven Pillars of Wisdom: A Triumph.* Although that "triumph" is everywhere undercut by warning and self-disparagement, it contains remarkable narrative peaks. His environment is like William Morris's in Victorian epic poetry, "filled with the . . . medieval glorification of certain loves, lusts, murders, wars, and vendettas, and the disparagement of others . . . a world of jealousy and conflicting loyalties on the part of both men and women, a world in which treachery, betrayal and vengeance abound. . . ."[44]

42. Tanya Hsu to the author, 16 May 06, relaying the recollection of Prince Nayef Al-Shaʿlan.

43. John E. Mack, *A Prince of our Disorder: The Life of T. E. Lawrence* (Boston, Little, Brown, 1976), p. 240. The author of "the authorized biography of T. E. Lawrence," Jeremy Wilson, *Lawrence of Arabia* (New York, Atheneum, 1990), provides abundant fact, but yields to Mack, a psychiatrist, on matters of motivation.

44. Mack, *Prince,* p. 101.

All that is true of Lawrence's literary environment, too, except for "women." Strike them all. There are *none* in a narrative of 660 pages, but for brief allusions to Gertrude Bell and Lady Blunt as "storied travelers." In the unfolding of scenes, plans, events, feasts, and scarifying encounters with Turks; in deep friendships and light alliances with Arabs, there are no females perceived. Lawrence would appear to have beheld no women across twenty-one months of action. He did not even film them, so to speak, in crowd scenes.

That is not to suggest that Lawrence was homosexual. Neither was he truly asexual. It is closer to the mark to describe him as an anchorite with a late-arising flagellation disorder, virgin until death. Raised among five bastard brothers, educated in all-male environments, including Oxford, he was happiest in camp life — archaeological digging, and in the post-peace routines of an enlisted man in the Royal Air Force. The womanlessness of Lawrence's writing is sometimes, but rarely, relieved by feminine simile, as in a description of Nuri's headmen, "famous sheikhs so bodied out with silks . . . that they rustled like women while moving in slow state like oxen." Or, more fully: "The Arab leaders showed a completeness of instinct, a reliance upon intuition. . . . Like women, they understood and judged quickly, effortlessly, unreasonably. It almost seemed as if the Oriental exclusion of woman from politics had conferred her particular gifts upon the men. Some of the speed and secrecy of our victory, and its regularity, might perhaps be ascribed to this double endowment's offsetting and emphasizing the rare feature that from end to end of it there was nothing female in the Arab movement, but the camels."[45]

Modern Travel in the Arabian Desert

My own interior travel in the Kingdom has been swifter than Charles Doughty's and wider than Lawrence's because of airplane and car — and for the same reasons, slighter. First: in November 2004, a day westward from Riyadh in a caravan of five well-used four-wheel-drive vehicles. We passed through massive machine-sliced cuts in the mountains, a vast roadside dune buggy emporium, miles of debris from marble quarries, and then undisturbed hills and cliffs and escarpments which flattened out until we rendezvoused at a gas station in the center of nowhere. There we talked

---

45. Lawrence, *Seven Pillars*, quotations, pp. 546, 214.

with a dozen black-jacketed men on Harley-Davidson motorcycles — Arab and European professionals of late youth and early middle age whose leader owned the BMW concession in Riyadh. They gathered and gunned off, a pack of roaring hogs, morning sun gleaming on leather and state-of-the-art engineering. Harley-Davidson, founded in 1903, is a year younger than the third Saudi state.

After a while we peeled off the macadam into the desert, dodging occasional sand traps, coursing mostly on hard rock and gravel. Our dust spun up to join the haze that filmed over a sunny blue sky. I had expected sensuous dunes in *Playboy* flesh tones, or the mad red cinema sands of *The English Patient*. But all was dun. After three hours of bumping and winding, we made our way into something more distinct and even welcoming: a ravine, arroyo, dry gulch? From its shale and gravel surfaces arose large acacia trees. Under the wide shade of one we built a fire, unfolded aluminum chairs, and pitched a picnic for twelve. The word is *wadi*. This was Wadi Jufair. I brought back a fossil seashell in the form of the Royal Dutch Shell logo, spotted by a German woman with a wide-brimmed hat, protection against recurrence of skin cancer. She generously gave me the bitsy thing with remarks on the Cambrian period, and the fact that central Arabia, five hundred million years ago, had been entirely under salt water.

Before the Kingdom of Saudi Arabia streamed highways through its deserts, abetting hajj travel and the petroleum economy, there was the Hejaz Railway, a north-south imperial venture of the Ottomans. And before those rails were laid, there were camel caravans immemorial. Charles Doughty, a solitary traveler and an inspiration to Lawrence, made his way there in 1876-78, keeping himself alive by dispensing simple medicines, and sketching with care places unknown then in Europe.[46] This "monumentally lonely man" knew the character of almost 200,000 square miles between Damascus and Mecca — built upon "plutonic rock," layered over with sandstone, then limestone; splashed with volcanic fields, and interspersed with veins of flint and strata of quartz. Deep sand deserts lap like great dry tongues throughout the peninsula.[47]

---

46. But it had been thoughtfully traveled for centuries by men of other cultures. See Abdulgadir M. Abdalla, Sami Al-Sakkar, and Richard Mortel, *Sources for the History of Arabia* (2 vols., University of Riyadh, 1977).

47. Charles M. Doughty, "A Sketch Map Itinerarium of Part of North Western Arabia and Nejd," endpaper to vol. 1 of Charles M. Doughty, *Travels in Arabia Deserta*, (2 vols., New York, Dover Publications, 1979; original Cambridge University Press edition, 1888). "Lonely": see Henry Green, *Surviving* (New York, Viking Penguin, 1993), p. 92.

Among the "discoveries" that Doughty made for Europe was Mada'in Salih, a complex of Nabatean monuments. To Petra, the Nabatean capital farther north, a recent Jordanian tourist focus has drawn hundreds of thousands of visitors annually, many pulled by cinematic memory of Indiana Jones seeking the Holy Grail. But Mada'in Salih is little different from when Doughty mapped and described the monuments and their inscriptions. A modern traveler may reach the place with some determination. In Jeddah I found Fahad Al-Safh to take me to it. In thirty hours — indecent haste — we flew to Medina, drove to the "Cities of Salih," and returned.

Charles Doughty required many arduous months to cover such territory. He carried an unholstered pistol strung around his neck under his Arab robes. His benign intentions were clear; only once did he come close to drawing his weapon. As "Nasrany," the Nazarene, or Christian, he took pains not to affront any Muslim believers, though he was queried sharply on his own convictions. One evening, among a great crowd for coffee, he was especially hard put in defense of the Christian faith. He answered contumelies as "fables . . . and old wives' malice of things unknown." During a spirited exchange in which he was addressed as *Khalil* (Friend of God), he finally declared, "We are as your elder brethren: — as for me I take every religion to be good, by which men are made better. I can respect then your religion." Privately, nonetheless, he saw Muslim ignorance of Christian scriptures as "cause why . . . the Koran itself is full of a hundred mad mistold tales and anachronisms." As for the charge that by "dividing the Godhead" Christians descend into idol worship, he gave up forbearance years later in his own published account: "Mohammedan theology is ineptitude so evident that it were only true in the moon: to reason with them were breath lost[;] will is their reason." But his disputants in the desert only felt sorrow for him. He had come far to be among them, but God had allowed a veil to be drawn before his eyes.[48]

As a veil across my own vision, I endured diabolic speed. There are to be seen, in southern near-coastal Arabia, trees of several kinds — lotus, jajub, juniper, acacia, pine cypress, casourina. And fruited: almond, apple, pomegranate, miscellaneous palms. Classified as "medicinal": the juniper, arrak, and henna.

48. Doughty, *Arabia Deserta*, 1:341-43.

But we went too fast to identify any of them, and I never dared ask Fahad to slow for seeing them. He had a modern schedule to keep, and so had I. Nine years before, he had founded against great difficulty the first tourist company in the Kingdom. A protected society does not encourage idle visitors. But now its cabinet allows awareness of the finitude of oil reserves; an economic keynote is diversification, and the Ministry of Information cautiously seeks Fahad's advice on tourism.

At 6:00 a.m. we set out from Medina. It struck me as an uncharming city, an assembly of buildings stingy with windows, reminding me of slaughterhouses, bowling alleys, Edwardian libraries afraid of light. Not knowing Arabic, I couldn't read signs, and so attributed minor purposes to what I saw. It is, however, a city of deep religious history, and a launching point for Mecca of what are now more than two million pilgrims a year.

Fahad soon hit his cruising rhythm. Catching only glimpses of the dashboard from the right front seat, I finally asked, "Are those kilometers per hour or miles per hour?" "Miles," Fahad answered absently, at 120 *miles* per hour. We were doing nearly bullet-train speed on concrete highway slashed through stone and desert. The only vegetation was trees, a few knotty growths no taller than a man. The rocks and low ranges were in colors of rust, tinged at their lightest toward green, the darkest near purple.

Houses were rare. I read and was told about decline of the use of the tent, which survives mostly in romantic tradition. Some of those once called Bedouins are now more accurately thought of as semi-nomads. Among them some prefer two-story houses, whose ground floor accommodates domestic animals and dogs. The family floor above has small bedrooms and a large general room with a crate for clothing and jewelry, brazier, earthen cookpot, large jar, crusher, skin canteen, and coffeepot.

I saw no farmland farrows, nor the spillways that the sedentary construct between them to preserve rain. I glimpsed no stone fortresses, nor heard any drumbeats to warn others of hostile strangers. With no evidence of the epics that seize Arab imagination — of *jihad,* of struggle, of solemn perseverance — we just drove, running on the hum of the highway, glued to the road as to a vast transmission belt. Too fast to see any wildlife but camels — none of the book-rumored creatures like wolf or hyena, or owl or hoopoe. We flew like a bat out of hell, but singularly straight, north and slightly northwest.

"What is the best technique," Fahad asked me, "for hitting a camel?" I had no idea. Bedouins had taught him that if you had any instant for maneuver, try to strike the hindquarters, which crumple more readily than the forelegs. His father had hit camels twice, once with a GMC and once with a Mercedes Benz, and luckily survived. The worst such accident Fahad ever saw was after an evening prayer, when a big speeding truck hit a wandering herd in the dark. They found five beasts writhing and shrieking in their "blood and meat." What does a wounded camel sound like? "You don't want to hear it." He searched for words. "It's like a big *scratch.*"

What could they do? "We had to cut throats," Fahad said. "You can't repair camel."

Late morning we arrived at Khaybar, where dark earth testifies to long past volcanic explosions. It is said by modern Arabs to be a "Jewish" town, inhabited by black people. Those incidentals nothwithstanding, glory attends the memory of Khaybar for having early been invaded by Muhammad. Doughty stopped there and was brought before the arrogant, illiterate local sheikh Abdullah, who had his camel-bags thoroughly searched before a crowd. With his books and maps confiscated, Doughty was pressed to disclose where his money was — French *livres* in the middle of his canister of tea leaves — and relieved of them for "safekeeping." At the bottom of a bag they found his empty pistol holster, which occasioned alarm, resolved by a spontaneous cry that the oppressor, Ibn Rashid, must have taken it from him. Doughty silently yielded to this explanation, glad to have no cause to use the pistol under his great Arab cloak.

Confined in Khaybar more than two months, Doughty gathered sights and tales, concluding, "easy are the Arab to forgive every treachery! *For they put all to the account of necessity.*" He passed dark days as "the black people meanwhile looked with doubt and evil meaning upon [me]." Intercession by new friends preserved him from an extended rampage of anger by Abdullah, but his books and papers were camel-expressed to the Turkish Pasha in Medina.

Eventually the Pasha (who knew his intention to map and to publicize antiquities of Arabia) wrote back in French a letter of deliverance, by which Doughty got restored his papers and books, and even his six French *livres.* His dearest friends, who had offered to "buy me . . . a great-eyed Galla maiden to wife," were sorry at his departure: "for he is a sheikh in questions of religion, and besides a peaceable man." He was missing only a Qur'an, an Arabic psalter, and a camel bag, stolen by a Turkish officer. When Doughty paid his great-hearted friend, Amin Mohammed, for all provisions consumed, "it seemed to him that I had taken away his good works"; and he feared that he had sinned against that man's "charitable integrity . . . [and] human affection." A last passage together, "and the world, and death, and the inhumanity of religions parted us forever."[49]

Khaybar in 2006: Fahad, having warned me that foreigners are not welcome, took me to an abandoned village at the edge of the city. Bishr is composed of houses of mud and stone, with a crumbling castle on its hill. Wooden doors, decaying in sun and rain and wind, hung open everywhere; and one iron door, rusting, stood closed. The government has moved these poor to a new settlement. We saw only a single other human, who came upon us in accusative loneliness: a black man in a gray thobe. "*Salaam aleikhum,*" we greeted him. His reply was half of that, and grudging. Fahad was not worried by him, but he was worried by a white jeep that marked our entering and leaving Bishr, and trailed us a ways afterward. The Interior Ministry was more suspicious than ordinary police. He watched for their spying vehicles all day long, and saw many. None stopped us.

Fahad paused longest in Khaybar over the "springs of Ali," named for the fourth Caliph, the Prophet's son-in-law. A hundred and thirty years ago, a guide to Doughty showed where Lord Ali's blade cleft the rock, from which sprang water.[50] Shi'ites for fourteen centuries had been coming to these springs to honor their martyr and to drink from its waters. But the government of the present Kingdom doesn't like Shi'ites, Fahad said. Two years ago they covered up the spring with earth and stone. As proof of the tradition he keeps his own photo of pilgrims drinking the waters.

Not that Fahad sympathized with Shi'ites. But the government shouldn't destroy places of historic and tourist value. As he put it later in the day, with greater vehemence, "What fucking business have the Wahhabis to say, 'history is *haram?*'"

But still, he didn't really like Shi'ites. Do you know, he asked me, what they do at the time of Ashura, the death day of their martyr, Ali? They gather in the dark at one of their mosques. The men, who usually go there in all-male company, bring their mothers and sisters and daughters. And then what? "In the dark, everybody make love, everybody do sex, with people they can't even see. And if any babies are born from this sex, they are 'the blessed of Ali.'"

49. Doughty, *Arabia Deserta*, 2:98-101; 143, 204, 207; 221-25; 233; 236.
50. Doughty, *Arabia Deserta*, 2:97.

Fahad waxed to his theme. And what do Javanese women do? They come to Mecca and Medina from Indonesia, and they look for Javanese boys, descended from immigrants who stayed after pilgrimage. And they have sex with these boys, so that they may have a holy child from a holy city.

Doughty heard Christianity likewise misunderstood, around coffee and the fire: Christians know no lawful wedlock, and with lights out in their religious assemblies "there is a cursed meddling among them in strange and horrible manner, the son . . . lying in savage blindness with his own mother," so that, one dared say directly of Doughty, he "cannot know his own father."[51] Fantasy multiplies faster than anthropological truth.

As for geography: Doughty heard "of a strange country in Arabia, southward of Mecca," only lately converted to Islam. The men have no beards on their faces." The place is called Java.[52] Placing it in the Arabian Peninsula misses by nearly five thousand miles. But many Muslims of Southwest Asia and Arabia are indifferent to the oceans and seas to their east. That Javanese men are mostly beardless is, of course, true.

Hajj had been the vehicle for accounts of travel in Arabia two centuries before Doughty; piety and politics dominate the perceptions of the best of them, by Awliya Chalaby, an Ottoman diplomat, and alleged songster and wit.[53] Hajj was only incidental for Doughty, who left a pilgrim caravan for individualistic reasons, non-religious, crypto-poetic, and elementary-scientific, hoping for recognition by the Royal Geographic Society. He did not correlate hajj and plague, but modern medicine does. Some *ulama* of northern Nigeria declared in 2003 that polio vaccine was a Western plot to depopulate Islam, and thus unloosed the infected among infectable people in the hajj crowds. The number of polio endemic countries, having been reduced from 125 to 6 since 1989, suddenly shot up. Nearly 96 percent of the world's one thousand cases of polio recorded by the World Health Organization (WHO) in 2005, until August, were from nations of the Organization of the Islamic Conference. That spurred the KSA, expecting two million pilgrims from abroad, to require evidence of revaccination in hajj youth under fifteen.[54]

51. Doughty, *Arabia Deserta*, 1:341.
52. Doughty, *Arabia Deserta*, 1:169.
53. Abdelgadir M. Abdalla, Sami Al-Sakkar, and Richard T. Mortel, *Sources for the History of Arabia*, esp. articles by Mustafa Bilge and by Carl Max Kortepeter, 2:213-27, 229-46.
54. Arab News online, 21 Aug 05; Crosswalk.com, Aug 05.

Hajj was a practical matter for my guide, Fahad, whose forebears had arrived from Lebanon for that purpose. Fahad's eight-year-old daughter was in the hospital with flu from a wave of sickness after the recent pilgrimage season. Aren't the millions coming on pilgrimage, I asked him, a great potential asset for your tourist business? "No. They don't stay. They are not interested in anything but hajj sites. And the government doesn't want them to stay." The Najdis, he said, with offhand bitterness, refer to Hejazis like himself as "the trash of the hajj."

We left the black lava rock of Khaybar, and the hills grew into mountains as we shot north. We returned to russets, at sharper heights with stronger profiles. Ages of weather erosion had left some arbitrary and striking shapes. Fahad told of a coarse Australian tourist who said they made him think of God as an artist dropping turds from the sky.

The Hejaz Railway still runs between Damascus and Amman, a steam-powered locomotive blowing black smoke along narrow-gauge tracks. That distance may be covered by car in two and a half hours, but the train takes seven to ten, depending on removal of goats and vagrants. Once its rails went all the way down to Medina, carrying hajjis of an earlier era, and connecting the Ottoman Empire to its southernmost possessions. It opened in 1908. In the First World War, Feisal's Bedouin troops made a repeated point of cutting its transport of military supplies. Lawrence was their chief manager of explosives. Lots of failures galled him, but one relieved him: charges not going off under a train carrying women and children. But blowing up a troop train, and watching its debris fly a hundred feet in the air, put him in high glee.

The southern sections of the railroad went defunct before Ibn Saud declared himself king. Their remnants are sometimes visible, winding on either side of the modern highway to Mada'in Salih. I asked Fahad that we stop and inspect its little crumbling stations; we saw a solitary abandoned tanker car, rusting on the side. Every wrenchable part had been pillaged. All the rails were gone, sold perhaps for scrap, and all the ties as well, usable for Bedouin house-building perhaps, or burnable in the winter cold. I did find, at Al Badiyah, some rusted tie bolts in the sands. I picked one up in my fist and showed it to Fahad. "You could sell these to tourists for five hundred dollars!" He picked up three. "I don't sell things. I give them to friends."

As a one-time gandy dancer on the Alaska Railroad, I explained tie bolts to him. These apparently made a simple screwed connection from rail flange to tie. My Alaskan labor included spiking rails to ties in four places each, to hold the much greater weights and speeds on those tracks. Near Mada'in we would see a displayed locomotive that confirmed my sense of Ottoman miniaturism. It looked almost like a Lionel train set. Was this the great imperial line of the Ottoman Empire to Southern Arabia? The scale seemed pitiful to me and not worth the deaths spent on it.

What were Lawrence's dynamite charges compared to the civic engineering in Jeddah now, which from the harbor throws the highest water jet in the world, illuminated by night? That a desert country can afford to blow water in the air was strangely cheering to me, for it is ultimately a sign of hope — unlike Lawrence's Lilliputian blasts of death for one bleak empire over an already broken one.

Al Ula contains mud homes a millennium old, with regal modern mosques in stunning white, and plenty of trees and orange groves in a craggy red-rock setting. We lunched and pushed on to Mada'in Salih, where we were to see only two other automobiles in its nine square miles — both of Pakistani families lingering after hajj. Fahad was dismissive of Pakistanis, saying that they carry their ignorant fundamentalism to the point of abjuring cunnilingus, "because the same tongue recites the Qur'an." "They don't know Arabic. They don't know Islam."

Salih, Fahad asserted, was a messenger of God. In the Qur'an his message is clear: *repent*. Secular sources are little help except to suggest that the Nabateans were a monarchical society with a variety of intermorphing gods. Their semi-supreme deity, Dashura, had no face or image, but was represented by an undesigned block of stone. Not monotheism, really; afigural oligotheism?

Salih's story is clear in the Qur'an, where it is told in overlapping but little elaborating ways in five different surahs (7, 11, 26, 27, 54). His people, called "the Thamud," are also portrayed in several further surahs as powerful, corrupt, and heedless of warnings. Salih's role, in the revelations given the Prophet Muhammad, is likened to that of Moses opposing the Pharaoh. In Qur'anic sequence Salih is linked with other ignored messengers, Noah and Lot, better-known names in Judeo-Christian tradition. Salih is given a giant she-camel as proof of his favor with Allah. His hearers, however, are defiant enough to hamstring and kill the camel. That brings down a lightning bolt from heaven upon them and their houses.[55]

We may not walk through Noah's ark, or explore Lot's city, or see his wife as a statue of salt. But we may walk through the "Cities of Salih." Over a hundred tombs survive there, built from the top down in a rock which is gnarled from millions of years of weather. The sculpture of Mada'in Salih, two thousand years old, is astonishingly sharp in relief. Damage is far less meteorological than vandalistic or theological. Modern iconoclasm and barbarism both smite the shores of tradition.

The isolated majesty of the place is not enhanced by the plastic signs which carry translations of tomb inscriptions. These insist on non-disturbance of the donor entombed, and his children and grandchildren to the end of time, at pains of everlasting curses. Shelves inside, however, are empty of belongings, and donor bones are dust under the floor.

The Prophet, in any case, speaking six centuries after the Nabataean tomb-builders, had inspiration strong enough for him to put Salih on a par with Noah. Repent; ask forgiveness and mercy; the day of reckoning comes. The reassurance of Allah to Muhammad may be applied to Salih and all the divine messengers: you are not required to control your people; you are only obliged to warn them.[56]

Between clumps of tombs, Fahad suddenly began short, sharp pulls on his steering wheel while gunning the motor. Pools of rainwater stood before us, and deep ruts in the sand. Jolted into dune-driving technique, he roared his Lexus through the hints of quicksand and bog, and parked on sun-cracked mudflats beyond. He shook his head. The government builds fences, but no roads.

Fahad resumed his disdain for the Wahhabis. "They say it is *forbidden* to go to Mada'in Salih. . . . They want to keep you close at home and ignorant. . . . *History is haram!* Don't ask about old things. Read about them in the Qur'an. *That's it.*"

Not only were the Wahhabis responsible for stopping up and stoning over the Springs of Ali; they have recently torn down the houses of the Friends of the Prophet. They have obliterated the old Turkish fort and replaced it with a shopping mall. They have destroyed the "Seventh Mosque" in Medina, because of the special reverence felt for it by Shi'ites. All of these things *recently*. And all such acts I again heard, later in Pakistan, criti-

---

55. *The Qur'an*, 27:45-52; 54:23-32.
56. For example, *The Qur'an*, 4:79-80.

cized by Kazi Zulkaddir, an eloquent Muslim businessman. He too is indignant over Wahhabi barbarism: "These are crimes against humanity . . . destroying places of Muslim history."

Fahad's peak story of dogmatic wrongdoing was the little-known tale of the Golden Ka'aba. A group of Jehani Bedouin expressed their new prosperity in the nineteenth century by building a replica of the Ka'ba entirely in gold (smaller, but mightily valuable) in the area of Omluj, five hours from Jeddah. I asked about their motives — worship, or attracting hajj trade away from Mecca? Probably both, Fahad answered. But when Abdul Aziz came to power in the twentieth century, the Wahhabi powers that legitimated his rule prevailed on him to bury the Golden Ka'ba. To avoid any division of focus or multiplication of entities, they persuaded him to have countless tons of sand shoveled over the shining artifact, so that it could not be detected in the shifting dunes of the region. Fahad tried to locate it once, asking around in the region, but "only grandfathers remembered that it existed, and got angry at questions about it from grandsons." So nobody, even in a country that likes to dig for buried treasure, is likely ever to find it. Another possible tourist attraction lost. He sighed.

The intolerance of powerful Wahhabi sheikhs was even now increasing. Fahad's anger went over the top when he cited the fire in 2002 at a girls' school in Mecca, where many had died because *mutawwa'in*, religious policemen from the Society for the Promotion of Virtue and Prevention of Vice, wouldn't let them out unscarved or let firefighters and police inside.

The repercussions were national, I later learned. Girls' School No. 31, with 750 students aged 13 to 17, was ill-equipped, with an average of only five square feet of classroom space per student. A girl caught smoking had tossed away her butt. When the fire ignited in trash, the illiterate guard with the key was away on a menial errand. The lights went out. Girls screamed in the dark, and some suffocated. Fifteen died and forty were injured. Crown Prince Abdullah, the actual power at the time, used the terrible incident to shake up the Presidency for Girls Education which had operated independently.

Abdullah knew the resistance to reform. He had initiated permission in November 1999 for women to have their own ID cards instead of appearing only as wards of their husbands. Because the ID photos would be unveiled, however, sheikhs attacked them as licenses for prostitution. But now the press, cell phones, and all the forces of outraged gossip were unleashed against the religious establishment. Not only against fossil thought, but also against corruption and rundown facilities in education. Prince Abdullah asked his next brother in line for the throne, Prince Sultan, to investigate unacceptable deaths, the result of negligent and incompetent officials. Prince Nayef, however, the powerful Minster of the Interior (and another brother), denied that the religious police had done anything wrong. He stands for the pro-clerical parts of the royal family, runs the state security apparatus, and presides over the Saudi fund for support of the Palestinian *intifada* against the "Zio-Crusaders." Against such forces, Prince Abdullah eventually managed to sack the overbearing, underperforming head of girls' education, and installed a respected academic secularist in his place.[57] After Abdullah became king in 2005, he eventually pushed through a number of reform appointments in 2009 — including a woman, Norah Al-Faiz, as Deputy Minister of Education.

Developing Saudi State and Society

The deeds by which Abdul Aziz, King Ibn Saud, unified Arabia are called by a Lebanese historian versed in Saudi sources "acts of expansion, plunder, conversion, slavery, and conquest." All of these the conqueror sanctified "as acts of *jihad*."[58] The title which he first preferred, from 1902 to 1915, was Sheikh, or Emir (prince); then, from 1915 to 1921, Imam (religious leader); then, for the first time, 1926-27, after conquest of the Hejaz, "King."

That last title, favored by British colonialists for their client ruling families, actually has a negative connotation for religious Muslims. In the Qur'an, kingdoms are not abodes of God; there the title "king" implies "arrogance, narcissism, and . . . self-importance." But feeling sufficient command in his hands led Ibn Saud to seek appropriate recognition from Northern powers. "King" contented him and his filial successors for sixty years, until in 1986 his son Fahd chose to become "Custodian of the Two Holy Mosques." Not consistent with his dissolute reputation. But the Kingship had been sharply challenged by Juhayman's 1979 takeover of the Great Mosque in Mecca, accompanied by the religious style of governance manifested after Khomeini's revolution in Iran the same year. King/Custodian

57. "The Fire that Won't Die Out," *Newsweek* online, 23 Jul 02; and miscellaneous online sources, including www.islamicawareness.com.

58. As'ad Abukhalil, *The Battle for Saudi Arabia: Royalty, Fundamentalism, and Global Power* (New York, Seven Stories Press, 2004), p. 21.

Fahd promised that "spending on Holy Places will be unlimited."[59] But whatever that may have earned him in the hearts of Saudis and among Muslims elsewhere was undercut by his inviting American forces, in 1991, to base themselves in Saudi Arabia for Operation Desert Storm.

Oil revenues had produced an extraordinary energy of material progress in Saudi Arabia. By 1980 its per capita income exceeded that of the U.S. Equally extraordinary dysrhythmia in development followed: by 2006 its proportion of American per capita income had sagged to one-third, while 20 percent of its males in their twenties were unemployed, and 20 percent of the whole population remained illiterate.[60]

For understanding such developmental phenomena, I relied on American-educated government servants. Dr. Mohammed Al-Jasser was then Vice Governor of the Saudi Arabian Monetary Authority (SAMA), who advanced to Governor in 2009. His gleaming white building is so beautifully proportioned that I was tempted to think of it as a religious institution. The central bank of the Kingdom had been located in Jeddah, as long as mud buildings were still prominent in Riyadh. Then in the early 1980s a building boom took place that reminded Jasser "of Shanghai *now*," in its profusion of cranes. The present SAMA edifice was erected in 1985, designed by Minoru Yamasaki, who also did the twin towers of the World Trade Center.

During the mid-1980s, thousands of Saudis were sent to the U.S. for education, in the greatest human resource development thrust ever undertaken by the nation. Even now, three-quarters of the Saudi cabinet has been educated in the States. "Our ways of thinking, management style, entrepreneurial approach, and no-nonsense directness make us closer to the U.S. than to Europe in style — closer than Europe itself is to America." All the more sharply disappointing, Jasser said in a gracefully brief parenthesis, to be treated after 9/11 with bureaucratic hostility in efforts to obtain an American visa.

Yes, there remain tribal weaknesses in the structure of the nation. Transparency is still deficient. But since the 1970s, life expectancy has gone from about 53 to over 70 years. Among high school and university graduates there are now more women than men. Religious education for women is still a big issue, but now "religious figures will pull [out] every stop to get their daughters educated, and then to get them a job." In national develop-

59. Abukhalil, *Battle,* p. 121.

60. www.nationsencyclopedia.com/economics/Asia-and-the-Pacific/Saudi-Arabia -POVERTY andWEALTH; IMF World Economic Outlook, database, Apr 06.

ment, these religious figures "may prevail until objective conditions overwhelm them." Although a practicing capitalist, Dr. Jasser, bright, still young, in a gleaming white thobe, used the term "objective conditions" with the trenchancy of a Marxist.

What about recent explosions set off by ultra-militant radicals? Jasser said, "It dawned on them [the religious figures] that this was not an Atari game." Going to Iraq on *jihad* was no longer acceptable. "The religious establishment is being transformed. . . . There are lines of violence they don't want trespassed." He insisted that the militants, though they do exist, should not be allowed to define Saudi Arabia in American minds. After all, he said, flashing a smile to accompany a brilliant reverse spin, "The Amish don't define Pennsylvania."

There is a massive complex of problems, Jasser continued, in resident immigration, education, and employment. There were only five million Saudis in the 1970s, and there are now, attracted for employment, that many legal immigrants in the resident population. They live, of course, among seventeen million native Saudis who require education and jobs. Motivation to acquire jobs and education declined for two generations because of oil wealth, but they are now rising. Educational ambition is becoming more innate; a new Ministry of Labor has been separated out from Social Affairs; and cultural changes are taking place. Young Saudi men are for the first time willing to become porters and doormen. He summed all this up as a steady progression: "the rejuvenation of motivation by objective conditions."

Another advanced agency of government is the Saudi Arabian General Investment Authority, or SAGIA. Its Director General for the Energy Sector, Dr. Abdul Wahab A. Al-Saddoun, also American-educated, is a graying, calm man in a beige thobe. His special concern is not "oil," but the "energy value chain." The Kingdom has proceeded far beyond Franklin Roosevelt's World War II embrace of Ibn Saud, an aristocratic harmony of misunderstanding in which both downplayed the importance of oil; and far beyond the Kissinger era, 1965-2001, when oil-guzzling was an unexamined premise of behavior both North and South.

Saudi Arabia's better thinkers now see their petroleum diminishing. Not all, of course, agree. When I used an assumption of twenty or thirty years' more supply with some Saudi businessmen and asked how they would solve the problems that would ensue when the oil ran out, I received three kinds of replies: diversify; muddle through; and "Allah will provide" — the American answer, the British answer, and the traditional desert answer.

Dr. Saddoun and SAGIA are distinctly untraditional; their answer to this question contains large components of the American one. I queried Saddoun on Saudi statements of total reserves, which had been unchanged for twenty years. He replied that a review of Aramco annual reports for ten years will show constant updating of figures for oil and for gas. That oil figure is now 260 billion barrels, and that it resembles the figure of two decades ago is no surprise. He would expect a similar finding in another ten or fifteen years because, at least in theory,[61] a combination of geological ingenuity in discovery and technological improvement in extraction will yield constants.

Saddoun stressed that the economy of the Kingdom is becoming diversified fast. It will add as much capacity in petrochemicals in the next five years as in the previous quarter-century. It is establishing a "mining city" south of Kuwait for bauxite, phosphorus, and steel, which will aim to increase the mining sector from 1 percent of the economy in 2005 to 9 percent in 2010. Desalination of water is strategic for Saudi Arabia because of very scarce underground resources. On the Red Sea and the Arabian Gulf, twenty-nine desalination plants already produce a greater global share of desalinated water (21 percent) than does the U.S. (19 percent).

These activities have raised the contribution of the energy value chain — petrochemicals, utilities, mining and mineral processing — which relies on natural gas or hydrocarbons as fuel or feedstock, from near 0 percent in the 1980s to 15 percent of the GDP. All this is correlative with driving down reliance on oil, greater than 60 percent of the economy in the 1980s, to just over 40 percent recently.

But SAGIA's goals are not merely to diversify. Saddoun concludes by stating their ambitious goal *to achieve a total economic growth rate double the growth rate in population.* The latter is dauntingly high, at 3 percent a year. So economic growth needs to be 6 percent to eliminate poverty and to enhance GDP per capita.

From my afternoons with Jasser and Saddoun I inferred that the government of the Kingdom of Saudi Arabia has ample brains and apt plans. But for smart plans to prevail requires weighing cultural lethargy and religious obstinacy against secular ideals of an improved society.

61. Serious doubts about such a theory burst forth in a posting of 9 Feb 11 on "Saudi Oil Production and Reserves — Reasons behind Wikileaks Concerns" (www.theoildrum.com/node/7465). Professionals in command of data and ways of evaluating it found the Wikileaks information trivial and Saudi government information dubious. Such debates on energy supply rapidly escalate in the comments to a competitive fury on theories of civilization.

The struggle for women's liberty and gender equality is alive in Saudi Arabia, but weakened by the presence of oil, and by Northern support for the royal government. "Women are doubly oppressed in Saudi Arabia because . . . *everyone* there is oppressed."[62] Except, presumably, the royals, their rich connections, and those well paid to protect the dynasty. But how long can this go on without at least subtle and gradient change? Women's levels of education have been steadily rising until their proportions nearly equaled those of men fifteen years ago, and now significantly surpass them. That puts them in a position to work for new levels of freedom *with* men, less hobbled by separation from men as now religiously and socially required.

Percentage of Saudi Women in Different Levels of Educated Cohorts[63]

	1970	1983	1995
Elementary	31%	41%	48%
Secondary	20	39	46
College	8	32	46

Saudi women, like other Gulf Arab women, have become increasingly convinced of their right to select their own husband, in proportions which refute both Western stereotypes of their inferior status and Islamic fundamentalist insistence on the same.

Percentage of Gulf Arab Women Who Prefer to Select their own Husband, 1981-82[64]

Qatar	90.3%
Saudi Arabia	90.0
UAE	87.5
Kuwait	84.0
Bahrain	77.8

All such cumulative change in opinion and in capacity to think has taken place to the discomfort of the religious establishment. The present Grand Mufti (a member of the House of Al-Sheikh) said in August 2003,

62. Abukhalil, *Battle*, pp. 162-63.
63. Abukhalil, *Battle*, p. 150.
64. Abukhalil, *Battle*, p. 154.

just three months after the first revolutionary bombing in Riyadh, "Rulers, even if unjust, should be obeyed."[65] This statement contradicted the Wahhabi inheritance from Ibn Taymiya, who had articulated most clearly in Islam a right of political revolt. Emphasis on obedience, however, has kept the Saudi-Wahhabi bond in high profile. Social articulations of obedience across a quarter-century came down from Abdul-Aziz Bin Baz (1912-99). He went blind in his youth, but only after he had memorized the Qur'an. He adapted to Hanbali legal principles the customary practices of Arabian society, and became the first nonmember of the House of Al-Sheikh to be appointed Grand Mufti.

Of moment to Saudi women, he promulgated innumerable *fatwas* on marriage and gender questions. Examples:

(a) Age differences between men and women are of no consequence in relation to their piety. The Prophet at age twenty-five accepted marriage from the widow Khadija who was then forty. He later, among his wives, consummated marriage with Aisha when she was nine years old and he was fifty-three.

(b) Birth control pills are not allowed except in cases of illness, because "Allah has sanctioned the means that lead to procreation and a larger Muslim nation."

(c) Marriage of a Christian man to a Muslim woman is invalid, and any offspring "are the children of fornication."

(d) Because in hadith the Prophet said, "A man is never alone with a woman except that Satan is the Third," a woman may travel nowhere with a chauffeur who is not a male relative.[66]

Certainly the thousands of pages of other rulings from Sheikh Bin Baz were earnest attempts to address troubling questions presented him by the faithful, and to strengthen the five pillars of faith. But orthodox requirements in Islamic tradition also include an Ibn Taymiya so interested to "make woman be able to control her lust"[67] that he endorsed female circumcision. Less inspiring, to be sure, than Ibn Sina and Al-Ghazali on divine and human love.

65. Abukhalil, *Battle*, p. 62.

66. Muhammad bin Abdul-Aziz Al Musnad, comp., *Islamic Fatawa Regarding Women* (Riyadh, Darussalam, 1996), pp. 65, 163-64, 172-73, 268.

67. Ibn Taymyah, *Fatwas of Muslim Women*, trans. Sayed Gad (El-Mansoura, Egypt, Dar Al-Manarah, 2000), pp. 25-26.

I was the first male ever to be given a tour of the Queen Effat Women's College in Jeddah. The college was an inspiration of the queen's daughter, Princess Lolowa. Founded in 1999, it was the first in tertiary education for women in the Kingdom. The princess honored her mother, who with the approval of the king had earlier started the first school of any kind for females in Saudi Arabia. That was in 1955, the year that the U.S. Supreme Court decided, in the case known as *Brown v. Board of Education,* that separate was not equal in the matter of facilities for black students. In Saudi Arabia, of course, "separate" continues to be mandatory with regard to gender, because it is divinely ordained. "Equal" is a mistaken idea of the Northern cultures.

Dr. Haifa Al-Lail was chosen as the founding dean of Effat College. She is the first Saudi woman to achieve a doctorate in the policy sciences, which she did at UCLA. A bright, smiling woman, she, with her husband, still considers two weeks in Los Angeles an inspiring vacation. Haifa wears a white *abaya,* with a hood to cover her hair. All other faculty and all students were in black *abayas,* with a hood or scarf. Those wearing black *burqas,* with only eye slits, I discovered later, were female security guards, who kept ahead of our tour to sweep the halls clear of incidental students, lest they see a man and he them. I asked how they had prepared for this "first" event. "We sent a general e-mail to all faculty and students," an administrator told me. "We were going to show you the swimming pool, but there are girls in it." She laughed. "We thought of asking them all to stay underwater when you came through."

I did visit library space, which was under-stocked and under-populated to my eye; but the computer labs were fully and industriously peopled, for Effat College, strong in business and management, was planning to introduce engineering.

It was my first day in Saudi Arabia, and my naïve American eye was keen for details of dress. A student named Sousan, who had been on American television the previous week, wore a gray and white scarf over her head and across her chin, mouth, and bridge of nose. A teacher of literature wore a white head scarf with her black *abaya.* A young American administrator from South Jersey, in high-heeled shoes, over six feet tall, had chosen a black *abaya* with floral designs scalloped into it that allowed a faint filtered view of her calves and ankles. An associate dean, with no such daring semi-transparency, wore garnet embroidery on her black. I asked about it. "Style," she shrugged. Each of these teachers and students some-how appeared to manage her own statement of style, however subdued. An American Ph.D. in psychology offered me further context. She had begun life in the United Church of Christ, become a Baha'i, and then in Syria converted to Islam. For work in Arabia the Saudi government made her take a test in proof of her faith. Having spent some time in Amish country in Pennsylvania, she happily likened women's clothing there to its counter-part in Arabia — all covered but hands and ankles, with head scarved in white, "to reflect praise to God."

The associate dean asked me about my shirt, which I explained was from Java: white, with high collar and long sleeves, and light blue embroi-dery along the button panel. I had chosen it over business attire: a dark blue suit, white button-down, red necktie. "I'm glad," she said, "to hear of men thinking about dress decisions."

From the day at Effat, two student opinions stay with me — classic statements, I would understand later, after hearing them repeatedly in con-servative Islamic circles. "Beauty should be precious to us women," said one. "Mine should only be revealed when I choose to reveal it, and to someone who deserves it." Sousan told me, "Beauty is like a diamond. It should not be buried, but it must be protected." I asked her, "Did you say that on American television?" "Yes," she answered, and pulled her scarf quickly, briefly, over her eyes.

Eyes, of course, should be met, if at all, only glancingly, and then as neu-trally as possible. I sought at the end of the tour to thank one of the little se-curity guards who had scurried to clear my path. I approached her and with American earnestness peered through her mesh to say *"Shukran jezilyeh."* What I could see registered fright. I realized that my gratitude was far too frontal in presentation. She appeared to feel less thanked than accosted.

In Riyadh, the foreign advisors and experts on which the kingdom has relied are gathered in compounds, now surrounded by walls increased to about eighteen feet, with razor-wire added. Big cement traffic blocks re-quire a five-miles-per-hour zigzag weave approaching armed check-in, where *iqama,* security documents, are required from visitors and held un-til departure. Armed personnel carriers with mounted machine guns circle in patterns. These stepped-up precautions arose from the invasion by radi-cals of three compounds on May 12, 2003. At one, Alhambra, murderous shootings culminated in a suicide truck blast at a Saudi-Western party within. The explosion was audible several miles away at Cordoba, where many Western medical personnel are living. Cross-checking, they afterward doubted the Saudi government reports of thirty dead. At King Feisal Hospital alone, they estimated fifty victims, from the first and most deadly of efforts to ignite internal revolution against a corrupt royal system. The militant organization involved is al-Qaeda in the Arabian Peninsula — chiefly returnees from Afghanistan, bidden by Osama bin Laden to take the battle to the Al Saud at home. In five subsequent years of the continuing struggle, a former American ambassador said that the Saudi government has killed 150 and captured 1,000 of its internal enemies.[68]

The related irony is trivial, but biting. The wife of a Mexican doctor bought and wore an *abaya* to the dining room in the Cordoba compound. Authorities descended on her and required her to take it off. Why?! I asked. The answer: no Saudiization of the prevailing Western culture is permitted in these compounds, which distortion might dilute their attractiveness to expatriate experts and their families.

Who owns these compounds? Very rich Saudis, one of whom was apparently targeted at Alhambra. What explains increasing Saudiization of professional positions and simultaneous anti-Saudiization of expatriate compounds? National control and financial advantage for Saudis explain both. Hence the uniquely privileged and constrained ghetto-life of supremely well paid foreigners: separate, and in everything unequal. Their salaries in their own terms may be "princely," which is why they come in the first place. They are paid far above a Saudi norm, and well beyond their own national level; but they may not imitate Saudi dress or pretend to be Saudi, which is by definition a superior kind of being. Trying to do so will make one unwelcome — an anachronistic Lawrence of Suburbia.

Seven Prominent Female Professionals

Madeha al-Ajroush is a pleasant, curly-haired brunette in her forties, a psychotherapist and photographer. Her *Flashes and Shadows,* a photo exhibition published in Riyadh in 2002, observes the Saudi-Wahhabi inhibition against showing the face of any woman. But her striking images of females averting their faces, and time-lapse photos of their swirling into dark interiors, call dramatic attention to what is not seen.

---

68. Wyche Fowler Jr. (Ambassador to Saudi Arabia, 1996-2001) and Mark Weston, letter to the *Atlanta Journal Constitution,* 7 Jan 08, forwarded by Elizabeth Greenberg to the author. See also Lacey, *Inside the Kingdom,* ch. 26.

Madeha was one of "the drivers" — the forty-seven women who, on November 10, 1990, sent their chauffeurs home by taxi, took over the steering of their cars, and defied the law in a caravan on the thoroughfares of Riyadh. They were seven more in number than the force with which Abdul Aziz conquered the mudhouse Riyadh of 1902 and initiated the present al-Saud state. But cultural advance is not decided by small numbers as readily as pistols effect dynastic change.

Saudis had seen women drive before. Bedouin women drove; Kuwaiti women drove. But the compelling moment came with the influx of American troops, invited to throw Saddam Hussein out of Kuwait and to protect Saudi Arabian oil flow. The example of truck-driving American females galvanized a group of Saudi women, including a few teenagers who had also learned how to control an automobile in Europe or America. Madeha expected to go to jail — which she did, of course. "We were actually detained less than twenty-four hours. Then, on the first Friday after we drove, we were denounced in the mosques as women of evil affected by Western thoughts."

The angry intensity of the repressive follow-up surpassed the expectation of most of the drivers. Those who were working in businesses were fired. Volunteers in NGO jobs were cut. Madeha was specially targeted as a photographer. "They came and burnt everything, including my negatives. . . . They had to punish us. . . . The world was focused on us. . . . The American military didn't like the uncovering of what kind of elite they were working with . . . so they attacked us [too], as well as the Saudi government and the Saudi public."[69]

Madeha had spent half her life in the U.S. She graduated from Columbia, obtained training, and practiced as a psychotherapist. She learned the orthodoxies, including Freudian, but inclined more to Harry Stack Sullivan. Her Saudi practice includes women, men, and children in unpredictable numbers, varying in their majority. "Manic depression and schizophrenia exist in all cultures," she says. "When I opened up practice [in Saudi Arabia] at three dollars an hour, it was a joy to provide a curative energy. If someone is anxious or depressed you have to get to the core of it. Cognitive therapy may get rid of the symptom. But without going to the depth, one cannot reach a cure."

69. Various subsequent efforts appear from Saudi women for the cause of driving: an online campaign, for instance, using YouTube, Facebook, and Flickr; thelede.blogs.nytimes .com/2009/05/07.

Her own bicultural depths move her to reflect on what she has seen in life and heard in therapy. "Americans portray themselves as open, easy-going, relaxed *individuals*. . . . But these are just *codes*. They are very hard to . . . penetrate. Americans don't really understand themselves [how regulated and predictable they are], because the pressure is so high to conform."

The U.S. and Saudi Arabia, as Madeha sees them, are two sides of a coin when it comes to sex and repression. On the Saudi side, woman is required to cover from head to toe, even face and hands, because she is so seductive. Her clothes may not even reveal the line of her shoulder. Recently she has even been made to wear rubber shoes, so as to *give no sound*. "I want to make sure," Madeha assumes the voice of a patriarchal religious authority, "that I delete her for all but her husband. *For **him** she is a sex object*."

On the other side of the coin is "the great Western man who has to be seduced. The *responsibility* of the woman is to get him." She must cultivate bigger breasts and lips, and maintain a slender body, as a sex object for the enjoyment of men. If she does not conform, she is rejected or despised. American culture tells the woman, wife or not, "*You must seduce*." Saudi culture tells all women, married or not, "*You must not seduce*." But in both cases, woman is ultimately a sex object — in America public and flaunted, in Arabia private and sequestered.

In the U.S., I reflect, women are commercially pandered and promoted. In Saudi Arabia, they are governmentally hidden and suppressed. A world theory of Eros lies in this contrast, which no Freud, no Marcuse, no Norman O. Brown, no Philip Rieff has begun to understand. Such commentators comprehend only *some* dynamics arising out of Mediterranean civilization and its transformations across the North Atlantic.

But Madeha is not interested in global theory. She wants to press home a point about the Middle East. "Contemporary patrilineal society is for the benefit of governments. Father and elder brother have the final word. This is very useful in [our region], because for the man to have the final word makes it difficult to contend with spousal abuse, and all else that is wrong." Madeha concludes with allusions to cases recently appearing in the *Arab News*, of women who contended against raging men and had all rights — and their children — taken away from them. "There is a horror story here: the lack of love, the lack of protection, the no-place-to-go. No shelters, no trained police to assist, nobody to hold her and help her."

Some of Madeha's insights came to life for me when a Saudi friend I'd made in America asked me over, with Mac Bosley, the American friend with whom I was staying. Refreshments at his house — I will call him Nabil — preceded a dinner elsewhere with his colleagues. "What would you like to drink?" he asked Mac, who replied by his long custom as a resident in the Kingdom, "orange juice." "No," said Nabil, a trifle disdainfully. "We don't have any. What would you like to *drink?*" For the first time in nearly eight years in Saudi Arabia, Mac was being offered alcohol freely and unabashedly.

As we left Nabil's house, he introduced his wife — who threw back her cowl to let long-waved hair fall in luxury. Nabil then hustled us out, lest the encounter degenerate into conversation. He had, I recognized from Madeha, presented to us his sex object; and with that moment of privileged sight we should be honored and content.

At the house of Nabil's friend, we were taken through the usual giant gate, with gateman, doorman, barman in turn ushering us through one kind of marble to another, past flowers and fountains to the flow of choice, American whiskey. I encountered a womanless arena of Arabian male privilege that is an indelible memory.

On three sides of the main room were long sofas and big chairs, with huge coffee tables in front of them. Except for those watching the end of a TV news show, all the men were lounging in the plump-pillowed, heavily brocaded burgundy sofas with gold fringe and tassels. Their posture was uniformly belly-forward, as if they had a large meal to rest, although dinner had not yet been served. Nobody sat with a straight back. Nobody was tilted forward with hands on knees. Seven men of the twelve I could readily see were wearing white thobes with classic Saudi red-checked white kerchief, bound with coil *(egal)* around the head. Others, including the host, were wearing gray or black robes. Four, including the host, wore no headdress. One, the young supervisor of the electronic system of stock trading set up in 2003, was dressed all in white with a white-only headdress, no red checkers.

A boisterous roar in the party came from having among them a famous commentator on the local stock market, himself also a prominent investor. He had just been shown on TV speaking about a big telecom IPO that had juiced up Saudi stocks 2.2 percent in one day. The investor-public commentator was now exuberantly free in his remarks, even if, in an American context, his presence among movers and shakers following his TV program might be seen as collusive, and those remarks a series of steroid shots to bulk up speculative values. The Tadawul Stock Index continued to rise for more than a year longer, topping 20,000. It broke in early March 2006, and closed 2008 at 4800, 76 percent below its peak value.

In the exuberant hubbub of the speculators that evening, Nabil asked me who I was going to interview the next day. Innocently I answered, "One of the drivers."

Nabil and others exclaimed, "One of the *drivers?*" and lapsed into a shocked and disapproving silence. When I told Madeha of the environment (but not that conversational detail) of the night before, she observed, "Oh, the whiskey group." They talk about money and politics, she said, but they will not speak out against prevailing social values. They like to show Westerners how modern they are, but they obviously don't want to shake the royal and religious system. To them, she said, "Real men are Saudis." Other men are something else.

So I learned, from opposing quarters, of an antinomy not in the books — of a deep antagonism in Saudi society beneath all the turmoil over oil and al-Qaeda: "the whiskey group" versus "the drivers." Both break the law. The men consume alcohol daily with impunity. The women went to jail for once handling an automobile.

Madeha al-Ajroush and the drivers celebrate an annual reunion on their motor caravan day. They are not otherwise organized, but they represent a rise of Saudi women in the professions and in business that was unimaginable fifty years ago. The variety of those professions itself is a marker of the development of Saudi society, and not merely the women within it.

The emergence of women in a variety of enterprises is not testimony to openness in Saudi culture, but a fused artifact of ingenuity in the women and the omnivorousness of business. Five percent of registered businesses are in women's hands. Perhaps 7 percent of the public workforce is female. Bright women will thoughtfully compromise to get ahead. The commercial profit motive — it would be too abstract to speak of "capitalism" — bends forces of all kinds to assure that income exceeds expenses.

Seema Khan, chief strategy officer of the Saudi Arabian General Investment Authority, is an example. She, like her husband (an ophthalmologist), is an Arab-American, now resident several years in Riyadh. Her bilingual fluency makes her invaluable in her agency, and her bicultural ease likewise. "As an advisor to my minister, I wear the *abaya* and the headscarf. I find it a great working uniform. Completely objective. It removes sexuality from the workplace altogether. How is a man going to pat my behind in *this?*" She smiled, having just come home from work in a voluminous black *abaya*.

There are dinner *abayas* now, she said, and evening *abayas,* and sports *abayas.* The Ministry of Religious Affairs issued edicts on measurements of everything and attempted to confiscate violations in manufacture. But their men couldn't go on the upper floors where seamstresses worked, so what could they do? Seema attested to Saudi women in their fifties with the maturity to defy the *mutawwa'in*. One clothed for business in a conservative woman's suit was halted on a main street and cane-threatened by a religious policeman. As a crowd gathered, she put up a verbal storm: "*How do you know that I am not religiously garbed?!*" Her defiant question contained large subtexts evident to the policeman and the onlookers: "Is *your* heart clean? Is your gaze *pure?* Because if you are making a judgment on my beauty and desirability, you have no business doing so!"

For Seema herself, "the whole concept of religious police is completely offensive." Why are rote learners, many of them former inmates of prisons, entitled to be judgmental in ways to which the Prophet never stooped? Seema generously gave my coordinates to several dozen women in her wide personal network, leaving it to those who wished to get in contact with me to do so. A good number did, from among whom I have chosen dialogues about different kinds of work and personal histories.

Sarah al-Ayad is a principal of SACCS, public relations specialists in Jeddah, with sixty-five employees in offices in Riyadh, Cairo, Amman, Kuwait, and Dubai. There was no work integration in Saudi Arabia until a royal edict in 1999 which, in accord with Islamic principles, defined certain women to be in the workforce. Of that female force, now 4.7 million women, only a small percentage are in jobs. Women who wish to work usually spend great effort reassuring their husbands and families that it's okay. More difficult for Sarah than the idea of working (she is a graduate of Aziz University in Jeddah) were the transformations required to do public relations work in the kingdom. Previously it was a matter of meeting visitors at the airport and issuing press releases. But client servicing had to be developed in detail. Women are good at that and now compose 60 percent of their office. Men's and women's offices are separate. There is a bi-gendered conference room.

Only two female employees have been lost. One resigned before she began; the other, who was given a completely secure office and permission to use the phone for everything in her work, was very good, but quit. "Perhaps she found it too fast and pressured." The firm has to deal with the fact that Saudi custom conceives a working day that only lasts from 8 a.m. to 2 p.m. Even for Sarah, who is comfortable working long hours, the Internet and cell phones ("even little kids are using them") make her feel that "it's spinning out of control. . . . Today we are one big humongous village. . . . In business we have no choice. . . . But some things change too fast for many Saudis."

Nadia Bukharji is an interior architect with forty-five members on her staff and an accomplished portfolio of 130 projects over a fourteen-year period. After graduating from King Feisal University in Dhamman, she trained in England and rose to a partnership with Prince Al-Walid from 1996 to 2001. Her university had a flourishing department for a few years until "they" drastically compressed its curriculum into soft arts and crafts such as painting on furniture, with the rationale that interior design as a field provided "no place for these girls to work." Then a prince of the eastern provinces reopened a college of interior design because his daughter wanted to study it. In Nadia's years there she saw a complete regeneration of the program. When she graduated in 1989, she spoke, gave a 3D presentation, and had mothers coming up to thank her for giving their daughters the courage to establish themselves in business.

With Prince Walid she did a "stunning Internet cafe" with a family section, designed as "*mutawwa*-friendly," with little shells upstairs for four people and food, and in the center an open, tented structure. Bachelors were not allowed. Downstairs, however, became so "popular, trendy, trafficky" that the *mutawwa'in* closed the whole enterprise before they could regain their investment.

Nadia is distressed that there are 2,000 businesses owned by women in Riyadh, but only thirty-two of those women voted for the council of the chamber of commerce. Voting preoccupies her. She decided to run for municipal council in 2004, one of three women in the whole country. No males put forth platforms, but Nadia published one in detail. She was interviewed on Arabia TV, at an unprepared moment in a hot room, where she recalls complex accusatory questions from the interviewer. But he afterward complimented her on a "beautiful interview . . . about her public duty." Her positive energy was part of what drove Prince Mansour, the government spokesman on the matter, to defend the official position that women were *not allowed to run*. He had to concoct a logistical defense, since there existed no written religious principle against it.

When I interviewed Nadia, however, she remained disturbed over a subsequent TV interview with CNN ("Kingdom on the Brink," August 2004) in which she had unwisely come downstairs at home with her headscarf in her hand while the cameras were on. She faults herself for being too relaxed, feeling this was her own home, with her husband's permission to be interviewed, and with a new baby. She asked CNN to "give her a digital *hijab*," but they cut the interview down, left her in the uncovered moment, and included a cheeky-sounding remark that she had made about it. A male cousin in an eastern municipality summoned pressure to declare that she was no longer part of the family, but her father gave him a deterrent tongue-lashing.

Head-coverage easily becomes front-page news. When the prominent private investor Lubna Olayan spoke at the Jeddah economic forum, she stressed the need for private companies to build up training for women as well as men, toward the next generation of Saudi and Middle Eastern leaders. But this key message was lost in the fact that her cowl slipped as she spoke. Nimah Nawwab was there. She saw it and understood. "My hair is very soft; the cowl slips all the time." She is sorry that Lubna's definitions of issues and solutions were lost in the fact that her hair cover fell. It was not, as some said, intentional. Nimah says Lubna was trying to manage her papers and her contact with the audience, and "it just fell." And just that made headlines.

Nimah herself is audience-conscious, having published poetry for a broad public. She is descended from a line of Meccan scholars. In photos, her eyes are almondine, and eyebrows, dark and thick, appear as arcs unusually high above her eyes. She has had book signings at Jarir in Jeddah and across the U.S., culminating in Washington, D.C. Just the same, she does not agree with Dr. Monera al-Nahedh, another of "the drivers," who, as a sociologist, discourses on violence against Saudi women. I described Monera, gesturing at her *hijab* drawn down and her hair released, having a cup of tea with me in the dining room at my hotel. "I look at these men and women [in the dining room] and ask: do they know me? And what do they think and what will they say? . . . That is violence against me, just to be here and considered that way."

No, says Nimah, it is not "violence" just to be in the public eye. But there are precautions one must take, and resources one must develop. "I don't look around. I don't like to make eye contact. I don't worry about what they will say. I put myself out in writing." And only with poems will she go into an audience, eye to eye, for that is appropriate to poetry, as it is to business presentations.

"I think of myself as a humanist, not a feminist." The biggest obstructions for women in Saudi Arabia, from Nimah's humanist point of view, are guardianship and gender segregation. Guardianship above all, for it requires a woman to get paper permission from her father or elder brother even to go to college. She has written a poem, "Life Imprisonment," on that.[70] She also manifested her powers of communication on the subject by helping to advance a petition to Custodian/King Abdullah against the forced divorce of Fatima and Mansour Al-Timani. Engineered as it was by half-brothers of Fatima, who ignored the love between the two and their two infant children, the decree of divorce resulted in Fatima's remaining in jail with her nursing child rather than yielding to the intrusive guardianship which alleged inferior tribal status in her husband. Globally, over 1,000 signatures joined in support of Fatima and the priority of Islamic legal principles over tribal custom. Five years after the lower court decree, the Supreme Court of the Kingdom overruled it in 2010, allowing the family to be reunited.

Beyond confronting such obstacles, Nimah says, there are plenty of personal challenges for her and for other Saudi women: to be a super-daughter, super-mom, super-wife, and super-worker. To be a cultural ambassadress. To help her teenage daughter get into college, when even the 80th percentile may be denied a place. To come home from work (external relations for Aramco) and then do time-consuming cooking — Malaysian or Italian or Japanese — and lay a *spread* before her family.

Soad Dabbagh is a well-groomed and humorous woman of ageless vivacity. Her son, Achmed, having completed his studies, is in a private sales business. He was our chaperone, Arab style, as we lunched in the tent on the lawn of her gated estate. Lunch was at a Saudi hour, 2:30 to 5:00 p.m.

Soad, after marriage, had started a gift shop with silver as her first staple, but trying a new idea as well: examples of traditional Arab fabrics. She had a private bet with her husband whether the new idea would succeed or not. He, lamentably, died in 1987. She would have won the bet with her first

---

70. Another Saudi poetess has taken on religious *fatwas* directly in her art. Appearing completely veiled except for eye-slits on Abu Dhabi TV, Hissa Hillal won third prize ($800,000) in a regional Arabic poetry contest. See Quanta Ahmed, *The Huffington Post*, 29 Mar 10.

show of traditional clothing in 1988. That occasion had taken her four years of preparation, with permissions from religious authorities the greatest obstacle. They said such a show would be *haram.* "They are against beauty," she said. But she managed finally to bring it off, including the training of models to parade on a runway. Her scrapbook of the event is dazzling testimony for the profusion of tribal designs in Arabia, which she has researched in all regions. Now her stores, "Lamsa," are a success in several cities. They have survived *mutawwa'in* coming into the shops with threatening looks. They told her male salesmen that they must not smile at female customers, and wrote them up if they saw such a thing. "Where in the Qur'an," Soad asks, "does it say 'Don't smile'?" No, the Prophet says that being pleasant to another is a gift, and will be rewarded in heaven.

We dined on the carpeted floor of her tent, semi-recumbent on pillows. I remember particularly the *kunafa* cake for dessert, with *chai akra,* green tea, while smoking *shisha.* The smoking was a commonplace for Doughty 130 years ago and is still; but for one who grew up breathing the industrial particulates of Pittsburgh and who never used cigarettes, the experience was new: inhaling, through a long tube bedecked with knotted silks, a water-cooled smoke from dried fruit, honey, and tobacco.

The *ulama* and the *mutawwa'in* worry and fluster continually about corruptions of any kind. All lowerings of women's status, says Soad, the dark veilings and coverings, date from the Iranian revolution and Juhayman's invasion of the Great Mosque in Mecca. It was not so before that. Women in the South worked unveiled and wore hats against the sun. Some old women, said Achmed, even worked bare to the waist. Covering is not a matter of Islam, said both mother and son. Religious manipulation of politics produces it — as does political management of religion.

I reached Dr. Majedah Al Bessar, as agreed, by phone at home at eight in the morning, because we had not been able to coordinate a face-to-face meeting. She answered in a voice still husky with sleep, a voice that grew more engaging and animated throughout the call. She is a pediatrician who also treats adults. She has an M.A. in international health and is active in the Human Genome Project. In Saudi Arabia she confronts autism and attention deficit disorder, and applies behavioral medicine to the best of her ability. "It is very common here to see anxiety and panic disorder, as well as obsessive-compulsive disorder." These apparently arise to a great extent from performance anxiety, triggered by a high rate of unemployment and sharp competition for university education. She sees young men and women under the stress of finding a place in life. (She herself, still young, sounded stressed but cheerful to me.) "I give priority to males, because if the patient is female, she has to be accompanied by her sister or mother, has to have a driver, and is unwilling to have others know they have a problem."

Dr. Al-Bessar's father was originally Lebanese, and also a physician. Her mother comes from Jeddah, "where people are more accepting [than in Riyadh]." Her father died young, and her relations saw her as a twenty-year-old liability. "Let's get the only daughter married, because her father is sick." The husband they chose for her, originally Egyptian, was abusive. She had two sons by him, now teenagers, before she divorced him.

Another interviewee, Dr. Mishael Al-Hegelan, roughly the same youthful age as Dr. Al-Bessar, says the first female medical doctor appeared as recently as 1975. All her own patients would call her "sister" in a tribal way until three years ago, or would even learn her father's name in order to call her "daughter of x-x." But there have been some rapid changes in such matters, and they are calling her "doctor" now. Still, when she goes into a patient's room as senior authority, they will ask a younger male assistant for his opinion (who then asks *her*), and wait in the end for *his* approval. Male physicians themselves, however, come to understand females as co-workers.

Dr. Al-Bessar notes the recently increasing number of Saudi females in pediatrics, obstetrics, and gynecology. There is a female chairman of pediatric surgery, seen by some as a "fierce personality." The matter of female surgeons touched my experience of my daughter's recent liver transplant, from which I came to know two American women surgeons specializing in such procedures. Would that be likely in Saudi Arabia, say, thirty years from now? "I hope," she answered. "But I don't think so." The subject moved her to talk about special burdens in Saudi society: beyond obvious sexism and racism, it is highly constricted by tribalism. "Unless you are a *tribal person,* you can't lobby effectively for what you need." She knows a Syrian by birth, trained in Japan for liver transplant. She believes him a genius. But he can't find here anyone willing to help him, because he has no tribe. "Believe me, it's very painful. It is awful, awful." She worried about her sons, then fifteen and sixteen years old, and full of hope. But they may run into barriers not yet felt. If Saudi society were only tied up in sexism, "it would be rationalizable. But the tribal thing is beyond repair."

How long, she asks, can we go on expanding our contacts with other countries, *but not with ourselves?* Najdis don't even work well with Hejazis, let alone with the foreign-descended who are in tribal limbo. "My former boss is allegedly liberal." When he became a Minister, she asked him for a letter of reference based on her two years of experience with him, but "He denied it. I didn't ask for a promotion, not even a letter of recommendation, just a mere letter of reference. 'No!'" Why? "Just because he *can*. There is no *accountability*. The moral corruption is so deep. . . . Nobody has ever checked them. They think they have a *God-given* right to behave this way." And the poison is not merely male: "Female Najdis in the professions and in charity work exercise huge discrimination based on tribe and contacts."

How does a society of God-anointed tribes, I asked Majedah, keep its public peace? Just now, she answered, by keeping the stock market active, especially from 5:00 to 7:00 p.m. "People are frozen in front of TVs to race and chase after the stock market. It keeps them busy, hoping to improve their situation." Only 5 or 10 percent of the population is wealthy. "But others don't have a hope of change. . . . This is *not* a freedom-of-opportunity society. Or even a freedom of movement society. Only Egyptians and foreigners go to public parks. There are no entertainment places. Coffee shops, when they opened, were a brief success, yes, but they are fading now." She casually predicted a downward correction of the stock market by June or July (in which she was later proved correct by a 30 percent plunge in the Tadawul Index). "What then? They will still have to keep the people busy."

In the U.S. in 2001 she had taken Professor Ronald Heifetz's course on leadership at the Harvard Center for Public Leadership. Afterward, she was elected among the top ten by all 120 students in the class, as one destined to change the world. (When later I asked Heifetz himself about the vote, he said it was on who among fellow classmates had influenced others the most.) Dr. Al-Bessar, recalling a hothouse of ambitious talents, says, "Some of us got depressed and suicidal in that class." But her retrospect of Harvard is fond, and she clearly would like to change the world. "I have lots of love inside me. . . . I can do whatever it takes to make things better."

After Osama bin Laden's capers, however, the Saudi government put more restrictions on travel of its citizens. For those with no tribal inheritance, this was additionally tough, and especially hard on the growing numbers of working middle-class women. Dr. Al-Bessar speculates on learning French or Spanish for the sake of diversity. She respects women who have *not* traveled outside, who marry, earn a good income, and are happy. Might she marry a younger man, even if it were against the social grain? She could meet such men at conferences, but is not keen on attending them. "I wish I were married," she has said to a male colleague, "so I could [now] get sixty days' maternity leave." When she was in medical school and bore her two sons, she received only three days' leave for each.

There is a big gap, Majedah concluded, between education in Saudi Arabia, in which the levels are high, and its civilization, where levels are low. Thirty-five-year-olds in Lebanon, Kuwait, or Oman are much broader in outlook, while materialism and careerism possess Saudis. "They think they will be happy, but they will *not*. Because happiness comes from exploring your humanity." If she were in the U.K. or the U.S. or France, she thinks, she would have a more successful career, because people there are "less shy or ashamed."

Suddenly she spoke directly to me, about me. "You are lucky to be who you are. I would love to meet you." I said, sincerely, that I would love to meet her, too. But there wasn't time. Dr. Al-Bessar added me to her international list of impersonal correspondents, about forty people to whom she sent frequent impulsive generic e-mails about values: common-sense intercultural values of hospitality, kindness, and patience, often beautifully illustrated with unfolding flowers or other wonders of nature. Robert Fulgham kinds of values — everything we know, in every culture, we learned in kindergarten. Occasionally a raunchy-funny joke or cartoon was thrown in. And so our moving conversation idled down (for she did not respond to my responses), stopped, and became a passing illustration of what several interviewees told me in different ways: Saudi women find the Internet an especially appealing way to connect, isolated and marginalized as they are, or forced by the arbitrary regimen of their society to "disappear." But monitored as they might be, it seems best to keep even Internet communiqués impersonal. Linkedin.com a few years later showed Majedah still connected to twenty-five different groups.

Sheikh Culture, "The Smile," and the Family

Mustafa Guma, a big Sudanese with black skin and a grand smile, was my driver, in his overused 1999 Suburban. He re-identified for me the major landmarks of vast, flat Riyadh. "Used to be TV tower was tallest building.

Now is Kingdom Tower number one [a silver-reflector building nearly 1,000 feet tall, which looks like an enormous Danish modern bottle opener]. Faisaleya Tower is two [which resembles a multi-lit and pointed television tuning wand]. TV tower is three, water tower, four." The first two, at more than eighty stories, loom high, regarding each other at the two ends of an axis of the city's center. I was amazed that the water tower was still on the list. "Do you have big wells in Riyadh?" "No," Mustafa answered. "Pipelines. They pipe water from Jebel in East." He smiled broadly. "Sometimes work; sometimes don't."

My first target of the day was the King Abdul Aziz Museum, huge caverns of marble with endless banners. A suave young guide in a white thobe pointed out Ibn Saud's three automobiles on display. The oldest, he said, was a black and white Pierce. "Pierce-Arrow," said I. "My grandfather owned one. And my great-uncle, too."

"*Cool*," he murmured — the only moment in the Kingdom when I impressed a young Arab.

After he floated away, Mustafa took over. On the grand walks of granite and sandstone with ranks of guards and keepers, in three and a half hours, we saw one Western man with two women. No Arabs. Saudi monarchy builds monuments to itself which no one attends.

The annual cultural fair of the Kingdom, however, was highly populated. The Janadreia festival was launched by the present king as crown prince in 1985, based on camel races, with horse races since added. In acres of displays, I gravitated to tents of the Educational Ministry. Every major educational planning document for fifty years was on shelf display, with all archetype models of primary schools. For a new one in Riyadh I saw a gray space nearly as large as the rest of the grounds. "What is that?" Parking lots for the staff, and for the girls' buses. Nearby, a separate model for a boys' school, with lots of playground space. I pointed back to the girls' school. "Where are the girls' athletic facilities?" They shook their heads. "Women need sports, too, don't they?" A bearded young man in brown, who had gone to a British college, answered me: "Not here."

Several other young men trailed along, some of them taking continuous videos of my cultural ambling and inane remarks for a course on TV. Finding no chalk at a whiteboard, I did 7^3 by teacherly gesturing with my finger — 343. They seemed to appreciate the invisible drama. I put myself to sleep that night by multiplying seven to the sixth power, which came out in my drowsy head as 117,649 — an index of my fatigue.

An exceptional effort has gone into Saudi Arabian education across the last fifty years, building something out of nothing. But I was conscious, from global newspaper reports, of biases in Saudi textbooks. First-graders are taught that "every religion other than Islam is false," according to the Center for Religious Freedom in Washington, which has translated twelve Saudi history and religion textbooks.[71] Since 9/11, in response to internal and external criticism, the monarchy has made reform of schools a priority. But Islam is at the core of public education, and occupies one-third to one-quarter of primary class time and one-sixth in high school. What will ever be said about Christianity, Judaism, Hinduism, Buddhism, and atheism — let alone Shi'ite and Sufi beliefs ("polytheism") and Sunni beliefs that are non-Wahhabi (which deviation can also lead to charges of "polytheism")? I might wish that the Prophet be quoted in his more forbearing mode, as in the Qur'an, 2:256, "There is no compulsion in religion." But the Saudi state does not sponsor interfaith discussion.

The annual report of the U.S. Commission on International Religious Freedom for May 2006 charged that there exists in the Kingdom a systematic theme of "hatred toward unbelievers" in a system that educates five million youth in 25,000 schools. The Department of State's eight "Countries of Particular Concern" worldwide included Saudi Arabia and Iran, pared from the Commission's own list of eleven, which included Pakistan, and its watch list of seven more, which included Indonesia. The Commission's report is studded with UN dicta and dogma, and concludes with a quote from the UN Special Rapporteur on the Freedom of Religion specifying nine different discriminations, stereotypes, ostracisms, and attacks on dignity which could undermine the rights of women. Religious freedom, in short, may not include indifference to the status of females.

The Saudi government in 2004, responding to such pressures, did create a Human Rights Commission to help assure, among other objectives, secure and diverse private worship. But in a public interview in October 2005, King Abdullah said that to allow non-Muslims places of public worship in Saudi Arabia "would be like asking the Vatican to build a mosque inside of it." There is no such pithy royal rejoinder to the Commission's urgings that the Kingdom stop funding religious propaganda abroad until it is satisfied that such activity does not promote hatred, intolerance, and human rights violations.[72] Despite bilateral understandings in 2006, and

71. *New York Times*, 24 May 06, p. A10.

72. Report of the United States Commission on International Religious Freedom, 2006 (online); inter alia, pp. 87-88, 190-97, 250. Quotation of King Abdullah, p. 193. Nina Shea, the

royal adherence to the UN Declaration of Human Rights, the Commission in 2010 found a rigid religious atmosphere still marked by prosecution for apostasy, blasphemy, witchcraft, and sorcery and by hate-preaching directed at minorities.[73]

At the Janadreia, an interesting primary school exhibit was a display called "Smile." I talked about it later with Dean Haifa and asked her if Americans smile too much. My further question, which she intuited, was why do Saudis smile so seldom? The primary school program is a good idea, Haifa said. Instead of scowling or averting your face — which she acted out — Bedouins have to be shown, or taught, how to get beyond being Bedouins. It's a hard life, she said. "You check *everybody* out," she stressed, making sure they are not camel thieves, before welcoming them into assured space. Automatic welcome with a smile, I realized, is a special correlate of affluent American space. Cloistered gender-space, a Saudi realm of infinite ingredients, allegedly justified by Islam, is beyond ready register by Western eyes.

Well after Ibn Saud's Pierce-Arrow era, automobiles began arriving in number in the 1960s. Now they appear definitive even of Bedouin rural life — white Nissan and Toyota pickup trucks are used in tending camels, cattle, and chores. As for the capital, Riyadh is a car city, laid out to grow in wide geometric grids.

As Mustafa and I come south from the Janadreia in winter's early dusk, the temperature drops fast from the sixties to the forties Fahrenheit. High winds snap festival banners and set off small booms in tent roofs. In the fast-fading light, dust rolls off the desert plains in waves like seaspray colored beige-gray. Along the roadside, piles of building materials giving no clue as to what might be built: sands of deep red, and tan, and, rarely, almost white; and assorted sizes of gravels. Then, suddenly, there are no human piles to see, only dunes, shifting heaps of desert, blown down, up, around.

---

major author of the report, supplies the biographical facts that she is a Dame of the Knights of Malta and holds an honorary degree from Alvernia Franciscan College in Reading, Pennsylvania. A former commissioner, Dr. Khaled Abou El Fadl, recently complained of the "rather suffocating" view "that victims of religious discrimination are invariably Christian."

73. USCIRF Annual Report 2010; Countries of Particular Concern, Saudi Arabia, 29 Apr 10.

Randomness then gives way again to arbitrary regularities, even square miles, of straight roads lined with street lamps unlit, having no houses or offices yet on which to bestow their beams. Lavish roads, fueled by oil to carry oil-propelled machines, disavow the desert. They run rectangular because the terrain, and perhaps the religion, too, does not encourage circles, curves, and roundabouts.

Saudi leadership for a century has been inducing Bedouins to settle down. But just as the rock writings of Arabia in pre-cuneiform characters are still unintelligible to Arab and Northern scholars, so the codes of Transatlanta are unintelligible to Bedouins as well as to many sheikhs. The single greatest penetration is in the term "okay," which at every level of this society is added to Arabic, the language pure and unsurpassable, yet in need of a term for easy, informal assent.

But "okay" is only a beginning. What will become of this Islamic society for whom thousands of native citizens holding American and European Ph.D.s cherish some non-Islamic and supra-Islamic goals of social development, and strategies to seek them? A post-Bedouin society may teem with Caterpillar tractors, but continue nomadic by nostalgia. It remains most respectful of those kings and sultans who know how to sit in their tents, receiving petitions with dignity, while mistrustful of those who generate them. Everybody has an appetite for democracy, but nobody knows the recipe.

Such a society is unlikely to be seized by any such outlandish idea as a Civil Rights Act, for its legislative body is appointed by the king on nomination from princes and sheikhs, and functions as a "Consultative Council." Saudi society will move forward in small publicly noted precedents such as in Janadreia in 2006, when boys and girls were gathered on the same public stage for the first time, to sing to the king. There is no social basis for understanding what Indonesia's learned Minister of Defense, Juwono Sudarsono, voiced in his blog at the time of observing the sixty-first anniversary of the Indonesian Constitution: "Eclecticism and syncretism [are] the keys to healthy pluralism and mutual tolerance."[74]

"There is no law against it." This spuriously hospitable utterance, favored by Saudi officials in power, sounds indulgent of what is asked, but requires

---

74. Juwono Sudarsono, blog site, 18 June 06, "Debate on Pancasila."

the asker to generate all the traction herself. There is no law against women driving vehicles, but neither is there a law for it, nor any body of regulation to shape such a practice in the absence of law. There is, however, a vivid precedent of forty-seven women imprisoned, publicly scorned by mufti as "shameless," and fired from their jobs for their unrehearsed impulse. Such a precedent infiltrates social memory with the presumption that women driving are "Satanic." And while "Satan" may be pushed slowly into technological retreat (once he was associated with cars themselves — now only with women driving them), and eventually into social retreat (one woman already flies a prince's private airplane), there remains a small body of men who define what is Satanic and what is Allah-blessed; what is *haram,* forbidden, and what is *halal,* permissible. With common law nonexistent, regulation amorphous, and precedent empty, the governor of changes is a male-assembled ad hoc amalgam of Qur'an, hadith, and *shari'a.* And because the Prophet Muhammad, unlike King Ibn Saud, did not own a Pierce-Arrow, it is hard for the sheikhs to assume bi-gendered legitimacy around owning and using such petrol-consuming machines.

A major organizer among "the drivers," Madeha al-Ajroush, sees far beyond the sheikh/royal and class/clan structures. She hears and observes in Saudi Arabia what she knows is universal — the tendency of individuals to over-infer personal limits from what they see around them, and to over-apply restrictions on their own personal growth as a consequence. Although she knows that such psychodynamics exist everywhere, she feels that their intensity in modern Saudi Arabia is so strikingly high as to warrant a special term. I suggested one: "self-inflicted oppression." She liked it, and said she might use it.

Nearly two decades after the famous initiative of "the drivers" and the sharp retributions they suffered for it, Madeha sees them as "mostly in a wonderful place." The stigma is still upon them, and none are being given any leading government positions. But they are major "social drivers" now, as NGO leaders and university professors. Some of the group founded "Mothers of Riyadh," an advocacy for needy and neglected individuals. Three core members of the drivers are founders of "Family Safety," an organization against violence within families, for which the king has accorded them headquarters at King Fahd Hospital. "Women are only verbally violent," says Madeha. Female violence against males is 2 percent of the total, she said.[75]

75. Martin S. Fiebert reports contrariwise, on phenomena almost entirely collected in

Looking back, Madeha recognizes, laughing, that "we didn't make a big change." They had sought discussion with the king and queen of the struggles of Riyadh women, but were denied it. Because they believed that a letter would be only filed, and they must do something visible, they *drove*. The government knew that driving was not against the religion or culture. "So they decided to ostracize us . . . to disseminate our names and our husbands' names all over the Kingdom at Friday mosque assemblies." They discredited women who want change as "prostitutes."

All the husbands of 1990 supported their wives, Madeha recalls. Many fathers did not. Her own husband stood defending her while her father attacked her. I had rarely heard a more vivid instance in which change begins, is registered, and resisted, all through clear conflict between generations.

Khalid Al-Awwad combines reserve and cordiality in quiet mastery. He has a wife and five children, and an American doctorate in the sociology of organization. In his mid-forties, he is a vice chairman of the Social and Labor Committee of the Majlis al-Sura, the royally appointed Consultative Council. Of this body of 150 members, 103 have Ph.D.s, which is almost certainly the highest component of educational attainment of any parliament in the world. Khalid was at pains to assure me that his Council is recognized by Arab, Muslim, and world parliamentary organizations, even though its members are not — he inserted, parenthetically, *yet* — elected.

Khalid is, in Saudi terms, a highly promising young man. In the Ministry of Education for a dozen years, where he rose to Deputy Minister, he saw the need for and established an educational planning section. He got himself sent to Harvard for six weeks, then dispatched colleagues there. Together they developed an educational strategic plan. Khalid enjoys such

---

English-language cultures. From a wide array of journals on aggression, violence, family, and psychiatry yielding an aggregate sample size of 221,300, he concludes that "Women are as physically aggressive, or more aggressive, than men in relationships with their spouses or male partners." *References Examining Assault by Women on Their Spouses or Male Partners: An Annotated Bibliography* (updated May 08). www.csulbedu/rimfiabot/assault.htm. Beyond Fiebert's bibliography, he has said that "women are more likely to be injured, but not a lot more," because they use weapons in domestic disputes, while men use physical strength. Men, he adds, are more likely now to admit when they are victims because the Western culture of patriarchy is breaking down (*Los Angeles Times*, 10 April 02, p. B4). The global epidemiology of domestic abuse is too complex and sharply contested to pursue further here.

teamwork. "Planning, vision, forecasting, all are big needs here." With such convictions he went to his minister.

Khalid: "You need to give me ten years, a budget, and requirements for spending."

Minister: "But we don't know future budgets. Oil revenues are unpredictable."

Khalid: "That's no excuse. We have to *plan* and adjust continually to changing reality."

His inability to get this point across disturbed Khalid. "Unless we have a national vision on more than the economy, unless we have it in education and health, and we share it . . . then what is the use?" Imitating Malaysia with its 20/20 plan, the Kingdom had a conference on the year 2020, but limited it to the economy. Khalid worries that oil cartels over-control all decisions. In the Consultative Council, he is in charge of working on a law for civil society organizations — for Qur'anic NGOs, and NGOs in culture, health, environment, everything. "We need government, business, and civil society [working together] in our future."

Khalid had lots further to teach me, especially on family in Saudi Arabia. Here all social phenomena are based on family, which in its largest extended concept is called "tribe." Arabian tribalism, he says, has been shaped by Islam, and by an environment whose basic dynamic was nomad-sedentary trade: Bedouins bartering with fabrics from their animals for dates raised by farmers. The Islamic dimension stresses obligations to parents and the shame to leave any parent in poverty. Children not only (mostly) enjoy that relationship, but they believe they will be rewarded for good Qur'anic behavior. The *zakat,* obligatory giving of one-fortieth of one's liquid wealth each year, begins with giving to make sure of parental security. The glory of this system, in which Khalid rejoices, is that among Riyadh's population of 4.5 million, only fifty persons, he said, are in nursing homes for the elderly. As an American, I could barely believe it, deluged as we are with facts about care and uncare for the elderly. For instance, 43 percent of Americans who turned 65 in 1990 will enter a nursing home at some time in their life. Just 25 percent of Americans will die at home surrounded by friends and family, although 70 percent wish to do so.

The strong recent movement to focus on the Saudi Arabian nuclear family does not mean ignoring the extended family. It means getting out of the parental house, but living nearby and visiting parents once or twice a week. Khalid instanced his own family, whose traditional center is in Diriya, where Abdul Aziz and his men thrashed the Rashid holders of the fort in 1902 and restored the emirate and flag of the Saud family, as in the eighteenth century. Yesterday afternoon (Thursday), Khalid says, the cousins of his father had their standing reunion, in which thirty of them meet every two or three months. Then at 6:00 p.m., all of his mother's children gathered, as they do weekly, with her: seven brothers and sisters, including him. At 8:00 p.m., Khalid dines with his own wife and five children. Today (Friday), and every Friday after midday prayer, all the family visit an uncle who, since the death of Khalid's father, is now the family patriarch. "We (Saudi society) are still very strong socially. Kinship is very strong. Very warm and generous."

As for his own children, Khalid's growth ideal is "to *protect* them from media and outside influences. . . . Remember, you are providing society with *good* or *bad* citizens." Among their five children are two sets of twins. His wife, Mona, has a full-time job giving them all love and education. It's okay, he thinks, if mothers go to work. But what, he asks, is the social gain or loss if ill-educated housemaids — he mentioned Indonesians or Sri Lankans — are brought in to take care of the kids at home?

The problem of female mobility — common globally, one assumes, to growing middle and upper-middle classes, and severe for the working poor — has a special Saudi component, dramatized by Haifa al-Lail at the Jeddah Economic Forum of 2006. There used to be, at such conferences, nearly complete visual and other gender segregation. But at this one, although seated separately, men and women were allowed to see each other through a glass partition between them. Haifa and her planners were proud of this "big advance." In her own paper in the gender session, she nevertheless focused on "glass walls and brick ceilings," of which the latter are important, and occlusive. Her point: women, including mothers, cannot see what they may aspire to, and therefore they don't know *how* and *where* and in *what ways* to try to grow. That brick above them must give way first to glass and then eventually to open air. Education is critical in giving women ascent, and sight of what they may rise to.

Okay, said Khalid. He accepts the metaphor. He does not argue against vision and opportunity for women. But, he insists, "Even for *men* there is a brick ceiling. What shall we be after twenty, thirty, fifty years? There is no national *vision*." And even where there is a national plan, nothing is done to make it happen. Khalid generously hosted a dinner for me three days later, where these questions could be pursued with legislators and with their chair, who is also a member of the Majlis al-'Ulama', the nation's supreme council of religious figures.

174

The Chair is Sheikh Salih bin Hamid. His red and white headscarf projects well over his forehead and temples, giving the impression of deeply recessed eyes behind his spectacles. His voice, firm but not especially resonant, was tired from a day begun in prayer at 5:00 a.m. His religious prominence is such that he is one of five imams in the kingdom who rotate in leading *khutba* prayer at the Grand Mosque in Mecca. Today, Sunday, is his day for holding public audience. About twenty-five people come each week with special requests and seeking opinions.

Sheikh Salih's hands are expressive. The fingers bend backward at will, conveying a sense that he sees in a curvilinear way what he nevertheless voices in mono-planar fashion. One of the two other young Asura members present said they regard him as a "liberal." What they would mean by "conservative," I did not have time to ask.

Dinner was preceded by discussion of the controversy over the Danish cartoons blaspheming the Prophet. This occupied us during passing of Arabian coffee in small cups, a manservant holding three in each hand: the guest chooses one and he receives from a long-spouted pot a yellow-ochre brew with cardamom (or alternatively, saffron) in greater proportion than coffee, whose Western variants are considered much too strong. To allay the bitterness of even this mild coffee, we had a choice of ginger, in four-ounce studded cylindrical glasses, or cubes of sugar wrapped in colored paper, or packets of Tropicana Slim.

Sheikh Salih launched a polite but pointed inquiry of me on the blasphemous cartoons. I cited and expanded on my (not printed) letter of objection to the Philadelphia *Inquirer*. That, apparently satisfying, led to a broad examination of cultures, in which the sheikh averred the negative cumulative impact of the Crusades, the Orientalists, media emphases, and curricular biases in Europe and America. I replied with good cheer that I had no part in the Crusades; I distinguished myself both from Northern Orientalists and from Edward Said's more extreme objections to them; and I observed that I had tried to counter my own urban press, which masticates controversy and spits it into the open maw of the public. I took responsibility for my share of our collegiate curriculum in its deficiencies, while declaring pride that it includes not only the humanities, of which religion is just one, but the natural sciences and social sciences.

This exchange seemed sufficient to aerate the cultural atmosphere. Khalid's brother and twin pre-pubertal boys then passed around incense — charred wood on coals in a censor gives off aromatic smoke for the guests to waft, with both hands, into their eager nostrils.

Dinner consisted of full plates served heaping to the diners: a salad of variegated greens; dumplings of several colors, shapes, and contents; and mounds of chicken and beef with rice and string pasta. Dessert, in due time, was a choice of one or more of a crème caramel, a black forest cake, and a heavy chiffon pie.

Eating allowed me to broach the subject of women's driving. Sheikh Salih proceeded into a conscientious procedural reply. As a social question, it was a matter neither initiated by the king nor raised within the Consultative Council itself. But because of its religious import, it had been considered and determined earlier by the Council of Ulama. The cabinet member who had recently spoken on it should have forborne from his remark, and confined himself publicly to a notation only of where the matter, in procedure, actually stood. (Which, I thought but did not say, was a ruling of the Council of Ulama in the time when Sheikh Bin Baz chaired, a blind man who had never held a wheel and was chauffeured wherever he needed.)

I asked: Are decisions of the Ulama not reviewable and subject to change by its own selfsame Council? The Sheikh gave a blurred answer, and his Secretary General apologized for the fatigue inherent in his long day — now approaching eighteen hours.

He and other guests launched one more query before departure, and much seemed to hang on it. Why had I come to Saudi Arabia, and what did I think of it? I answered with late evening candor. I had decided, for my book, to "throw myself into Saudi Arabia," even though I had "dreaded it," not only on my first visit, but this, my second. That remark raised eyebrows. But my negative emotions, I said, were being drained away by conversations such as this one. It evoked in me an "I and Thou" kind of understanding. I cited the great Jewish scholar, Martin Buber, to convey his sense of mutual spiritual anthropology and, distinct from dissection of issues, the discovery of souls. Solemn nodding suggested understanding and gratified agreement.

We rose and shook hands and wrapped up loose ends. I was happy but for one omission. I had met three of Khalid's seven brothers, but none of his four sisters. I had met his two sons, but none of his daughters. I had enjoyed his three male guests, but no females. I had been served by numerous men, but with no woman apparent. Most notable for me in absence, although present in felt graces, was Khalid's wife, Mona. In this long and weightily sociable evening, women were completely invisible.

176

For propelling the modern development of Saudi Arabia, oil has been the indispensable fuel. But the piston chamber is pre-modern: the structure formed by pact between the first Ibn Saud and Muhammad Ibn Abdul Wahhab two and a half centuries ago. And the ignition spark that must be struck remains the most literal and puritanical in all of Sunni Islam.

Neither democracy nor freedom for women is natural to such an engine. King Abdullah is considered relatively broad-minded, but his edict of succession issued in 2006 aims to guarantee dynastic continuity, and not a constitutional monarchy in Thai or British style. His brother Prince Nayef, the powerful Minister of the Interior, stands strongly against electing the Majlis Al-Shura, the appointed Consultative Council. In such circumstances, it is wisely remarked that if in the future the electoral principle would ever take hold, what would ensue is not an Arabic-speaking version of the Swedish parliament, but a Sunni analogue to the theocratically marked legislature in Shi'ite Iran.

For women, then, there are no natural advocates or forums. Women are expected to act as a visible symbol of the monarch's piety.[76] Lawyers, lawmakers, and judges are all agents of that piety. The case of "the girl from Qatif," a nineteen-year-old Shi'ite, illustrates the point. Having married, she met a former suitor to retrieve from him a photograph of herself. A gang of seven young men abducted them and raped her fourteen times, making videotapes on mobile phones. Four of them also raped and videotaped her ex-suitor. The men were given sentences ranging from ten months to five years in prison. She and the ex-suitor, also treated as sexual offenders, were sentenced to two months in prison and ninety lashes. In an appellate hearing, all sentences — of rapists and also of victims — were roughly doubled: hers to six months and two hundred lashes. International outrage was instant, and helped carry the matter to the king. Even George Bush weighed in, observing that if such a thing happened to one of his daughters, he would be "angry" with a government that did not protect the victim. King Abdullah ultimately pardoned the young woman and the ex-suitor, and set in motion a judicial inquiry. The inquiry has not surfaced yet, but the case itself threw open every major contradiction in Saudi society and law for global inspection.[77]

76. ". . . visible symbol of the monarch's piety": For this quotation I am indebted to Rula Jurdi Abisaab, review of Eleanor Abdella Doumato, *Getting God's Ear: Women, Islam, and Healing in Saudi Arabia and the Gulf* (New York, Columbia University Press, 2000). The review was emailed to me by Nimah Nawwab, 19 Feb 07.

77. Lacey, *Inside the Kingdom,* pp. 306-15; *The Economist,* 14 Nov 07, p. 52; Abeer Mishkas,

The Identity of God

Life in Muslim nations challenges the Western believer or seeker. T. E. Lawrence rejected his parents' evangelical enthusiasm, and gave such fervor as he had to the Arab revolt. Across its two years, Lawrence only prayed once, a sham to mislead Turks who had his men under surveillance. His literary forebear, the explorer C. M. Doughty, developed his thoughts to a point summed by his biographer as "deep, but agnostic, reverence for religious creeds." Doughty himself said he could have been a disciple of Confucius, but never of Mohammed. It would abrogate Reason to accept that "fatal Arabian's solemn Fools' Paradise."[78]

"Who are the greater Fools?" is often an underlying question for the religious seeker. Laura Collins created her own successful business, Saudi Solutions Consulting, with an eminent partner and clients. She was born of an American with a Vietnamese wife, which mother divorced four times altogether, including twice from Laura's father. She then came and joined Laura's Arabian household as the second divorced mother-in-law in residence, for Islamic and Saudi duty had already required Laura to take in her husband's mother. Laura, when I interviewed her, had four children, ages two to ten.

Her capacities to enjoy variety, to tolerate strife, and to find her own gravity of conviction all emerged early in the American Catholic schooling her father thrust on her. She says she wrote herself out of religion classes with essays against praying to Jesus. "If Jesus was God, why would he allow himself to die? Why pray to this bloody naked man to take my sins away? It just didn't make sense to me."

She thought, "Maybe God doesn't exist at all. . . . But I got through the agnostic phase. I felt there must be something more. Look at the stars! . . . Look at the vastness of the universe. [While camping] I heard the wolves howling and saw the stars, and said I can't be given this brain for no reason."

In college she met a Saudi, her future husband, whom she knew for five years before marrying him. "He had one God. And his prophets included Jesus. The One God had Bible, Talmud, and Qur'an. I always considered myself logical, and this made sense, while Catholicism was all over

---

29 Nov 07, www.ordoesitexplode.com; Abdullah Shihri, Associated Press in Riyadh, *The Guardian*, 18 Dec 07.

78. D. G. Hogarth, *The Life of Charles M. Doughty* (Garden City, New York, Doubleday, Doran & Co., 1929), pp. 202, 169, 133.

the place." Still it was eight years before she converted. "Five prayers a day, fasting . . . hajj, alms, that's a lot of stuff. Once in Islam, if apostate, you are condemned to death. I liked my wine, pork chops and ham. [But I said] 'All right, God, I'll take it easy. I believe in all your prophets. . . . It took me a long time to give up the good stuff . . . [and] to learn how to pray, to give up the drinking, to put on the *hijab*. But *Alhamdulillah!* It comes. . . . I teach the kids how. It's still a hard path; you struggle with yourself. But now my dad gives me space and respects me for it."

Some things still trouble her. Why a black *abaya*, like a solar panel absorbing sunlight; why not white or pink? Why cover the face and hands when the Prophet never required it? Why let prisoners vote and deny the vote to women? Around the rest of the world prisoners cannot vote, but women *can* vote. Why let prisoners out to become *mutawwa'in*, like the one who struck her with a stick going around the Ka'aba: "'Woman, cover your face or get out of here!' I was really *mad*, but I worked out of it."

Her Vietnamese mother felt very much at home when she moved to Saudi Arabia — seeing sisters and brothers taking care of each other and of their old father. Her Asian values were realized far better than in America. As for Laura's father, he recently married another Vietnamese in Washington, D.C. Attending the ceremony as a Muslim, Laura felt "out-of-body, almost sacrilegious." She was given a speech to read the night before the wedding, but found she had to hand it over to an uncle. "I'm really *sorry!* I just couldn't give honor to any other God in the speech. . . . But there was my Dad, burning incense, bowing to bowls of fruit, leaving perfectly good food to rot before a manmade statue. . . . It was really funky! I felt I had nothing to say but (laughing) 'Congratulations, Dad!'"

Laura identifies with Muslim women everywhere who are cross-taxed with business demands, duties at home, and campaigns for rights. "But we need to pause" — and this is true of women everywhere, of whatever religion — "and ask what is really important? Our family, husband, God, children, and the poor. We must not forget that."

Tanya Hsu, born English, married a Chinese-American and raised two sons with whom she stays in close contact after her divorce. In the Kingdom of Saudi Arabia she feels she has found a kin-culture, that of the Najdis. "They are taller, more dignified than the Hejazis," who are a mix of traders and stayers-after-the-hajj, envious of the style of Riyadh and the royal family. "Coming from England, I see Najdis as extremely polite, putting others ahead of themselves, very hospitable, while remaining very private. . . . Having lived in the U.S. for twenty years, I was accused of arrogance when I was trying to be polite. Then I understood that the Najdis are well-mannered and gracious in an English way. . . . I realized, when I wept on return, landing at the airport, that *this is my culture*." And, she carefully posits, this culture that she loves is a Wahhabi culture.

Tanya sharply distinguishes among controversial Saudi elements. Osama bin Laden was a wealthy Najdi grown violent under the influence of Ayman al-Zawahiri, who intruded the politics of the Muslim Brotherhood (not Wahhabi). Bin Laden did not live in the past; he lived in a technological future in which he included equality for women. Salafis wish to return the present to the seventh century, the time of the Prophet and his companions. Some are violent; some are pacific. (I chimed in here with like distinctions between salafis and violent militants as made by Sidney Jones regarding Southeast Asia.[79]) A true *mutawwa,* of the circle from which Tanya draws her closest friends, honors in clothing and style the life of the Prophet. Men of that group dress in short thobe and long beard and do not wear a band in their headscarf. They are aware that the Prophet said the beard should only be a "fistful"; but long beards, she says, they choose as a cultural option. These purists she cherishes. While not despising the *mutawwa'in,* those of the guardians of vice and virtue who serve as religious police, she implies strong class and educational distinctions between them and her social circle.

There is no such thing as "Wahhabi religion," Tanya asserts, just as there is no religion called "Branch Davidian." Both are journalistic descriptions. "Wahhabism" arose as a term of contempt from the Ottomans, who had to contend with them for control of Mecca and Medina. The Ikhwan, as she sees them, were not truly Wahhabi either, but pure Bedouin, fierce tribal warriors that Abdul Aziz picked as his fighting force for years, until he had to defeat and dismantle them.

What about Muhammad Ibn 'Abd al-Wahhab himself, then? "There is no difference between 'Abd al-Wahhab and Jesus Christ. 'Abd al-Wahhab destroyed idols and ransacked temples where they were buying and selling goods — what Christian heroes such as Martin Luther have done — stopped the cheating, lying, prostitution, gambling outside the gates of Mecca."

79. "Indonesia: Why Salafism and Terrorism Mostly Don't Mix," International Crisis Group (Brussels), Indonesia Backgrounder, online report of 13 Sept 04 (42 pp. printout).

The same way, I asked, that Juhayman, with his Ikhwan background, tried to do in 1979? No, she answered. Juhayman was very different — also influenced by the Muslim Brotherhood from Egypt, and strongly anti-royal-family. Tanya's Wahhabi, I began to see, were definitely not Bedouin. They were not international Islamists either, but, as religious royalists, might be comfortable with aristocratic Brits.

With these several religio-cultural identities scattered on the table of discussion, I wished to know how, in Tanya's estimation, a pure Wahhabi would behave. With a genius for timing, just before I had to depart, she got me invited to dinner by her archetypal Wahhabi prince.

Our host was His Highness Prince Nayef bin Sultan bin Fawwaz Al-Sha'lan. The hour of his dinner, after 9:00 p.m., reminded me of social and business schedules of Spain and Argentina. The hours of 2:00-5:00 p.m. are devoted to siesta, after which shops reopen and social gears resume their mesh, with the variant here that the last two of the five daily prayers consume parts of late day and early night hours. The Prince's meal itself did not begin until after eleven, at which time he distributed the six Colombians, Venezuelans, and Spaniards also present — and happy to be in the company of a royal and learned Muslim — at the farther ends of his long narrow dining table. This was slightly bent at the center like an archer's bow, and looked out at a swimming pool. His own place was in the middle, at the archer's palm, as in old refectory tables that can be seen in the American Southwest. Tanya he placed on his right, me on his left, and the Hispanologues to the lengths of the bow. Spanish is among his tongues, but so is a fluent, precise English, which he announced would be the language of the evening. It is also a major language of his study of the Torah, the Bible, and the Qur'an, volumes of which were at hand.

Arriving at the "palace," which Tanya was happy to call it, had been like entering a rich gated residence in Euro-America, with driver stopping under the porte-cochere. The Prince himself, with an attending servant or two, came out and amiably shook our hands. He wore a white headscarf. His short beard and moustache were stylishly and closely trimmed. His build was slight; his manner intense; his eyes, large, untender, unaggressive. He is a thinker. I learned very little about him except that he had declined posts in the government, and has owned various businesses — banking, information technology, and media — as well as an Arabian horse farm. He did disclose that he had simultaneously earned doctorates in international relations from Princeton and in engineering from the University of Miami. I remarked that such a feat deserved recognition in the Guinness Book of World Records — to which he mildly replied, yes, he had been noted there at the time as the youngest double doctorate-holder in the world. One private query established that he had not had boyhood instruction in Islam, but had been educated in Catholic schools. At what age, I wanted to ask him, did you first immerse yourself in Islam? But he was not taking questions.

Before the Hispanic expats came, Prince Nayef discoursed with Tanya and me on a long L-shaped sofa. He sat at the angle of the L with a multi-extension telephone beside him and a mobile one in his pocket. Before him was a strange little plastic table with legs of jagged blue ice. Upon it lay what looked like the helmet decoration of a Roman centurion, and two fat sculpted peanuts about a foot long. The giant peanuts were, I suppose, bronze, but the luxury of the surroundings and the headgear guarding them suggested to my pliant imagination that they were peanuts of gold.

Talking with the prince, my own appreciation of Muhammad Ibn 'Abd al-Wahhab took leaps ahead. Nayef has thought through the oneness of the Qur'anic God and His subordinate prophets to a point of apparent seamlessness, which allows him to expect the return of Jesus at the end of this world — from the heavenly company in which only the Prophet Muhammad is more intimate with Allah.

On Judgment Day, across the bridge to Paradise, some will streak like lightning — as the prince intoned the lesson — and some will roll like thunder, some will clump like camels, and others will walk and crawl. Those who have not earned Islamic heaven will fall off the bridge into eternal fire. But, he stressed, God, having sent down among us one mercy which can be split into trillions, has in reserve ninety-nine more mercies to dispense if he wishes.

Across the evening, Nayef's discourse privileged Islam to a point that began to be dismissive of Christian belief, which he called "Paulism," or "Pauloismo," to some agreement from the Hispanics. At a certain point I made a simple declaration for myself, quoting Jesus on loving God with heart, soul, mind, and strength; and your neighbor as yourself.[80] Nayef congratulated me, "You are a good Muslim." That is because all of us are born Muslims, he said, and the essence of faith is love of God, which means good deeds for his sake. Be warned, however, that if you know how to become a better Muslim and don't choose that way, you are in deep jeopardy.

80. Matthew 22:34-40; Mark 12:28-34; Luke 10:25-28.

The prince demonstrated his command of scripture by translating at sight from an Arabic version of the four Gospels, while then handing me an English version and directing me to read chosen verses from St. Matthew. He intended to contrast two selections in particular — verses almost adjacent to each other. In one, Jesus calls Peter "the Rock" upon which he will build his church (Matthew 16:18). In the other, Peter entreats him to power, but Jesus says, "Get behind me, Satan!" (Matthew 16:23). Here, Rock; there Satan? Nayef invited us all to be as incredulous as he was. "Rock" one moment; "Satan" the next? "Doesn't that prove that Jesus was a schizophrenic?"

The Prophet, of course, enjoins against criticizing other religions. But to my host I only observed that Jesus might speak differently to the same man in wholly different situations. Nayef, I thought, wanted Jesus to be as consistent as his own tightly engineered Islam, or to forfeit divinity. I protested it was a mechanical requirement to make two utterances square with each other when they were part of a circle. Nayef, however, brushed aside objections.

I found later occasion to make two further forays, both against Nayef's interruptions. At the table I said that the Jesus I treasure is the person who, incredibly for his times, a man and a Jew, asks a Samaritan woman for water. A needy request of a woman, and of a despised Samaritan, shows a man who does not recite by-laws, but reads souls. Nayef changed the subject. He did not mention anyone or anything feminine all evening.

To the prince's hard drill on the Oneness of God, I had agreeably assented. I felt I must venture the assertion that Jesus and the Holy Spirit were manifestations of that One. Nayef responded by scorning a "triune God." I put out three fingers of my left hand and swatted them out of sight with my right. "'Triune' sounds like a fork with three tines. But God is One," I insisted. I sounded dogmatic to myself, and only much later found an essay in a "Common Word" exchange which describes One God, beyond number, internally differentiated into divine trinity.[81]

In sheer volume of exposition and declaration, Nayef was probably 80 percent of the evening's voices and the Hispanophones 10 percent. Tanya (a self-styled "Salafiyah of the Najd") and I were the other 10. After one in

---

81. Miroslav Volf, "God is Love: Biblical and Theological Reflections on a Foundational Christian Claim," in *A Common Word: Muslims and Christians on Loving God and Neighbor,* ed. Volf, Ghazi bin Muhammad and Melissa Yarrington (Grand Rapids, Eerdmans, 2010), p. 131.

the morning, the party began to dissolve. Determining to make a last effort, I caught Nayef standing between goodbyes. I asked him to consider the risen Christ's different treatments of Mary and Thomas with regard to his corporeal nature. To say "Touch me not" was a way of keeping Mary's love at a respectful limit. To say "Touch my wounds" was a way to dispel the doubt of Thomas.

As I said these things, I looked into Nayef's eyes. His discomfort with my observations was palpable, and his rejection was audible. I said that the two apparently contradictory entreaties do not conflict in any real way. Both attest to Jesus' mastery of human nature, and to the mystery of his divine nature.

Nayef chose to scoff at mystery. Clarity is the goal, he said, and the reality of Islam is perfectly clear.

Thus ended four hours of dialogue, sometimes contentious but always polite.

I had met a princely example of the *muwahhidun*, worshippers-of-the-One-True-God, and I was grateful for the encounter. Yet I felt that this proud, sophisticated, articulate Wahhabi was a restless doctrinaire whose studies day and night gave him little peace of mind or soul.

Discourse with Prince Nayef remained with me as a peak experience of Arabia, epitomizing its rise from the "blood-spattered monotony" of tribalism to a cosmopolitanism with oil-stained luxury. My image of him would have persisted simply, perhaps, with holy books and telephones beside him, were it not complicated by a Googled discovery four years later. In May 2007, Prince Nayef bin Sultan bin Fawwaz Al-Sha'lan, a grandson of Abdul Aziz, was found guilty in absentia by a French court of using his Boeing 727 jet and his diplomatic status to transport cocaine. The plot, developed in 1998-99, focused on smuggling two tons of coke from Colombia to a stash house in Paris. The penalty could not be exacted on the prince because there is no extradition treaty between the Kingdom and France. But he was sentenced to ten years in jail and a fine of $100 million.[82] He denied all charges and said that the Saudi government had cleared him of wrongdoing.

Four years later, on Nayef's appeal, the case remains before the French supreme arbiter of such matters, the Court of Cassation. Gag orders on all involved prohibit distribution of documents. Prince Nayef, in his palatial

82. ABC News online, 9 May 07; U.S. Drug Enforcement Agency, News Release, 3 May 05; miaminewtimes.com/2005-10-13.

residence in Riyadh, continues to study the Abrahamic religions. First a fugitive from justice in 1984 (narcotics charges in Mississippi), he is now listed on the Internet by Interpol as "wanted" for the French conviction — for drug-related crimes and criminal conspiracy. An informant is quoted as asking him why, as a non-user of alcohol and tobacco and as a strict follower of the Qur'an, he wanted to sell cocaine. Nayef answered that "the world is already doomed and that he has been authorized by God to sell drugs. . . . [His] true intentions for trafficking narcotics [will become clear later]."[83] We continue to wait for more on this expected revelation from the Satan-stressed and God-tormented prince.

83. www.Interpol.int/public/data/wanted/notices/data/2002/93/2002-49793.asp; www
.indybay.org/newsitems/2009/11/16/18628884.php?show. The latter source is a video documentary entitled "Royal Inquest: Princely Trafficking," by Edward Schillinger and Mike Dang.

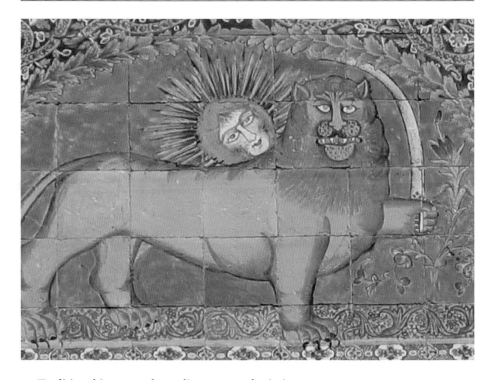

4.1 Traditional iconography — lion, sun, and scimitar. *Photo: William Grassie, 2005*

4.2 Post-revolutionary iconography, Tehran. *Photo: William Grassie, 2005*

4.3 Grand Ayatollah Khomeini; Qom, September 1979. *Photo: Abbas/Magnum*

4.4 Revolutionary mob, Tehran, January 1979. The mob has just torched the red-light district with "Islamic Purifying Fire." It now exhibits the burned body of a presumed prostitute. *Photo: Abbas/Magnum*

4.5 Young Basiji receive military training (December 1979) on property in Tehran confiscated from Baha'i. *Photo: Abbas/Magnum*

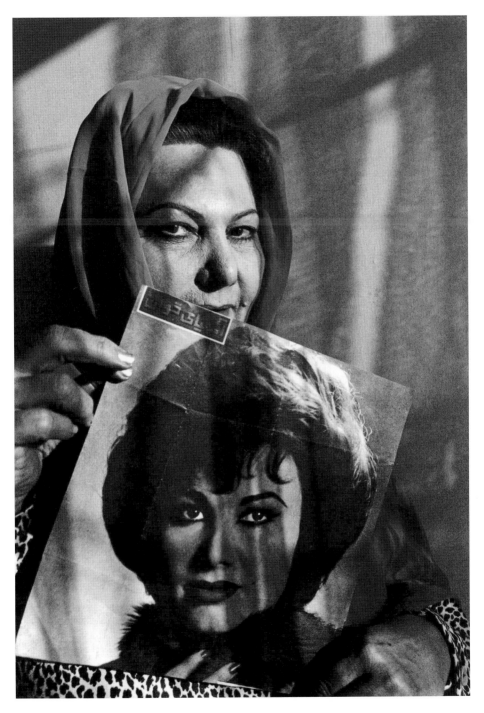

4.6 Irene Zazians, 1998, a famous actress before the revolution, shows a cover from the time of her glory. *Photo: Abbas/Magnum*

4.7 On Ashura 2005, in Khorramabad, a woman wears her black chador imprinted with a muddy hand, to mourn the martyrdom of Imam Hussein. *Photo: Abbas/Magnum*

4.8 Tehran University, May 2000. Female students protest for freedoms. Theirs was a particularly courageous stand in view of forceful repression of demonstrations the year before, which had spread to several other cities until, in mid-July, President Khatami "dis-
owned" them. Several persons were killed, hundreds injured, an estimated 1,200-1,400
detained, and more than seventy "disappeared." There followed a variety of laws, including penalization of "thought crimes," which were later invoked against the election protests of 2009. *Photo: Abbas/Magnum*

4.9 An ayatollah at the microphone, first Iranian national conference on religion and science, April 2005.

Photo: William Grassie

4.10 On a walk in Darband, North Tehran, behind the park of the former Pahlavi residence, Faézé Woodville eats lima beans bought from a street vendor. *Author's photo*

4.11 Woman at grave of son killed in war with Iraq, 1980-1988 (2005).

Photo: William Grassie

4.12 Hazrat-e-Masumeh, Qom: shrine dedicated to Fatemeh, daughter of the seventh Shiite imam, and sister of the eighth, Imam Reza. *Photo: William Grassie*

Chapter 4

IRAN

Challenging the "Sacred System," 2009

In the dynamics of post-revolutionary Iran, fire and smoke often rise from its uncertain blend of theocracy and democracy. Ayatollah Ruhollah Khomeini came back to Tehran from exile in Paris in 1979 as the personification of his own resolution of the problem: *vilayet-i-faqih,* "Guardianship of the Jurist." Deposition of the Shah was followed by constitution-writing, which put Khomeini and his theory on top, and sprinkled mullahs throughout the system as leaders of ministries, councils, and institutes.[1] The voice of the people would be heard through popular election of a president and a parliament, with candidates and balloting vetted by a Guardian Council composed of mullahs. Two other key institutions helped amplify the system: the Assembly of Experts, a council of virtuous and learned men who chose a new Supreme Leader (Ayatollah Ali Khamenei) on Khomeini's death in 1989, and who can reprove or replace that preeminent official; and an Expediency Council, which Khomeini later invented to resolve disputes between the parliament and the Guardian Council.

So much for councils, whose multiple mullahdom may produce equivalents of fog chambers. What about money and guns? The Supreme Leader has oversight of all finances, and also selects leaders of the powerful

---

1. For historical perspective: Abbas Amanat, *Apocalyptic Islam and Iranian Shi'ism* (London/New York, I. B. Tauris, 2009); Ray Takeyh, *Guardians of the Revolution: Iran and the World in the Age of the Ayatollahs* (Oxford/New York, Oxford University Press, 2009); and Kenneth Pollack, *The Persian Puzzle: The Conflict Between Iran and America* (New York, Random House, 2004).

religious-charitable foundations. Conventional military and police forces report to the Supreme Leader. So do the units vital to internal security: the Islamic Revolutionary Guard Corps, famous for suicidal attacks against armored units in the war with Iraq; and the Basij, military reserve and ideological youth corps, often plainclothes vigilantes armed with truncheon or bicycle chains. Plus the Quds Force, clandestine units connected to Hezbollah and Hamas for export of the revolution.

What powers are left to the president? He appoints the Council of Ministers and oversees executive functions, but he has no veto power and does not control the leading bloc in parliament, which can dismiss his ministers with a vote of no confidence. He is responsible for national performance, without the distinguishing powers of a British prime minister or an American president. In effect he is the chief operating officer of the Republic, while the Supreme Leader is chief executive, chairman, senior pastor, and voice of God.

The president can nevertheless use his position as a pulpit. Given the cautiousness of Khamenei as Supreme Leader, there have been many national tone-setting opportunities. Khatami (president, 1997-2005) failed to use his opportunities well. Mahmoud Ahmadinejad, elected in 2005, uses them powerfully to express messianic convictions ripened by his service as a mid-level commander on a battlefront in the war with Iraq. Before the UN General Assembly in 2005, he even prayed to God to "hasten the appearance of the Imam of the times" and to grant victory to his followers and martyrs. He thus brought to a major international forum the voice of Shi'ite apocalypse, in which a messiah delivers his people from the burden of history.

The working effect of Iran's structures may be simplified as an Islamic polyarchy, still under post-revolutionary trial. Thus far it is driven more clearly by the Supreme Leader's perception of the will of God than by any test of the will of the people. Apparent checks and balances turn into a system of bucks and valences, in which frustration of reformers is accomplished by key positioning of mullahs to insist on conservative clerical values. Against any threats of itinerant messianism or sudden mobocracy, there remains the authority of the Supreme Leader. His word would be authoritative on the timeline of the eventual divine showdown. He would presumably insist on the ultimate rather than the imminent advent of the Hidden Imam (unlike Ahmadinejad, who sometimes poses as the Mahdi's deputy). Or, in immediate clashes on the streets of Tehran, he may call in security forces, regular and/or irregular.

But what if the Supreme Leader makes a big mistake? Khamenei appeared to err grandly when he acclaimed Ahmadinejad's landslide victory in the June 2009 presidential election only hours after the polls closed. He should have waited, by law, for certification three days later from the Guardian Council. They, deluged with complaints about irregularities, eventually conceded that discrepancies involved up to three million votes, but not enough to overturn the outcome. To many voters and informed observers, however, the announced results had appeared instantly incredible. Ahmadinejad's "63 percent" looked astoundingly high, given that his four-year term had produced slumping growth, rising unemployment (from 10 percent to 17 percent), and increasing inflation (from 10 percent to 24 percent). Mir-Hossein Moussavi's "34 percent" looked incredibly low, given waves of enthusiasm for him in weeks preceding. And the "2 percent" ascribed to Moshen Rezaie and "1 percent" to Mehdi Karroubi appeared unbelievably meager.

Television debates had sharpened issues in pronounced ways. Karroubi, former speaker of the parliament, had declared that Ahmadinejad's denial of the Holocaust had undermined Iran's international reputation. Rezaie, former chief of the Revolutionary Guards, challenged Ahmadinejad's nuclear foreign policy as provocative. Moussavi, prime minister during war with Iraq, and respected for his internal policies at that time, promised economic reform, freedom of expression, a campaign against corruption, and a curb on the power of the Supreme Leader by taking control of security forces. He also criticized Ahmadinejad's crackdowns on dress that had led to warnings or prison for hundreds of thousands of women and men, and he broke all precedent by having his famed wife, Zahra Rahnavard, an educational leader and artist, campaign in public with him, often holding hands. Her intelligent fire included a demand for apology from Ahmadinejad for lying about her, and promises that her husband, if elected, would appoint women to cabinet posts and ensure that they were no longer treated as second-class citizens.

Was Khamenei trying to convince the public with highly manipulated vote totals that a runoff was not needed? Did he fear that a second vote would pour over into clear victory for Moussavi, who had opposed him more than twenty years before and pledged to curb his powers now? Whatever his motives, and whatever the electoral facts, hundreds of thousands went to the streets in peaceful protest, many of them women. Moussavi bolstered them, declaring that this "performance by dishonest people is shaking the pillars of the Islamic Republic," and if continued it would "transform all key members of this regime into fabulists in confrontation with this nation . . . seriously jeopardizing them[selves] in this world and the next."

A massive protest procession three days after the vote proceeded in stunningly orderly silence. According to journalists, it was five hours long, and according to the mayor of Tehran was the biggest since the revolution. Despite beatings by Basiji, brutal invasions of university dorms, and lethal shootings outside their headquarters, the demonstrators continued. Foreign journalists were ordered off the streets and their visas left unrenewed. Against regime command and blockage of standard Internet sites, reformists parlayed overseas connections to YouTube, Facebook, and Twitter sites. A countering crowd summoned for Ahmadinejad swelled to fill the squares. But cell phone, text messaging, and word of mouth brought out reformist demonstrators in countering numbers.

The incumbent president and declared winner had plenty of ballot and crowd indications to consider himself the voice of the people, popularly chosen as the toughest possible negotiator with the West. Moussavi's followers, however, sought Iranian democracy through annulment and a new election. Their silent marching by tens of thousands, even after tear-gas, beatings, and shootings, was more intimidating than noisy protest. The Supreme Leader warned that continued illegal demonstration would be met by force, and that any bloodshed would be on the hands of opposition leaders. Now he had to reckon with a populace which, after dark and out of reach of Basiji, was shouting from its home rooftops, *"Allah-u-Akbar!"* The cry that "God is great!" had punctuated deposition of the Shah, but reformists were not asking for another revolution. Their signs by day asked, "Where is My Vote?" At night cries even emerged of "Death to the Dictator."

Moussavi and his councilors commanded no army or police, no irregulars or thugs. But they did have at their call that extraordinary resource of Iranian and Shi'ite history, the will to martyrdom. Would they need to invoke it? What would it achieve? The day that the Chinese government used its army to crack down harshly on youth protesting for democracy in Tiananmen Square, June 4, 1989, was the same day as the Ayatollah Khomeini died, to massive manifestations of national grief. Could reformists in Iran, thirty years after their revolution, achieve anything more enduring than demonstrators in China did forty years after theirs?

Moussavi said, "I am prepared for martyrdom. Go on strike if I am arrested."[2] Ten days after the election, however, it appeared clear that a harsh calculation would prevail: the government's readiness to kill if necessary far exceeded the protesters' will to martyrdom.

Iranians had felt a continuing pride, since 1979, in not only having defined their own political system, but also in uniquely shaping their destiny in the form of an Islamic, Shi'ite, republic.[3] They had broken the mold of classic modern revolutions: French, anti-clerical; Russian, atheistic. They had installed in power the solemn, angry, pious longtime exile, Ruhollah Khomeini, as Supreme Leader, with his unique doctrine of the "Guardianship of the Jurist." He was addressed as "Imam," a title which no Shi'i figure had assumed since the Occultation of the Twelfth Imam eleven centuries before. Indeed, while awaiting his return — the Mahdi, the Lord of the Age — his vice-regent on earth (Khomeini himself) must be upheld as a temporal authority superior to all other powers.[4] These hungers and expectations focused upon the Supreme Leader. Khomeini exercised his pre-apocalyptic authority with confident power. Six months before his death, he wrote Premier Gorbachev, who was still trying to hold the Soviet Union together, an astonishing letter in which he condescended instruction in Islam in order to shore up a system collapsing from the weight of its godless materialism.[5]

Violent revolutions, however, go awry. As the narrator remarks in Conrad's *Under Western Eyes,* such revolutions pass away from the scrupu-

---

2. For details on polls, election, protest, repression, May/June 09: New America Foundation with Terror Free Tomorrow, poll concluding 20 May and webcast panel review, 22 June; *New York Times,* PBS, NPR, and FARS News Service, *passim;* unemployment and inflation, *New York Times,* 10 June 09, p. A6, citing Saeed Leylaz and the Central Bank; Zahra Rahnavard, Times [of London] Online, 8 June 09; Mousavi 1388 on Twitter, *passim;* "Iranian Presidential Election, 2009"; Wikipedia; Occident.blogspot.com; huffingtonpost.com; images from many sources, including tweets, especially "The Big Picture," *Boston Globe,* 15 June 09. Excellent interim summaries by Roger Cohen, op-ed., *New York Times,* 21 July 09, and "Iran: The Tragedy and the Future," *New York Review of Books,* 13 Aug 09, pp. 7-10.

3. Hooman Majd, *The Ayatollah Begs to Differ* (New York, Anchor Books, 2009), p. 6 and *passim.*

4. On Khomeini's claims of authority, see Amanat, *Apocalyptic Islam and Iranian Shi'ism,* pp. 65-67.

5. Imam Khomeini's Letter to Mikhail Gorbachev (December 1988); www.ghadeer.org/english/imam/letter%20Imam/callto/callto2.html.

lous, the unselfish, and the just, who become victims "of narrow-minded fanatics and of tyrannical hypocrites." Such was the experience of the simple man who had once been Khomeini's designated successor. Grand Ayatollah Hossein Ali Montazeri had been his chief representative in Iran and endured numerous jailings under the Shah. But across the first decade of the Republic differences emerged between them, erupting when Montazeri learned that almost 4,000 prisoners serving time for earlier convictions had been put to death. Montazeri wrote Khomeini denouncing criminal abuses by the regime: "This is not what we fought for."

Montazeri's sustained honesty led to the stripping away of his title, ransacking of his home, and house arrest until 2003. He used his detention as freedom to speak truth to power, and he expressed it scathingly to his former protégé, Grand Ayatollah Khamenei, the second Supreme Leader. Now Montazeri regretted the doctrine of the Guardianship of the Jurist which he had helped to fashion. On the contrary: all power in an Islamic state must arise from the people. He declared that Baha'i should enjoy equal rights. He deplored nuclear weapons as immoral and anti-Islamic. He condemned the election results of June 2009, and dismissed the government of President Mahmoud Ahmadinejad as illegitimate.[6]

It remains possible that Ahmadinejad did indeed win by a large popular margin. After all, he was a lower-middle-class puritan, consistent in dress and manner, who had chosen his enemies carefully: America, the Great Satan; and Israel, infamous Zion, which should be removed from the pages of history. As Holocaust denier and as Satan's challenger, he cut out for himself a large role in which no one could surpass him. Just to make sure of allegiances, he scattered state revenue from oil money among deprived classes and built up his institutional alma mater from the war against Iraq, the Revolutionary Guards, as a corporate power and as national enforcers. They in turn were backed by Basiji, underclass zealots serving as a volunteer paramilitary force. Perhaps one million men and women could be mobilized as Basiji if necessary. Many more claimed registry for benefits and as a job-hunting tool.[7]

These forces Ahmadinejad relied upon to grind down the fervent protests that followed his election. At the same time he continued to whip

6. Abbas Milani, "The Good Ayatollah," *Foreign Policy,* Mar/Apr 10, pp. 25-26; *New York Times,* 25 Dec 09, p. A26.

7. Numbers of Basiji: Wikipedia, citing Globalsecurity.org and Center for Strategic and International Studies (Washington, D.C.).

up popular sentiment where it might be lagging. His choice of emphasis is revealing: not such much on the revolution, not on the *vilayat-i faqih* which backed him in the person of Grand Ayatollah Khamenei. The revolution, after all, was thirty years old, and a high percentage of the population had been born since then. And the Guardianship of the Jurist was a central part of the problem, if one longed for democracy or a Western lifestyle, or both. So Ahmadinejad leaped over such appetites and declared himself the agent or precursor of the Hidden Imam, Lord of the Age. Who would contest the glad tidings inherent in a message central to Shi'ism? Ahmadinejad, having already characterized himself this way in a speech to the UN General Assembly, went much further in hints and thrusts and public prayers at home. Adding to historic condemnations of America and Israel were now routine attacks on Baha'i and Wahhabis.[8] Such a combination of orthodoxy and hatred, backed by military, police, and vigilante forces, was proving impossible to counter with democratic incrementalism or bourgeois possibilism. Eventually, human-rights activists in Iran later said, 18,000 people were arrested. The Green Wave of protest broke upon the shore of repression and began to sink into the sands of time.

Initial critiques on the part of international observers were difficult to sustain after foreign press offices were ordered closed and photographing protests was treated as criminal. University faculties were purged. Reform media were shut down.[9]

One of the most reliable international reporters, Nazila Fatih of the *New York Times,* left on July 1, 2009, after being surveilled by numerous hostile men, some armed. With two toddlers to protect, she pulled up stakes and returned to Toronto, where she had done graduate work several years before. What finally drove her away? A warning by phone that she could be the target of a sniper.[10]

There remained, as a theoretical resource, several emotional days on the calendar of protest, from December 2009 to March 2010: National Student Day, Ashura (commemoration of the Martyrdom of Imam Hussein), the anniversary of the revolution, and the Zoroastrian Feast of Fire. National Student Day ignited the strongest demonstrations in the nearly six

---

8. UN speech and attacks on Baha'i and Wahhabi, Amanat, *Apocalyptic Islam,* pp. 241, 247. Historically, of course, Ahmadinejad was far from the first self-declared "precursor."

9. *New York Times,* 2 Sep, 8 Dec, 23 Nov 09; 2 Mar 10.

10. Nazila Fatih, "The Exile's Eye," *New York Times,* 17 Jan 10, WR p. 1; "Iran: The Deadly Game," *The New York Review of Books,* 25 Feb 10, pp. 12-14.

months since the elections. Posters of Ahmadinejad and Khamenei were burned. Students marched, chanting, "God is great!" and "Death to the Dictator!" Against them police fired tear gas and stun guns, and Basiji wielded truncheons and chains. Feeling was geared up for the death of Montazeri two weeks later, when hundreds of thousands turned out in angry mourning. The regime banned further memorial services and arrested dozens who violated the ban. Hard on the heels of these clashes came Ashura, with notable violence. The government reported the deaths of eight protestors and followed up with the jailing of Ibrahim Yazdi (Foreign Minister early in the revolution), three aides of Moussavi, and several other notables, among hundreds of protestors who were arrested.[11]

A parliamentary panel's report against a major prosecutor varied the tenor of the news. Three deaths from beatings in prison were defined under his responsibility, although a larger number was certainly suspected. Charges of rape were made by at least three former detainees, but such claims were dismissed by the panel as "illusions of a mother." The national police chief followed up by declaring the era of "mercy" was over, and promoting harsh crackdowns on those organizing and publicizing protests. As an index of serious prosecutorial intent, hundreds of protesters have received harsh prison terms, and several death sentences have been handed down. Two protesters have been hanged for the crime of *moharebeh* — warring against God.[12]

As a result of repressive intensity, the turnout on the anniversary of the revolution was disappointingly small. Indeed, a fizzle. An overseas contributor to protest chat observed an end to "euphoric buildup" and recognized that "fighting a government as determined as the Islamic Republic of Iran will require much more than Facebook fan pages, Twitter clouds, and emotional YouTube clips."[13]

Mir Hussein Moussavi tried to rally his forces by denouncing "rule of a cult that has hijacked Iranianism and nationalism." But such rhetoric seemed not to be as effective an energizer as government actions were de-

---

11. *New York Times*, 8 Dec 09, p. A6; 21 Dec 09, p. A6; 27 Dec 09, p. A6; 28 Dec 09, p. A1; 29 Dec 09, pp. A4, 7.

12. Jon Lee Anderson, "After the Crackdown: Talking with Mahmoud Ahmadinejad — and the Opposition — about Iran Today," *The New Yorker*, 16-23 Aug 10, pp. 60-69, esp. p. 60; *New York Times*, 11 Jan 10, p. A4; 16 Jan 09, p. A9. Iran's use of the death penalty is second in the world to China's. It had already quadrupled in the first term of Ahmadinejad. *New York Times*, 28 Nov 09, p. A6.

13. *New York Times*, 15 Feb 10, p. A4.

motivators. An announcement timed before the Zoroastrian Feast of Fire declared the sentences of six who had protested on Ashura: *death*.[14]

The Feast of Fire had been anticipated on the Facebook page of Moussavi's wife, Zarah Rahnavard. It is the festival of light against darkness, she said. But if that were meant to be a mobilizing political metaphor, it echoed faintly on the occasion. Fireworks went off. A few posters of Khamenei were burned. Brigades answered ordinary alarms. A media blackout covered Iran. The Supreme Leader had banned the festival itself as corrupt and counter to Islam.[15]

Ten months after the election, matters stood just where Rafsanjani, in a major Friday prayer sermon, had positioned them. If it were only Islam, Iran faced a ruinous desert. If it were only a Republic, corruption would destroy the body politic. Religious values and democracy must proceed hand-in-hand.[16] But who would lead those listening?[17]

Divine Banquet and God-Tempest, 2005

What I saw with the rest of the world electronically in 2009, an Iran in severe crisis, I was able to understand better for having been there myself in 2005, just prior to the previous presidential election. I hoped I could return to Iran after the upheaval, and indeed I was invited back in 2011 to a conference on psychology, religion, and culture. I accepted the invitation and drove myself to produce a paper, which was welcomed by the organizers. Later, however, they apologized: the Ministry of Foreign Affairs had rejected my application for a visa because of "security reasons." I inferred that interviewing some dissidents in 2005 had branded me as subversive. Whatever the case, to consider an independent writer nearly eighty years old a threat to the security of the Islamic Republic of Iran is simply laughable, or evidence of an insecure regime, or both.

During that three-week visit in 2005, my two companions and I saw no other Americans, or Europeans, either. We were immersed in a nation

14. *New York Times,* 16 Mar 10, p. A10.

15. *Los Angeles Times,* 13 Mar 10, 8:59 a.m.; Guardian.co.uk, 16 Mar 10, "Iran Protests: Festival of Fire/weblog."

16. Anonymous Irani, www.salon.com/news/feature/2009/07/21/tehran_dispatch.

17. Hopeful expectations at the time are found in http://roomfordebate.blogs.nytimes .com/2009/06/16/where-will-the-power-lie-in-iran/; Abbas Amanat is followed by Meyra Wurman, Mohsen Milani, Djavad Salehi-Isfahani, and Janet Alfari.

whose capital city was full of graphics against the U.S., and whose neural-gic political cry was "Death to America." My country had earned that chant, first by helping the British in 1953 overthrow Prime Minister Mossadegh for no greater offense than trying to get a larger share of the price of Iran's own oil, of which British Petroleum was drawing off seven-eighths while paying employees "a pittance and treating them like slave la-borers."[18] Then, in 1979, the American government's support and comfort of the Shah incurred popular rage when he was deposed. In a mad inter-lude, students occupied the U.S. Embassy and held its employees captive for 444 days. If American-Iranian relations were not already sour enough, the Reagan administration then curdled the mix by supporting Saddam Hussein's use of chemical weapons in the Iran-Iraq war.

I was a trustee of the Metanexus Institute on Religion and Science, an organization in Philadelphia admired by a group of Iranian scholars on those subjects. When they held a conference styled as "the first Iranian na-tional dialogue on religion and science," they used us as a model in repair-ing Darwinian breaches in the arches of human knowledge. Once a won-dering inquirer could have seen the spans of theology, physics, and biology as converging toward an apex of the dome of learning. But now the roof was open and the elements were raining on the floor.

When William Grassie, Executive Director of Metanexus, received an invitation for the conference, he asked me as a trustee to join him. Faézé Woodville, an Iranian émigré, offered to be our "interpreter and fixer," while her husband took care of their two sons. Her Iranian passport would get her in easily. Billy and I, however, waited uncertain for months for our visas. I prepared two papers to qualify for the conference: one about a multicultural program on religion which I knew in Central Java, and the other a lay summary on brain scans of meditative states of mind. I won-dered if either would be well received in a Shi'ite theocracy, for the first, ar-guably, diluted Islam in cross-currents of other faiths, and the second could be misunderstood as reducing religion to electronic wavelengths. Anxious as I was on those two fronts, my main concern was something else.

I feared that my daughter might be dying. She, Timmie, had been di-agnosed a decade before as suffering from a rare liver disease, rarer still for women — primary sclerosing colangitis. No cause could be discerned, for this was an "autoimmune disorder." Now her energy was sagging. Her doc-

18. Pollack, *Persian Puzzle*, p. 51.

tors concluded, as they had predicted ten years before, that only a liver transplant could save her. To our happy astonishment, two volunteers came forth from within the family as having the right blood type, not to mention a friend who was excluded as not young enough. The operation was scheduled for late May 2005. Timmie was still coping with the sudden death of her mother as she faced a surgical procedure which was only five years in practice. Her San Francisco surgeons, a wife-and-husband team, had performed a hundred of these operations. But I still feared that in addition to having lost my wife of forty-three years, I might lose my youngest child and only daughter, whom I immoderately loved.

Our visas came through with a week to spare, but anxieties remained. One was fed by a Baha'i friend whose family, on both her side and her husband's, had lost several members to Iranian prisons, torture, and executions. The Constitution of 1980 had effectually criminalized the Baha'i faith, which considers Abraham, Krishna, Zoroaster, Moses, Buddha, Jesus, and Muhammad all divine messengers. Khomeini's revolution had led to continuing destruction of Baha'i religious and cultural monuments, confiscation of property, loss of livelihood, and demise of education.[19] Why go to Iran at all? As an American I would be a focus of mistrust. Baha'i know about that — suspicion of their education, their wealth, their faith. They have paid for it in unjustifiable torture and deaths.

A second, and special, anxiety resulted from my determination, in time separate from the conference, not to go on the tourist route intended by our friendly minders from the conference organizing staff, to Isfahan and Shiraz. The architectural gems of the Safavids, who made Persia Shi'ite in the sixteenth century, and the pre-Islamic ruins of Darius the Great — those glories I could travel with coffee table picture books. I wished to go to Mashhad, in the northeast corner of Iran, not far from Afghanistan. That big city contained the tomb of Imam Reza, the only one of the Twelve Shi'ite imams actually buried in Iran. Faézé, who had never been there, was interested to go and to be my interpreter. A renowned Baha'i scholar counseled against this anomaly — a Western man traveling with a much younger, and married, woman. Too risky. Shi'ite religious police will not understand. Don't do such a thing in Iran, where you do not wish to be asked questions out of the ordinary, and where police supply their own answers to questions.

---

19. A full account may be found in *A Faith Denied: The Persecution of the Bahá'is of Iran* (New Haven, Iran Human Rights Documentation Center, 2006).

The third anxiety was truly mortal. Would my daughter pull through? The doctors said that the chance of death from the operation was 5 percent. That was much higher than for my wife, who had expired in allegedly simple heart surgery to replace a mitral valve.

Faézé was careful to warn Billy and me that revolutionary Iran abjured symbols of Western formality. And also Western informality. There were neither neckties in Iran nor blue jeans. No bright colors or patterns. Men's business clothing was optimally a white shirt open at the neck and a plain, even drab, suit. For informality, shed the jacket. Women, of course, if pious, wore a black *chador* from head to toe, revealing at most temple to chin, and possibly less. Faézé, a professed atheist and occasional Episcopalian, would wear a minimal headscarf and a *manteau,* a shapeless garment like a raincoat — by her choice, tan. Lipstick was prohibited, and wearing it suggested prostitution. Alcohol was, of course, outlawed. Dogs were defined in the Qur'an as unclean, so do not expect to see them as pets. Chewing gum was prohibited, not because it was unsanitary and unsightly, as in Singapore, but because it stood for the self-indulgent habits of the childish West. Credit cards and travelers' checks were useless. There had been no financial relations between the U.S. and Iran for more than two decades. I had to carry dollars, which were welcome in value, for all expenses I might encounter. There were no safes in hotel rooms. My suitcase became my bank. Nothing, in the end, was stolen.

My postmaster had questioned me: Did I really know what dangers I was getting into, going to Iran? "I don't care," I answered him. "But I'll find out." So I displayed to him and to myself two sides of a widower's mind — fatalistic indifference and eager curiosity.

In Tehran, Faézé stayed in a family apartment in a more northerly section of the city. The hotel for Billy and me had been taken over from a Western five-star chain a quarter of a century before. It reminded me of a big Beijing hotel in 1977, before Deng Xiaoping's getting-rich-is-okay policies set in. The food was banal and colorless, one level above grub. Dormitory-style décor prevailed, with dull maroon bedspreads. The service, however, was notably sharp in relation to communist staffs — egalitarian disconcern in immediate post-Mao China, and grudging contempt in post-Soviet Prague.

A bellman stood smartly at each elevator, and the chief duty manager roamed the lobby carefully. I got to know him in the in the course of changing my dollars into rials. Mr. Assidi wore close-cropped white hair and a black moustache with a tightly trimmed bilateral slant. He smiled with aplomb, while his eyes clicked — banker's ice, liar's dice. I had later good reason to think of him as the plainclothes chief of a radiantly costumed police unit. But for now he seemed to be the captain in charge of stopping, at three stars, or two and a half, the hotel's descent from its once five-star rating.

Two hundred and forty societies modeled on Metanexus had grown up in forty-two nations, competitively selected and with their own matching funds, to pursue their own discourses about science and religion, and in the charming phrase of William James, to "gossip about the universe." Such a society, based in the University of Tehran School of Medicine, had launched this conference. A former assistant minister of health, whose name I will change to Nosrat, was given control over the event, prepared by his junior associates. As a professor of medicine and psychiatrist, he would later disclose to us his idiosyncratic view of Allah, science, and the mind of man.

Apart from the conference, I came to respect Professor Mehdi Golshani, a physicist with a doctorate from Berkeley, an authority on science and religion, and leader of his own Institute for Humanities and Cultural Studies. His book, in its third edition, was entitled *Can Science Dispense with Religion?* Holmes Rolston, a prominent American contributor, answered that title question simply: yes, science can dispense with religion, but human beings cannot. "Science *explains,* but religion *reveals;* science *informs,* but religion *reforms.* . . . The task of religion is to examine [the] self in its relationships with the world, unmasking illusions and false cares, reforming it from self-centeredness, centering it on that which is of ultimate worth."[20]

Golshani's own view pictures Galileo, Newton, and Leibniz all sharing a conviction that might be expressed in Newton's words: "This most beautiful system of the sun, planets and comets could only proceed from the counsel and dominion of an intelligent and powerful being."[21] Then scient*ism* began to arise, with its conceit that science can explain everything. Darwin, in the mid-nineteenth century, disputed the special creation of

20. Rolston quoted in Mehdi Golshani, ed., *Can Science Dispense with Religion?* (Tehran, Institute for Humanities and Cultural Studies, 1998, 3rd ed., 2004), p. 325.

21. Newton quoted by Golshani, *Can Science Dispense with Religion?* p. 4. See also Golshani's own full reasoning in *Issues in Islam and Science* (Tehran, Institute for Humanities and Cultural Studies, 2004).

humankind, fundamentally questioned the real distinction of humans from other animals, and challenged the argument for God from design. By describing natural selection, Darwin provided a powerful analytical concept, even if it does not comprehensively explain order and disorder in the biological world.

Twentieth-century empiricists of various stripes and spots carried scientism further: primacy of sense experience, rejection of metaphysics. The quoted voice of Richard Dawkins, oozing atheistic acids, is permitted several appearances in the book. Moving in the direction of mathematical physics to explain everything, however, is checked by Gödel's proof that the consistency of mathematics cannot be proved.

Where, then, do we emerge? Golshani feels that the science-religion dialogue in the last thirty years has moved from the paralysis of conflict to freedom for intellectual traffic to proceed both ways. Two of his contributors mention Pierre Teilhard de Chardin, the French Jesuit paleontologist, who erected a structure of twentieth-century thought to help guide inquiry and reverie. John Haught, a theologian at Georgetown University, says that the careful scientist will avoid changing empirical discoveries into ultimate explanations, which would be to attempt to turn science into an alternative religion. Meanwhile the thoughtful religionist will continue his/her efforts in the distinctly different realm, content that every kind of naturalistic inquiry proceed in areas ripe for scientific exploration. True unity differentiates. Teilhard demonstrates how science and religion constitute a differential unity.[22]

Golshani's total list of interviewees comprises seventeen Muslims and forty-five Christians (Catholic, Protestant, or Orthodox). No Baha'i. No Jews. No Buddhists or Hindus. No women. Few Asians (two Malays, one Indonesian); no Africans; no atheists. Dramatically exclusive; but still contributory to easing discourse between Eur-Americans and Arabic/Farsi speakers.

M. Kamal Hassan, Rector of the International Islamic University, Malaysia, notes that in revealed religion, physical objects are "signs of God," the domains of scientific activity are aspects of "worship," and the products of that activity are "virtuous deeds." Such a view of the cosmos means that "a good scientist and a pious religious personality [may be] embodied in one person."[23] Islamic history is full of such integrated examples. So was

22. Haught, in Golshani, *Dispense?* p. 169.
23. Hassan, in Golshani, *Dispense?* p. 152.

Christian history, until the aberrancies generated by Darwinians in hyperscience, Freudians in quasi-science, and Marxists in pseudo-science. Their combined yield includes the hypertrophy of every kind of empiricism and the strangulatory extremes of logical positivism. All this went on while tangible and abstract resources grew, enabling humans, in deploying raw materials and capital with astounding impact, to ignore God and their own poor while congratulating themselves on Faustian triumphs.

In consequence, at the outset of the twenty-first century the so-called "advanced industrial nations" are teeming with examples of anorexic thinkers and bulimic consumers. But people of science and faith exist everywhere. H. Hassan-Zadeh Amoli, an Iranian ayatollah, distinguished in Islam's philosophy and gnosis, also pursues research in jurisprudence, poetry, and traditional medicine, mathematics, and astronomy. He quotes the Prophet with relish and approval — "science is the guide to action." At the same time he highlights for the reader a gem from the Messenger of God: "Verily this Holy Qur'an is the banquet of God, so learn the manners of this banquet as far as you can."[24] In table manners of everyday life, in the how much of this, and the when of that, is found an essential tension of the dialogue between science and religion. But, as several tempered minds point out in Golshani's compendium, tension need not be conflict.

Golshani's sixty-two respondents deepened my understanding of the complementarity of science and religion. One, by providing a fresh translation from the Greek in the New Testament, opened up worlds to me: "In the beginning was the Pattern (Logos), and the Pattern was with God, and the Pattern was God." The same Danish theologian, Niels Henrik Gregersen, goes on to demonstrate how far beyond Newton modern science has brought us. A clockwork cosmos has been replaced by a network cosmos, and by the "sciences of surprise."[25]

Before the conference, Faézé located a group of distant relatives, elderly women who intended a pilgrimage to Mashhad the weekend our conference ended. Would they embrace her in their troupe, and incidentally me, an elderly blue-eyed male, so that I might pray for my daughter and pay my respects to Iman Reza, eighth of the twelve great Shi'ite Imams? (He

24. Ayatollah Hassan Hassan-Zadeh Amoli, in Golshani, *Dispense?* p. 155.
25. Gregersen, in Golshani, *Dispense?* pp. 131-33, esp. p. 132.

was killed by a caliph twelve centuries ago, it is alleged, by poison in his pomegranate juice.) Word came back to Faézé that she and I should not try. "You will be bugged and watched. And everyone you see will be watched and bugged." Don't make difficulty for yourselves, your relatives, and others.

Okay. How, then, would we do it?

I could not do it alone, for I don't speak Farsi. Should I be a good camper and just accept the Isfahan-Shiraz tour southward which had been prepared for us by our warders? I persisted against that, and remembered counsel from my friend the senior Baha'i scholar. He had advised me to press my age: "Say, 'I am an old man, and I may never see Iran again.'" Test their hospitality and generosity. But, he added, do not travel solely with a much younger woman. It is fine for her that she has her husband's permission, and his willing understanding. But that will mean nothing for the two of you in a punitive theocracy. Yet I persisted. We determined to risk it.

Dr. Nosrat launched the conference by summarizing the split in the Occident between science and religion a century and a half ago, of which repair had begun in the last thirty years. Here in the Orient (so he called it) a similar bridging was required, as, for instance, to recall and employ spiritual aspects of treatment in medicine, and his own field of psychiatry.

Nosrat's junior associate summarized their invitation of papers in five dimensions: cosmology and theology, evolution and genetics, humankind and health, family-sex-ethics, and environment and technology. Nearly 400 papers had been received, and 216 accepted, 80 of which were to receive roundtable discussion. More than half of all papers were from outside Tehran. Sixty of the accepted papers were from women. He quoted a master Iranian theologian on science as the external revolution and faith as the internal revolution. Then he closed with ascent to a Shi'ite perspective. "The management of Satan, the Fallen Angel, is part of our management responsibility. . . . as we await the purified, clean life and institutional justice with the advent of the Twelfth Shiite Imam." Thus was opened to me the supreme importance of Satanic management, and the dramatic expectation that, whereas we on the human track dwell in the two disciplines of faith and science, after the advent of the Twelfth Imam we will have twenty-five disciplines opened to us. I enjoyed the prospect of expanding the curriculum of human consciousness more than twelve-fold.

There were five ayatollahs at the conference, I was proudly told. Presentations from these white-turbaned, brown-robed, long-bearded eminences were usually thick with Qur'anic authority and thin on science. The least impressive of them was a short feisty character who went well over his time limit. The chair gently admonished him, and granted him another five minutes. "Another five minutes?" he shot back. "I want another five bucks." This coarse riposte revealed why many ordinary Iranians are fed up with mullahs, whose social authority often exceeds their wisdom, and is sometimes undermined by their grasping appetites.

I was given a lift by a presenter who observed that most papers thus far were "religion" or "science," but not "dialogue" between them. He concluded by generating a metaphor of two complementary wings of human endeavor, science and religion, which work together to enable the body of humanity to fly. One of the most empirical papers came one from a young scientist who showed slides of fetuses, and quoted the Qur'an on humans "coming from a black layer of mud." Despite this earnest effort to show, scientifically, that "all prophesied things take place," a commentator treated the slide and the Qur'anic allusion to mud as upstart, renegade, disrespectful science. The two wings beat here in contrary ways.

Billy Grassie's "Constructive Theory of Evolution" unfolded criticisms of simplifiers of theology who invoke "intelligent design," as well as atheistic deniers like Dawkins, author of *The Blind Watchmaker,* who arrives at a universe of no good, no evil, no purpose. A commentator supported Billy, observing that Dawkins misses the point in saying there is no watchmaker. There may be, simply, "no watch" — because clock is a poor mechanical metaphor for life-in-time.

Faézé was listening with special tastes in mind. She latched onto a philosopher from Qom named Alizamoni. A fortyish, quietly charismatic speaker, he wore a short, scraggly Hezbollah beard. He paid homage to modern science as the most powerful generator of culture in our times, while expressing his devotion to an Islam in which no scientist has ever gone on trial for his beliefs. The core of his thinking was poetically Shi'ite in its stress on *ranj-e-shirin,* "sweet suffering." The greatest of all sweet sufferings is that of the lover for reaching his beloved.

Faézé sought out a private conversation with Alizamoni to explore that special humanistic dimension. He pictured rising levels of faith which bring out rising capacities for love. Because suffering is coextensive with life, the capacity for creative suffering, and the enjoyment of it, rises in proportion with faith and love. Death, for Shiites, is a way of joining God, and therefore welcome. In Christianity, too, the willingness of Jesus to die to join his Father is a "sweet suffering."

I asked Alizamoni about Hallaj, the extraordinary Arabicized Iranian

Sufi who was tortured and executed in 922 C.E. after a political trial. He had returned to Baghdad "to die there in the confession of the Cross" — seeking to be a Muslim Jesus, and thereby to order a single spiritual radiation through all humanity, from Covenant to Judgment. His extreme conviction — a victimal desire to be "absolutely poor, transparent, annihilated" — sought a guilt, condemnation, and death that might point with Jesus toward the Hour of Judgment.[26] Hallaj was flogged and had his hands and feet cut off before being exhibited, living, on the gibbet; then decapitated; trunk soaked in oil and set on fire; ashes thrown into the Tigris. Alizamoni did not comment on Hallaj's exclaiming from the gibbet, "I am the Truth." Perhaps he thought the ambitions excessive — to supervene the Prophet in reordering time, and to surpass the martyrdom of the Prophet's grandson, Husayn. Alizamoni merely replied to me that whatever Sunni might think of it, for Hallaj his suffering was sweet.

The idea of a Qur'anic Christ is highly disturbing not only to orthodox Sunni, but to orthodox Shi'i for their own historic reasons. They see the lines of martyrdom arriving at an apex with Husayn at Karbala. As the grandson of the Prophet in a line dislodged from the Caliphate, his is the archetypal story of legitimacy undone; and of courage vanquished by overbearing might. Martyrdom is inevitable. Suffering is sweet. Martyrs out of Shi'a context, however, are suspect. Hence Hallaj on the gibbet, a presumptive Christic Sunni, is a grotesque anomaly.

Special modern sufferers are the Baha'i. In the mid-nineteenth century, the Persian calling himself the Bab declared that he had come to initiate a new prophetic cycle. He was executed by firing squad. One of his students, Baha'ullah, declared himself to be the Promised One foretold by the Bab. Despite prison and exile, he lived until age seventy-five, expanding his appeal to the messianic expectations of other faiths, so that now Baha'iism is an independent world religion with five million adherents. That makes it a target, along with Judaism, for orthodox Iranian mullahs and their theocratic government. The UN Commission on Human Rights has repeatedly commented critically on discrimination against Baha'i, including a formal statement by Asma Jahangir, Special Rapporteur on freedom of religion and belief, in 2006.

Even for a sophisticated Shi'ite, the Baha'i faith may be a problem.

---

26. Louis Massignon, *Hallâj: Mystic and Martyr,* trans. and ed. Herbert Mason (Princeton, Princeton University Press, 1982 [4 vol. trans. of French ed., Paris, 1973]; abridgement, 1994), pp. 15-23, 70-71.

Seyyed Hossein Nasr, the elegant Iranian descendant of the Prophet, teaches at George Washington University; the jacket photo of his most popular book includes a vase of roses. Baha'i, he says, is "a modernist religious movement seeking to attach itself to certain of the prophetic and universal principles of Islam, but not in the way Muslims understand those principles."[27]

The God-tempest that I found in Iran moved me still further to seek to understand gender as conceived there. One eminent interviewee, an exile returned to Tehran, said flatly and smilingly that "the Iranian women are better than the men." I searched to see that, for it was not demonstrated at the conference. Most female presenters seemed awed by male dominance and by turbaned presences. They failed to engage their audience with eye and voice, and their papers, read in faltering tones at an incantatory pitch, seemed like prayers to an angelic presence hovering near ceiling height.

An invitation to visit the Muslim Women's Research Organization seemed to promise real discourse. Its founder, Dr. Sorayya Maknoon, had twelve years previous launched an intensive reexamination of rules and roles for women, with the ambition of defining an Islamic psychology which is "universal." I found her colleagues, a small cell of women in black *chadors,* bent with the gravity of their endeavor, unstinting in hope, and surrounded with paper. The walls were tacked and plastered with successive position papers on their "Model of Women's Dignity"; and their oral arguments were accompanied by gestures at the walls, as if to say, "There it is, manifest, and to any right-minded person, irrefutable." What does one say to a cadre of women whose courageous aim one approves, while feeling that they are without traction, like geese on a frozen pond? They believe they have worked out a comprehensive syllabus of life, "beyond gender and religion." In developing it they have ascribed value weights of 4 to feeling, 2 to action, 1 to thinking, as correctives against male underappreciation of emotion and overemphasis on reasoning. I heard unfolded at some length this model, which stresses enjoyment and mercy, without neglecting power, in

27. Seyyed Hossein Nasr, *The Heart of Islam: Enduring Values for Humanity* (New York, HarperCollins, 2002), p. 79. Baha'iism may be assessed on its own terms through the writings of Baha'u'lláh, trans. Shogi Effendi, *The Kitáb-I-Íqán: The Book of Certitude* and *The Hidden Words* (Wilmette, Ill., Bahá'i Publishing, 2003 and 2002, respectively).

realizing the Divine Will. Male thinking can certainly take female correction, I thought; but what follows from these calligraphic posters?

Tentative conclusions, they emphasized. Tentative against what contingency? I asked. Toward what tests? I felt urgently that their work across a dozen years not be lost, but become grounded in social reality. My sallies of questioning, however, only revealed that publications thus far had been minimal. There were no survey instruments, nor was there any social-science strategy for empirically testing their hypotheses. There was no evidence at all of public discussion. It felt stale.

Billy entered the room very late from another meeting and hit the same wall at once, but kept his American game face on, unaffectedly congenial in his desire to be a Quaker-for-all-seasons. Faézé, who had been there silently from the start, later described this cell of research endeavor as "insane." No, quite sane, I thought; but futile in its sequestration. It took me a long time to feel the faith and hope in their work, and to trust that it was attended and blessed by nameless angels.

Dr. Nosrat promised to provide new insights by inviting us three Americans to a private seminar in his psychiatric hospital. What he chose to show us was accompanied by his comments as a practical man, a presentist, a results-oriented administrator. I discovered that he could not escape the Iranian past: the strongly pronounced nineteenth-century male view that shaving of the beard was double trouble — it made one look like a boy, implying catamite; and it made one look like a woman, implying a European dandy. Religious authorities weighed heavily in favor of the traditional beard, for the sake of shari'a and nativism, and against perverse and foreign effeminacy. By the 1920s, however, the battle for the beard appeared to be lost. And by the 1930s Europeanization had reached the point where Riza Shah's reign unleashed a compulsory campaign for unveiling women. His son's prime minister for fourteen years, Amir Abbas Huvayda, was persistently rumored to be both Baha'i and passively homosexual, twin designations in orthoprax Iran for otherness and perverse excess. The theological revolution of 1979 appears to have brought back late-nineteenth-century stereotypes. Homosexuality and moral corruption are again conflated with Western cultural imperialism.[28]

28. Afsaneh Najmabadi, *Women with Moustaches and Men without Beards: Gender and Sexual Anxieties in Iranian Modernity* (Berkeley, University of California Press, 2005), pp. 16-17, 142-45, 241-44, 304n.16. Janet Afary has written a powerful interdisciplinary consideration of *Sexual Politics in Modern Iran* (Cambridge/New York, Cambridge University Press, 2009). Among other subjects, she treats gender history, women's rights, and same-sex relations as

Dr. Nosrat's slide show for his guests was astoundingly blunt and strangely interesting. He narrated a series of images depicting an initially effeminate-looking young man who came to him for advice about seeking sex-change surgery. Dr. Nosrat apparently considered himself engaged in a frontier skirmish in the psychosexual wars of his nation. He undertook all-out persuasion, short of hypnotic suggestion, against the young man's pursuing his desired course of action. Nosrat's slides then documented, over a few months, the transformation of the young man's face from a clean-shaven longhair (presumably a feminized European dandy) into a bearded short-hair (a proper male product of the revolution of 1979).

Billy and I murmured our insincere appreciation at this psychiatric feat, with a query about what would have been the consequences of letting the young man pursue his instinct and original aim. That idea was clearly antisocial to Dr. Nosrat, and possibly even counter-revolutionary. Nosrat himself, bald and mustachioed, conveys gender in part by prowling and growling. His own defensive sense of maleness was clearly aroused in opposition to his patient's wish. I felt that his sense of public standing as a former sub-cabinet official was also involved. In our immediate micro-environment (three men, one woman), Nosrat even allowed his felt male prerogative to venture upon insinuating comments to Faézé.

I cannot remember any reply from Faézé, although I did see her lips firming together and her eyes flaring. Had she broken into speech, it might have been eloquently contemptuous, given her very first reaction to meeting Nosrat earlier: "That man would not have been permitted to serve tea in our house." I cannot evoke the now overturned social distinctions which moved her to that remark; but I felt that Nosrat had reacted to her at once in counter-rejection. His body language seemed to say that those who, in the Shah's time, were expected to be servants had now become educated cabinet officers.

Revolution Now: The Cooled Volcano

The occasional extended quotation from Hafez, which might have helped me at the conference, occasioned silence from the interpreter in my ear-

---

part of the (p. 360) "marriage crisis in Iran." Less persuasive, because in the end it backs away from its subtitle, is Pardis Mahdavi's *Passionate Uprisings: Iran's Sexual Revolution* (Stanford, Stanford University Press, 2009).

phones because, he said, "Hafez is untranslatable." Daniel Ladinsky's superb versions disprove that cliché.[29] Certain tangled moments moved the conference chair to proclaim Bismillah, "to purify the air," at which point all Muslim participants obligingly went into prayer. When the first Iranian national dialogue on religion and science ended, I was free to pursue interviews.

The first that Faézé lined up for me was Makan Zahrai, scion of parents who had initiated publishing and bookselling firms forty years before. His perspective on Iranian reading culture was broad and cheerful. Before the revolution, 5,000 titles a year were published in Iran. After the revolution, 80,000 a year. More books are published in Iran than in the entire Arab world.

For such productivity, there must be lots of publishing houses — 4,200, in fact — and Makan told me where to find a huge center of them, which I did. At the "rear end" of the University of Tehran, there is a big research publisher just opposite the gates, and a great density of other publishers, bookstores, and distribution centers, thinning out into small think-shops next to micro-restaurants and laundries, dribbling away into student and faculty residential areas. Each of the Harry Potter books, said Makan, has had 300,000 readers in a Farsi population of 70 million — a much higher proportion than in the English-speaking world.

Makan swiftly summarized Iranian history since 1979: three "black" years; eight of war with Iraq; eight of Rafsanjani's presidency (a "mysterious character," but he did allow advance of the "cause of the left"); and the eight recent years of Khatemi, the best in getting "out from under that all." He had no prognostications on the presidential election immediately before Iran in 2005, but he still clearly trusted some form of continuing "Dialogue of Civilizations" as initiated by Khatemi. He was proud of Iranian civilization. Where else can you find 3,200-year-old chairs, 4,000-year-old forks and spoons, a 4,500-year-old carpet, and speakers of poetry every day?

I asked about the status and progress of Iranian women. The only ones with problems, he said, are on the borders of Arab states. "We are a cultural flower among thorns and weeds." Thirty percent of the large number of publishers are women. Only two of them put out "progressive" books

29. Daniel Ladinsky, trans., *The Gift: Poems by Hafiz, the Great Sufi Master* (New York, Penguin, 1999). A fuller sense of the Iranian tradition is conveyed by *The Hand of Poetry: Five Mystic Poets of Persia* [*Translations from the Poems of Sanai, Attar, Rumi, Saadi and Hafiz* by Coleman Barks; Lectures on Persian Poetry by Inayat Khan] (New Lebanon, N.Y., Owega Publications, 1993).

on women's issues. There is, he admitted, a governmentally "closed space" on women's issues, but female publishers are doing their own thing, proudly. They don't have "Western issues" or need to advance women's rights and roles. They particularly develop two strong genres — romance and spiritual novels for women. Makan assembled and brought out a stack of two dozen romance novels, all with sedate covers and properly veiled women. He answered me that the contents were "not quite as veiled"; but books, like movies, generally treat sexuality in delicate and discreet ways.

Fourteen different editions of Khalil Gibran's *The Prophet* have been published in Iran, and the one by the house of Zahrai has gone through fifty printings. They have a large research team working on an edition of Hafez. "The only people who don't read," he said, "are those who don't have the money to buy books."

Makan led us forward to the cash registers, remarking that theirs was "a serious bookstore. . . . We don't publish trash. But we gladly *sell* trash." The more serious titles are read by men, he said. My quick visual sample picked up ten people in line to pay for purchases: one male, five women in *chador* (of whom only one was face-veiled), and four women with head-scarves showing a lot of hair. Makan was happy: "At 9:15 p.m., busier than a bakery in here!" He flashed his hospitable smile. "People are buying bread for their heads."

I asked Faézé, in setting up interviews, to include conservative men and women, and a particular Islamic feminist member of parliament. But her natural connections pointed in other directions — so much so that when she returned a year later, she encountered our reputation for inter-viewing "dissidents."

One connection, Dr. Ibrahim Yazdi, was a distant relative of hers. As a youth he had been a leader of underground resistance to the shah. Then, in the U.S., 1961-79, he was a founder of the Freedom Movement and an ally of Ayatollah Khomeini. In February 1979, just after Khomeini's return, Yazdi rounded up several hundred Tehran University students to liberate the U.S. Embassy from Marxist students who had seized it. But the more famous and enduring takeover, of November in that year, signaled a revolution beyond Yazdi's tempering. Yazdi, then Deputy Prime Minister, went out with his Prime Minister, Bazargan, their cooperative posture toward the U.S. having branded them as poisonous moderates. With a thousand others, he eventually declared himself a presidential candidate for the election of June 17, 2005 — but the Guardian Council only recognized a hand-ful for the purpose.

Yazdi is a molecular geneticist. He held weekly Qur'an meetings in which he might gently correct the reader's pronunciation of Arabic, and would discourse on the meaning of the verses read. Allah created the Earth, "but if you want to know how he did it, study nature." His own hypothesis for the origin of life involves an environment of clay and minerals and, under certain conditions, polymerization of complex molecules. "Science is science," he says. Islamization of science is meaningless.

Another strong and sharp distinction: "There is no Islamic democracy." Democracy means people governing themselves. America, France, and Germany each do it differently, and Iran differently from them. Religion and politics cannot be totally separated. Even in the U.S., churches play a strong role in elections. "But we don't have a church, we have priests." The danger for Iran is "krytocracy." (The term, derived from Greek, means government by judges; but in Iran the judges are mullahs.) He and other oppositionists say that the revolution was for the sovereignty of the people; but the conservative clerics deny that.

In the modern history of Iran, the shah never ruled alone; it was always the shah and the clergy. In 1979 the clergy joined the intellectuals in fighting despotism, and now the shah is gone forever. "But the clergy don't read history." They need to learn from the story of the companion of the cave in the Surah of the Calf. There, a man in isolation emerges after thirty years and tries to use money and concepts no longer valid. This is an allegory for present times; "The Prophet's Medina cannot be replicated now."

The greatest new forces in Iran are youth and women. Seventy percent of the population is under the age of thirty. And 63 percent of the college enrollment is female. They are active and capable, as were their mothers, who became highly politicized and joined men in the revolution. Yazdi even looked in a sanguine way on the Revolutionary Guard, which stands for hard power and supposedly for blind obedience. But in the presidential election of 1997, he said, against the recommendation of their commander, 70 percent of them voted for the liberal Khatemi. I left Yazdi, thinking: a man of hope, sidelined by history. Following the protests of the election of 2009, he was jailed three times by the regime, which finally released him in March 2011.

Isa Saharkhiz had been, under Khatemi, Deputy Minister for Islam and Public Guidance. He was energetic in the approaching election of 2005 as an advisor to Mostafa Moin, former Minister for Science and Technology, a reformist and man of reason. Saharkhiz gave us his own capsule history of modern Iran, focusing upon "movements from the inside" which changed or tried to change Iran, and influenced the whole region. First was the constitutional revolution of 1906 (in which Faézé's grandfather had been a factor), through which Iran, first in the region, built a parliament to balance power against its monarch, and an independent judiciary. The second was Mossadegh's attempt as prime minister, 1951-53, to nationalize the oil industry and to justify that action by parliamentary support. Against him were the military, the monarchy, and conservative clerics, in a coup supported by the oil interests of Great Britain and the U.S. The third was the anti-shah revolution of 1979, which removed the monarchy forever, with waves of dramatic influence throughout the Muslim world. It left behind the continuing tension between clerical power and popular sovereignty. "The fourth move," said Saharkhiz fondly, was in 1997: a reform for pure democracy, to take some mullah power away and give it to the people. (If he saw the election of 2009 as a "fifth move," the regime tried to curb his enthusiasm with jailing and torture. He is now in a wheelchair, serving a three-year term for "insulting the Supreme Leader" and issuing anti-government propaganda.[30])

His sub-cabinet job under Khatemi had been to see to the expansion of politics and culture; to issue, for instance, permissions for new newspapers. The circulation of the largest, *Iran,* jumped from 100,000 to 500,000. Total journalistic subscriptions nearly tripled in one and a half years, with a marked influence on parliament through press lists of candidates and editorials affirming certain ones. Saharkhiz interrupted himself to quote an Iranian proverb, "Once the tooth falls, you can't put it back."

In fact, however, his personal narrative unhappily illustrated clerical dentistry, and its unrelenting bite. He had authorized and supported the paper *Zan* ("Woman"), owned by Rafsanjani's blonde-streaked feminist daughter, Faezeh Hashemi, which was a reformist organ for expanding women's roles.[31] The clerics closed it. When, at a press festival, he let *Zan* participate despite its closing, he was tried for a possible five-year term, and resigned his official position. His office had been rifled and his hard disks stolen. He spent time in jail.

The government in one day in the spring of 2000 closed eighteen reformist journals, including twelve dailies. In the period 2000-2005 they

---

30. http://www.rferl.org/content/jailed_iranian_journalist_appeals_to_un_rapporteur/24264623.html; *New York Times,* 29 Sep 10, p. A10.

31. Elaine Sciolino's excellent book, *Persian Mirrors: The Elusive Face of Iran* (New York, Simon & Schuster, 2000), captures Hashemi, pp. 118-21.

shut down 110 book publishers with court proceedings (all of which contributed to a steady public neutering of President Khatemi, the reader of Tocqueville). Saharkhiz and his friends consolidated their interests in various ways, and created in the autumn of 2001 an Islamic reform magazine, *Aftab,* with contributions from writers of the Iranian diaspora and translations of others with global fame such as Fatima Mernissi.

Saharkhiz appeared to be assuring himself, as well as us, that such efforts as *Aftab* signified the existence of a "dual state," but it seemed to me less of a shadow government in the British sense than the specter of an opposition. Saharkhiz said they were studying the Portuguese, Bulgarian, and Czech "revolutions" to capture examples for a "semi-coup movement." I wondered silently what could this amount to. A "semi-coup" would get its throat cut.

The fate of Moin's presidential candidacy is instructive. The Guardian Council, noting the 60 percent of the population under the post-revolution age of 25,[32] with unemployment surging, became coarsely pragmatic. To distract attention from the economy, they relaxed social restrictions. Headscarves were allowed to slip, *manteaus* grew tighter about the hips. Out-of-wedlock pregnancies increased, and so did drug and alcohol addiction. As the election approached, the Council did not even include Moin among the original six (out of 1014) that they endorsed, including Rafsanjani, who had announced with some panache that he was going to run in any case. But the Supreme Guardian, Ayatollah Khamenei, added two more: Moin and Khatemi's vice-president. Why did he boost a pair of reform candidates screened out by his council? Not out of fair play, I suspect, but to dilute reformist vote totals and thus enhance the chances of his own hard-line protégés, Mahmoud Ahmadinejad, the populist mayor of Tehran, and Ali Larjani, former head of the Islamic Republic of Iran Broadcasting.

In fact, in the first round of voting, if one attributes votes to three sectors of public opinion, reformists won nearly 40 percent. That includes Moin, the only candidate quoted by the *Tehran Times* as outspoken about women's rights. (He came in fifth, with 13.6 percent.) Pragmatic conservatives won over 35 percent (including Rafsanjani with 21.2 percent, leader of all), and hard-line conservatives just a quarter of the total ballots (with Ahmadinejad second overall at 19.2 percent). By segments of opinion,

---

32. Pollack, *The Persian Puzzle,* p. 371. A demographic statistic only half as youth-heavy is given by Ali Gheissari and Vali Nasr in *Democracy in Iran: History and the Quest for Liberty* (New York, Oxford University Press, 2006), pp. 153-54.

then, hard-lineism came in last of the three slices. But by the rules of the game (and despite a variety of allegations, the rules appeared largely to have been followed), the rigidly conservative Ahmadinejad joined the flexibly conservative Rafsanjani as the candidate in the second round. Reformists, the most numerous by segment, were maneuvered completely out of the picture in the runoff.

After we left Iran, Ahmadinejad trounced Rafsanjani, 62 percent to 35 percent. By giving ground on social purity and manipulating the political context, the Supreme Leader and the Guardian Council had preserved their regime. They channeled anger over the economy into a hard-line surge for Ahmadinejad. He ran as a downtrodden outsider and man of the people. Forty-eight years old, short and slight, with a Hizbollah beard, he began press conferences reading from the Qur'an. As mayor, he had turned some cultural centers into prayer halls. He was a pothole-fixer to his detractors, an effective and accountable public servant to his supporters. He promised militant Islamic socialism and a Third World-oriented foreign policy. Humble image and spartan campaign, promises of continuation of state subsidies and redistribution of wealth, all seemed to reawaken the "Jacobin policies of early years of the revolution."[33] He appealed to the urban poor and to disadvantaged provinces, while Rafsanjani's middle-class support trickled to a minimum. Not yet fully manifest was Ahmadinejad's occult and aggressive irrationalism that by 2008 had begun to make some mullahs highly uneasy.[34]

As a political father of Iran's nuclear program, Rafsanjani had the credentials for proceeding to accommodate a possible American policy of massive financial aid, unfreezing assets, settling claims, and removing sanctions in return for deceleration of nuclear enrichment. He had already performed a number of Persian reversals, as one might call the unfolding origami-like quality of policy-making at the top in Iran, when it hinges a contradiction to an assertion in order to establish both flexibility and gravity. But this artistry was unwelcome to an electorate that wanted a new sheet of paper. Who could care passionately for a magician of the pistachio concession, a man without enough facial hair to constitute a true beard, a fat-cat mullah whose greatest asset, in the words of one of my informants, was that he "can be relied on to double-cross his friends equally"? The Su-

---

33. "Jacobin policies," Gheissari and Nasr, *Democracy in Iran*, p. 154. I owe my election statistics to their Epilogue, pp. 148-56, but the shape of analysis is my own.

34. Nazila Fatih in the *New York Times*, 20 May 08, p. A8.

preme Leader had manipulated candidacies to yield his desired result. But, it could be argued, he concluded thenceforth that runoffs were too risky.

From Daryush Shayegan flow ideas born of worldwide experience and study. His physical being and clothing signify a transcultural man of many layers: wavy white hair worn long in casual disarray, silk scarf at his neck, shiny French loafers on his feet, jacket open to reveal a reddish magenta silk lining.

He left Iran in 1979 during what he calls its "counter-reformation," but after living in Paris until the early 1990s, he returned to his native land, because "even though there is *no* juridical or political security at all, here there is more emotional connection, and communal life." In his youth he studied Sanskrit, and he became a professor of comparative philosophy and theology at Tehran University. He says he would have become a Buddhist, "were conversion to have any meaning. But I am an Islamic Persian — I don't dream of Buddha."

Shayegan is highly sympathetic to the Mughal Indian Dara Shokuh, a prince, poet, and philosopher whose own brother, the emperor Aurangzeb, had him cruelly killed. Why? For his theory of monism, picked up through his Advaitya schooling and from his grandfather, the emperor Akbar, still famous for his ideal of religious tolerance. Dara Shokuh's "The Mingling of Two Oceans" apparently influences Shayegan's own Buddhistic stress on monism within Hinduism, which is in turn compatible with his own hospitable form of Islam, and antithetical to (the unmentioned) Wahhabia.

He speaks affectionately of his "occult country," Iran, and the convulsions of its last century. He believes that the future of all countries, including his own, is democratic. But democracy in what form? The ideas of 1906 are still the best ideas, because they reconciled modernism, the monarchy, and shari'a. He speaks of "Westoxification," *gharbzadi*, as do many mullahs, but he gives it a concise definition of his own: "being bitten by the West, but not understanding your infection."

"Not understanding" is a fundamental ailment in itself. Dismissive as Shayegan is of a youth culture infatuated with Michael Jackson and Madonna, he reserves his deepest, calmest fury for Islamic leadership everywhere — and above all in Iran. He sees a great many "second-level people" in the government, and "nobody . . . believes in the theocratic experiment. They think it's bankrupt. They don't know what to do." If there were a referendum now on church and state, 90 percent would vote for separation, and the regime could get only 6 or 7 percent for their principle. "But they can mobilize two or three million *in the streets*."

Almost all of what the Shah attempted in the 1970s was what Southeast Asian countries, with pragmatic nationalism, accomplished in the 1980s. But the "imperialist stooge" label was affixed to the Shah, and it stuck. Tehran was in a huge confusion in 1979, for which Shayegan resorts more than once to volcanic metaphor. A hot explosive energy propelled Iran all the way to a theocratic state, while Pakistan remains awkwardly stuck between modes of polity, and in Turkey, at most, 20 percent want Islamic law.

For the problems of modernity, "Islam as a religion has no collective solution to offer. There is no Islamic capitalism. It is a religion with laws of the seventh century which cannot be adapted. . . . So many paradigm shifts in knowledge have occurred that Islam can only answer questions about which we have no knowledge — where we come from, and where we go after death."

In psycho-political metaphors, Shayegan's book, *Cultural Schizophrenia: Islamic Societies Confronting the West* is a sophisticated exercise. The Iranian revolution of 1979 was equivalent, in the Indian caste system, to a *brahman* coup d'état against the *kshatriyas* (warriors). "But the monarchy has not been eliminated in favor of secularism or some kind of democratic government. On the contrary, one *myth* has been substituted for another, but it is a myth which, in the economy of the symbolic vision of forms, can only function in the presence of its *complement*. In banishing the king, the clergy did away with its own other half. . . . and offered itself as fodder to all the demons of temptation. . . . [This] situation, in which the priest crowns himself without becoming king, is the worst possible solution."

Shayegan takes some of the phenomena since characterized as "lipstick *jihad*" and gathers still more of them as a seething magma of discontent. "Under the old regime, militant Islam was the underside of the opposition movement, the refuge of the oppressed; now, after the explosion of our collective unconscious and the ensuing flood of vomit, it is modernity . . . that seethes in the secret underground life of Iranians."

The real danger of the Islamic revolution is that its lava cools in formless ways as heavy caps of obstructive rock. Its deepest threat is not in "its excesses, its random changes of direction, its blind groping, its utter obsolescence, but in the fact that, *being incapable of setting up a structured historical order,* it produces chaos; and this favors the most subversive and sinister elements who loiter in the corridors of power waiting for their time to come."[35]

35. Quotations above from Shayegan's book (1st French ed., 1989; 1st English ed., Lon-

Among crazed visionaries thrust to power by modern chaos, he mentions Qaddafi and Pol Pot. But their populations are a fifth and a tenth of Iran's, their GDPs a sixth and a sixtieth of Iran's. Iran, a prime early civilization, is now a pivotal modern state. The successor state to Persia would soon throw up Mahmoud Ahmadinejad as its elected president, a former commander in the Revolutionary Guard, reliant on Basiji thugs, a ranter against the Holocaust and the existence of Israel.[36] What will be his effect in time, I wondered. A shaper of history? Or just another noxious puff of pyroclastic ash from the volcano of Iran?

Shayegan had no comment on Ahmadinejad, for like all my interviewees he did not even imagine him becoming president. He uttered words of hope, from a totally different angle: "The women of Iran are far superior to the men . . . and more intelligent. . . . They have resisted, educated their children, done everything they could when men have given up."

Women in Mythology, Movies, and Investments

Of the thousand self-declared candidates for president of Iran in 2005, many were women. Although several might by global standards have been considered well-qualified, the all-male Guardian Council validated none of them to run. One of them, Dr. Nahid Tavassoli, helped found a women's party. She is also a leader of the Association for Women Journalists, and founder and publisher of the literary artistic magazine *Nafeh*. She later would become a founder of the campaign for "One Million Signatures Demanding Changes to Discriminatory Laws." As an expert in ancient languages including Sanskrit, Pahlavi, Sassani, and Avestan, she brings to the clamor of modern Iran her own voice and views, confident in her sources of learning, and in feminine values with far more ancient roots than those of Gloria Steinem. But she concludes, in her present work in progress, *Is Eve Really Missing a Rib?*, that the ancient cultures with which she has familiarized herself are of no use to modern women.

---

don, Saqi Books, 1992; Syracuse University Press ed., 1997); "Brahmin revolution," p. 174; "explosion of our collective unconscious," p. 96; "incapable . . . of structured . . . order," p. 99. Emphasis supplied in the last of these.

36. Nazila Fatih, reporting from Tehran, quoted Ahmadinejad, early in his regime, that Israel "must be wiped off the map." *New York Times,* 27 Oct 05. Others translated his Persian differently: "must vanish from the page of time." See Wikipedia, "Ahmadinejad, Translation Controversy."

All the other female party founders wear heavy *chador*, she said, except herself — even though she is a descendant of the Prophet from both parents. I noted that she had clothed herself in a white *manteau* with stylish gray stripes, and covered her hair with a plain white scarf. She had been in the U.S. on a fellowship in 1962-63, where she began to ask herself about Iran under the Shah: "Why are we under veil, with no authority in our lives?" She unveiled herself; but in Khomeini's time, "I wore first a little scarf to show I behaved in the revolution. If the Shah had stayed on, we might have become a little like Turkey. . . . But I didn't want *either* the Shah or this very prejudiced government." On veiling, on principle, her views are energetic. "The Qur'an *first* tells men to keep their eyes pure. If they did so, women would not have to pay the price of men's impure gazes. . . . Only because men are stronger and more aggressive does the Qur'an instruct women to cover themselves *defensively*."

As we talked in the lobby of my hotel, she suddenly asked me to note two men who had set up a camera on tripod some feet behind me. She said she was used to being followed and observed, but would feel more comfortable in our conversation if those men were not there. I rose and approached the two and told them that we would be happier not to be in the plane of whatever they were recording. One who spoke English asserted that they were just taking photographs of transactions at the cashier's desk, to which he vaguely pointed. Okay, I said, but please take us out of the angle of your lens. They picked up their equipment and moved. I did not see them relocate for another view of the cashier's desk.

Dr. Tavassoli, eyes gleaming through gold-rimmed spectacles, rolled on with her convictions, challenging an Iranian proverb that declares women's dreams to be *"false"* (which key word may also be translated as "left, wrong, flipped, or distorted"). Her articles and interviews, she took satisfaction in saying, are collected at the Center for Dialogue Among Civilizations. Her perspective on Abraham's religion, and on sacred Zoroastrian writings, is directed against *nezameh*, or patriarchy. She speaks passionately of "twenty-five hundred years of despotism here in Iran," causing women to suppress their abilities, or to fail, *ever*, to feel their potential. Nothing is holding back women in the U.S., Dr. Tavassoli feels. But it is vital to give Iranian women self-confidence, "while men change their minds."

As a deplorable example of how the male power structure works, she cited the case of a woman with a four-month-old embryo discovered to be malformed and threatening to her life. The parliament accepted and passed a bill by which severe handicap to the child or mortal danger to the mother demonstrated by that time could be resolved by abortion, if three medical specialists and legal experts agreed on that course of action. The Guardian Council, however, said *no* to the legislation, and without documenting its opinion, vetoed the bill as contrary to religious law. Tavassoli reacted by writing an article declaring that the Guardian Council itself, in this instance, had exceeded its constitutional prerogative. But when it was submitted to the editor of a major paper, he would not print it.

Qur'anic imperatives for purity begin with the story of Satan insinuating himself in the hearts of Adam and Eve — both of them — to eat from the forbidden tree and to make them consciously aware of their own sexuality: "And Satan began to whisper suggestions to the two of them, so that he might expose to them their private parts which had been hidden from them."[37] The imperative of purity is a key part of the teaching of Mulla Sadra, inseparable from the seventeenth-century percolation of Sufism through the Shi'ism introduced and sponsored by the Safavid Dynasty. His insights continue in genealogical transmission among mullahs, strengthening group cohesion and pride in being a spiritual elite. Their training in adolescent discipleship leads to accusations of homoeroticism by anti-clericalists. The very intensity of discipline in purity carries masters of this style far beyond the quietism associated in the West with mysticism, and it may produce men like Ayatollah Ruhollah Khomeini, who was indifferent to materiality, utterly confident of his own perceptions, and unwavering in following through on his personal will.[38]

Dr. Tavassoli's views of pre-history, myth, the Qur'an, and the present are vastly at odds with those of Mullah Sadra, his modern apostles, and the mindless among their followers. Sadra said woman is a beast to satisfy men's desires. He was completely wrong — "Eve is an awareness inside Adam," says Tavassoli. "She encourages Adam to eat the fruit of awareness, which distinguishes humans from all other creatures on earth." Only if a woman accepts a special part of a man, his sperm, to merge with an egg and grow in her body, can she create something new. And only if men accept their own *anima*, the feminine spirit inside themselves, will they be able to create something new.

As for power: a truly feminine woman in high responsibility would

---

37. Quoted without textual note in Roy Mottahedeh, *The Mantle of the Prophet: Religion and Politics in Iran* (Oxford, Oneworld Publications, 1985, 2005), p. 181. I cannot locate the identical language, but in Q20:120-21, Satan whispers, "'Adam, shall I show you the tree of immortality and power that never decays?' and they both ate from it."

38. Mottahedeh, *Mantle of the Prophet*, pp. 138-44, 183-84, 242-43.

not express an instrumental kind of male power. Instead she would try to demonstrate the transforming power of love. If women want to engage with ruling, they must do it *with men,* in mutuality and collaboration.

On this note of female *animus* joined with male *anima,* we concluded. We may have been photographed, or even recorded, but there were no domestic spies any longer visible to us.

Dogmatic religious practices, and the predominance of males as theater-goers, greatly inhibited cinema-making in Muslim nations. The "theme of women who fall when left without an owner" long dominated Iranian and Turkish films, from 1918 into the 1970s; and even when prostitute and vamp movies faded, other themes were oppressive in other ways. One was the rural woman of tears and suffering; another, especially notable in Turkey, was of the lower-class urban migrant woman who accepted humiliation. "She is someone who errs; who has to be physically punished. . . . She is honourable only when she does not live."[39] Even after mass urban migration greatly complicated society, top female stars had to play their various roles as if wearing a mask in Japanese *kabuki.* They were given no psyche. It took the combined impact of TV, video, and the Internet to bestow character — including sexuality — on women.

Ayatollah Khomeini did not advance artistic maturity. In the last year of the Shah's reign, fundamentalists burned an Iranian theater, killing hundreds of people. In the fervor of the early revolution, more than 180 theaters were burned. Several filmmakers were indicted as corrupting the public; others went into exile. Of 2,200 films re-inspected, only 200 received screening permits. For a while production stopped.[40] As Minister of Islamic Guidance and Culture, Muhammad Khatemi dared to say that the cinema was not the mosque. He was forced to resign under pressure in 1992, but then was twice elected president, 1997-2005.

In this environment Mrs. Tamineh "Bati" Milani grew up. Her parents wanted her to be a doctor or an engineer. She became an architect, but started working for a famous film director and then for herself; in the late 1980s she directed the first of what by 2006 were nine feature-length films. All of them, she said, are about the social and psychological problems of

---

39. Gonul Donmez-Colin, *Women, Islam and Cinema* (London, Reaktion Books, 2004), quotations of Ali Özgentürk on pp. 25, 34.

40. Donmez-Colin, *Women, Islam and Cinema,* pp. 7, 96. On fundamentalism against cinema, see also Hamid Naficy, "Poetics and Politics of Veil, Voice and Vision in Iranian Post-Revolutionary Cinema," in David A. Bailey and Gilane Tawadros, eds., *Veil: Veiling, Representation and Contemporary Art* (Cambridge, MIT Press, 2003), pp. 136-59.

Iranian middle-class women. She broke into a wide, big-lipped smile. Vitality bursts from her eyes and her laughter. Her movies generate a lot of fans but also frighten and anger critics. The label "feminist" is applied to her, which tag by itself stirs anger in many men, hatred in many women. For herself the term doesn't mean much. "What is 'feminist' in this society, when [for] abortion they can kill you?"

Faézé was with me to interpret, but Mrs. Milani, at home with her young daughter who was playing nearby, preferred to run off her thoughts in English. I got her point: if the shari'a penalty for aborting an unwanted child is execution, all the boundaries of independent action for a women are sure to be constraining. In Islamic theocracy, there is no room for a book entitled *Our Bodies, Ourselves* — a breakthrough essay in self-expression which I bought for my wife, on my own initiative, at its appearance in 1973.

The most daring of Milani's movies, because the most political in content, was entitled *Hidden Half* (2001). In it she tried to show what happened during the four years when "universities were closed" at the onset of the Shi'ite religious revolution. The cultural minister at the time she conceived the movie was Ayatollah Khatemi, and he gave permission to make and show the film. But the judicial system has always belonged to Khomeini and his ideological successors. "Bati" found herself tried, judged, and convicted of heinous crimes against the state. The formidable result was four death penalties against her.

Her hopes dwindled down to her friendship with Khatemi, who by then had been elected president. "He loved me. He tried to find me. But he didn't know which prison!" Testimony to an opaque society, that its president cannot learn in which jail a convict may be found! It turned out to be Evin: since the time of the Shahs, the most terrifying of all four-letter words for incarceration, and still so today. Khatemi eventually did find her, and after two weeks got her released — testimony to the power of friendship in any society. But nobody else has attempted that kind of movie since hers.

Having learned how dangerous it is to try to deal artistically in the underside of the 1979 revolution, Bati has since confined herself to her natural genre: the middle-class woman, and her male counterpart. She observes that because of the imposed religious culture, "all the time in Iran, women have two faces, one inside [the home], one outside. Not just religious people, all traditional people." Even worse: "Our women also have two faces *inside* the home — the image of what their spouses . . . want them to have, and what is [really] inside of them."

She believes that most educated women are, nonetheless, really "modern" in major ways, or even most ways. "But our men are traditional, want to change women, stop modernism. Mad! Foolish!" When *Two Women* was shown, she says, "Housewives came first thing in the morning, weep leaving the theater, weep all day long, send me e-mail, 'Now, Mrs. Milani, we feel we are part of humanity.'"

Her husband, she says, smiling, is exceptional. So was her father, "a really *democratic* man . . . and fortunately I had good brothers too." Brothers in our society, she said, have a major role in their sisters' lives, which can be constructive, "although sometimes they kill them if they have lover." One of her brothers, injured in the war with Iraq, came home a quadriplegic. She took care of him for ten years.

She is not anti-family, she stresses, responding to some of her critics. "I have good family." But the themes of her movies are about varieties of failure in families. *The Fifth Reaction* is a critique of a religious law that requires a widow to give her child to her father-in-law. *Unwanted Woman* is about a wife who lives simply in her house. Her husband goes philandering, gets AIDS, and then leaves her. Such a husband "abuses your faith, your love, your life." Why shouldn't he be criticized, even harshly?

Other husbands drain their wives' energies. But when Bati is sad, she says, she phones her husband, to whom she has long been married. In her one political movie, *Hidden Half*, she let her husband play the lover to Niki Karimi, a superstar in Iran for a full generation. "Women exclaim to me, 'Why? How can you do that!?' But I *trust* him."

A sympathetic man such as he is in danger, among Iranian males, of being considered a wimp. If a husband washes dishes for his wife, or takes special time to be her good friend, he may draw upon himself terms of dismissive opprobrium from other males. Considerate behavior threatens others' masculinity to such a degree that they will call him *zanzalil*. The word has such force that Faézé declined to translate it when it arose. "Afterward," she murmured. Later, when I inquired, she told me what it meant: "pussy-whipped."

"I continue *willingly* to do the traditional [woman's] role," Milani told me, "because it is the best way the family relax." After all the day's household chores, she rises from sleep at two a.m. to start writing, then sleeps a little again before waking at six a.m. to take her daughter, Gina, to school. Of the movie she was planning next, *Unwanted Woman,* she was "100 percent sure" that it would start fights in all families. It later won best director and best film awards at the Arpa International Film Festival in Hollywood.

She went on to make *Cease Fire,* a divorce comedy that set Iranian box office records.

Having found the regime too cruelly powerful to criticize, Milani would rather flaunt the professors, the critics, the intellectuals, "who are not real intellectuals. . . . They have sex problems. . . . They live like their fathers." Or the religious columnists who, trivially, say she is jealous of men having four wives. Or Abbas Kiarostami, the famous director of *Taste of Cherry* and other films. "Kiarostami hates my movies because he hates women. . . . He makes festival movies, maybe ten thousand come. But my movies, ten million come!" Bati threw back her head and laughed, happy with her own zest and daring and controversial popularity.

Later that day I asked Makan Zahrai, the publisher-bookseller, his opinion of Bati Milani. He replied that she dwelt too much on shortcomings in Iranian society. Then, smilingly: "She threatens your life, so you are willing to accept a high fever!"

But I had found Mrs. Milani insightful, with inspiring gusto. I had concluded our morning in her living room by asking, "If there were one handle to Iran which could change it by your taking it and turning it with others, what would that handle be?" She thought very briefly and answered with force: *"A cultural revolution led by women."*

What did she mean by that? There are more than 100,000 runaway girls in Iran. They run away to love, to have ten boyfriends, "to avenge their mothers and grandmothers." They may live in a subway, underground. Theirs is not necessarily the best way, but even if they achieve little, they are a sign of ferment in the society, and its deep dissatisfactions. There are also, in millions presumably, women who do not run away, who are settled and stable and yet also highly dissatisfied with the culture. "We have a lot of women like *me*. . . . They work alone, they do what they want. . . . [Because of my movies] they know me. They work apart from each other, but they feel together."

An authority on cinema involving women and Islam attributes to Tamineh Milani a courageous breakthrough in giving women in her films individuality and inspiring the generation to follow her with more daring film.[41] Still more broadly, I understood Bati, through her movies, to be feeding enzymes of cultural revolution into the Iranian system. But there

41. Donmez-Colin, *Women, Islam and Cinema,* pp. 152-53, 187-88. Among the many books of Hamid Dabashi, including several on film, is *Close Up: Iranian Cinema, Past, Present and Future* (London/New York, Verso, 2001) — a provocative, highbrow history covering the twentieth century.

has already been one religious eruption in her lifetime, and she has the experience of Evin prison, under death sentences, to remind her of the price of being adjudged as "counter-revolutionary."

Mrs. Mahnaz Nobari may be nearing fifty years of age. She receives us at midday in her office with a polite smile, not radiant but genuine. A *chador* frames her handsome face, a suitable study for a Rembrandt character portrait. Elements of softness and strength, passion and patience flicker across her countenance in subtle tension and counterplay, none allowed to dominate, because this is an experienced CEO who knows that the face she brings to her staff, her customers, her guests, may need to be at moments a mask, but even then a constant and readable reality. Just visible under the cowl of her *chador* are a stylish few dyed russet strands in her black hair.

Mrs. Nobari founded Donyayeh-Khobreh, the first and only investment trading firm in Iran led by a woman. This securities company serves nearly 2 percent of the Tehran market, and 15,000 customers, both retail and institutional. "I avoid publicity," she says, but she is gladdened by having once been written up in the *New York Times.* She is proud of her firm having been chosen by the board of directors of Iran's stock market as number one in the nation in quality of service. She "came to the stock market" under Rafsanjani, when there were about 200 Iranian firms involved. At that moment there were 422 companies.

Of the seven children of her parents, Mrs. Nobari is the only one not educated abroad. It was her own choice, not to immerse herself in American standards and expectations, but to do her best with the resources and limitations of Iran. At Tehran University she learned English and got an M.A. in accounting. She has been working ever since age seventeen, except for one year after the revolution. Her assiduity in learning remains impressive to her younger brother, with whom I later talked in San Francisco. He remembers the sound of her footsteps walking the flat roof of their home, end to end, with a book in hand to memorize the lessons required. She had calculated the number of paces involved so she did not have to look up and would not fall over the edge. Her disciplined intensity was so great that she developed knee problems.

Mrs. Nobari and I talked of Taiwan's market volatility (Iran is different, with much activity in price and volume, but not such dramatic rates of turnover) and of Jack Bogle's lectures to the mutual-funds industry on transparency. The latter subject appeared to worry her. "We are trying hard," through a market supervisory committee, to oblige companies to provide the public with trustworthy figures, quarter by quarter. There was a bad crash several years previous. Her own company had to struggle for three years afterward, but survived.

Was she constrained in any way as an executive by being female? "No limitation. I am free as a woman to do as I want. But I have to regard the principles of my country." She expressly averred that the government was not a problem. Her greatest preoccupation had been with her children — three daughters now in their twenties, of which two have doctorates in engineering from Cornell, and the youngest is studying art.

Coming from "a workaholic family," she established a pattern for her company a decade ago by arriving at the office at 4:45 a.m. Important meetings of staff are at five a.m., three hours before the market opens. "I worked on learning how to sleep less . . . how to get down to five or five and a half hours a night." I looked at her again with this in mind, and thought I saw, not a face of fatigue, but a look of prevailing discipline, capable of tolerating lesser achievers.

Our hostess for lunch was clear that her daughters are of immense value to her. She works hard so that they have "not just mother-daughter relationships," but profound friendships together. As for her employees, "With my life I want to show them they can accomplish anything they want. . . . Talk is cheap, so I try to show in work life and in family life what I mean."

Influence on society is always in her mind. "In every decision I make, I am trying to consider what is its legacy. . . . Your debt to society is only paid if what you do is viable and continues to have an impact." Gender questions do not trouble or impede her. She reads many books on women's issues. Problems of work/life/family are extant not just in the U.S. and Iran, but everywhere. "If you believe in yourself," she summarizes, "the society will believe in you."

I was struck by her forceful simplicity. Whereas a dramatic advocate like Bati Milani is constantly sketching webs of contradiction and drawing lines of confrontation, Mahnaz Nobari, far less visible and vocal, works like a laser surgeon, cutting straight through to what she sees needs doing. Faézé said to me afterward that Mrs. Nobari could be achieving more for Iranian women in the long run than Mrs. Milani. But that may reflect Faézé's own MBA training. Hope certainly abounds in undereducated cinema-goers as well, many millions of them.

Protestant Pilgrim in the City of Martyrs

History, properly written, is the story of salvation. That's not me speaking, nor am I quoting a megachurch Christian preacher. My friend Mahmoud Ayoub, a Lebanese-born Shi'ite, takes this view, having done a classic study of redemptive suffering. Small and almost completely blind, Mahmoud was raised in a Christian orphanage and trained how to read. He did so well that he became a scholar, with a tremendous capacity for memorized texts. He read himself from Christianity into Twelver Shi'ism, the largest branch of what Sunnis consider heretical schismatics.

The history of religion may be traced as theological writings, but is better viewed through popular piety and modes of devotion — ways in which men and women cast their souls before God in love and fear, for judgment. Instead of men arguing on paper about the nature of God, we might better study women and men on their knees, deep in hope or lamentation.

My fear for my weakening daughter and the imminence of her surgery for liver transplant made me an abject supplicant. Having lost my wife less than two years before, I did not know if I could bear losing my daughter, too. I told God this in my prayers, but there was no sign of being heard — only a feeling that at least I was telling the truth. I wished for an old cathedral in which to pray, such as Elizabeth and I had found in Siem Reap after two days at Angkor during the Vietnam War. Later Pol Pot had it pulled down as part of his moral cleansing of Cambodia, which turned to bones a quarter of its seven million people. Khomeini's absolutism was energized with reading the Qur'an rather than Karl Marx. But whatever the atmosphere, I wanted some *place* to tell God just how helpless I felt, and to ask for cosmic love to aid my daughter. So the intended trip to Mashhad became for me a Protestant pilgrimage in Shi'ite territory.

Mahmoud Ayoub told me a story of his own visit there in the early 1970s, which made me feel strangely ready to accept whatever I might find. When he reached the tomb of Imam Reza and made his prayers, a big Iranian convulsed in tears challenged his sincerity by asking, "Why aren't you crying?!" Mahmoud looked up as if squinting into the sun and answered, "I think that I am so small, and Imam Reza is so great, that perhaps *he* should weep for *me*."

Weeping is no incidental matter for a true Shi'ite, as Mahmoud's own book vividly details. The martyrdom at Karbala of Husayn, the Prophet's grandson, is the central event in time, through which all preceding and succeeding moments flow. Imam Reza told one of his disciples that he had been told by his father, on the authority of fathers before him, that when Husayn died the heaven rained down blood and red clay. If his disciple shall make a pilgrimage to Husayn's tomb and weep for him, God would forgive any sins, however grave or innumerable. Four thousand angels are charged by God to guard Husayn's grave and weep for him until the day that the Imam Mahdi appears as the avenger of his blood. Then they shall join him with the war cry, "Revenge for the blood of Husayn!"[42] Until that time, the duty of all human beings is to participate in the unending stream of tears. Weeping for the martyrdom of Husayn is to flow toward salvation. The indifferent will be damned. All time present is redeemable by sorrow for Husayn, until that future moment when his martyr's death is avenged. Understanding this helped me to see that Sunni and Shi'i are not merely separated by "beliefs." They are sundered by a blood feud twisted in every fiber of history. The Sunni, in the Shi'a view, carry a heritage of murder, whereas they themselves sacralize time and space with remembrance and acts of martyrdom. But Shi'ites, in the Sunni view, are dangerous deviants who unforgivably distort history and mangle tradition.

Husayn indeed, by conscious sacrifice of himself and his family, achieved a massive transformation of Muslim religious consciousness. Victory through sacrifice is everlasting. Sanctification through suffering is insuperable. The shrine of Husayn himself is in Karbala, southwest of Baghdad, troubled with modern tumults in Iraq. Imam Reza, the Eighth Imam, is in fact the only one of the twelve imams buried in modern Iran. His tomb, in the city of Mashhad ("place of martyrdom"), is the greatest pilgrimage site in that nation. There I would be in a genuine human stream of suffering, repentance, and supplication.

Mahmoud Ayoub had said to me, "If Shi'ites were Christians, every day would be Good Friday." I took that as an amusing exaggeration from a wise man. But what should be the power of Professor Alizamoni's theory of "sweet suffering," as a way of justifying love through redemptive pain? Such questions would later lead me to American female critics of Christian theology who understand abused children and battered spouses. They point out the dangers of the doctrine of atonement: letting oneself be

---

42. Mahmoud Ayoub, *Redemptive Suffering in Islam: A Study of the Devotional Aspects of Ashura in Twelver Shi'ism* (The Hague, Mouton, 1978), pp. 146-47. Ayoub, in his culminating arguments, pp. 229-35, shows the martyr Husayn not only as terrible judge but as compassionate pardoner.

locked in another's pain is misuse of the bond of empathy, which may make one captive to another's unjust demand. Rather than taking Christ's pain and sacrifice as supreme, they would exalt his love — "love [as] the wisdom of life that knows when connection can heal and when separation will make life flourish. . . . Love directs the use of specific powers in response to particular circumstances, for the sake of creating, sustaining or healing life."[43] From that point of view, not only is suffering without love a gross aberration of Christianity, but the pivot of Shi'ism on martyrdom might constitute a tragic flaw of that faith, and Alizamoni's "sweet suffering" a temptation to romantic masochism. Why concentrate on Good Friday, these critics ask, just one day of the year in which the violence of the Roman Empire prevails? Every day requires love, faith, coping, non-aggression, and intelligent self-defense. What would they do with the millennial, annual, and daily structure of Shi'ite self-flagellation and celebration of martyrdom? Abjure it, perhaps, or counsel flight from it.

But I was heading right into the heart of it, a stranger in an occult land, a seeker surrounded by apocalyptic faith; an ignoramus desperate for a holy place, where he might pray for his daughter and have his supplications amplified by the sacred appeals of others.

The conference organizers attempted to dissuade me from Mashhad. Their time and services as "minders" — responsible to their government if we should be spies, or trouble-prone klutzes — would be best fulfilled by my following their plan for us Americans to see Isfahan and Shiraz, with a side trek to Persepolis. All great architectural stuff, of imperial and secular import. But I wasn't seeking encyclopedic knowledge and tourist photos. I wished to approach wisdom by begging for my daughter's life. I knew that God saw into me and through me. By submitting myself to God, perhaps I would see in a flash a diagnostic image of my own soul.

My Baha'i friends, understanding my motives, had nonetheless counseled against such a trip. One of them later told me that she prayed for me. On my return she revealed the story of a British consular officer who had gone to the shrine of Imam Reza without the right motives and auspices, and was torn to death by a mob. Despite the buoyant mythos of the Imam himself, which includes the sympathetic title, "protector of the deer," there is a history of violence attached to the shrine. Reza Shah, the military seizer of power and founder of the Pahlevi Dynasty, had his soldiers in 1935 fire

---

43. A. Rita Nakashima Brock and Rebecca Ann Parker, *Proverbs of Ashes: Violence, Redemptive Suffering, and the Search for What Saves Us* (Boston, Beacon Press, 2001), p. 198.

upon a crowd protesting his edict that women not only might, but *must* unveil. They killed over one hundred people within the very grounds of the shrine.[44]

I sought, in peace, to go to Imam Reza's tomb. The prospect was daunting, but the introductions were helpful. Mahmoud Ayoub sent an e-mail to Mehdi Golshani, describing me as "a pious and decent man." Golshani, in eventual reply, sent me the telephone number of an astronomer in Mashhad, Farhad Rahimi of Ferdowsi University. Preoccupations of the conference for some time held me back from calling this stranger and invoking the credentials attributed to me. In any case, I considered my piety eclectic and my decency limited, but my need strong.

Getting about in Tehran, with its fourteen million people, took me through some of the most congested traffic I've ever seen, and certainly the most anarchically willful. (The fact that Ahmadinejad has a Ph.D. in traffic engineering appears irrelevant.) At a multiple intersection without a traffic light or a policeman, cars and trucks will all assume right of way and will grind gears and nudge fenders for a two-foot advantage. Taxi drivers working in this environment are likely to be frazzled wrecks or men of character. Faézé and I were lucky to wave down one of the latter just before leaving for Mashhad. He already had three other passengers, whom he dropped off one by one on the way. Then he asked Faézé about me and learned where I was from. America! He had relatives there. He hoped some of his seven children would go there.

Why was I in Iran? Going to the shrine of Imam Reza?! He pondered that. I asked what Imam Reza meant to him. "Justice! And miracles!" He exploded in wrath at the corrupt government. Tears streamed from his eyes as he railed against the wrongs that make life so hard for working men. On miracles he pressed his emotional accelerator again. Yes, he knew people who had been cured by praying at the tomb of Imam Reza. All the while we talked, I was leaning forward and he was flashing me looks through his rear-view mirror or turning his neck at the stops. When we disembarked I had his visage unforgettably in mind: steely gray hair, grizzled gray face, and narrowed glinting eyes. He asked that I pray for him to Imam Reza.

44. Over a hundred killed: Mottahedeh, *Mantle of the Prophet*, p. 60.

In the tarmac bus for getting on the plane for Mashhad I counted ten women in black *chador* and four with colored scarves, including a dark green and a dark blue worn by women otherwise completely in black. One young woman wore a tight pink dress and a pink-and-white scarf and had a young man beside her. Honeymooning, I thought, allows variation. Faézé's filmy olive scarf had been whipped about by the wind at the airport, requiring frequent re-tyings. There were no hand straps to clutch on the bus. When it lurched into motion, Faézé was thrown backward. I caught her around the waist before she crashed into the honeymoon pair behind us. I asked her the Farsi term for *excuse me,* and turned to the honeymooners. *"Bebakhshid,"* I said. They both smiled — the first smiles I had seen in the airport.

There were indeed very few live smiles anywhere in the capital city, although the billboards with messages from the presidential candidates, affected by American political culture, mostly sported smiling faces. When had political faces changed, historically? FDR's jaunty grin, I thought, broke the old mold. Dewey's toothbrush moustache, a fainthearted throwback to William Howard Taft, weighed down his mouth and lost him the election to a purse-lipped but congenial Truman. Eisenhower's wide smile established the ideal American political face thereafter as sunny and hopeful. Iran was just beginning to experiment with its face. On a journey to Mashhad, and in the city of pilgrimage itself, I expected no such play of countenance, but gravity to prevail, or sorrow.

Traveling toward a highly conservative city made me reflect further on headgear. The only rigidly enforced code I had seen was within the University of Tehran. All women, faculty and students, wore long black clothes with full or nearly full cover. "Government money," said Billy. "Enforcement shows where the power is." Some young women even take exclusion of hair to a medieval kind of wimpole, tight around the ears. One young female researcher, I was told, had an invitation to the U.S., but declined to comply with the American visa photo requirement that it reveal the ears. No visa for her; no research in the States.

We had been introduced to Roya, who runs a chic jewelry shop, with her own brightly crafted designs. Her scarf was even sparer than Faézé's, and her hair more abundantly displayed. The police had entered one day, and on a charge of immodesty, taken her away for sustained questioning. Professions of loyal citizenship got her nowhere; they closed her shop. Then she found four pieces of gold for them. The shop reopened.

Painful rebuke may strike at even modest variations from a severe norm. Roya's friend Cimine was praying in full black with a decorative pin to hold her *chador* cowl to her hair, avoiding constant adjustment. A female monitor suddenly swatted her with a stick and accused her of worse-than-laxness, wearing the forbidden. In telling such stories, stylish women sometimes reflect on the lack of education in their monitors, or their possible previous prison records, or the charge on which they might have been imprisoned — prostitution, perhaps?

An Indonesian under Suharto's dictatorship in the 1990s said to me, "We are only a police state six hours a day" — an amusing assertion of freedom combined with anxiety. In a like spirit, I wonder how many more hours a day Iran under Khamenei is a police state. Political surveillance and thought-control clearly attempt to be more comprehensive than clothes-policing.

Mashhad sits five hundred miles east of Tehran, a city of three million at the craggy border corner near Afghanistan. It was once a stop on the Great Silk Road. Now it is best known for attracting 12, or some say 20, million pilgrims a year, most of them too poor to make the hajj to Mecca.

We were booked at a former Hyatt, half an hour outside the center. But on a hunch in the taxi from the airport we redirected the driver into Mashhad itself, and after a bit of looking settled on a post-Edwardian hotel — ornate but clean-looking, with a campy color scheme, and large fountain and pool that won out over chairs for lobby space. The desk clerk asked Faézé what our relationship was. She told him we were attending the same conference. Only in my room, at last, did I make a phone call to my ultimate contact, the astrophysicist at Ferdowsi University. It was his day off, Friday. He said he would come instantly.

Farhad Rahimi proved to be a tall, muscular, balding man in his fifties. He strode into our hotel purposefully with an inquiring face. We sighted each other fifty feet away and, heading right into earnest conversation, decided to go to the Imam Reza complex immediately for the time of midday prayer.

I was now in the company of the two people who were enabling me, a Pennsylvania Presbyterian, to approach the great Shi'ite shrine — Faézé, by language, and Farhad, by male authority. There would be so much to take in that I here split my memory in two parts: Saturday night's return there with Faézé, and our original Friday afternoon visit with Farhad.

Faézé is a tri-cultural person. She lived for a while in Paris before coming to the U.S., where she graduated from Amherst College. She got an MBA and worked in New York for Lloyd's Bank before marrying, in her mid-thirties, a bright and courteous Boston Brahmin, Richard Woodville. Faézé remembers North Tehran, the skyline of the Alborz mountains, and high-walled family enclosures, none of which I ever entered. ("Back there," she would point, as we shot past a curving alleyway in a taxi.) Her nostalgia includes the kinds of rural memories pictured by Terence O'Donnell, of wood-chopping, and juicing pomegranates, sour cherries, and limes, among a poor and forgiving, poetic and voluptuary people. There is no word for "romantic" in Farsi, O'Donnell says, or for its opposite, "realist": "No Iranian would so limit his sense of the world by being one or the other."

Faézé's memories of France seemed to be best evoked by guitar-playing songsters, male or female. She was an early fan of the sultry fatalist, Carla Bruni. Her views of the U.S. are savvy and aggressive. When George W. Bush finally realized early in 2006 that he had better talk to the American people about a foreign policy they saw gone awry, his staff chose the City of Brotherly Love as the setting. Questioners were not screened ahead of time, and in the audience, Faézé caught Bush's eye immediately. Her direct and doubting query on Iraq made the front page of the *Philadelphia Inquirer* and other major newspapers.

The Faézé who volunteered to accompany Billy and me to Iran was already accomplished in adventure travel. Before marriage she had made her way alone deep into Amazonia, joining up there with a group of pistol-wearing, freely cursing naturalists. They accepted her because she could do her part hacking open a path with a machete. She managed their combination of protection and menace, and achieved the feat of bathing alone, naked in the Amazon, the acme for her of all that is primal, green, and wild.

In an even more dangerous adventure, after she had become a mother, she traveled alone in the Chinese provinces, without knowing the Chinese language, and made her way illegally to Tibet. There she was eventually apprehended by police, held, and interrogated for hours. Despite even more intimidating all-male company, the possibility of prison, and the most severe indignities, she negotiated a bribe with them for her unmolested exit from Tibet. She cites with triumph what she whittled them down to: twelve dollars to let her go.

Now she was our guide in her native land, which remained officially hostile to America. Billy was off in Shiraz with the minders. Mashhad for a pilgrimage was foreign to Faézé as a non-religious aristocrat, and she belittled my ultimate destination as "Imam Reza's mosh pit." But its popular sanctity, its very strangeness, its alien golden mass, made it a magnet for me. Even so, without Farhad Rahimi I would not have reached my goal.

Three major financial foundations express Iranian beliefs. Each of them is also a complex political network with leaders at the top who command extensive employment patronage for their beliefs. Endowment of the Shrine of Imam Reza, estimated at a value of $25 billion, surpasses the two other largest, the Martyr's Foundation ($20 billion) and the Foundation for the Downtrodden ($15 billion).[45] These asset values suggest the uppermost order of priorities of Shi'ite theocracy: first, building and support of a massive worship and cultural center for pilgrimage (exceeding even Vatican City, which is less than 60 percent of its size); second, glorification of those who die in politically prescribed holy struggle; third, alleviation of the plight of the poor.

Mashhad's giant religio-cultural complex is beyond full reckoning by a stranger on his first visit. Faézé and I went back on Saturday night for 7:30 prayer. Again the complex was swarmed by thousands, but fewer than at Friday midday. We sensed more clearly the vastness of the main marble assembly square and the only slightly lesser vastnesses of the several other prayer courtyards. Just the prayer rugs and staff needed to shake them out represented an enormous investment of money and time.

At last I took in the Persian mirrors, which Faézé chided me for not having noticed — the myriad embedded fragments of mirrored glass, mosaics that threw back the lights of giant chandeliers, while also reflecting the silver and gold of major structural elements and decorations. (I later reckoned that I prefer God as a still, small voice to any deity of bedazzlement.) The total impact was a crackle and snapping of light upon light underneath a dark blue mountain sky.

People swarm around the squares and corridors, supplying human warmth in the cold. Shoes come off at the areas of prayer carpets and are carried in a plastic bag. Men and women divide at entrances; merge; redivide for gendered internal halls of prayer; part definitively for access to the golden latticed tomb of Imam Reza. There, on the male side, always, a jostling, weeping mob. Women are a mob apart, segregated in religious ecstasy.

Before going to the women's side, Faézé, dressed in a white *chador*

---

45. Estimates on foundations: Gheissari and Nasr, *Democracy in Iran*, p. 123.

with black flowered designs, had said we should meet outside the golden dome. Now trying, I realized I wasn't sure what she meant. I turned back and proceeded straight ahead until I encountered gold. After a thronging confusion I came out under a golden arch. Dome? Arch? Maybe she had spoken loosely. I waited there about fifteen minutes, watching the women emerging from their devotions. Among the many hundreds of all-black *chadors* I saw dozens of white-and-black. But none of them was Faézé. Okay. Not *arch*. I put on my shoes and went a long distance looking upward for a golden dome. When I finally spied a massive and unmistakable domelike thing, it was clearly at the other extreme of that temple, opposite the outside which I was now on. So I reversed my path and proceeded through all the now semi-familiar turning points, checking stations, and guards with feather dusters for crowd control. I saw no Western faces at all, and not the one familiar Persian face. I worried about Faézé having to walk all the way back to the hotel on the rocky road in her stocking feet. I had picked up her shoes.

Finally, in my zigzag confusion of places, in a hall of women who had been praying, framed in a *chador,* a familiar countenance. It looked serious. I smiled at the face. Faézé smiled back.

For the hike returning to the hotel, we had first to get out of the massive Imam Reza complex. Even she had to ask directions of the guards — three different times.

The *Lonely Planet Guide* to Iran, that adventurous modern guidebook, cautions the fair, six-foot, blue-eyed Christian against trying to get to the Inner Shrine. Four warnings in two pages, concluding with "Do not attempt to enter the actual shrine unless you are a Muslim."[46] But in Farhad Rahimi we had a prominent scientist of the Imam Reza complex to accompany us. Without lunch, we three set out on foot from the hotel along the crumbling sidewalks toward the gold. Always it glinted above the low-profile city horizon against its mountain backdrop. In our half-hour walk he chatted with me in English. I told him about my daughter, whose liver transplant was just nineteen days away. Farhad then dropped back on the narrow broken sidewalk to talk with Faézé in Farsi. He asked her, "How long has Dr. Friend been a Shi'ite?"

46. "Do not attempt to enter": Oct 04 edition, pp. 323-24.

She answered him, "He is not a Shi'ite."
He thought a bit and asked, "How long has he been a Muslim?"
"He is not a Muslim."
Professor Rahimi left it there.

First he took us to the Science Museum, adjacent to my goal. This was his home in the grander-than-Vatican shrine center of Shi'ism. In it we saw stunning, disparate collections of armor and weapons; of coins back to Philip of Macedonia, and older; of opaline bowls and all kinds of seashells, including a large Cyprae Tigris, whose stripes inspire its name. There were giant golden and ivory doors inscribed with holy calligraphy, and previous gold-latticed tombs with sarcophagi for Imam Reza, the grandeurs of which had come to be seen, from time to time, as insufficient. His current place of rest (2001), just a few minutes away from the museum, represents the upscalings in the last thirty years enabled by petro-gold.

After a superb astronomy section, which Rahimi had assembled himself, he brought us down to a room where we were served sweetened tea. He explained an arrestingly ugly mummified fish which had caught our notice. The mounted object was about eighteen inches tall, with a gown-like fish-tail, a royal torso, a crown-like cap, and a bare skull with a conspiratorial smile. There is a myth about her, Farhad said with a smile. He attributed the myth to the imagination of a guard in the science museum itself. She represents a woman turned to a beast by her lust and anger. She passionately desired a particular man in marriage, but he was denied to her. In fury, she tore up the pages of the Qur'an. For that blasphemy she was transformed into the bestial figure of the mummified fish.

"Sad fate," I said, "for a disappointed woman."
Faézé corrected me: "A *devastated* woman."

After tea, our only midday nourishment, Farhad walked us through giant prayer courtyards, each drawing in thousands for the climactic prayer of the week — Friday. Attendants were unrolling, snapping out, and throwing down prayer rugs. The *muezzin* was beginning his loudspeaker call, imperative and harshly pure. At different places we took our shoes off; at others put them back on, proceeding from cold marble to hot carpet and back again. At certain checkpoints Faézé would be peeled away, later to rejoin us. At these early places Rahimi was recognized, and he easily nodded me through as a friend. As the crowd thickened, he pulled out his white shirttail and beckoned that I hang on to it. Even so, we were cut apart twice by men barging between us in the crowd.

Now we were carrying our shoes in small plastic bags provided.

Guards with bright feather dusters were signaling which way to go, and fluff-tapping any loiterers to urge them onward. Faézé's white and black flowered *chador*, an affluent contrast to the all-black worn by most women, was now dissolved in a flow beyond our sight.

Suddenly, around a bend, the golden tomb of Imam Reza was visible. But not fully visible. Between a gold base and ornate gold roof, tall, tightly latticed windows of precious metal — white gold, perhaps, or silver — surrounded the tomb to the height of a basketball rim. Whatever lay on the floor within the windows was obscured by throngs of men eight or ten deep, pushing to get close enough to touch the lattice, to throw their votive offerings through it, and in the cacophony of sobs and wails, to pray. Rahimi told us later that occasionally he had shoveled out the tomb, knee-deep in currency, coins, mementoes, and flowers.

We stood a moment at our entranceway watching the struggle. Farhad took back his shirttail. He gestured that I was on my own now. I saw a man resting his head in the cavity of a doorjamb, weeping and shuddering in his unique ecstasy. If anyone had swung that giant gate closed, it would have crushed his skull.

I eased my way in, then muscled along, using the advantage of long legs and long arms. Nobody said *"Bebakhshid."* Those who tried to bump me aside ignited my soccer reflexes, a swiveled hip in return. I kept my hands high so that I would lay them on nobody. My elbows were free for defense and offense. All action was impersonal, to meet dumb physical challenges, to keep basic psychic space. I slid and shoved toward the tomb to save my daughter by desperate supplication. When I got close I saw men with young sons on their shoulders leaning forward to let their boys grab the lattice. I realized I was as tall as a man plus a perched boy — but with a longer reach. I need not battle to breathe against the gold. I could stretch over the heads of two layers of men and clutch the lattice, which I did. And reached with my other hand into the pants pocket with the paper money in it, which I fished up, uncounted dollars and rials, and, several lattice squares above other hands, flicked it all into the dark within.

Thus my *nazr*, supplicant gift. I prayed inchoate prayers for Timmie, her life, and the health of her donor. I prayed for all associated with me. I prayed for those new acquaintances in Tehran who, learning of my pilgrimage, had sought prayers on their own behalf, including the taxi driver who took it as his right to expect from Imam Reza both "Justice! and "Miracles!" These prayers took a short and telegraphic time.

I edged out sideways. Other men surged in, swiftly sucking up the trail

I left behind. I slipped back to Farhad as he stood composed beyond the commotion. He asked if I would care just to watch the people. I said I would. He remained a little behind me and to my left in the din. After a minute I heard his friendly deep voice in my ear: "If you want to cry, it's all right."

My eyes on the golden lattice, I broke into sobs. I hadn't known the sobs were there, waiting to get out. They burst forth abruptly in a helpless seizure, and tears streamed down my face. I did not repeat my prayers, but I suddenly remembered and cried for my deceased mother, my departed wife, my endangered daughter, and the women I love. In a life-flashing-before-me, as it is said to do at the moment of death, came my loves and fears, my longings and concerns, and I knew myself powerless before them. Weeping, I entreated Allah/God to take care of the faces that flashed past me.

When I was done sobbing, I turned to Farhad and embraced him in a bear hug. He held me and kissed me on the cheek. Later he told Faézé that he felt Allah had appointed him to be with me that day, and that he wanted to press me to his heart. Over our protests he took us to his home for lunch. His wife hadn't sufficient food, so they sent their children out for kebab and rice. He opened his beat-up computer to me, where I tried to answer family messages, while he played backgammon on the floor with Faézé. She won. We ate with delight. Twice more before we left I hugged Rahimi and called him my brother.

Afterward I wondered to Faézé how Farhad had got me past the last and most serious of the guards, who questioned him carefully just before the tomb. They had talked about it. She said, "He told them, 'He is a new Shi'ite.'"

I am touched by Farhad's untruth — indeed, his daring lie — which enabled me to pray for my daughter at Iran's holiest shrine. He, blessed man, took an interest in her welfare. For the operation, at the University of California San Francisco Hospital, all of Timmie's family were there, and naturally all of the donor's family — the donor was her husband's stepsister. There is a photograph of sixteen of us in the family waiting room. A senior operating nurse gave us instruction in what to expect. "Liver transplants are messy and fun." That got our attention. Messy because there is blood everywhere, all the time. "And fun, because miracles are fun."

Farhad, for an astrophysicist, seemed to me remarkably interested in miracles. I was thrilled that Timmie came through having her liver carved out of her body and half of Kim Webb's sewn in. The days of her intensive care, the pain and the fear, are past now, but they harrowed us all. The big studs on her belly are long gone too, but four dozen of them had been needed to clip together the skin where her gut had been gashed to let the fingers of the surgical team do their work, and dozens more of smaller clips remain inside. The husband cut the diseased organ out; the wife sutured the healthy organ in. Astonishing. Five years of practice on adult-to-adult live liver transplants, ten hours in the operating room, as the culmination of half a millennium of modern medical discovery. The gallop of surgical advances in my own lifetime and the teamwork of nurses, researchers, and doctors seemed to me miraculous, and so I told Farhad by e-mail.

Dr. Rahimi, however, wished to ascertain the possibility of a different kind of miracle. He asked me to inquire of my daughter's state of spirit at the very moments I was praying and weeping for her, half a world away at the tomb of Imam Reza. I did ask Timmie, allowing for the eight-hour time difference, any recollections she might have of those minutes; but they were all a blur to her, in preoperative nights of sleeplessness.

This I told Farhad. And I reasoned to him that miracles need not involve simultaneity, as in biblical examples, such as Jesus to the hemorrhagic woman who touched the hem of his garment: "Thy faith hath made thee whole." Or Jesus, hands-on with the blind man, using mud and spit and restoring his sight.

Mashhad, however, like Lourdes, seems devoted to the instant miracle. If my taxi driver, as well as many modern people in Tehran, are to be believed, such miracles occur. As for me, I am endlessly thankful for the cumulative miracle that my daughter's surgery represents: her new liver grew from 750 cc to 1300 cc in three months, and immunosuppressive medicines in perilous balance keep her body from rejecting Kim's precious gift. I remain grateful for the continuing miracle of her return to life — loving, laughing, and working. Two years after her transplant, she bore her first child — a miracle compounded.

There remained an Iran less beautiful than the fountains of Isfahan, or Faézé's childhood memories of family compounds, or the kindnesses of Golshani and Rahimi in getting me to Imam Reza's tomb. As we walked away from the complex on that Friday afternoon, I heard the loudspeaker come on again, and not in summons to prayer. I caught the name Khamenei and the word "Engleesh." Faézé translated for me, part of a sermon on the wrongs in Palestine and Iraq, which called for death to America, England, and Israel. I said I thought that incitement to war from the *minbar,* pulpit, was profane. But I was told that the government pays the clerics to make it happen.

When we returned to Tehran, we were on our own routines, hastening toward the end. An afternoon before departing, Faézé, on the way from her family's apartment to join us, chose to buy me a bunch of lilies-of-the-valley, for which she used the French word *muguet.* She waved at Billy, who was having tea in the lobby, sashayed into the elevator, and came up to my room, where I was sorting through notes and papers. She put the flowers in a glass of water on my table by the window.

We were seated there, planning an interview, when a loud knock sounded at the door. I opened it to see two uniformed bellmen and the duty manager, elegant Mr. Assidi. The burlier bellman barked at Faézé and beckoned her to come. I appealed to Mr. Assidi, who ignored me. In a trice they were gone. I shoveled my papers into my briefcase and ran out to the elevator. It took eternity to come up, and forever going down.

A shaken Faézé was talking with Billy at his tea table. He'd seen the duty manager grilling her from behind a desk while the bellmen stood over her.

"I come from the *moon,*" Faézé told them.

"You are *Irani,*" they said. "You should know better than to be in a room with a man not your husband."

"I come from ten thousand miles away."

"You are Irani and must live by Iranian rules."

Billy saw the agitation on Faézé's face. He came over and asked what the problem was. One of them told him. "She's our interpreter," Billy said. "There's nothing out of order here." With severe warnings, they let her go.

"At least," said Faézé, "they didn't stone me to death."

"I'm six feet two," Billy said, in that moment no longer a Quaker pacifist. "And I would have ordered in a nuclear strike."

By e-mail from America I was able to tell Farhad Rahimi how well the surgery had gone for my daughter and her donor. Farhad wrote back: "Your face is often against me, especially the moment that you started crying, and I embrace you as my brother. I thought that was a miracle . . . by itself. That was a moving and impressive moment. I found that you let go of all your inhibitions. It was a pure act."

I answered Farhad that whatever the moment was, his purity of hospitality enabled it to happen. Now that moment seems like a micro-storm on the perimeter of a true and brilliant miracle, the renewal of my daughter's life. In any case, I told him, you will always be my brother.

Surgers against the Systems, 1844-2009

What was going on, socially and politically, before the tumult in the streets, 2009, and its quelling? Iran's population, growing fast, was approaching 75 million. In the 1950s only a quarter of it had been urban, a factor that had increased to half by the time of the revolution. Now four-fifths of Iranians are urban or semi-urban. They are also mostly young: born after the revolution, and not old enough to have served in the defining war with Iraq. They are educated; not only the largest cities, but middle-sized towns have at least one center of advanced learning. They are technologically savvy, as proven among crowds by instant transfer of handheld video images of protest and repression, and invention of a verb, "bluetoothing," for that act. Women are preponderant among the educated, and prominent in protest.

What kind of a society does such a young and savvy population desire? Abbas Amanat, a professor of history at Yale, notes that such a society cannot isolate women from the Internet or insulate them to be unpolitical. The bi-gendered blend of ferment that results, in his belief, wishes to be a stable and balanced society, not a pariah among nations. It may wish a more secular society.[47] Certainly it is not at all levels entranced with the idea of an End-of-Days society advanced by Ahmadinejad — although the undereducated and the overzealous respond to him.

To say that Iran has a totally new and much larger middle class than it had at the time of the Revolution is surely true; but what does that amount to? The rise of a middle class does not guarantee salvation to any nation. And, in Iran's case, it may be offset by considerable lower-middle and

---

47. Kathryn Day Lassila, editor, summarizes her interview with Professor Abbas Amanat in the *Yale Alumni Magazine*, Jul/Aug 09, p. 2.

underclass millenarianism. Disaggregating the dynamics, one may conceive of young, urban, educated, and female-invigorated sectors of society as thinking differently from the clerical patriarchs of Qom and other cities likewise networked; and also differently from the Revolutionary Guard veterans of the war with Iraq, who pursue the corporate and fiscal momentum which their benefactor, Ahmadinejad, has helped enable. And yet: not all young are kind — men under thirty make up the Basij. And not all women are peaceful — there are female corps of Basiji as well.

Demography alone will not tell us where Iran is headed. But the will to repress has clearly prevailed since the protested election. The will to reconstruct may eventually surpass it, but not on symbolic acts alone. Heavy costs may have to be paid. To stuff a rose in the barrel of a gun will not work if the wielder of the weapon is willing to pull the trigger.

Historical perspective helps. Across the last century and a half, Iran has several brief times pulsated with challenges to existing systems, sometimes failing, sometimes leaving accomplished reform, and once erupting in transformative revolution. Common to all those challenges, and contradistinctive to the histories of the other nations in this study, is the Shi'ite historical consciousness, which insists on the value of martyrdom. And coiled within the martyrology is a tensile alloy of ideas about the end-of-time and establishment of justice. The Hidden Imam (the Twelfth, in occultation now for over a thousand years) will reappear as the Mahdi, the Islamic messianic savior, to defeat the Deceiver, redress all wrongs, and transform the material world. The spiral spring of such ideas is capable of leaping forth unpredictably, with power.

Reform was notable and practical in the Constitutional period, 1905-11, when the Shah had to accept a national consultative assembly and the first elections ever, in 1906. Reform was truncated and foiled by Anglo-American imperial force in 1954. Mossadegh was confined to his home, and a cruel and vacillating puppet shah, the last Pahlevi, was put in power for a quarter-century.[48] Shah and imperialism were both routed in 1979 in a volcanic explosion. The Islamic Republic of Iran preserved 1906 elements of democracy, while capping the volcano with Grand Ayatollah

---

48. On 1906 and 1954: William R. Polk, *Understanding Iran* (New York, Palgrave Macmillan, 2009), pp. 92-93, 113ff.

Khomeini's unique theory of the Guardianship of the Jurist, with Khomeini himself as the first and far-reaching definitive guardian.

Against this last structure have contended what may be called 1906 democrats (not to over-label them as Western liberals) and the ever-growing proportion of Iranian young who have not suffered for the Revolution or the subsequent war against Iraq. For what proportion of the regime's critics does Zahra Rahnavard speak? The wife of Mir-Hossein Moussavi broke precedent by campaigning with him and being photographed holding his hand. In her own right, she is an artist, and was the first female university president in Iran. When Ahmadinejad challenged her credentials, she denounced him as a liar. But even if she was the woman in highest Iranian political focus in 2009, she was far from emanating the charisma of Quarrat al-ʿAyn (1814-1852), the first modern Muslim woman anywhere symbolically to remove the veil.

Born as Fatima Zarrin Taj Barraghani, Quarrat al-ʿAyn was married at age fourteen to her uncle's son and bore him three children. She was such a youthful prodigy of religious learning that her father, one of many well-known *ulama* in the family, lamented she was not male. The philosopher Rashti, absorbed in messianic prophecies, named her Quarrat al-ʿAyn (Solace of the Eye) in tribute to her beauty and sublimity of mind. After her unveiling raised vicious rumors of unchastity, the Bab himself named her Tahira (the Pure One). Her religious thirst as an intelligent human and her severe boundedness as a woman of that time fused in dream and poetry with a passion for the justice that would come with the Mahdi. While she never met the Bab, she saw him as that savior, and eloquently advocated his cause even after his execution by firing squad in 1850. She had made her case for religious independence and political revolt unforgettable in 1848 at a conference of Babis by removing her veil in the middle of a speech. That symbolic act of defiance embraced all shariʿa. "I am the word that the Qaʾim [the Emergent Imam as Deliverer] will utter, the word that shall put to flight the chiefs and nobles of the earth."[49]

She began to brandish a sword to emphasize sacrifice rather than prayer. In audaciousness she put herself ahead of male followers of the Bab, and even perhaps the Bab himself, by dressing unveiled in men's clothing, mounted, and waving a bare sword. The government eventually detained her, and finally asked for a death sentence. In the middle of a

---

49. Abbas Amanat, *Resurrection and Renewal: The Making of the Babi Movement in Iran, 1844-1850* (Ithaca, Cornell University Press, 1989), ch. 7, *passim*; quotation, p. 326.

night she was strangled in secret by a drunken black slave. She offered him her own scarf. He jammed it down her throat.[50]

Qurrat al-ʿAyn, in rejecting the Islamo-Persian social order, expressed her soul as "enamored with torment," and a learned mind so intent on dynamic progress as to embrace martyrdom. She did not know of European suffragists, and her entire worldview was religious, without any secular concept of women's emancipation as much later found in Iran.[51] She was closer in spirit to Joan of Arc than to her American contemporary, the pan-social activist Lucretia Mott. She was not merely the first female unveiler in recent Islam. She was a model and advocate of independent will and action, not only for women, but on religious grounds for all believers.

The rebellious new faith, after many executions, retreated from the ideal Babi political revolt, and carried forth the Baha'i religion. Its universalist and pacifist doctrines have preserved it as a worldwide faith. But if an Iranian, male or female, were to look in national history for an example of resistance to arbitrariness by the state, obscurantism among the mullahs, and torpor in the society, Qurrat al-ʿAyn might serve as a worthy model.

50. John S. Hatcher and Androlla Hemmat, eds., *The Poetry of Táhirih* (Oxford, George Ronald, 2002), details, p. 11.

51. Amanat, *Resurrection and Renewal*, pp. 330-31.

5.1 Atatürk with his wife Latife. They married early in 1923. He divorced her two and a half years later.
Photo: Radikal, *Ankara*

5.2 Atatürk (mid-1930s) with one of his adopted daughters, Sabiha Gökçen. She became the world's first female combat pilot. *Photo:* Radikal

5.3 Lunch honoring former President Suleyman Demirel, Ankara, June 2004. From left, Prof. Talat Halman, author, Nezir Kirdar, Demirel, Rector Dogramaci of Bilkent University. *Author's photo*

5.4 AK Party demonstrator wearing a çarşaf; Kahramanmaras, Southeastern Turkey, **2002.** *Photo:* Radikal

5.5 Prime Minister Tayyip Erdoğan and his wife Emine, who is, as requested, bestowing on him an award from the Intermedia Economy Group, Ankara, 2003. *Photo:* Radikal

5.6 Prof. Ali Bardokoglu (in white), Director of Turkish Religious Affairs, with Patriarch Bartholomeos (on his left) of the Greek Church, after an iftar dinner, Ramadan 2004.

Photo: Radikal

5.7 Duygu Asena, in her office as journalist, about 2000. *Photo:* Radikal

5.8 International Women's Day, March 2005: police with batons disperse demonstrators, Beyazit Square, Istanbul. *Photo:* Radikal

5.9 The family of Fatma Benli was part of the vast Turkish rural-to-urban movement of the late twentieth century. She received her university degree and law training before secularist regulations forbade covered heads on campuses and in court. Now she must argue cases through associates. A great public cause takes much of her time: the use of the brains of Turkish women regardless of what they wear on their heads.

Photo: Author's collection

5.10 Kurdish women gather in a park in the city of Konya. *Photo: Abbas/Magnum*

5.11 Dervishes (hatted), one of them a woman, gather among Alevis in their prayer house on the anniversary of the death of Atatürk, Istanbul, 2002. In this one image are suggested several elements that may blend in the energy of Turkish syncretism: Zoroastrian, Hindu, and Shi'ite rituals fused in the Alevi minority form of Islam. Also: hospitality to Sufism, modern feminism, and Kemalist secularism.   *Photo: Abbas/Magnum*

Chapter 5

TURKEY

Atatürk's New Nation

In Istanbul, I was told of a kindergarten girl who said, "Mommy, when I grow up, I want to marry Atatürk." When I repeated the story to an Istanbul feminist, she thought about it for a moment and commented: "*Marry* Atatürk? Why doesn't she want to *become* Atatürk?" The sequence illustrates the extraordinary power of Mustafa Kemal in the minds of the people he willfully shaped into a nation. Despite his modern critics, and regardless of his ideological packaging by the military, Atatürk lives on as a demigod. The enduring clarity of his ideas contends with a new socially and politically muscular Islam which has gone beyond his vision.

The reputations of Atatürk's famous contemporaries have shrunk. Jinnah will always be faulted for dying too soon, leaving Pakistan an orphan. Reza Shah Pahlevi, who tried to imitate Atatürk for Iran, could not pull it off, and left a weak and arbitrary son as monarch. Abdul Aziz (Ibn Saud), Atatürk's contemporary in birth who lived fifteen years longer, most nearly approximates him in forming Saudi Arabia; but to prevail among warring tribes does not measure up to countering Britain, France, Italy, Greece, and Russia all at once, while overthrowing the internal stranglehold of the Ottoman bureaucracy. Sukarno, with his five principles of Pancasila, rivals Atatürk in ideological heritage, but Kemalism's six principles are undergirded by strong policies and overlaid with courageous personal example. Indonesia still struggles to overcome the institutional deficit in which Sukarno left it, while Turkey evolves institutions that are Kemal's heritage.

How did Atatürk himself become Atatürk? The boy, Mustafa, "chosen," was born in Thrace (now Greek territory) in 1881 to a father who was a forest warden. His mother, Zübeyde, was blonde, blue-eyed, pious, and veiled. His father died when he was seven years old, after having gotten his son into a suspect Western-style school whose style of learning liberated him from rote. His performance there moved him to add a governing name, "Kemal," which means "perfect." He got himself into a military academy, continuing to excel, and graduated into the atmosphere of the Young Turks, trying to modernize against the arthritis of the Ottoman bureaucracy and its supreme governing institutions, the sultanate and the caliphate. After decades of stalled reform, the Balkan Wars of 1912-13 and the First World War thrust on the Ottoman Empire seven straight years of regional convulsion. The next four years (1919-23) produced bloody trans-Anatolian spasms, out of which modern Turkey emerged by a breech birth. A Caesarian knife might have made things simpler, but there was no surgeon who knew how to slice into the belly of history to deliver the thing forming.

Mustafa Kemal's roles in this were at first purely military. At Gallipoli he achieved fame as a front-line corps commander who contributed to the eventual Allied retreat, and to Churchill's resignation as Lord of the Admiralty. In one battle, a piece of shrapnel struck Kemal above the heart and was stopped by the watch in his breast pocket. Astonishing luck confirmed his own sense of destiny.

The Allies took advantage of Ottoman chaos to impose, in the Treaty of Sevres (1920), a complete carving up of that empire: eastern territories to Armenia, western ones to Greece and Italy; and colonial spheres of interest to the south — present Syria, Iraq, Jordan, Palestine, and Arabia — to France and to Great Britain.[1] "Sevres" is a term of lasting infamy to modern Turks. But the Turkish nationalist army, led by İsmet (İnönü) and Kemal, proudly responded, attacking from the ruins of the Ottoman Empire. They forced another assembly at Lausanne in 1923. Here their delegation was offered only subordinate seating. İsmet, its leader, first insisted on

---

1. Nicole Pope and Hugh Pope, *Turkey Unveiled: A History of Modern Turkey* (Woodstock/New York, The Overlook Press, 1997; 2nd ed., 2004) contains an excellent map of the Sevres divisions of Turkey, pp. xiv-xv, as well as balanced analysis throughout. Andrew Mango, *Atatürk: The Biography of the Founder of Modern Turkey* (Woodstock/New York, The Overlook Press, 1st American edition, 2002) contains several maps, pp. xvi-xxi, from Ottoman Empire, 1881, through final frontiers of the Turkish Republic; and in factual comprehensiveness is unsurpassed.

armchairs of equal status, and then stubbornly, with intentional deafness, negotiated to the basic present borders for a nation of Turks. Problems of dealing with Kurdish, Armenian, and other minorities were ignored at the time. They still remain.

İsmet's colleague, Mustafa Kemal, was meanwhile trying to galvanize ten million Turks, a disorganized mass, chiefly of illiterates in poverty, who would soon grow to forty million and now are nearing eighty million. The failing sultanate called for Kemal's death. Kemal called for a new Turkey. From first national meetings at Erzurum in the far east of Anatolia, he and other nationalists gathered momentum, and established a legislature in Ankara, in the central West. In just over four months beginning in late 1923, he brought off essential redefinitions that continue to shape Turkey and to haunt the Islamic world. First he sprang a resolution for a republic, to which the Assembly supplied 159 votes, with over 100 abstaining. He proceeded within days to abolish the sultanate, forcing Mehmet VI, who held both that position and the caliphate, into immediate exile. A cousin was selected as caliph. After allowing a brief time for digestion of this dramatic change, on March 3, 1924, Kemal moved abolition of the caliphate, once called "the shadow of God upon earth. The caliph was forced to depart Turkey the following day. Kemal now had a clear path, leaving absolutists of succeeding generations like Osama bin Laden hungry for a caliph — and with ulcerous indigestion.

The man driving Turkish reform was of medium height at five feet nine inches, but his self-possession and innate sense of command made him stand out in a gathering. His fair skin, blond hair, and blue eyes placed him among minorities found all the way from Transylvania in Romania/Hungary through Macedonia-Thrace, Kemal's area of birth, across Anatolia into Iran, trickling into Afghanistan and Northwest Pakistan. The trail of the anomalous blue-eyed blonds tracks roughly with the route of the army of Alexander the Great, which conceit of descent, had it been offered to Atatürk, might have pleased him grandly.

Early photographs of Mustafa Kemal show a slight strabismus, which, in power, moved him to present his left profile to photographers. The combination of faintly deviant focus, intensely felt will, and unusually intense blue eyes made Atatürk's gaze hard to hold. No one, it was said, could look at him without blinking, any more than one could stare at the sun.

Intimate commentators observed his delicate hands and feet, and the exquisite grace of his dipping a biscuit into his tea. In his military youth he grew a full beard, at a time when "In the Near East . . . only eunuchs had no beards or moustaches."[2] He trimmed it back, as a general, to a moustache; and as a reformer went entirely clean-shaven. His speaking voice was not powerful or musical, although his words could be spellbinding. He demonstrated his love of talk, including speculation and disputation, at dinners far into the morning. Islamic injunctions against alcohol he grandly ignored, and eventually banished.

In Mustafa Kemal's carriage, manners, and moods, men and women found integrated both feminine and masculine characteristics. His orchestral harmony of human appetites and passions, his combination of commanding power and gentle conduct, made him hard to resist and easy to follow.

His aggressive virility was of mythic dimensions. He eventually wed, at age forty-two, the accomplished Latife, twenty-four years old, who spoke several languages, including French and English, and whose organizational power in her parents' household he admired. He proposed marriage — or commanded it — after his first visit to his mother's grave, but soon felt his young wife's will as engulfing of him as his late mother's. His own accounts, and his friends', represent Latife as her stiletto heels echoing overhead, or her banging on the floor above the guests late at night to bring all-male talk to a close and her husband to the bedchamber. The picture is overly shrewish, not cognizant of her presence of mind and breadth of culture. But Kemal divorced her after two and a half years, under the Islamic law which gave the husband a unilateral right of dismissal, six months before Turkey adopted its new civil code.

The president never again married. To fulfill his fatherly instinct, he adopted daughters — eventually eight of them: Sabiha, Zehra, Rukiye, Afet, Sabriye, Nebile, Bulent, and Ülkü. "It has never been established," say his psycho-biographers, "how many of these women had sexual relations with the Ghazi." Afet and Sabiha stayed close to him. Most clearly Latife's surrogate, and making the others most uncomfortable, was Afet, who, not long before Atatürk's death, was allowed to go to Europe for a doctorate. She eventually became a university professor and made a notable contri-

---

2. "Only eunuchs." Vamik Volkan and Norman Itzkowitz, *The Immortal Atatürk: A Psychobiography* (Chicago, University of Chicago Press, 1984), make this remark. They are also the best source of physical descriptions and moods of Atatürk.

bution to the history of women's rights in Turkey. Sabiha became a military pilot and participated in bombing missions against Kurdish rebels. Sabriye became a judge. The last adoptee, Ülkü, at the age of a granddaughter, he treated like a pet. Seventy years before Saudi educators attempted policy on the matter, he told his daughters to *smile,* and not to trust those who didn't. He hired a Swiss woman to teach them manners, and a black eunuch to serve them.[3]

His mother, said Mustafa Kemal, expressly and in metaphor, was Turkey. To give that mother rebirth, he applied his utmost energy. Two weeks after putting Latife aside — for fifty years afterward she lived a life of dignified non-commentary — he launched on the first of a series of major social reforms. Headgear was symbolic of sex, of status, of culture. The fez had been introduced a century before by the then-sultan. Atatürk ridiculed it. He wore and waved a panama hat, promoting Western headgear as a shield from the sun. Crowds responded with bought and improvised headgear, waving them at him in an imitative enthusiasm not yet called globalization. Severe hat laws generated riots among turban-wearing religious conservatives, who were in turn adjudged rebellious. In a year of 138 death sentences, about twenty emerged from the hat riots.

Even more delicate was the subject of the veil. "Friends," Mustafa Kemal preached to the crowd, "our women have minds too. . . . Let them show their faces to the world, and see it with their eyes. . . . Don't be afraid. Change is essential, so much so that, if need be, we are prepared to sacrifice lives for its sake." He stopped short of a general ban of the veil, but officially discouraged it, and let the government prohibit it under civil service regulations on official premises, including school. The loss of the veil to some who wore it was a loss of security, or mystery, or both; it led to unprovable but informed allegations that suicide among Turkish women rose to new levels in the 1930s.[4]

Mustafa Kemal pressed, by example, the conceits of Western music and the Western style of ballroom dancing. Reaching more deeply into potential opposition, he closed dervish lodges, shrines, and mausoleums, speaking with disdain of those who pray to the dead. He was also concerned, as his military successors remain, about the capacity for extremist

3. Adoptions and sexual relations, Volkan, *Immortal Atatürk,* pp. 259-61; "smile," p. 286. Mango, *Atatürk,* pp. 438-39, 514, differs on the number of adoptions. Modern Turks, dependent on received stories, also differ on which were close to Atatürk and which were not.

4. "Show their faces," quoted in Mango, *Atatürk,* p. 434; new levels of suicide, Volkan, *Immortal Atatürk,* p. 294.

political movements to be bred within the special Islamic associations called *tekke* or *tarikat*.

Turkey's assembly adopted, beginning January 1, 1926, the twenty-four-hour clock and the International Christian calendar, which replaced the (administrative) Muslim solar calendar and the (religious) Muslim lunar calendar. Then, in swift succession, the assembly passed a new civil code based on the Swiss model; a new penal code, Italian-based (but retaining the death penalty, which Italy had discarded); and a new business code, inspired by Germany. Nowhere did Mustafa Kemal speak in mere imitation. Always he implored the joining of a universal modern civilization, to which the alternative was to be "crushed." An old Arab proverb says that when a stone drops on an egg, the egg breaks; and when an egg drops on stone, again the egg breaks. Atatürk was trying to strengthen the thin structure of Turkish society; to make it stone to meet stone. Three generations after him, the question would become whether Turkish stone was admissible in building the edifice of European Union.

Alphabet reform was another major initiative of the 1920s — one which brought out the teacher in Atatürk, and the oral examiner, who would put his dinner and drinking guests on the spot at any time over any subject he fancied. With the introduction of the Roman alphabet, he and his coterie sought also to minimize Arabian and Persian terms and heighten reliance on Turkish. A modern Turkish novelist, Elif Şafak, protests against this "language cleansing" for being as brutal and arbitrary as ethnic cleansing. But few disdain the achievement, abruptly launched and rapidly advanced, that gave Turks an alphabet of 29 letters, omitting Q, W, and X. It uses diacritical marks to convey sounds special to Turkish and achieves an orthography which, if not as easily phonetic as Spanish or Indonesian, is vastly simpler than English.

In unveiling the work of his alphabet commission in August 1928, Mustafa Kemal implored his listeners to teach the new Turkish letters to "women and to men, to porters and to boatmen," and to overcome the shame of a nation that consisted of "eighty or ninety percent [a later census proved 90 to be more accurate] of illiterates." He then raised a full glass of raki in a toast that decried the Ottoman elite, which "two-faced impostors in their dunghills used to drink this secretly a thousand times more. I am not am impostor. I drink to the honor of my nation."[5]

Turkey in the 1930s was at peace with all its neighbors and enjoying, at

5. Quoted in Volkan, *Immortal Atatürk*, p. 284.

least in urban settings, a culture unimaginable in the days of the sultan and caliph. After Turkey conquered central Islamic lands in 1517, Ottomans for four hundred years had been "Protectors of the Holy Places of Mecca and Medina." World War I having sprung the Ottoman Empire apart, Mustafa Kemal was letting the holy places look after themselves. Saudi governments took over that responsibility when they got their tribes in hand. King Fahd assumed the "Protector" title in the mid-1980s to give himself competitive status against the Iranian leader, Ayatollah Khomeini. Turkey, however, relieved of those burdens and indifferent to them, used the 1930s to enjoy the yoyo and the Charleston, the tango and Freudian theory.

Of Mustafa Kemal's culminating reforms, one was giving women the right to vote: locally in 1930; in village councils, 1933; and in parliamentary elections, 1934. Eighteen women, in 1935, became members of a parliament (of nearly four hundred) which was actually appointive. Their numbers decreased when later elections became more truly free. But the official recognition of women's political rights could only help reinforce the gradual improving of the social treatment of Turkish women.

While fooling rather uselessly with national historical theories, Mustafa Kemal continued effectively to promote language reform. Then in 1934 a new law made surnames compulsory for Turkish citizens, a useful step for a growing modern society; traditional titles and distinctions were abolished. After putting Ottoman honorifics in their place, a further law banned clerical dress outside of places of worship and religious ceremonies.

Mustafa (the "Chosen") Kemal ("Perfect") now added the surname Atatürk ("Father of the Turks"). *Ata* signifies the progenitor of a line. The assembly passed a law restricting this surname to his use only.

Atatürk in 1935 was elected president for the fourth time. His energy of achievement was ebbing and symptoms of cirrhosis of the liver were appearing. He succumbed to that disease on November 10, 1938, at 9:05 a.m. Still, at that hour on that day each year, traffic is halted and all human motion is arrested in Turkey. Within his mausoleum on a hill, completed in 1953, there is a huge block of pink Turkish marble, shaped like a coffin, weighing forty-four tons. But Atatürk's body is interred on the floor below, so that stone does not weigh down upon him.[6]

When Atatürk died, four-fifths of the population still lived in villages, many in mud brick houses. But fighting disease had increased the population by nearly a third to 17.8 million in the first census, 1940, after his

6. Coffin and mausoleum, Volkan, *Immortal Atatürk*, p. 348.

death. In his fifteen years of presidency, literacy doubled, from one-tenth to one-fifth of the population. National income per person remained extremely modest, but also doubled.[7]

Atatürk left behind two kinds of revolution that did not seem reversible. One was a formal political structure within which democracy could grow, and in which women and men could both flourish. The other had been brought about by what for Muslims was a revolutionary act — abolishing the caliphate in 1924. All the rules of religion were in effect abrogated except those relating to worship. With the privacy of worship there was to be no interference. But the republic, led by Atatürk, had declared its independence from Islam. That act intended to allow the republic to grow by its own best principles, while permitting Islam a natural growth in its own private modes, contained within a secular public capsule. Seven decades after Atatürk's death, Muslim political leaders were refining techniques by which they might win elections and then manifest their religion in power without imposing it — and do so short of provoking military intervention.

Demirel's Fifty-Year View

In the long run, other post-Atatürk leaders will be remembered as having had greater impact than Süleyman Demirel: Özal on the economy, Erdoğan on politics and society. But Demirel provides a unique half-century overview. He was a peasant shepherd boy in his mid-teens when Atatürk died. The bright, burly youth would make his way to the top of the Turkish political heap, get slugged off, and return again and again. In his study are several carvings and a big romantic painting of a white horse, symbolic of the Justice Party that he led; daggers and swords on the wall, presented him by Arab potentates; and photographs of hydroelectric projects that he commanded as an engineer. A photo of Bill and Hillary Clinton on a visit. And books. "Many decisions have been taken here," he says, looking around the study. His home address in Ankara, Güniz Sokak, constant for decades, means to Turks the street where Demirel lives. He was their prime minister six different times and finally their president for a seven-year term, 1993-2000.

In his mid-eighties, he looks back over the years since 1949 when he entered government service, shortly after American aid to Greece and Tur-

---

7. Data on development, Mango, *Atatürk*, p. 533.

key began flowing in to offset attempted Soviet incursions. He had been in the U.S. briefly as a trainee in a Marshall Plan program. He suddenly saw his native land as "a sleeping country." Its population of 21 million then had a per capita income of $150. Eighty percent of the people were still peasants. There were only three universities in all of Turkey. Of 35,000 villages, including his own in Isparta province, only thirteen were electrified. "The country was in dark at night."

The elections of 1950 changed the government for the first time since 1923 and put the whole system under review. "We started building dams." There was only one, for local supply in Ankara, built in the 1930s. He was managing ambitious dam-building when selected in 1953 for an Eisenhower Fellowship, a new, private, American exchange program with extensive professional appointments designed around each individual selectee. He said he was "too busy here," and only agreed to go when told he was not being sent to acquire more engineering knowledge. He should see how the society worked, how federal and state governments function.

I asked him in retrospect the question he carried with him then. "What is the basis of development in the USA?" He answered promptly from his own, never-forgotten, one-page report: "The persons, the citizens, the society, the states, and the federal government are all based on the preamble of the Constitution — 'We, the people.' Everything is for the people, by the people, of the people."

Demirel was struck by the fact that the U.S., as recently as the 1930s, had been an underdeveloped country. National rural electrification had only begun in 1935. "How the U.S. developed; became a superpower, this is a *miracle*. . . . A miracle created by free individuals . . . [putting] their skills and energy into developing society over *years*."

He thought of his own Turkey, short of roads, still reliant on camel transportation, as he saw the irrigation projects in the Sacramento River Basin, and what the Tennessee Valley Authority, in twenty years, had done to alleviate poverty. He studied universities, farmers' cooperatives, the New York Port Authority. "I saw how hard ordinary people work . . . conscious to *produce* something. . . . In my opinion, no power is stronger than [belief in] *getting the job done*."

On his return from the States, Demirel was made director of all hydraulic works and power plants. He left the government at the time of the military intervention of 1960, did his compulsory military service, and launched a private construction business. But "I felt responsibility to help put the country back on track" — to development and democracy, the two themes of his life. In 1964 he became chair of the Justice Party, and in 1965, with 53 percent of the vote, prime minister. His aims were, using Atatürk's language, to bring Turkey "to the level of contemporary civilization, and to defeat misery." He pronounced the last word "myze-ery."

Over four decades he did his part to bring Turkey to where it is today. "There is no village, no person, in Turkey without electricity, telephone, television. There is no place you cannot go without beautiful highways. There is no child without school." Turkey has grown from 20 million to nearly 80 million people, from three universities to eighty-two, and from $150 per capita income to $5,000. Farmers are down from 80 percent to 30 percent of the population, and tractors are up from two thousand to one million. Turkey builds all kinds of industrial goods, much for export, including cars, trucks, and ships. Whereas in 1965 there were 100,000 tourists, there are now a stunning 25 million a year.[8] I reflected that whereas, before Atatürk, the Ottoman Empire was known as "The Sick Man of Europe," now Turkey is flourishing as the Florida of Europe. The big question remaining is whether Europe will let Turkey become, structurally, part of itself. Demirel is proud of Turkey's freedoms in elections, universities, press, religion, and expression; in judiciary, assembly, and association, all of which enable Turkey now to negotiate from strength as a candidate for the European Union. But this had to be based, he is convinced, in getting across the idea of "We, the People." He liked to tell them, "You are the *owners* of this country, not its guests." Far less its servants, as in Ottoman times.

That flavor of ownership remains distinctly Turkish. I had seen Demirel's power with a crowd in Antalya, on Turkey's southern Mediterranean coast, in 1992. I rode from the airport to the central square with his chief of staff, who advised me to roll up my window. Sometimes peasants slaughter buffalo in Demirel's honor as he drives by, and if they wait until the last moment to cut the jugular, "you don't want blood pumping through the window." At the edge of the square, he pulled out his shirttail and advised me to hold onto it tightly, so as not to get separated in the crowd. We pushed our way through fifty yards of people. I held on against buffeting until we reached the small bus atop which Demirel would speak. We climbed a ladder up its back and stood on its platformed roof while he addressed the square full of mobbing enthusiasts. He took off a soft black chapeau, his post-Atatürk trademark hat, and waved it to the crowd, which roared in recognition. Under the steaming sun he spoke with fervor, his

8. All data as received from Demirel, 21 Sep 06.

huge bald brow glistening, jowls working with passion, his face a cartoon-ist's dream of Cubist planes in animation. To his antiphonal questions the masses roared back the answers he sought. The bus trembled with pres-sures upon it and seemed to breathe the dialogue. Later he said casually, "Sometimes it is good to rock the crowd."

Demirel was never able to soften the problem of Armenian memory of losses incurred while they sided and fought with the Russians in the First World War, when the Ottoman army and policy had punished them with massacre and murderous exposure. Nor was he able, despite having an ex-cellent assimilated Kurd, Hikmet Çetin, as his Foreign Minister, to resolve Kurdish separatist tensions, to which Atatürk had reacted by letting his daughter pilot a bomber against the rebels. But there was a period of peacefully promising foreign policy after the dissolution of the Soviet Union, during which Turkey took a non-imperial, avuncular stance with the several Turkic republics that were establishing their sovereign indepen-dence. In this era of the early 1990s, the trustees of Eisenhower Fellowships, recognizing Demirel's three decades of leadership, made him the first for-eign awardee of the Eisenhower Medal for Leadership and Service.

I wrote the citation, which epitomized his moving from engineering control of water power to his evocation of the power of his people. As the large Philadelphia hotel luncheon ended, and with the medal still about his neck, his bodyguards surrounded him. American Secret Service leading the way, we exited through the kitchen to avoid Armenian protesters at the front door. Demirel stopped and turned to me with a big smile and said, "I must kiss you." In the steam and clatter of crockery washing, he bussed me on each cheek, man-to-man, Turkish style.

Demirel summarized his own public career to me as prime minister for six years and president for seven (a total surpassing that of Turgut Özal and far exceeding that of Bülent Ecevit)[9] — plus parliamentary deputy or op-position leader twelve years, and suppressed by the army for another seven. Had he an accomplishment like translating T. S. Eliot and Tagore, as Ecevit did, he might have won more respect from intellectuals. Had he creatively

9. For insights on Özal and Ecevit, see Pope and Pope, *Turkey Unveiled, passim,* and Steven Kinzer, *Crescent and Star: Turkey Between Two Worlds* (New York, Farrar, Straus and Giroux, 2001, revised, 2008), *passim.*

fulminated for free enterprise like Özal, he might have attracted the piety of policy experts. But on his own simple terms, he worked for development and democracy — not with genius, but with devotion. He relished that his people called him "Baba," father.

"What would you do differently," I asked Demirel, "if you could do things over again?"

"In politics," he replied, "you can only use opportunities. Did I use them in right directions? I'd say generally yes. . . . Without these military interventions, Turkey could have gotten more from us. . . . We should have better governance, better working of the state, of administration and the economy." He smiled, still eager in his eighties: *"I could do something more on that!"*

The Military and Kemalism

"These military interventions" have been four, across forty years. I was privileged to feel the convictions behind them from a just-retired general, Hurşit Tolon — tall, broad-shouldered, clean-shaven as all military must be, and now in a soft gray business suit. He had been commander of the Army of the Aegean, and of the First Army (Istanbul). Generals don't give interviews in Turkey; they give, in pre-studied uniformity, press conferences. But Tolon was no longer on active duty. Free to speak, he was zealous to communicate his own cherished view of Kemalism: "The republic has rules that cannot be altered. "Independence, sovereignty, secularism, and unity — these are the cornerstones, and they cannot be moved. . . . These revolutionary acts cover all areas of life in Turkey." Protecting secularism especially concerned him. If bureaucrats publish regulations saying that men and women cannot be treated by doctors of the opposite sex, then intrusive religion must be opposed. If *tarikats* (independent Islamic associations) start growing again, then a secular need to protect the republic must be awakened.

The people, Tolon insisted, expect the Armed Forces to take action to ensure democratic development. That is not necessary in the West, where populations have long ago digested democratic needs. But the EU critics of Turkey must learn to appreciate this: "The Turkish people entrust their political vision and expectations to their politicians, but their security is entrusted to the armed forces." The military has earned that trust by its four timely interventions — 1960, 1971, 1980, and 1997, each followed by deliberate return of governance to the civil sector. The first time, said Tolon, involved everyone from general staff down to foot soldiers. The last time was the most delicate, although he dislikes the journalists' term for it, "the post-modern coup." I realized that the second and third times both displaced Demirel, and that the casualty count of terrorism before the 1980 intervention — many thousands dead and wounded — fully justified military action in the minds of most of the population.

Turkey is more finely tuned now. When the Islam-based Welfare Party rose to power in 1995, the Armed Forces watched with concern as the high priests of ideological secularism. A meeting of the National Security Council (created by the military constitution of 1982) was called on February 28, 1997, and the prime minister, with key aides and cabinet members, was summoned to it. Certain developments gaining momentum, they were told, were anti-constitutional. In the memorable euphemism of General Tolon, the military "coughed." The Turkish verb that he used, *öksürmek,* can mean to clear one's throat, and by implication, to politely object. No need for display of troops. The military *coughed,* and the government resigned.

The capacity of Islamist politicians to take a hint is now well established. When another Islamic vehicle, the AK Party, ascended to power in 2002, with Recep Tayyip Erdoğan as prime minister, it showed great care not to overstep in the ways that had discredited its predecessor. Meanwhile the public was also growing in acumen about where it might indicate power limits to the military. The Turkish armed forces, over half a million, among NATO countries were second in size only to those of the U.S. When they announced plans for $50 billion of spending on updating of forces and weapons, public outcry and editorial protest slowed down their zeal.

The Turkish polity was growing more complex and sophisticated. It could not be guided solely from the officers' club in Ankara, dreary with opulence, where General Tolon hosted me; nor by the didactic oratorical tone which marked his delivery across our three hours together. Certainly not, most Turks hoped, by associations of General Tolon with General Veli Küçük and others darkly involved with the so-called "deep state," which manifested itself violently in the name of hyper-Kemalism.

At least three newly contending elements were at play in Turkish policy life: genuine contests among political parties, a secular judiciary, and a new critical culture. As Erdoğan's prime-ministership approached a decade in length, those three elements were far from comfortable with each other. But in a creative flux with other forces they were helping to shape a new polity, undreamed of by Atatürk — non-religious in its dynamics, yet led by a man who had served four months in jail for reciting in public a defiant poem that pictured the mosque as "our barracks."

Multi-party politics had been artificially launched, but aborted, as early as Atatürk; then sincerely cultivated by his intimate associate, İnönü, after the Second World War. Meanwhile the judiciary continued to try to emerge from the compromised condition of many Third World courts. The parliament, in choosing a successor to Demirel as president, picked Ahmet Necdet Sezer, the Chief Justice of the Constitutional Court. He had astonished his countrymen the year before when he denounced the military's constitution of 1982 as undemocratic, declared that the government had no right to ban education or broadcasting in Kurdish, and supported repeal of all laws restricting freedom of speech. Opinion polls showed that the presidency now surpassed the armed forces in public respect. But the military's jealousy of its guardianship and its defenses of Kemalism were unchanged. Nor were they, by far, the only voices for secularism. In November 2006, more than one hundred pro-secular organizations assembled and marched to Atatürk's mausoleum, waving Turkish flags and chanting slogans. Such demonstrations, alarmed at the popularity of the AK Party, would then grow into hundreds of thousands.

The military threatened to intervene if Erdoğan were to succeed a secularist in the one-term, seven-year presidency. Erdoğan instead advanced his Foreign Minister, Abdullah Gül, for the presidency — a Europhile as well as a devout and observant Muslim. In the national elections in July 2007, the AK Party won 47 percent of the vote, with supporters from all regions of Turkey — the first incumbent victory with enhanced vote totals in half a century. Parliament then elected Gül as president. Military leaders openly fumed, but they did not dare formally to "cough" as in 1997. Turkey now had two top leaders who drank Coca-Cola rather than alcohol, and who understood the compromises innate to democracy.[10]

Turkey's per capita income has almost tripled during Erdoğan's tenure. No surprise, then, that the trumping of Kemalism continued in the next national elections in 2011. The AK Party again raised its share of the

---

10. An excellent summary of contrasting novelties in Turkey's post-2007 politics, with more subissues than I choose to deal with, is by Nilüfer Narli, "Turkish Politics: More Democracy and Europe or more Islam?" FRIDE (Fundaciòn para las Internacionales Relaciones y el Diálogo Exterior), *Comment,* May 08.

vote, to nearly fifty percent. Fears were voiced about "Islamization" and "autocracy." But electoral triumph of a Muslim bourgeoisie in no way threatened the principles of a secular republic. Erdoğan's appetite for a more powerfully executive presidency certainly deserved focus. Yet his party was still forty-one seats short of the super-majority (two-thirds) that would enable him to redesign the constitution over the opposition in Parliament. The fact that fifty-eight journalists remained in jail, however, manifested his hyper-sensitivity to criticism, as well as his capacity for a rage that some called "sultanic."[11]

Attempting a Judiciary

Although the comparison may not be a grand compliment, Turkey's secular judiciary surpasses those of most Muslim countries. Among its eloquent spokesmen is Sami Selçuk, former President of the Court of Cassation or, very roughly, chief justice of the supreme court of appeals. He acknowledges that in swiftly adopting European models from the top down, Turkish legal reformers left its system with many inconsistencies. Yet, on the caravan principle — it's up and moving, join or be left behind — it sorts itself as it proceeds. Selçuk is eloquent on behalf of the rule of law and the separation of powers, and equally eloquent against the death penalty (which "cannot be rectified, it cannot be made up for later"); against torture (which diverts justice from its orbit, estranges the people, and shames a nation with its brutality); and against alleged thought crimes (Turkey frequently has led the world in its number of journalists in prison). Selçuk reveres the Atatürk who said, "I don't want doctrine, we might get stagnant." He desires the Kemalism which is "not trapped in the 1930s but produces an infinity of futures in the light of science."[12]

11. *The Economist,* 19 Jun 11; Atul Aneja, "Turkey's Election & Arab Spring," *The Hindu,* 15 Jun 11; "Turkish PM Erdoğan Withdraws Lawsuits against Journalists," http://www .hurriyetdailynews.com, 16 Jun 11; Gerald Robbins, "Understanding Turkey's 2011 General Election Results," Foreign Policy Research Institute E-Note, 29 Jun 11.

On repression of free speech: another source says there were "more than 60" journalists in jail in Turkey (Sebnem Azsu, *New York Times,* 13 Jun 11, p. A7). Meanwhile, in Pakistan, the murder of Saleem Shahzad, in which the ISI denied involvement, brought the total of journalists *killed* in that nation since 9/11 to thirty-seven (*New York Times,* 5 Jul 11, pp. A1, A8).

12. Dr. Iur. Sami Selçuk, *Longing for Democracy* (Ankara, Yeni Turkiye, 2000), quotations in order of appearance in my text: pp. 210, 90, 74.

With shallow law, Selçuk observes, the public terrain is pocked with craters ready to explode. With deviant law, every family needs protection from earthquakes that will seize upon the fault lines. But with laws nationally enacted and reasonably reviewed, with a democracy whose life in law is devotedly pursued, then there is little to fear from criminal initiative or ideological excess. The goal is humane life together, as Nazim Hikmet in his poetry envisioned it: "To live free and single like a tree and in brotherhood like a forest."[13]

But, I asked Selçuk, does not the constant threat of military intervention compromise those ideals? He replied firmly. In three of their interventions the military officers stated that they were relying on the Internal Service Law. It is certainly a law, he said, but it is not organic to the basic constitution. The cabinet may be dismissed by parliament, but constitutionally cannot be dissolved by the army. "I am a lawyer and I cannot lie," he said — a statement which I had never heard from an American lawyer, but which I took as Selçuk's own rehearsed answer to any possible interrogation by an official of the armed forces. "The democratic military does not have the mission to take protective measures unless ordered by the executive." As in the broader world (by which he meant Euro-American), so in Turkey now, it must be the same. Although we were availing of a political scientist as an interpreter, Selçuk chose here to frame his thought carefully in English. *"All military interventions are illegal and illegitimate."*

The matter was of high import, for three military leaders had recently sounded off in rehearsed succession on perceived dangers in the society. I therefore repeated my question in a new form toward the end of our dialogue: Is Turkey going to be ruled by the nervous systems of its generals, or by a body of law? By gut or by writ? Selçuk again responded firmly in English: "Although the intervention practice of the military is established here, it is *wrong.*"

I wished to test the judge with the example of the "Susurluk event" of 1996. I stated my understanding of it: late at night, near an Anatolian village, a speeding truck had crushed a limousine containing a remarkable constellation of four Turkish personalities — Istanbul's former vice-chief of police, a leading Kurdish member of parliament, a notorious mafia hitman (allegedly once under secret service hire to exterminate Armenian assassins who had killed two dozen Turkish diplomats), and a prostitute with

---

13. Crater and fault line, Selçuk, *Longing for Democracy,* p. 75; quotation from Nazim Hikmet, p. 229.

a fake identity card. In the luggage of the car was a load of weapons. My question was, did this event ever get to court? I later found an acknowledgment of mafia influence in Selçuk's writing, quoting Brecht, because of "justice which is stagnating and growing stale."[14] But his answer on the spot was not philosophical. There are events like Susurluk everywhere, including the United States. Yes, parts of it got into prosecution, but the courts needed more concrete evidence, which proved hard to obtain.

Selçuk appeared concerned that my respect for Turkish law was affected by its inability, regarding Susurluk, to get at underlying systemic corruption. He concluded with an unsolicited statement touching some of my deepest levels of apprehension. In forty years of legal experience, he said, he had never received advice from the executive branch in any case before him.

In farewell, Selçuk presented me with a book of his, translated into English. He formulates there what Turkish jurists like himself are striving for, and with equal vigor, struggling against. The history of Turkish state attitudes toward religion has included theocracy, hyper-secularity, and *laicité*. Theocracy in Ottoman times meant determining all private and communal life by Islam — which caused divisions, conflicts, and inequalities. One reaction to it (*not* Atatürk's) was absolute, antagonistic separation of state and religion, in the manner of France of the Revolution. The rationalism of Descartes and the positivism later articulated by Comte merged in a reactionary state, determined to wipe out clergy and religion. But a mild resolution is preferable to a vindictive revolution. In pluralist democracy, an impartial state is equidistant toward all faiths. The mild and middle way is best. "In pluralist democracy," Selçuk writes, "different ideological or religious identities cannot be destroyed, ignored, monopolized or forced on others. Every religion, every faith has the right to define its own destiny." The application of pluralistic democracy to education is vital. "Religious schools cannot be opened by the state. However, neither can the opening of religious schools by communities be prevented. Religious education cannot be impeded; on the contrary, new vistas are opened for it. . . . Lessons in the curricula are not to indoctrinate; they will be tailored according to pluralist, agnostic and skeptical principles; and the individual will be of free choice to opt for any religion." The state will monitor

14. On Susurluk, see Yael Navarro-Yashin, *Faces of the State: Secularism and Public Life in Turkey* (Princeton, Princeton University Press, 2002), pp. 171-180. Selçuk quotes Brecht in *Longing for Democracy*, p. 75.

schools — for public order, security, morality, and health — and disputes will be settled by an independent judiciary.[15] But first, such a judiciary itself needs to be secured.

Islamic Bureaucracy, Turkish Pieties, and the Pope

The building that houses the Diyanet in Ankara has no analogue in America, or Italy, or Saudi Arabia. It is the Presidency of Religious Affairs. With American separation of church and state, such an edifice is unthinkable. Encapsulation of the Roman Catholic faith in a city-state of its own, the Vatican, makes a "Diyanet" in Italian civil government superfluous. In Riyadh, the historical conjunction of royalty with Wahhabi theological authority is so woven into history and present levels of ultimate power that there is no need for a building to contain it. That tapestry of thought, so to speak, hangs within all government buildings, and if you cannot finger the texture on the walls, you will sooner or later perceive the weave in the minds of the leaders.

Turkish history, however, requires Turkish institutions. Atatürk abolished the caliphate, yet allowed Islam to be designated the official national religion. He banned the *tarikat*, the independent Muslim religious orders, but in a speech in a mosque in Balikesir he described how the Prophet had "possessed two dwellings, two abodes for his endeavors. One was his own house, the other was the abode of God." Atatürk wanted illumination to arise from the house of God. "Mosques were built for discussion," he said — "for consultation, of what had to be done in religious and worldly affairs, as well as for obedience to God and prayer. It is indispensable for everybody's mind to be occupied with the affairs of the nation."[16] Lest there be muddle or madness, he later founded the Diyanet. Today its budget is exceeded only by that of the armed forces and education. It builds mosques; it pays their imams, and sends them weekly texts to read to their congregations, and monitors their sermons. With the ministry of education, it regulates religious schools and their texts for teaching. It stands less for "separation of mosque and state than a subjugation of mosque by state."[17]

15. Selçuk, *Longing for Democracy*, pp. 52-60; quotations, pp. 55, 56.

16. Quotations from Atatürk, Volkan, *Immortal Atatürk*, pp. 228, 229.

17. On the Diyanet: Kinzer, *Crescent and Star*, pp. 60-61. Quotation from Colin McMahon and Catherine Collins, "Special Report: Struggle for the Soul of Islam," Chicago *Tribune*, 24 Oct 04, available on Lexis/Nexis.

The external secretariat to the inner office of the President of Religious Affairs contains three tall growths of roses trained in bonsai style. Desks are piled with maroon leather folders under constant stocking, shuffling, and filing by the staff. My appointment with its president, I thought, would be assisted by an aide fluent in English, but that aide, this morning, had a dental emergency. The president, Ali Bardakoğlu, received me in blue suit, white shirt, and reddish decorated tie. We plunged into discussion in English. In a recent speech, Pope Benedict XVI had made a quotation from a fourteenth-century Byzantine emperor.[18] His use of its content implicitly minimized reason among Muslims in relation to the might and mystery of Allah, and maximized historical conversion to Islam by violent means.

Dr. Bardakoğlu, who was expecting the pope's first visit to Turkey two months from the moment we were talking, had immediately given the press his sharp critical reaction to that speech. Prime Minister Erdoğan had shot off even stronger objections to get his licks in before the pope apologized. Benedict XVI actually never withdrew his remarks, but uttered mollifications. "Four 'I'm sorry's' equals one apology," I said playfully to my Turkish friends. "No, it doesn't," they said, too often wounded by condescension from Europe.

Now Bardakoğlu and I were sorting the matter out, he with a candid energy of conviction that overrode his problems with English syntax. He wished to meet the pope in a non-political atmosphere, expressing Turkish hospitality and respect.

Bardakoğlu's good will firmly established, he went into the specifics of the pope's remarks. (Some Turks saw them as more inflammatory than the Danish cartoons blaspheming the Prophet, because Benedict XVI is *the pope*.) In tackling the concepts involved: "[The pope] claims that in Islamic faith the Almighty Transcendental God may pressure the freedom of reason. But that is *wrong*. 'Transcendental' . . . means that we can't qualify God with any physical attributes, or our own words. It doesn't mean that God is *not* reasonable. It means that there is no other human authority between God and individual."

Bardakoğlu went on in a remarkably trans-ecumenical vein. "There is no limit to the freedom of speech, thought, or faith. . . . Every human being can believe as they learn. . . . This means that rationality is *very strong* in Is-

18. Full English text of speech of 12 Sept 06 available through Catholic World News (CWNews.com), 20 Sep 06.

lam (although there are marginal groups who claim that God conducts all our affairs and limits our freedoms) . . . and Islam means rational human beings in freedom."

Violence? It does not arise from the Qur'an or the Holy Prophet. The real reason for violence is in the human being, his lack of education, his selfishness, his hopelessness for the future. There is no holy war in Islamic history. Wars are of nations and politics; we can't blame holy values for it, or elements of religion.

The source of the Crusades? It is not Christianity. It was not holy values, but persons, events, and evils. We cannot prevent the negatives in the modern world: the main responsible groups are regional politicians, international policy makers, and selfish factors. "Our job is to help reduce the tears."

This mustached, bespectacled, influential man was brimming with a positive energy that made me wish to usher in the pope then and there, and to dissolve the whole international word-hassle with smiles and glasses of orange juice (no tea offered in the Diyanet).

We went on to the question of new activity among the *tarikat,* about which high military officials were sounding warnings in the media. "They are forbidden by law since the beginning of the Republic," said Bardakoğlu. "But mystical movements are always alive. We see them [as part of] . . . the freedom of religion. But they are not allowed to be organized politically." He described several of them recently mentioned in the newspapers, casually minimizing their influence, while acknowledging in a few cases those which had their own TV channels.

Mystical, cultural, and folkloric movements are all natural and understandable manifestations of Islam. But — his aspect and tone changed — "The Wahhabi approach is not acceptable in Turkey." The Turkish people oppose Salafi thought, because Salafis try to explain Islam by separating history, culture, art, and feelings of the people so much that we can't see religion anymore.

"If we ignore . . . the historic basis of Qur'anic verses and their context, and the total concept of the Qur'an, we can't understand it. They choose one sentence and separate it and misuse this sentence for their special purposes. . . . To understand Islam correctly, we have to see Qur'an, sunna, hadith, and history *all together.*

"In every time and region, every religion takes on different colors. For example, North Africa, Turkey, South Arabia have different psychological colors of Islam. Just like in Christianity, if we want to *eradicate colors,* all will disappear. Or one subjective color will continue as the approach. The Wahhabi thinks, claims, his frame has no color or additional culture. But his color . . . [actually dominates] the frame."

The multicultural aspects of modern life require us to respect all colors, all cultures, all human beings, without hierarchy of value; and to respect *all* channels of belief. "I visited Shinto and Buddhist shrines in Japan two weeks ago, but I never thought to judge about their faith, because the ultimate God gives us liberty of choice of religion, of faith and of unfaith. He made us responsible for our choices. We cannot limit God's freedom."[19]

I felt I should turn the focus back to the meeting which he would face if diplomatic timidity did not cancel it, or mindless violence make it impracticable. "The pope," I interjected, "is not a Wahhabi. But he ought to loosen up his mental framework." Something about that thought tickled the Turkish President of Religious Affairs. Ali Bardakoğlu laughed. He repeated, "The pope is not a Wahhabi."

In a private sequel to our meeting, Bardakoğlu's aide, Dr. Şemsettin Ulusal, stressed that the *tarikats* are totally civil groupings. "Their sheikhs are not working for us. We cannot check them. That is the work of police officers or soldiers. But we can say that 99 percent of our [76,000] imams, for whom we are responsible through our inspectors, are far away from fundamentalisms."

So I was reassured. What shall one say, however, of religious regulations which, when Mel Gibson's movie *The Passion of the Christ* was released in Turkey, applied an age limit of sixteen to attending the film; and systematically, country-wide, through the Diyanet's commission on sermons (consisting of clerics, theologians, academics, and a retired general), promulgated a sermon entitled "Christ in the Koran"? The Diyanet and the State reminded Muslim worshippers that Jesus was a servant of God but not the Son of God. He was put on earth not to redeem men, but "to remind them of the rules of the Torah."[20]

The actual visit of the pope, November 30, 2006, was secure in a predictably monitored Turkish way. Prime Minister Erdoğan shot to the airport to meet him, on his own way out of the country; and later told the press that the pope said, 'We want you in the European Union." Publicly, the pope himself never said anything declarative on that matter.

19. A still fuller range of Bardakoğlu's thinking is available in Ali Bardakoğlu, *Religion and Society: New Perspectives from Turkey* (Ankara, Diyanet Isleri Baskanligi, 2006).

20. McMahon and Collins, *Chicago Tribune*, 24 Oct 04.

Bardakoğlu never got the face-to-face private conversation he wanted with the pope. Instead, two delegations of eleven persons assembled together at the Diyanet with a Turkish film actress as their interpreter. While the pope wore a white skullcap, Bardakoğlu in his own official hat, red and white, made a speech that lightly touched on the Regensburg error: "The so-called conviction that the sword is used to expand Islam in the world, and growing Islamaphobia, hurts all Muslims." Benedict XVI confined himself to remarks against violence everywhere, and for "authentic dialogue between Christians and Muslims based on truth . . . respecting differences and recognizing what we have in common."[21]

The complex response to the pope, the arrest of Hirşit Tolon for alleged plotting of an anti-AKP coup, even a plot to kill the Nobel Prize-winning novelist Orhan Pamuk, are all clues to the complex nature of belief and observance in Turkey. In counter-gravity to each other, there appear to be two opposed fundamentalisms, an official religiosity, and an assortment of pieties. One major fundamentalism, military Kemalism, is fully armed, but the public has been steadily drifting away from that. A second major fundamentalism was represented by the crowd of 25,000 protesting the visit of the pope late in 2006. The number of dogmatic and determined Islamic believers should not be estimated by either crowd size or the weak electoral figures of the Felicity Party, but by the much stronger index of its grassroots organization and its provincial social impact.

The pivotal religiosity on the scene is that of the Diyanet, neutered but omnipresent. Cynics say that its job is to "foster Islam in order to minimize it." In the tradition of Atatürk, however, the Diyanet trains imams, prepares standard instructional texts, and issues weekly sermon themes so that the religious appetites of the citizens may be fulfilled without their giving way either to toxic emptiness or to hypertonic enthusiasms.

Several shades of piety may also be observed, in their attempts to color in the religious picture. One is a secular liberal piety, not "religious" at all, but influential, and fervid in its expression of values because of the comprehensive contest in Turkey to prevail in public space. There is also an international conservative piety which (like the secular liberals) employs an "Amerikan model" of discourse, including conferences, symposia, and

21. CNN.com, 29 Nov 06; *The Economist*, 2 Dec 06, pp. 53-54.

roundtables. The wealthy organization of Fethulla Gulen, resident in eastern Pennsylvania, is prominent here, with 2,000 schools and seven universities across 90 countries. The Homeland Security Agency sought to have Gulen expelled from the U.S. as failing to meet standards of alien worker status in education; but in 2008 a district court judge held that he met high standards in theology, political science, and Islamic studies. Critics, nonetheless, label Gulen's organization "Jesuitical" or "dissimulative," for assumed intentions to wield power behind the AKP, or even preparing to accept power itself in the future.

Most dramatic yet are the manifestations of the ruling AKP itself under Prime Minister Erdoğan. It dares not be overtly religious, for it is fully cognizant that even marginal overzealousness could end its life, like that of its predecessor, the Virtue Party. It therefore maintains a precarious balance which may be called conservative nationalistic piety. Sometimes the thin skin of Erdoğan himself threatens the balance, as in his personal suits against critics, including cartoonists. Sometimes his party officials lean to thin-skinned initiatives, as in the comprehensive roundups of various figures under the journalistic label of Ergenekon, referring to a myth in which a she-wolf leads the first Turks to their Anatolian home. Indeed there may be hypernationalists, militarists hungry for action, and unreconstructed communists, all suspicious of the AKP. But the bouillabaisse of successive arrests lends credence to the worry that the AKP is trying to intimidate its critics of all colors by incarceration. Faithfulness is endemic in Turkey, but contrary value systems keep the nation dancing on shattered glass.

Duygu Asena and Feminist Achievers

His country, Suleyman Demirel proudly says, is not like other Muslim states. "The great Kemal Atatürk put women in society; and that *doubled* Turkey's power." Of 1.5 million students in the universities, he says, half are women. (A researcher for the European Stability Initiative [ESI] has found otherwise: four out of seven students of Bosphorus University are male; and at less progressive universities, the proportion of females is even slighter.)[22] Of the judiciary, 40 percent are women — judges, lawyers,

22. Nicole Pope to the author, 4 Mar 07, on the basis of her work with the ESI. At elite Koc University, however, genuine gender balance exists. I am grateful to Prof. Cigdem

prosecutors. Of the medical services, almost 40 percent are women. Other countries, I replied, even Pakistan and Saudi Arabia, have also achieved large numbers of women in higher education. Demirel nodded, but with reserve. "Pakistan, to reach Turkey's levels [of development], will require another fifty years." Demirel may be right about that; but the relevant comparison, chosen by Turkey itself, is with Europe. In urban labor force, Turkish female participation is 17 to 18 percent, much lower than OECD countries, and even low by world standards.[23]

For Turkey to become Turkey, of course, it has generated strong women for a long time. Fatma Aliya in 1895 published a book with the title *Misean Islam* (Women of Islam). She became well known by challenging an Islamic sheikh, in high office under the sultan, who declared that the Qur'an *ordered* men to marry four wives. Her textual destruction of his argument might not have won on scholarly logic alone; but, the woman who told me the story said, "As the daughter of a highly educated official, she had the status to get away with it."[24]

Semiha Berksoy (1910-2004) was a painter and opera star who performed in the first Turkish opera, commissioned by Atatürk in 1934, and subsequently was the first Turkish prima donna to perform onstage in Europe. She received the title of "State Artist" in Turkey in 1998, and at the age of ninety performed in a dramatic scene at the Lincoln Center in New York. Her individualistic life included an affair with the world-famous poet Nazim Hikmet, and a daughter by him.

Duygu Asena, born in 1946, carried the meaning of the independent woman still further, advancing her gender's cause more pointedly than earlier illustrious women. When fired from a Turkish newspaper in the 1970s for an affair with a male colleague at an associated paper, she realized that had she been a man she would not have been treated that way. Later, as editor-in-chief of a publishing house, she was responsible for creating a succession of women's magazines, of which the best known was *Kadinca,* "A Woman's Way." From the 1980s onward she became a leader of the movement for women's rights and status. The first of her eight novels,

---

Kagitcibasi of that institution for sharing with me her draft sociological essay, "Gender and Age Distribution of the Scientific Community in the South." She shows the multiple factors playing into Central Asia, Latin America, and East Europe being at or near parity in female participation in that research community. The EU is at the world average of 27.7 percent. Far below it are the Arab states, Japan, and Korea.

23. Nicole Pope to the author, 4 Mar 07.
24. Nükhet Sirman, 20 Sep 06.

published in 1987, *Woman Has No Name,* has gone into fifty-nine editions. Nükhet Sirman, a feminist, both admirer and critic of Duygu, thinks it a "wonderful book" because "it shows intimately what it is like growing up as a girl in this country." Females are addressed as "daughter" or "girl," distancing appellations that make it hard for women to win names, careers, or even places in Turkish society. Duygu was "very beautiful and soft-spoken," she says. But as a journalist she had a sense of the streets — where to eat or drink, what was hip in Taksim, where she met with friends and followers. The fortieth edition of *Woman Has No Name,* 1998, was banned by the government as obscene, undermining marriage, and dangerous for children. But its reappearance demonstrates feminism not suppressible by bureaucracy.

Nükhet believes the movie made from that most famous of Duygu's books was a very good one. "Nudity is not tolerated in cinema here," but the heroine in the final scene sits down in front of a typewriter, naked. Memorable. Still, Nükhet asks, "You take off to write? No, you have to realize what you have *on,* to write." She presses the matter: "Naked may mean not being civilized." She carries her critique of Duygu further. Her glossy magazines, some of whose elements followed leads of *Cosmopolitan* and *Ms.,* trivialized feminism when they focused on leg-shaving, and did it a disservice with advocacy of pub-crawling and cruising for men. But in telling young women they could do everything a young man could do, they did not degenerate into "an eye for an eye" vengefulness, but kept a sense of humor. "She had anger, like Germaine Greer did, but she mastered it, and became a very powerful writer." She did not just criticize men, but rose to the higher need of criticizing Turkish society.

Hers was a critique not always appreciated: in 2001 she was fired from her column at the daily *Milliyet* with the excuse of financial difficulties — in the very year that the paper became part of the Doğan group, the largest media conglomerate in Turkey. A few weeks later, a friend recalls, she went with female journalists, writers, and artists to try to help reduce ethnic tensions with Kurds in Diyarbakir. For the welcoming committee, "we were the 'Westerners' visiting the East. . . . [They asked for a talk.] Duygu was the right person. Without any preparation, she spoke to the large crowd with her calm and warmth. Most of these women were illiterate, but they all seemed to know Duygu. Her message was clear: 'only we women can stop violence and hatred.' The crowd responded warmly and enthusiastically. I'm sure they felt she was one of them. People always felt like that with Duygu. She never preached feminism. She shared the pains of the common women. There was such an intense, loud, and long applause that I would never forget."[25]

At Duygu's funeral (she died of brain cancer in 2006), women shouldered her coffin and bore it to her grave. One of them, who had been falsely accused of bombing a spice market and spent three years in jail before her recent acquittal, spoke tellingly. As remembered: "Although Duygu often said something that we criticized as too popular, untheoretical, too *concrete*... we have come to realize that this was the way she *succeeded*. This was the way she disseminated the idea of the equality of women and men."

For a Turkish woman born twenty years after Duygu Asena, life is a little less constrained, but far from as straightforward as a man's. Rengin Akillioğlu feels no need to describe herself as a feminist, but as a self-confident professional she inherits the momentum of those who have done so. She remembers, as a little child, watching the first landing on the moon. "When they put the American flag there, I wished it was the Turkish flag." She hadn't even heard of Turkish Airlines, the only national company "close to the skies," but her ambition was to put Turkey's flag in space. At age eight, however, she realized that a childhood case of mumps had left her deaf in her left ear. She could not be an astronaut.

There were no aeronautical engineering courses in Turkey, but degrees from Istanbul Technical University and Bosphorus University enabled her to join Turkish Airlines in 1987 as a finance specialist. After two thorough investigations of her work at different stages — evaluations fraught with the kinds of controversy common to corporate executive positions — she was promoted to Chief Financial Officer in 2004 (actually the *second* woman to hold the title of CFO there). Then, in 2006, the CEO changed, and the new man assigned her to head the Chicago and Midwest office, which was a kind of lateral demotion. He also launched a third, conflict-laden evaluation of her work. The AK Party was influencing top executive choices, because Turkish Airlines is government owned, but Rengin declines to think that her case is one of AK Party against a Kemalist. She simply repeats what she has said in key in-house discussions: "I love this company and want to work for it."

25. Zeynep Atikkan to the author, 29 May 08.

Life got complicated for her, her husband, and their grade-school son. She could try to minimize passenger complaints from Chicago, but doesn't she, I ask, have some complaints against the way things are working out?

"Companies are not human. They are not breathing. They have no destiny. The company's life depends on the people for its life. . . . Somebody will see you. Do your best. Don't listen to gossip. I like to be deaf for that reason. . . .

"When I was made CFO, I was surprised, but it happened, like a miracle. I believe in God, so [even] if no one is watching, I know God is watching. He can send dead people who will notify me. I never lose my hope or my willingness, because of people who I don't know. . . .

Q. Angels?
A. Yes. . . . I am Muslim. My God is Allah. He is beyond everything. . . . Our capacity of thinking, our wisdom is not enough to understand Him or define Him. . . .

Q. What is your idea of womanhood?
A. I never see anybody in business life as a man or a woman. I don't check sexual differences, but compare others' attitudes with my actions, and not as a check on my body. . . . Personal development seminars show everything as a mirror of your *self*. So if I behave like a *woman* in my business life, they will not see my professional personality. I am a *human*; not a man, and not a woman except in my private life.

The investigation was demoralizing, Rengin said, without a sigh or altering her tone. She closed our conversation with her unwavering space-faith. "God says explore more, so you will be closer to me. . . . The always expanding universe is unscrolling itself . . . but one day it will be rolled back. It is written in the Qur'an. When, we don't know. But to explore is a holy thing." Space exploration and space technology have a divine motive. They drive "the Internet, development of space foods and beverages, and space clothes," which in turn affect earth life and habits.

Teilhard de Chardin, the Jesuit paleontologist, said we need a bigger idea of God. I felt that Rengin, in her personal Muslim faith, had accommodated a mighty and growing God, and done so comfortably and practically.

The Scarved, the Uncovered, and the Transparent

"Should women cover the head, or not?" — is the great social as well as political discussion of present-day Turkey. Covering may be an observance of faith, or style, or male wish, or all three. Not to cover, to be *açik,* or "open," is much more than a declaration of style. It suggests what kind of man the woman associates with, as well as her openness of mind, whose shades may vary enormously from secular dogmatism to liberal Islam to skeptical modernism. For a foreign observer, Turkey's progress in transparent legislation on sexuality may appear more important than the emblematic arguments on head-covering, but for those within the society, the dispute on covering remains radioactive.

Women of every age and persuasion are critically tuned to the continuing debate. They may consider the AK Party the champion of their modesty and mystery, or the constrainer against their freedom and personal growth, or something in between, or a mix of both. Şule Kılıçarslan is a politically sensitive young woman, now the leader of a small NGO, who let herself be persuaded to run as an AK Party candidate in a municipal election, and won. Now she looks back laughingly, and considers that just part of the Quixote in her character. It was a disappointing experience. She felt she had no influence, and was being used by the Islamists as a symbol of their openness. To speak of their "veiling" their true intentions by her presence on the ticket would be a poor pun. But her sense of being "used" was real, strong, regretted, and unforgettable.

Açik, or "open," women are far from a majority. On many streets in Istanbul one would think them preponderant. In Konya, however, a careful count of some alternate sections of a large audience for dervish dancing told me that exactly one-third women were unscarved. Why does covering prevail, statistically, despite eight decades of Atatürk? First, some traditions have never changed. Second, Turkey is still rural in character, despite steady urbanization. And third, the world Islamic revival that accelerated in 1979 had an impact there as well.

A responsible survey in 1999 showed that twice as many Turkish women wore the headscarf as went uncovered. The proportion of covered women exceeds two-thirds when a new element of scarving is included: styles of *turban* (15.7 percent). These *turbans* are in effect newer, larger, more colorful headscarves, more likely to be pinned under the chin and more fully draped over the shoulders than the older *başörtüsü,* which resembles a Slavic babushka. *Turbans* are popular with university students and with younger women of the lower-middle and middle classes. In individual cases they may express the growth of Islamization, personal style, and changing demographics of age and class, or any combination of those factors.

A more recent poll by the same organization shows the rapid growth of the uncovered, but the headscarf still prevailing:[26]

	1999	2006
Headscarf	53.4%	50.0
Uncovered	27	37.5
Turban	15.7	12.0
Full body veil	3	1.0

These numbers, of course, cannot convey the variety of cross-cutting regional and gender tensions, religious and political trends, and changes of view in one lifetime that individual women may go through. A quotation may help with nuance: "Without a doubt, for us in the east [of Turkey], our elders don't accept you if your head is uncovered. 'You, you're going to hell, or you'll be a whore. . . .' I am not free, my daughter is not free [because of such attitudes]. . . . [But] nobody goes to heaven or hell with their clothes."[27]

The numbers in the surveys certainly help orient a foreign observer. But when I presented them to interviewees, they elicited no interest, disbelief, or disdain. The last was reserved for *çarşaf,* or full-body veiling, which might leave only chin to forehead exposed or, indeed, only the eyes. That style, to an *açık* woman, might suggest association with a *tarikat,* one of the outlawed but thriving urban brotherhoods of Islamism, and could be possible cause for quiet alarm.

26. Data for 1999 from Anna Secor, "Islam, Democracy, and the Political Production of the Headscarf Issue in Turkey," in Ghazi-Walid Falah and Caroline Nagel, eds., *Geographies of Muslim Women: Gender, Religion, and Space* (New York, Guilford, 2005), pp. 203-25, esp. pp. 207-8; based on A. Carkoglu and B. Toprak, *Turkiye'de din, toplum ve siyaset* (Religion, Society, and Politics in Turkey) (Istanbul, Turkiye Economikve Sosyal Etudler, 2000). The Carkoglu and Toprak follow-up data for 2006 are taken from the ESI Report *Sex and Power in Turkey* (Berlin-Istanbul, 2 Jun 07), pp. 31-32, n. 172, 173.

27. "heaven or hell . . ." Secor, "Islam, Democracy, and the Political Production of the Headscarf Issue in Turkey," p. 209.

A conference in New York late in 2006, prompted by the demise of Betty Friedan, brought together in reconciliation contending American feminists from the 1960s and 1970s. Friedan, in her column in *McCall's*, had called Bella Abzug and Gloria Steinem "female chauvinist boors." But death and speeches and old photographs were mellowing their followers.[28] Divisions of course also exist among Turkish feminists, the most active in the Muslim world. But the conditions they contend against do not reward schism, nor do they honor cliques. Contexts for action are limited because social visions differ markedly between secular and veiled women, and within each group.

By the account of a variety of feminists, however, Sibel Eraslan is the first effective large-scale organizer of women in modern Turkey. Eraslan admits, with a positive nod, to the figure attributed to her — half a million women (total) marshaled in demonstrations for Refah (Welfare), the predecessor of the AK Party, for which she worked from 1989 to 1995. We met in her office in a crowded old section of Sultanahmet, west of the Golden Horn. She arrived late from the outskirts, delayed by traffic, wearing a dark purple scarf, brown jacket, white blouse, and black skirt. She spoke in measured tones, without the downcast eyes or avoidant gaze common in some Arabic cultures.

In the 1970s Eraslan had studied law at Istanbul University. Only in her senior year did she arrive at the decision to cover her head, and she managed later to do graduate work wearing the headscarf. The ban against covering, tightened in 1998 after the military intervention, now prevents her from practicing law. "It makes a woman weaker socially and financially because she can't work. I have experienced this also in politics. You can be at the core of it, but you can't run for parliament because of your covered head."

I asked if it was difficult to contend with two forces against scarved women in politics at once — Kemalists because of secular convictions, and Islamists for patriarchal reasons. She confined her answer to the secularists. In twenty-five years of leading demonstrations for the headscarf she has learned that she is "protesting against discrimination by someone who is *not like you*. . . . Seculars and us watch the same movies, hear music, read the same books. . . . But then the headscarf splits us apart."

Discriminatory events — a woman fainted in a protest outside the university and was not admitted to its hospital because of her scarf — led Sibel to the Refah Party. While Erdoğan, now Prime Minister, was its chair

---

28. As reported by Kate Julian, *The New Yorker*, 13 Nov 06, p. 42.

in Istanbul, she was the chair of its women's branch. Their aim was to take scarf-wearers, feeling discrimination in education and the professions, and ally them with uncovered women from the whole metropolis who were complaining about city government, its streets, water, electricity. Until 1994 religious people were seen as "poorer working class," but then Refah's vote shot up from 5 percent to 20 percent in that single year, and kept growing. Meanwhile, in cities like Konya and Kayseri, new Muslim entrepreneurs were succeeding in furniture, fabrics, sugar beets and other fields, generating new social and economic structures. Previously, Sibel implied, critics of the secularists had been intimidated by the Kemalists' relative wealth and confident consumerism. But "Green Capitalism" dissolved class restraint and diffidence. Erdoğan, in 2002, went further and blew away the idea of the government as "the shepherd of employment" by insisting repeatedly in his speeches, "Don't ask for a job."[29]

Sibel and my young interpreter, Melis, in an animated side discussion, agreed and declared to me that now the Louis Vuitton or Hermès *turban* is not only a religious distinction, but contains a style statement in part (Mrs. Erdoğan, the prime minister's wife, wears one with Gucci sunglasses). Add implied demonstration of consumer capacity, for social status.

Q. What is your personal psychology, Sibel Hanim, in scarf wearing?
A. I see it as part of my identity, like the color of my eyes. It is not an ornament, but like an arm or a leg. There was a dialogue between Allah and myself. . . . But because of political and social obstacles, the scarf became still more part of my identity, in worldly struggle. . . . My dialogue with Allah got overcome with politics. . . . Now the headscarf symbolizes for me [an unresolved] political feud.

Q. Your eyes can't change their color. But your headscarves can. How many headscarves do you own?
A. [Not directly answered.] The color of the scarf doesn't matter. It's wearing it that is part of you.

Here we went into commercial particulars. Sibel does not buy from Tekbir, a Turkish company which specializes in styled religious garb. Melis

29. Erdoğan quote (p. 22) and other impressions from "Islam's Calvinists: Change and Conservatism in Central Anatolia" (34 pp.) (Berlin/Istanbul, European Stability Initiative, 19 Sep 05). Nicole Pope kindly provided me this report.

posed the problem of a scarf from Vienna, portraying Klimt's painting of "The Kiss." Sibel answered that it was contradictory to Muslim values, and doubted that men would dare use it as a necktie. Even if not sensual, in Islam no human figure is permitted. She received a Hermès yacht-scarf as a gift, and enjoyed its portrayal of boat, steering wheel, and flag. But one day she noticed a woman on it and never wore it again.

I thanked Sibel Eraslan for allowing me to ask about her personal values, and asked her where, in her career, she was going now. She answered pointedly: "I am no longer active in politics. It was very tiring. There is little chance of success for a covered woman." She views national events now from the "outside," writing for newspapers. And like other women who have given up on politics, she is involved in several international NGOs, for victims' rights, for women's rights, for anti-discrimination, and for student women in particular, to enable their study abroad; also in providing legal advice to young women, and advice to them on housing, tuition, "everything from A to Z." So Sibel Eraslan, a national leader whose dialogue with Allah had for years suffered submersion in the din of Turkish struggles for power, continues her lifework as a religious feminist.

Fatma Benli, a generation younger than Sibel Eraslan, is a *turban*-wearer. Since she attended a religious high school in her very early teens, she has been convinced that God, as indicated in the Qur'an, wishes her to cover her hair. She graduated with a law degree from Istanbul University in 1995, when university rules said students were free to wear what they wished. But after the "post-modern coup" of 1997, the state, citing Atatürk, has required the universities to ban headscarves. University compliance with the state has prevented Fatma from completing her master's degree.

She patiently controls frustration for herself and her clients about not being allowed to argue in court with a headscarf, but permitted only to advise. Fatma considers that Atatürk wanted women to develop and to participate in public life. The state, in her view, is thwarting Atatürk's higher design. And, because there is no specific law on which the current ban is based, rulings tend to be arbitrary and inconsistent. Even the European Court of Human Rights has rejected the case of a Turkish woman who had worn a headscarf in her civil service job for eighteen years, and then, after 1998, was fired from the position for continuing to cover her head. Another teacher covered a thin scarf with an abundant wig, a stratagem which often succeeded. When an inquiry about her discerned the fact, she took off both wig and scarf to hold her job. But she was fired anyway, as "insincere," and has been jobless ever since.

I proposed a hypothetical case to Fatma, in which a female state employee has to undergo chemotherapy for cancer, loses her hair in consequence, and chooses to wear a minimal headscarf for cosmetic reasons. She prays to Allah for her recovery, and with sincerity believes that her ensuing wellness is in answer to her prayer. She therefore continues to wear the scarf as her hair grows out beneath it. Fatma shook her head. "Basically there is no tolerance at all for the headscarf. She would lose her job."

Examples multiply, and affect the heights of power. Prime Minister Erdoğan's wife does not appear at official functions, nor do covered wives of AK Party cabinet members and parliamentarians. The Erdoğans sent their daughters to college in the U.S., where they could wear what they wished.

Deep down, issues of class and of patriarchy are intertwined with freedom of religion. Ever since Anatolians began flocking to cities, a share of their women have been taking jobs as cleaning ladies while continuing, as before, to wear headscarves. Subservient roles "cover" them in another sense — no questions asked. But an educated cleaning lady will run into problems. A certain NGO woman who considers herself *aydin*, "enlightened" (a self-description of many educated seculars), treats Fatma with condescension, despite her level of education and published scholarship. Fatma, however, endorses the view of the female columnist who asserts that if the "secular has the right to expose his/her body, others should have the right to cover it." To bear home the point of absurdity: "Why are women wearing bikinis and drinking raki along the Aegean Sea entitled to consider themselves more enlightened than scarved women, whose men doing barbeques in city parks are seen as having 'hairy arms, short legs, and big bellies'?"[30]

When a provincial governor's office opened cases against imams with full beards, as suspect of anti-Kemalist fundamentalism, they shaved their beards the next day. "While women have to plead in court like thieves," Fatma said, men she knows to be more religious than she go through universities and can practice law without constraint. "They are protected by patriarchy." Or at least by the aggregated power of maleness.

The headscarf issue in Turkey appears to involve at least three major

---

30. Tugçe Baran, in *Vatan*, 22 May 07.

issues: freedom of religion (and its personal expression), democracy (equality of class treatment), and women's rights (including non-suppression by patriarchy). Which of these three principles, I asked Fatma, does she expect to prioritize across the next thirty years of her career?

Fatma answered promptly. The ban on the headscarf violates all three principles. But for her the worst offender is its violation of women's rights to make personal decisions. Her father, a simple man with only primary education, feels that, and pointed out that Fatma's seven-year-old niece can choose her own clothes, but she, at age thirty, cannot. Her basic stance is simple: "God made men and women equal. Neither can impose on the other. Both answer to God."

Fatma continues to publish studies for Akder (Organization for Women's Rights against Discrimination). Her writings give full weight to selective illiteracy (its rate four times higher among females over twelve years than among males); to minimal female representation in parliament (4.4 percent in 2002) and maximal male ownership of GDP (84 percent); as well as exposure to physical abuse, ranging from marital rape (for 16.3 percent of Turkish women, "frequently"), to murder cloaked as "honor killing," most common in Eastern Anatolia. But the headscarf issue is easiest to discuss, because the ban is not only discriminatory and disproportionate, but is seen and felt daily. It has cost "thousands" of civil workers their jobs, and "hundreds of thousands" of university students their education.[31] When the parliament by a four-to-one vote in February 2008 lifted the ban on headscarves at universities, Fatma seemed to feel it was just another stage in an endless emblematic contest.

Her resigned attitude, however, may not be consonant with the actual progress of Turkish women. A report of the European Stability Initiative, a think tank based in Berlin, sees Turkey, like Spain and Ireland before it, on the path to a post-patriarchal society. Yes, more people than ever declare themselves to pollsters as "very religious." But at the same time, the numbers of those favoring adoption of shariʿa law have decreased sharply;[32] those accepting arranged marriages are also decreasing (to only 10 percent among young unmarried Turks); and while headscarf debate continues, the proportion of women appearing in public uncovered continues to increase.

---

31. "Assessment of the Women Condition in Turkey, According to the Statistics and the General Impacts of the Ban on Women" (14 pp.), (Istanbul, Akder, 2005).

32. Kinzer, *Crescent and Star* (rev. 2008), p. 242, says from 21 percent (1999) to 9 percent (2007).

More significant than polled attitudes may be the massive revision of the penal code in 2004. Public consultation in drafting it was a major innovation in Turkey. Cooperation between the governing party and the opposition was a positive feature of its support. This widest discussion of sexuality in the history of the Republic signified the arrival, at least for the instance, of transparent democracy. The new penal code no longer treats sexual crimes as offenses against traditional family, society, or public morality, but as violations of individual women's rights. Among many other features, it criminalizes rape in marriage and sexual harassment in the workplace. It eliminates sentence reduction for honor killings. These astonishing advances were nearly derailed by Erdoğan's last-minute attempt to criminalize adultery. Hostile reactions within Turkey and across Europe forced him to withdraw that amendment, leaving a sour taste. In net overall impact, however, Turkey continues to digest its first major post-patriarchal legislation.[33]

Prosecuting Honor Killings

Vildan Yirmibeşoğlu is a striking woman in appearance, and splendid in her achievement. Yet her bearing is modest, like her account of herself. She hasn't the voice of a public advocate; her tones are not deep or especially resonant. But like a good lawyer — she was trained at Istanbul University — she lets the facts tell the story, and she trusts our interpreter, Nilüfer Narli, a friend of each of us, to expand where she wishes. Vildan comes from a conservative Muslim family of Istanbul, who respected Atatürk. She married a fellow student of law, and in 1984 she moved with him to Gaziantep, in the deep Southeast of Turkey, where Kurds prevail in number. There she worked as a lawyer in the mayor's office and raised their two daughters. Vildan was surprised to find women meeting only in their homes, never going outside, strikingly invisible on the street. She encouraged them to a possibility never considered — meeting with each other in coffee shops. (As in Japan, she said, there were no women in nightclubs except entertainers.) In awakening such timid social awareness, Vildan felt like a "cultural ambassador." She proceeded to organize conferences on social and political issues, the first such held in Gaziantep. She encouraged

33. ESI, *Sex and Power in Turkey: Feminism, Islam, and the Maturing of Turkish Democracy* (41 pp., Berlin/Istanbul, 2 Jun 07).

women to take part in debate, and started a chapter of the Contemporary Life Association, an influence for modern values throughout Turkey. She headed it for five years.

In her municipal job, she found many women seeking assistance on violence — economic deprivation, beating, torture, even honor killing. She established a "People's Day for Women" so that once a week they might vent and debate their problems. In this consciousness-raising, she included Kemalist and Islamist equally, made no distinctions by party or class, and encouraged illiterates from neglected wards.

Through her job, Vildan had already become aware of many battered women seeking a "green card" for free medical treatment from the municipality. She began to notice anomalous and unresolved case files. On further study she recognized a common theme of ultra-violence, largely unpunished. She assembled many cases that appeared to be murder. She analyzed the records: What were the conditions for "assignment" of the killing? What was the "decision-making process"? What loopholes in the law were used by defendants, lawyers, and judges to mitigate or escape punishment? What was society's response to the *lekeli*, the "stained" girl and her family? Here Nilüfer, who knew these stories already from Vildan, threw in her own heated commentary: neighbors threw stones at the house containing the alleged miscreant and cried, "Kill the bitch."

Vildan's study,[34] the result of a dozen years of work, makes a clear and strong distinction between "murders of love, passion, and reaction" and "organized killings" for the sake of family "honor and dignity." The first group of murders are individual in motive and often instantaneous, springing out of envy, rage, or self-defense. The second, little-studied, group has no bibliography, because the basic sources are silent: women deliberately killed to satisfy tribal custom. Vildan, however, established context and pattern for these unresolved killings — over 300 of them between 1995 and 2000, out of a larger total — aborted, or concluding in minimal punishment. They affected nineteen Turkish provinces, eighteen of them in Southeast Turkey, ranging from Adana in Central Anatolia on the Mediterranean Sea through two, three, or even four layers of provinces along the entire borders with Syria and Iraq, bending northward along the border with Iran, and jumping to Kars on the border of Armenia. The nine-

---

34. Vildan Yirmibeşoğlu, ms. English summary of her book, *Toprağa Düşen Sevdalar* ("Desires Fallen to Earth"), published by Hürriyet, Istanbul, 2008. In author's possession, courtesy of Ms. Yirmibeşoğlu.

teenth province was geographically disconnected — Istanbul, where those practices arose in ghettos of internal migrants from the Southeast.

The trial that prompted Vildan's first public involvement was that of the murder of Sevda Gök, in Şanlıurfa in May 1996. "Why was she killed?" Vildan asked the mother. Weeping, she replied, "She liked hanging around too much; she was seventeen and no one had asked to marry her yet." In other words, her family considered her defective. No matter that forensic medicine determined she was a virgin. Males in council had concluded she was defiling the family. On a crowded street, two members apprehended her and bent her to her knees on the sidewalk, whereupon a fourteen-year-old male cousin slit her throat.

Attitudes? A policeman told Vildan he was personally aware of the killing of more than thirty women in the last four years, and was unfazed by Vildan's query about measures to stop Şanlıurfa from being "a slaughterhouse of women." Sevda Gök's grandfather grew angry with Vildan when she said "condolences" to him, because he believed that by her death family honor had been re-dignified. The prosecutor in the case said that the event arose from the socioeconomic structure of Şanlıurfa, which provides the mitigation of custom. The judge found further mitigation in the age of the boy-killer (chosen for that reason) and refused to allow broadening of the investigation to those who held Sevda's arms. Vildan's request to intervene was refused because she was "not damaged by the crime." The sentence of the killer was so light — two years and eight months — that she concluded, "another murderer-hero is added to society."

As she examined court archives, Vildan was agonized by "the short lives of many women each of whom remained in my throat as a sob." She resolved to see that the laws of the Republic of Turkey were applied to defend the right to life of other women. Her researches included surveys, interviews with police, public prosecutors, judges, and lawyers, with perpetrators of honor killings and the family councils that determined the killings — over 600 people in all.

Vildan concluded that in Southeastern Anatolia patriarchal and feudal structures prevail. "The woman is regarded as an item purchased and sold by the family." A woman's body, if affected by relations unapproved by male authority or the family council (or even just besmirched by gossip), is lowered in value — specifically with regard to marriage money. So "damage to the social and economic status of the family [becomes] . . . an important ground for honor killings." Ignorance, lack of education, and religious zeal prevent the changing of customs dominated by tribal law and characterized by "social and cultural introversion." Yet, she is at pains to point out, Turks, Kurds, Arabs, Yezidi (Zoroastrians), and Ashrani (Christians) all practice honor killings. They are therefore not a matter of religion, but clearly of tribal culture. In the Southeast, Turks follow the practice less than others. But Kurds and Yezidi are heavily represented in its pursuit.

Nilüfer took the cultural point further. She had spent a year in Malaysia and had never heard of honor killings there. I had been traveling to Indonesia since 1966, and had heard of none in its bilateral family culture, influenced by Sufism. But such killings are numerous in Pakistan, vividly reported in Iran, well-known in Saudi Arabia, and predictably extant among Arab peoples in Iraq, Jordan, and Palestine. So it is clearly possible to trace patterns of tribalisms within different cultural Islams, showing how traditional values justify such murder.

Premodern values in many parts of the world, including Judaic texts, justify it. Recent emigration has carried Islamic honor killings to some European countries. And it is certainly possible to see modern dowry deaths in Hindu India and "crimes of passion" in parts of Latin America as comprising further parts of a worldwide continuum of violence against women, wherever females are seen as family property. The killings are done by males within the family, and the matter is viewed without judiciary context, but with family as the court.

Vildan's legal files and interviews left her clear about what she was dealing with. In Turkey's Black Sea region, when a woman is raped, the family may move in to kill the rapist. But in the Kurdish region, "they must kill the girl." When Vildan moved back to Istanbul in 1998, she became part of a larger feminist network, motivated by the Beijing conference on women in 1995. Together they mounted pressure that brought central changes in Turkish law — in 2003, abolition of the statute allowing crimes of passion to go unpunished or minimally punished; in 2005, changing of the sanctions law to allow charges against the family in these cases, which had previously been impossible.

The media, at last, now took a role. Why, I asked, had they been slow to do so? Vildan answered that they were mostly men, unwilling to open the minds of the people. They were supporting the guilty because "they had the same view"; they were sad for the killer, not the victim. National legal reform helped to change reporters' minds. A journalist can now advance himself with such a story, where only a few years ago he would look like a deviant or a sentimentalist for writing one.

Looking back, I asked Vildan for deeper causes of this cultural phenomenon. She answered that pre-Islamic law treated woman as a commodity. The corrections of Islamic law have not yet reached into tribal areas, where feudal structures remain. Kurds who migrate to their cultural ghetto in Istanbul continue to do honor killings. But if they ascend to the middle class, they adopt new standards. Kurds of the Southeast, however, in *all* classes, commit honor killings, because their tribal network is the controlling grid of values.

Nicole Pope, who is researching a book on honor killing, offered observations from her sources that help explain to me a psychology otherwise repellent. What if you live in a neighborhood where nobody will buy things at your store, nobody will talk to you outside the mosque, nobody will allow their young to marry yours, unless you exterminate your offender? The metaphor offered by the honor killers is that of a diseased limb on an otherwise healthy tree. What do you do? You hack it off. Then the family tree can be healthy throughout. Obviously that culture is still strong. In Turkish urban settings alone, within police jurisdiction from 2000 to 2005, there were 1,091 honor killings.[35]

Vildan has heard all the justifications, but she is a lawyer and advocate seeking to end the practice. She continues to go further in prevention and rehabilitation. Just after my second conversation with her, a police and community cooperative was launched in which three Istanbul police districts would specialize in prevention of these crimes, by special access to premonitory reporting, and with counseling. She also helped launch a new NGO *for men,* who need counseling either for guilt over cooperating in an honor crime, or for fear of committing one.

Vildan may properly feel herself a key actor in the movement against honor killings, which brought about a parliamentary commission of investigation and then, based on its report, a circular issued by the prime minister. The years may have taken their toll on Vildan, but part of her beauty is her courage. At the corners of her mouth are three dimples, which will deepen with age. The first appears to be of humor, the second of chagrin, and the third of skepticism. Her smile, depending on how she is moved, may travel swiftly over a wide range of affect, and back to her resolute humanity.

I had just asked her what the impact of her campaign had been on her own life, when a senior Turk required my attention elsewhere. So Nilüfer

35. Figure from ESI Report (2007), p. 22.

put my question to Vildan and jotted down a brief English translation of her answer. "She received threats because of concern for 'woman's modesty' and 'family honor.' . . . Some papers published articles criticizing her. They had negative effect on her family life during the marriage. Later she got divorced. She has two daughters [whom she is educating through college]. She never [felt too] discouraged to do her studies."

The New "Critical Culture"

Rising education at all levels, a greatly expanded university system, and a diversifying socio-economy have fertilized new patterns of thought. In the last twenty years a "critical culture" has appeared in Turkey, not unlike that of some advanced industrial societies, but with its own distinctive premises.

A journalistic manifestation of new attitudes was to dub the military intervention in government of February 28, 1997, a "post-modern coup." The belittlement in that term was galling to the military, who like to be seen as guardians of the Republic. Did they not intercede in a carefully measured way to sustain the Kemalist core against irruptions from Islamism? Shouldn't they hear gratitude for having refined their methods since 1960, when they moved with full military and judicial force, leaving Prime Minister Adnan Menderes, among others, hanging by the neck until dead? And did not subsequent stability prove their wisdom in 1980, when polarizing violence in Turkish society had required judicial executions of several on the left and a few on the right?

But a new perspective, neither Islamist nor Kemalist, not socialist or capitalist, but independent in its views and diverse in voices, was articulating its own variety of hopes for Turkey.[36] This new culture showed its courage by daring to assert its own findings and convictions on Turkish history, and to reassert them in the face of legal challenge. The novelist Orhan Pamuk is an outstanding example. With ten significant works in Turkish behind him, with translations in more than forty languages, including six books in English, he was awarded the Nobel Prize in Literature in 2006, at the age of fifty-four. That day he ventured to say that "Culture means a mix of things from other sources. . . . Istanbul, in fact, and my

---

36. Both editions of Kinzer's *Crescent and Star* (2001, 2008) conclude with eloquent "blues" codas on capacities for disappointment.

work . . . is a testimony to the fact that East and West combine culture gracefully, or sometimes in an anarchic way come together, and that is what we should search for."[37] His memoir of Istanbul seizes the city with *hüzün* — a melancholy which becomes a weapon of ownership. In one sentence spread across six pages and connected with fifty-seven semicolons and a colon before arriving at a period, he iterates "everything being broken, worn out, past its prime."[38]

Pamuk had found it painful, however, to allow himself to be quoted by a Swiss journalist about "30,000 Kurds and one million Armenians killed in these lands." Ultra-nationalists rose against him for specifying the human costs of events ninety years past, especially Turkey's struggles against European imperialism, in which Armenians sided with Russians. Pamuk's trial for "insulting Turkishness" ended eventually in dismissal of his case on technical grounds. But the same forces proceeded against the columnist Murat Yetkin, whose careful — and sympathetic — reporting of Pamuk's case led to a charge of "interfering with the judiciary," with a potential four-and-a-half-year sentence. Also dismissed. Then Elif Şafak was tried for having one of her fictional characters utter the words "Armenian genocide." Finally dismissed. Among what are now several dozen cases resolved or still proceeding, the female journalist Ipek Çalışlar was grotesquely prosecuted for her biography of Atatürk's wife, Latife. It includes the story of her helping her husband to escape an attempted assassination by dressing him in a *çarşaf* to leave the house with other women, while she, in blurred silhouette, remained in his study as if he were still there. The moment is a tribute to Latife's ingenuity and her husband's realism. But the idea of the great leader in a woman's garb led ultra-nationalists to initiate a case against the author for "insulting the memory of Atatürk." The petty advocate who argued the case maximized its triviality by adding to the charges that of offense against his own masculinity. In December 2006, Çalışlar was acquitted. The minister of justice in 2010 reasoned that his ministry had only granted a sanction in 7 percent of the 1,252 cases filed with it under the "insulting Turkishness" statute. That statute, Article 301 of the penal code, although modified, remains in place.[39]

Harassment of the new critical culture did not deter so much as moti-

37. http://nobelprize.org/nobel_prizes/literature/laureates/2006/pamuk-telephone.html.
38. Pamuk, *Istanbul*, trans. Maureen Freely (New York, Knopf, 2005), pp. 94-99, quotation, p. 99.
39. *Hurriyet Daily News*, 25 May 10.

vate and strengthen it, until, perhaps, the murder of Hrant Dink, a leading Armenian journalist. One may nevertheless hope for a future Turkey that can see its own history clearly and debate it concretely. Meanwhile, to the muscle and nerve of a modern nation is being added a component neither military nor religious nor overtly political, but simply "critical." Among its prominent exponents is a high proportion of educated women, taking risks for truth without regard to gender. One such woman is Ayşe Gül Altınay. She approaches "state-making as a gendered cultural revolution," which in its post-Ottoman and anti-Ottoman trajectory includes powerful elements of nationalism, militarism, and, she also stresses, masculinism. The citizen-soldier in a military state becomes an object of reverence, not to mention a symbol for obedience. For Altınay, however, the "state" is a front, and the "military-nation" is a myth. The state is what really makes things happen and/or hides those things, and the nation is those to whom they happen, trained to either represent or respect military virtue.[40] Altınay leaves her reader with an impression of a state as a hum of military activity behind a mask, and at worst a cannibalistic grinding of teeth behind a festive face-piece.

Much of the story is prefigured in the life of Sabiha Gökçen, one of Atatürk's adopted daughters. As a young woman she sought to undertake flight training, and with his enthusiastic blessing was given special instruction, because she was shorter than her male counterparts. When she volunteered for a special operation, her commander said that only her father, the president, could give such permission. She flew to Ankara and convinced Atatürk to let her take part. He required that she accept his own pistol, and if anything put her "honor to risk," she was to use it against others or to kill herself.

Sabiha had already imagined the dangers of a forced landing in enemy hands. Taking the pistol, Gökçen kissed Atatürk's hand, then kissed the weapon, and vowed a lifelong promise as he wished. She became part of a Turkish force of 30,000 fighting against Kurdish rebels. Sabiha put in a full month of operations, dropping bombs in a campaign which, according to official figures, killed five thousand.

When she returned from the Southeast, she was highly honored, and her father was thrilled. Then, at his urging, she put her modernist case to the chief of the military, Marshal Çakmak. Dressed in her military uniform

---

40. Ayşe Gül Altınay, *The Myth of the Military Nation: Militarism, Gender, and Education in Turkey* (New York, Palgrave McMillan, 2004), p. 6 and *passim*.

for the annual Republic Ball, she asked him to advance a law so that young Turkish female patriots could become soldiers. To her surprise, he refused. To avoid crying, she kissed his hand and backed away. Her own father chose not to oppose his chief of staff on the matter, but to respect his responsibilities in the chain of command. After Atatürk died a year later, Sabiha resigned from the military. She worked for a civilian organization to develop aviation in Turkey, and taught flying to air force cadets.[41] She volunteered again for service in the Korean War, and was declined. Turkish women were finally admitted to the military in 1955.

Sabiha Gökçen was not only Turkey's first female military pilot, but the world's first female combat pilot. One cannot avoid feeling the pathos of her risking her life for Daddy's republic, followed by her frustration at not being able to open the way for other women. In the end she became an image deployed to reinforce the myth of the military nation.[42]

Part of the present feminist critical approach to militarism and Kemalism includes an appetite for debunking Atatürk himself. Altinay, in conversation, ascribes to him the assassination of Fikriye, his consort before marrying Latife, by having her shot in the back. The evidence appears to me to be chiefly opinion long after the fact, in the absence of a coroner's report on trajectory of the bullet. Atatürk as a soldier certainly knew professionally how to kill, and as a politician was not above influencing judicial executions. But to murder a lover that he had rejected seems to me out of character for him: too tawdry in motive, and too terrible in means. Fikriye's volatile despondency, however, is not inconsistent with suicide.[43]

The feminist project in Turkey has a long history and does not need to turn Atatürk into a common murderer in order to succeed. In the period of pre-Republican ferment, 1908-23, Turkish women generated twenty-seven women's journals and forty women's organizations, including a special unit that provided support at the Republican battlefront, carrying ammunition and sometimes fighting the enemy. Sabiha's disappointment at the Republic Ball may be seen actually as an incident in the *wane* of Turk-

41. Zeynap Atikkan to the author, 12 May 08. Ms. Atikkan's mother was a friend of Gökçen.

42. Altınay on Gökçen, *Myth of the Military Nation*, pp. 34-48.

43. Altınay informs me that Ipek Calişlar's biography, *Latife Hanim* (12th ed., pp. 283-84), gives both versions of Fikriye's death, that is, by suicide and by murder; and while tilting to the former by predominance of evidence, leaves substantial insinuations regarding the plausibility of the latter. I find the reasoning in Mango, however (*Atatürk*, 2000, pp. 409-10, 606n58), compelling on suicide and dismissive on murder.

ish feminism between its two great waves of the twentieth century. The first wave threw up the Turkish Women's Union, which in 1926 joined the International Women's Union, founded in 1902. In 1935 Turkish women organized in Istanbul the twelfth congress of their international union, within a year of Turkey's Grand National Assembly granting women's suffrage. *After that they were asked to dissolve themselves, and they did so.*

Not until the last quarter of the twentieth century did Turkish women begin to assess themselves and their condition systematically. Duygu Asena became a leading voice in the dimensions of sexual freedom and independent initiative, broadening the grounds for Turkish feminism. In the critical culture which has more recently emerged, feminism is a bold component. One example is Altınay's book, which describes the state as overstrategizing politics, overmechanizing education, and overmilitarizing national pride. It summons out of silence the feelings of ethnic minorities — Kurdish, Armenian, Greek, and others — and religious minorities — Christian, Jew, Alevi, and others. It presumes to say that conscientious objectors to military service are also honorable people. And it may be inferred that homosexuals, transvestites, and other psychological minorities are not only decent citizens of the Turkish state, but may also be creative resources for the nation's future.

Rumi and Old Anatolia

From Istanbul to Ankara I slowed my life by taking an overnight train, and woke to fields sliding by, of loam and harvested grains. Friends then drove me to an ancient caravan stop on the Silk Road, built in the bilateral symmetry of Selçuk geometrical style, nothing more than three stories high, for fear of quakes. The women tended stalls in full skirts and colored headscarves, while grizzled men in grays swilled coffee in lordly discussion outside a corner shop. It was Ramadan, a month when national GDP surges and Turks gain weight, their nighttime feasting overcoming daytime fasts.

A thousand internal migrants a day arrive in Ankara, two thousand in Istanbul, stressing urban environments already in crisis. Some are wholly traditional; others represent "Green Capitalism," or new Islamic entrepreneurship. Contractor teams on Sundays continue to steam away at subsidized government housing for arrivals, their excavation claws digging and swinging for eight- to ten-story apartment dwellings, and, in the exurbs, four to six stories. "Earthquake topology," my friend said about the road we were traveling, with allusion to a recent rumble near Istanbul that had killed twenty or thirty thousand people. "But," gesturing at cranes and trucks, "Turkey itself is an earthquake."

I proceeded alone for Konya, the long-time home of Jalaluddin Rumi, thirteenth-century Sufi mystic. Through excellent translations he became the largest-selling poet of late twentieth-century America, and on his 800th birthday (2007) was honored as the most popular poet in the world after Shakespeare. A secular skeptic in Istanbul laughed at Konya: he said that commercial data showed the highest per capita sales of mail-order sex objects there of any city in Turkey. But the idea of conservative religion correlating with sexual experimentation at home was strangely cheering to me.

I had no choice but to go more slowly still: by bus. The station in Ankara is a great modern stadium of sixty-some gates, in which dozens of small companies operate. A few words, eyebrows raised in query, and a smile of thanks got me to the right counter with the correct reserved ticket soon in hand. Ten American bucks for a seat to Konya.

Little concentrates the mind as fiercely as discovering, seven minutes before departure, that the bus itself has no WC. The Turkish word is *tuvalet.* That, with an urgent look at my wristwatch, got me hand directions from the driver. I jogged a couple of hundred yards through three turns and up one floor to a welcome 35-cent opportunity. For that price the lemony liquid soap was working, but not the hand dryer. No paper towels. So shaking my hands, I ran back, drying them with my geriatric speed.

The bus left, with Japanese efficiency, exactly on time. I settled in to its loudspeaker — Sufi pop and arabesque, some chipper advertisements, and a succession of female voices backed by strings, whose emotion and phrasing seemed to me well above American standards. But it may help not to know the language.

The driver packed us into the front half of the bus, as if we were a small military detachment that had to be kept compact. Overhead was too narrow for storage. My overnight bag filled the space under my seat and thighs; my briefcase bulged out beyond it, under my knees and behind my calves. My patience was unlocked for a three-and-a-half-hour journey. Despite air-conditioning, the temperature rose from 19°C to 24° (75°F). The land stretched on, plowed and unplowed, harvested and fallow, looking like Kansas or Dakota. No features other than smoke from distant brushfires. On the horizon, softly contoured hills.

We passed a tractor hauling a wagon of potatoes. Then, after a while, two red trucks with tarpaulins over their potato-loads; close enough to see muddy black tires turning close to really big tubers. Occasionally we saw a gas station. Once, a town with four gas stations.

Eventually the driver announced "Konya." We parked on the edge of a metropolis. I needed a taxi to my hotel. How to pronounce "Rixos" when there is no "x" in Turkish? My taxi driver curtly corrected me: "Reek-sose." It lay back outside the city, twenty-five minutes away, rising two dozen floors. I was not, to my disappointment, in a cozy quarter of a medieval town. I could not even see as far as Konya from my hotel room. I spent two nights in a marble palace in the potato fields.

I saw distant mountains and close-up housing developments. Again, the square and rectangular buildings, four to eight stories, clumped in symmetrical blocs, all standing out against agri-land. Everybody had a balcony. Laundry was hung out the windows to dry. On top of each building, an anarchic throng of chimneys and satellite dishes. A palette of pastels prevailed; some few structures featured white on grays; most ran light yellow to light blue. There were noble efforts at variety: red stripes on orange buildings, a vertical beige panel on olive. Extremely rare to see any curve or decorative figure. In incomplete condos, gaping black windows. Turkey's earthquake of construction was heaving up residences more solid than toys, but not designed for the ages.

Rumi lived in Konya eight centuries ago. Persian in his original culture, he made his home and trained his heart here in Anatolia. Turks cherish him as "Mevlana," the Master. I had first sensed his meaning to them a dozen years before, when I was trying to raise money for an Eisenhower Fellowships program from Nejat Eczacibaşi, an eminent industrialist. Our talk flowed into culture and religion. Mr. E., seventyish, gray-haired, cinema-handsome, rose from his desk to demonstrate the dance of the dervishes. To illustrate what the Mevlana was about, this Westernized billionaire spun slowly about in the middle of his office, arms extended, left palm upraised to receive divine energy from heaven, right palm downturned to relay it to earth.

The dean and three professors were kind enough to receive me at Selçuk University's Faculty of Theology. I had three questions, and the group was forthcoming on them all. "Live in love's ecstasy," I quoted the Mevlana, "for love is all that exists." Then I asked, "Is this good theology? Or merely good poetry?" All were eager to reply, and their answers converged. If love means love of Allah and love of the Prophet, then it is good theology. In Sufi understanding of these matters, it is important to remember that when in love you are not to forget religious rules. Thinking "I am God" is dangerous. The Prophet Mohammad said: First I am the *servant* of Allah, *then* I am his prophet. Only in service is union with him possible. As Muslims we must love God and the Prophet before and beyond all else. And the Prophet is careful to warn against idolatry in love.

I raised the phenomenon of Ayesha (Turkish: Ayşe), Mohammad's favorite wife, as a test of principle and proportion. All present agreed that the Prophet strained to make sure that his love of her did not interfere with his love of God.

Two specialists in Sufism present stressed that when Sufis are in transport they may see and say unintelligible things; "But then they wake up." Consciousness of servanthood must prevail. They all agreed on compelling love of Allah, with a negative digression on the Wahhabis, who have gotten lost in textual empiricism and hyper-rationalism. The Prophet was quoted, "We are a *moderate umma*." I tried to summarize all this, in borrowed Quakerly terms, as the necessity of blending love with faith and practice. "You are on the right road," I was told.

In a heart-city of historical Sufism, two of my interlocutors returned to love as the reason for our creation. They quoted the Prophet, revealing Allah: "I was a hidden treasure. I wanted to be known, and therefore I created all human beings." This is not a fully proven hadith, they said, but Sufis believe it is a vital one. I certainly liked the idea of a lonely Creator making creatures with which to share love, even if the motive seemed more human than divine.

We came back to the Mevlana as the Master of Love. Asking again if it were good theology, I quoted Rumi on his spiritual travels, in search of Allah as his Beloved. He looked at Christendom, but "He was not on the cross." In Indian temples, but there was "no trace of him." And in the Ka'aba, but "he was not at that sanctuary." Then, in his own heart — "He was there and nowhere else."

Rejoinders: Love *should* be in the heart first. But you can also see God's power all through the universe. If you have that love, you *can* go to the Ka'aba and see it. Without it, you can go to the Ka'aba and see nothing. It must be in the heart, or everything is *"void."* Love by itself is zero. But Allah is everything by which and for which love exists. The female among my four interlocutors, a Sufi philosopher herself, stressed blending the understanding of things exoteric (physical and sensual) with things esoteric (spiritual, or containing hidden meaning). When they are combined, "God is everywhere — on the cross, in the Ka'aba, in a tree, in you and me. If you understand this exoteric/esoteric combination, then you are okay. If we combine love, faith, and practice, we are *increasing* our love."

My third question was a broad inquiry into the standing of women in Turkey, and in all of Islam, as they perceived it. The dean in particular wished to stress that at the time of *jahiliya* (ignorance before Islam) women were treated as slaves, and because they were mere property, they themselves enjoyed no ownership. The Prophet made a point of their rights, and of their lives, *mutually shared* with men. In that way, Islam was a revolution. I knew the common understanding of *jahiliya,* and was glad to hear it in this setting. Then the dean quoted the Prophet as saying, "one half of the world is women."

If he expected me to be impressed with the quotation, he was disappointed, for I found it anticlimactic. To make my own point I quoted the Chinese proverb, "Women hold up half the sky." Whether Confucius first said it or Mao Zedong, the practical condition of women in China needs great advancing. What accounts, I resumed my inquiry, for the descending position of women in Turkey, as Atatürk found it in the late nineteenth and early twentieth centuries?

The dean answered straightforwardly. "People lost their conscience and sensitivity about women." That led to a discussion of the relative standing of women in Turkey compared to other Islamic nations. The faculty sought my own opinion. I summarized it by saying that Turkey, overall, is not surpassed by any Muslim country in the condition of women. In Indonesia, however, women are anthropologically more secure, because of their bilateral family system. Turkish women are liberated by statute, by Kemalist exhortation, and from time to time by feminist initiatives; but they always have to struggle against a patrilineal system and patriarchal ethos.

My hosts had triumphed by letting me feel knowledgeable on one matter, while drawing me along as a teachable novice in all others. I thanked them fervently for one of the most heartwarming of conversations in all my travels.

I had never seen a dance meditation, or what in tourist language is called whirling dervishes. The dean of theology determined there was an event that night at 9:30 p.m., free of charge. I arranged a taxi in, with driver to wait and bring me back. He, Mustafa Koç, I determined by my phrase book, was 58 years old. When I told him I was 75, he exclaimed, "Maşallah!"

He chose to watch the performance too, and provided me a bottle of water and choice of colored Chiclets.

The Mevlana Cultural Center, a modern amphitheater, was half filled, with about a thousand people. Middle-class families, I judged, and middle-aged, with a good many youth and some romping children. I saw no white-haired men except Mustafa. It interested me that all these people were not at home watching television.

Proceedings began late: a twenty-five-minute lecture, and a five-minute reading from the Mevlana, about Shems of Tabriz, his profoundest human inspiration. Then an orchestra of twenty filed into place, robed in black, with brown, cylindrical hats. An aged man of short stature then led on a troupe of thirty males who filed around the edge of the circular dance floor. When the drums, flutes, strings, and chanting began, the troupe took off their black robes, revealing white skirts. They filed past their leader with mutual bows, and one by one, slowing unfolding their arms, swung onto the dance floor.

The eleventh and twenty-first dancers were, from their size, early teenagers, used as punctuation for the second and third phalanxes of ten slowly whirling men. A large middle-aged man, muscular, nimble, and tireless, struck me as being like a graceful rhino in a steeplechase.

In addition to the stationary leader, one other man retained his black robe. He navigated slowly among the dancers in ways that suggested his presence was to keep them from congestion. In addition to traffic management, I wondered if he were also scanning countenances to detect any flawed concentration, or dizziness. After perhaps ten minutes of a steady bedazzlement of whirling men in white skirts, all slid back to the perimeter in pairs and trios.

Then they filed forward again, into another prolonged stream of gyrations.

After another return to the perimeter, to my amazement they opened their wings and flew a third time.

On musical beat there was an astounding fourth flight, this time half of the dancers, while the others rerobed themselves in black and watched.

On completion of their fourth hypnotic flow, these last dancers donned black and joined an amphitheatric quiet. Expert sources later told me that I had seen four salutes: truth through knowledge, the splendor of creation, total submission to God, and coming to terms with destiny. But in attendance I was not absorbing lessons; barely self-aware, I was more than half in a dream.

A startling voice broke the silence. The lead baritone had been noticeable among the chorus. Now, solo, he launched on a vocal tirade of great volume and engrossing tonal range. Unable to recognize a word that he uttered except "Allah," I couldn't discern a logical message. But are denotations needed when one is seized by an extended carnal cry of rage, abasement, grief?

His flowing chords and sudden stops lingered with me for a full day. I am broken, the voice said to me. We are broken. We are shards on the field of the Almighty. We cannot assemble ourselves. He will fracture all our designs so that his own may be realized. Let us find a reverent voice for our pain, for it comes again and again, inseparable from life and its pleasures. Rejoice in the round of pain, inevitable as the course of the planets and rotation of the seasons. Allah, accept our song. We long for you. Let us belong to you completely.

Popular Culture and National Poise

I was trying to reach Pelin Akat, a young TV producer, who had four shows going at once. By e-mail she replied that she was very busy the day I suggested, when two new shows of hers would open. Yet, she wrote in capital letters, "THERE'S ALWAYS 'BUT' . . ." By phone she suggested meeting at the Hilton for a celebration of fall shows hosted by Star TV. How would I find her? "I am tall and blonde," she says. "Too bad," I say, laughing with her. "I may be recognized as formerly having lots of curly brown hair."

Half a dozen searchlights were washing the sky, and security was thick. Two hundred yards of red carpet was rolled out to draw one to the lawn party side of the hotel. In an awninged corridor over it were colored panels displaying Turkish TV stars in characteristic costumes and antics. They giggled, dreamed, shouted in panic, frowned in comedic concentration. They were in business suits, blue jeans, kitchen frocks, sports garb, slinky dinky teen stuff. There were as many women as men. None were scarved. I recognized only one character, a large-headed man of late middle age with a stiff broom of pepper-and-salt hair and a large irregular black mole, like a burnt island in the Aegean of his cheek. I had seen him as I channel-surfed, playing a careworn husband and father.

Beyond this gallery were gathered hundreds of people, younger and slenderer than those at the Hilton poolside on weekends. Men were in dark suits; two-thirds wore neckties. Percentage of décolletage among women was high. Lots of swiveling necks as each sought a prime contact, or a new connection. An outspoken female of middle age was wearing dark glasses and a black getup that her friends said recalled "The Blues Brothers." John Belushi and Dan Aykroyd had not made an impression on me with their film of 1980, but apparently they are remembered in Turkey and in worldwide musical festivals.

Three tall feminine icons, assembled for publicity shots together, presented me their shoulder blades. A photographer jostled past me to join the blaze of guns at the willing victims. A dwarf gaffer trotted back and forth sorting out cables on the grass, ten or a dozen black snakes here and there banded with wire twists.

From a table displaying J&B, Chivas Regal, various vodkas, and red and white wine, I took two swigs of vodka with pineapple juice, my only hard liquor during this month in Turkey. In the lobby at the appointed meeting time with Pelin, the concierge recognized her name and seemed honored to dial her cell phone. She would come "in ten minutes," I was told, and was asked to sit in a sofa opposite.

Half an hour later I was sleepy when a figure came up from the opposite end of the hall and paused, with eyebrows raised: "Dorie?" I rose from the depths of the sofa, comforted that, especially tall as she was for a Turkish woman, I uncoiled two or three inches higher. Her eyeballs and teeth were dazzling white, as if scoured by a magic cleanser. Her irises were a warm brown, with a tender humor. We went downstairs and joined the mob.

The music grabbed for throats and guts. In Pelin's conversations with others, I studied her features. Long head, finely carried on a long neck, in a lissome body dressed in a high-collar fawn gray suit. Diamonds hung on her ears as if she had been born with them. Her nose was long and narrow, in keeping with her head and body. All her proportions seemed to suggest a dancer without pronounced muscle, but with elegant tone. In amusement, she winced with humor around the eyes, wrinkling the top of her nose. To speak through the noise she sometimes flared her lips, as if they had special muscles for unmistakable diction in crowds. And yes, her hair was blonde, fine strings of silk falling to her lower back.

She introduced me to Zühtü Sezer, Manager for International Business Development of Doğan Media Group, which owns Star TV and much else. Her famous "May I Call You Mom?", a show featuring daughter-in-law aspirations and problems, had recently closed after eight years. The next day she would take it to Romania to launch it there.

"She is a genius," Sezer said to me. "She has her finger on the pulse of the woman in the street. And the man in the street. She knows what they feel. She knows what makes them laugh and cry." In my channel-surfing, I said, I couldn't discern plot lines, but I could feel a lot of sadness. "Yes, that's Turkey," Sezer said cheerfully. "People like to sit alone in their living rooms and weep." He smiled. "Or laugh. Or both together. . . . She is very good at reality shows." I described an American reality show, competitive and cruel. He shook his head. "That's not her kind."

Pelin herself answered some personal questions directly. She had started in advertising, before television. She was divorced, with a ten-year-old son. "You must have married at sixteen," I said. She laughed: "I am thirty-four." The noise, the press of the crowd, the acrobatics of waiters with trays were all intensifying. She had somehow lit a cigarette without my seeing it. She dragged on it with her face averted, and then stubbed it out in a yellow ashtray on a little table piled with red bunny blankets, a favor for each guest.

"You've had a hard day," I said.

"I'm fine," she said mildly. "I'm fine." At later inquiries from others, she said so two more times.

"There are lots of people here," I said, "behaving like kings or queens. Like princes and princesses, too."

"That's Turkey." She looked up, as upon a familiar reality, neither detestable nor admirable. "Everybody wants to be somebody special. On top. Somebody royal. But they are not. Not in the big world. This is just Turkey."

"Everybody wants to be an aristocrat," I added. "But Atatürk ended hereditary titles [Pelin nodded], and you can't just *grab aristocracy*." I seized the air with my hand, and Pelin nodded again. "Our hero, Thomas Jefferson," I paused, and she acknowledged him with a third nod, "said that the only aristocracy is made up of talent and virtue." On talent she nodded once more. On virtue she gave off no expression. She had to get home to her ten-year-old son.

I caught up with Zühtü Sezer again some weeks later, to try to understand what Turks look at in their living rooms. "I've thought a lot about that," he said. "There is no umbrella 'television.' All markets, even the market for breads nowadays [lunch in his skyscraper cafeteria offered several], are diversified. . . . There is mainstream entertainment [his own major interest] and there are niches for kids, ladies, sports, news, business, et cetera." He gave as an example CNBC-E, which is a business channel by day, but if it persisted in that mode it would drop to zero share in the evening, when people want to get away from business. So that channel picks up and shows things like "Desperate Housewives," with Turkish subtitles. But the imported desperation achieves only 1.2 percent in the ratings.

"During the day, we all go out wearing a mask, or a costume, like a necktie." (He fingered his own Western-style cravat.) "When people come home, they take their masks off, become a more natural person, in privacy. They don't have to show off. They want to empty their minds." In letting themselves go, mainstream TV is a big factor. "All day long, expected to be rational? Impossible. It's psychologically healthy to let themselves go. 'Entertainment' really means 'emotional content television.'"

I suddenly glimpsed Zühtü as a co-manager of secular therapy to his nation. He returned to my questions about Pelin Akat's shows. Her generating and managing four shows at once was an achievement. Now *six* shows, even more impressive. But it's like advertising, in which business they first met each other. Only half of what you spend proves worthwhile, and you never know which half it is.

She must have real executive capacity, I observed. "Yes, she has that. She also has the talent of knowing what will go with the public. She has (he pinched his fingers beneath his nose) — she has *the smell.*"

For her show that ran eight years, she put twelve girls and five mothers living in the same place, with five marriageable sons located nearby. In the twelve weeks of the program, based on interpersonal emotions and dynamics, the moms and the public voted off a girl a week. The winning girl, and boy, won a money prize (larger if they actually married) and advertising gifts in kind. There were lesser prizes for the runners-up.

Pelin also developed "Second Life," in which widows, widowers, and divorcees in their forties and fifties competed for several weeks, with eliminations, "Survivor"-style, as they proceeded. They had a jury on which Pelin herself, once an actress, served. If the jury voted someone out, the public by text messaging could overrule and "save" them. The winners, again, got a bigger prize if they married.

She has her own kind of "Wheel of Fortune" show. And now in production is "Cash Cab." (It had actually originated in the U.K. the year before, and was now spreading around the world.) An ordinary-looking taxi cruises for customers who, if picked up, have hidden cameras explained to them, and their chance to "be a millionaire" by answering questions to follow. Their progress is registered on the specially calibrated taxi meter.

"In our business," Sezer stressed, "you must get the viewer emotionally involved. And that carries over to [profit on] the advertising belt. . . . People want not only to laugh, but to cry. Not just at horror, or sadism, or masochism. Where moments of real drama occur, they *can let themselves cry,* where at the office they would be regarded as *weak* persons." I thought briefly, without speaking, on the international phenomenon of armies at the office, softies in the living room.

Sezer explained the laugh-cry television business as "*not* didactic, *not* teaching, *not* raising the standards of Turkish society." He spoke with respectful dismissiveness of the five government television channels. "Raising standards of knowledge? That's up to them." CNN Turk follows a mission of news and education. "But it has only a 1 percent share in prime time. That's how much the Turkish public wants it."

The holding company for which he works, Doğan, owns both the No. 1 rated Channel D, whose prime time rating is 14.9 percent, and the No. 3, Star TV, at 12.7 percent. The other two general entertainment channels, ATV at 13 percent and Show at 12.5 percent, bring the mainstream big four to over 53 percent of the Turkish market, which is 41 million people. Thirty smaller channels split about 36 percent and numerous "others" the last 11 percent. Why can't the five government channels do better than, collectively, 5.7 percent? Even though subsidized, they are the lowest in Europe. BBC at 21 percent viewer share and Italian TV at 22 percent are neck and neck with their biggest private competitors. But Turkish state television, which was the only TV in Turkey until 1990, had a huge chance to enlighten the villages mentally, as Demirel's infrastructure transformed them electrically and physically. It failed.

Why? I asked. Sezer shrugged. "Bad management. They did not take it seriously. They didn't *learn how to do it.*"

There are several religiously oriented channels. Their top three, collectively, do three times as well as the five government channels, but only one-third as well as the four big mainstream channels (18 percent versus 53 percent). Sezer is not triumphalist about his mainstream culture trouncing religious channels, which in turn trounce the state channels. Instead, he is always trying to sniff out motivation in the public. Look at the AK Party, he suggested. It gets far more votes than religious channels draw a percentage of TV watchers. In the local elections of 2004, its share of votes was 44.6 percent — more than double the TV share of religion.[44] So, he im-

---

44. Obviously there is no necessary mathematical correlation between votes and share of viewership. But Sezer is making a social/political point, which is all the stronger when one considers that many TV viewers are below voting age.

plies, these votes convey marginal political preference rather than deep religious motivation.

Sezer clearly believes that the best index of what Turks want and need is registered in what they do at home. Ninety percent of Turks watch TV during dinner. Our conversation occurred during Ramadan, so he cited another research statistic. In 87 percent of Turkish households, there is at least one person fasting. "But fasting has nothing to do with fanaticism." (Iran and Iraq he saw as fanatical nations.) Rather, it has to do with familism. Even if only one member is fasting, all the others want to break the fast in the presence of that person, which generates togetherness. Multiplying the two above factors suggests that family religious togetherness and television-watching converge in fasting for three-quarters of Turkish households. So the mainstream stations, always observant of state guidelines on language, on showing of flesh, on misleading children, from 6:30 p.m. onward in Ramadan are especially careful about nudity.

Pelin Akat, to an American reporter, once differentiated Western television from Turkish television very simply: "In a word, it's sex." In 2005 the government cancelled a popular television talk show whose producer claimed that her professional guests were making women aware of their rights in home and workplace, and providing basic information about health and domestic violence. But the showdown in principle had come over another women's program. A guest on it had complained about domestic violence. When she went back to her village, her 14-year-old son shot her five times — the second shooting in a month attributed to that show. According to the Turkish press, before pulling the trigger on his mother, the boy said, "You ruined our family's honor."[45]

Such factors, however, don't make those who work in mainstream television into missionaries. Zühtü was emphatic: "We are not priests. We are not clergy. . . . It's very wrong for intellectuals to expect us to be clergy." He resisted my implication that TV had a development task to enlighten, analogous to the thirteen electrified villages in 1950 having become 35,000 today. I quoted Demirel on the half-century previous: "Turkey was dark at night." Sezer rose to a map and pointed out Demirel's own province, Isparta, in Southwest Anatolia. "That's a good metaphor. But there was lots of kerosene burning then."

"Between 1950 and now," I asked, "has TV made a better life for

---

45. Akat on sex and boy on honor: Catherine Collins, special to the Chicago *Tribune*, 1 Jun 05, p. 8.

Turks?" Sezer dug in against my persistence on this question. "We are *not* trying to *change* people's lives. None of the top four are trying to change them *politically.* The anchormen are not even trying in a subdued, subtle way. That is not our *couloir.*"

He expanded his answer far beyond the Demirel range of housewifely gratitude for refrigerators and clothes-washing machines, which I had found in middle-aged or older women. "The villagers who never leave their villages, they go outside by TV. They start to know what is happening in other villages, what is happening in cities, in the whole country, the world. That is not our mission, but *indirectly* we educate them and we raise their *aspirational levels.* Youth take their education more seriously. They want to do more than push a plow. They want to become an agricultural *engineer.*"

I seek more examples. He readily supplies two more in conclusion. *Tooth-brushing:* a peasant sees an implement on TV that can keep his teeth clean. So he buys and uses one, having learned personal hygiene from a TV commercial. And *women's programs,* which fill up much of the day. There is a medical element in them. Not special programs on health, but phases of interviews with doctors, which dramatize, for instance, regular check-ups against breast cancer. So mainstream TV follows its mission of emotional engagement, while as a *by-product,* it *educates.*

There he rested mainstream's case. And there I saw the limits to worries about military Kemalism and about militant Islamism. Nicole Pope had told me, warningly, that the army enlists peasant boys, "teaches them how to brush their teeth, and has them for life." But now TV teaches all peasants how to brush their teeth. Military sons come home to peasant parents whose tongues are not exploring bare gums, but who can articulate questions about what's going on in Iraq or in Europe.

Nilüfer Narli had fretted about the advance in the last ten years of religious TV, along with growth in fasting, mosque-going, *umra,* and exhibition of religion among the urban middle and upper-middle classes. Iftar dinners are a much more prominent phenomenon in Istanbul life than a decade ago. The number of courses on the Qur'an doubled in East Turkey just this year. Statements of soccer players and female pop singers about personal faith and practice have become a staple of the news. All of this she focuses on religious television, which nourishes themes initiated by Islamic groups fifteen years ago in children's stories, comics, and Ottoman history, where God's word lay behind Turkish victories. Now those children grow up to Islamic channels like Samanyolu, TV7, and Mesaj TV, and programs like "The World of Secrets," in which divine justice punishes a car thief. Mesaj is very clear, Nilüfer says, that mystical forces organize life. She, a Kemalist, political scientist, and widely sought media commentator, is disturbed.

But I am not dismayed. Spongy religion is evident on American tubes, too, as in "family-friendly Christian TV" and other brands of religion offered by twenty or more religious networks in the States. Their products, however, do not threaten to undermine the culture as much as, say, potato chips with their addictive fat and salt undermine health and contribute to national obesity. A greater threat may be visible in that segment of the American populace which soaks up Armageddon religion on TV, as promoted by figures like Pastor John Hagee, with his tendentious readings of biblical texts, his anti-Catholicism, his enthuasiam for advancing the "End Times," and his bellicose challenges to an Islam that he does not begin to understand. His program, nevertheless, runs far below the fandom that followed "Touched by an Angel" for its nine years of life, ending in 2003. The latter program's bland spirituality, its nondenominational angels and vague reassurance of unexamined spiritual premises, made it unthreatening to American society.

Nilüfer Narli worries that religious TV stations in Turkey have "become liberal mainstream TVs" in their popularity. The most cogent reply to such a worry is that it is not factually true. The collective viewer share of religious TV in Turkey is only one-third that of what professionals define as "mainstream." And the mainstream is not interested in combative interpretations of the Qur'an or in the hidden agency of Allah. The mainstream simply wants to go home to relax, alone or in family, and there to laugh and cry.

The passivity of family dining table and television is obviously unlike the activity of national policy debates, but their relationships are reciprocal. Popular values drift up to councils of deliberation, and critical decisions sift down into portable public consciousness. Even in tension there is a creative relation between the two planes. What is rejected in popular culture will be reflected in national poise as the equivalent of autoimmunity. A nation that fails to recognize its own parts, and treats components of itself allergically, will fall far below its optimal energy. Such a condition was threatening Turkey in the opening decades of the twenty-first century.

Of the five Muslim nations with the greatest GDP, Turkey and Indonesia are the only two so far with analyzable data for popular culture as revealed by television audience measurement through AGB Nielsen Media Research. Indonesian appetites shifted in an Islamic direction after American invasions of Afghanistan and Iraq, but eventually began to bounce off invisible limits to Islamism, moving back toward what some indigenous analysts see as "universal values." Visions of modernity prevailed again over ideas of eternity.

Reality TV shows in Indonesia revealed that shift. They multiplied in number (seventy-nine of them are now made by local production companies), and overtook other genres, especially soap operas from Latin America, India, and East Asia. Every subgenre of "reality" was explored: talent contests, dating shows, reunions, and social experiments like extreme home makeovers. Eko Nugroho developed *Tukar Nasib* ("Fate Swap"), where a poor family and a middle-class family temporarily switch houses, and *Badah Rumah* ("House Change"), in which a deserving poor family gets a radical improvement of their home. From his successes Eko believes he has learned that everybody in the world has "the same dream, no matter who you are, what nationality you are."[46] Would his belief stand comparative testing? Turkish data might support it to some degree. But Pakistan, because of the distortions of much deeper poverty, and Iran and Saudi Arabia, because of the controls of religious orthodoxies, would be dissonant.

Whatever spectrum of appetites — or dreams — are revealed by family television, its "consensus," a marketable commonplace, is qualitatively different from another kind of consensus: the national poise needed for decisions to overcome national crisis, deprivation, or doubt. Turkey is the best current test example of crisis — as contained in secular-religious tension (overly reified as Kemalist-Islamist strife), whose eventual resolution will ultimately supplant the assumptions of Atatürk's rule three-quarters of a century ago. Indonesia, having passed three electoral tests in the last decade, is in free run. Pakistan's anarchy is severe, and lacks a traction point. Crises in Iran and Saudi Arabia are under-defined and over-controlled. Iran's bloody repression of June 2009, and female prominence in protest, prove the costs of patriarchalism. The Saudi kingdom will find monarchical minimalism regarding women hard to sustain indefinitely.

Turkey, meanwhile, is in semi-paranoid suspicion of possible coups

46. Norimitsu Onishi feature article in *New York Times*/Asia Pacific, 22 May 09; print, 25 May, p. A4.

from opposite directions. The first public statement of judicial closure proceedings against the ruling AK Party, in January 2008, was followed in one week by broadening of stale investigations of the Susurluk event into a sweep against what was mythically labeled "Ergenekon." The first wave of government detentions had some consistency: retired generals and officers clearly hypernationalist, a lawyer who had led the effort to jail Orhan Pamuk, and figures connected to Susurluk by cell phone records or supposition. For baroque elaboration there was included the vocal granddaughter and scion of the self-appointed patriarch of the Turkish Orthodox Church, a dynasty without clergy or worshippers, who own religious property that displays only lit candles and drying laundry, and is blogged with allegations of hidden ammunition.

The decision of the Constitutional Court in July 2008, barely failing to remove Erdoğan and Gül from public office for five years, continued the coil and countercoil of tensions. The vote of justices was actually 6-5 to make the AK Party illegal, in a situation where 7-4 was required for conviction. Widely shared rumor, not reported by the media for fear of retribution, had it that two of the six votes had been bought by agents of secularity.[47]

Further endangered by electoral losses, the AK Party government, which had built a case of nearly two thousand pages, pushed its detentions toward two hundred persons with a large passel of roundups in May 2009. These were composed chiefly of university rectors, professors, media executives, columnists, and leaders of NGOs, one of which had developed a "Daddy Sent Me to School" campaign for the education of young rural girls, a program which had recently won a UN Special Award in 2007. By early 2011, "more than 275 people, including 116 military officers, ha[d] been charged in the Ergenekon trial." Investigations, home searches, and accusations continued, but no chain of command or cell structure of "Ergenekon" had yet been defined, or any proven violence attributed to it.[48] The sudden joint resignation of top Turkish generals in late July, 2011, including all service chiefs and the chief of staff, dramatized tension over the case. But self-abnegation by the military created no waves of sympathy.

47. Confidential conversations, May 09.

48. For the accumulating detentions in 2009, my web sources include: Hurriyet Daily News, Today's Zaman, Radikal, Bianet, Ebru; Al Jazeera English, Al Arabiya (English); Newsweek World, Eurasia Daily Monitor, Jim Meyers Borderlands; ESI Picture Stories, Southeast European Times, and Spero News. For 2011, the quotation is from Berfu Kiziltan, "Ergenekon: The Power of a Legend," Hurriyet Daily News, 10 Mar 11.

Erdoğan and Gül replaced the generals with aplomb, having won a big stride in the continuing tug-of-war.

The puzzled citizen might be forgiven for thinking that the case that had begun against militant secularist plotters had now elaborated into a vast effort by the AK Party leaders to harass and intimidate its opposition, whatever contrary stripes it wore. "Ergenekon," once a self-congratulatory in-group name affected by nationalist conspirators, could not describe the corral of defendants gathered by 2009 who, as one foreign observer said, if put in one room together would try to kill each other.

The gray wolf of myth, which connected Atatürk to the founding of the first Turkic state, was an incongruous symbol for the arraigned. The critics of the AK Party are various in their distaste for any religious dimension of power, but poorly coordinated in opposition. Having several types of enemies, nonetheless, seems to produce in the government a political analogue to what in cephalopods is called the *blanch-ink-jet maneuver:* it lightens its own color while propelling defensive blots of ink against its predators. Such maneuvers, of course, cloud public discourse. But they may across time have the unintended effects of allowing women to manifest themselves as women in multiple ways, and minorities likewise to express themselves as minorities. "Victory" in a politico-military sense may eventually come to mean much less than it did in a state founded by a general. The integrity of Turkey may slowly be advanced by pluralism.

C.1 "After the Meeting" (Toledo Museum of Art, Ohio). Cecilia Beaux painted her friend Dorothea Gilder after a meeting of suffragists in 1914. The right of American women to vote and hold office was secured by amendment to the Constitution in 1920. Among currently independent countries, New Zealand was the first to legislate women's suffrage (1891). Turkey did so in 1930; Indonesia, 1945; Pakistan, 1947; Iran, 1963.

A century after the painting by Beaux, the Kingdom of Saudi Arabia has no suffrage for women. A Gallup poll press release (December 2007), however, states that polling had determined Saudi reactions to the statement, "Women should be allowed to hold leadership positions in the cabinet and national council." 66 percent of women agreed; 52 percent of men agreed.

C.2 "Three Liberties." This drawing by Saul Steinberg illustrates his impression of America's women — who "embodied all the drive, panache, appetite, self-regard of their era, whether outdoing one another on the sidewalk, or incarnating Liberty (the statue and the mode of life) on their straphanging way to work." Quotation from Joel Smith, *Saul Steinberg: Illuminations* (New Haven, Yale University Press, 2006), p. 104. The drawing itself appears on p. 105. *Saul Steinberg, Three Liberties, 1949. Ink and watercolor on paper, 14 × 23 in. The Saul Steinberg Foundation. © The Saul Steinberg Foundation/Artists Rights Society (ARS), New York.*

C.3 Yenny Wahid (b. 1974) is a daughter of the late Indonesian President Abdurrahman Wahid ("Gus Dur"). At the time of this photo with the author in the garden of the Hotel Oriental (2005), she was director of the Wahid Institute, a major NGO for "seeding plural and peaceful Islam." She later also became Secretary General of the PKB, Party of National Awakening. *Photo: author's collection*

C.4 Professor Dr. Siti Musdah Mulia was a senior advisor to the Minister of Religious Affairs in Indonesia (2000-07). Her searching scholarship drove a comprehensive updating of shariʻa law, which although not approved by the Parliament, remains a monument of Islamic modernism. A critical and historical reading of the Qurʼan led her to draft provisions asserting gender equality, forbidding polygamy, and allowing interfaith marriage, with children permitted to choose their own religion. Since 2007, Siti Musdah has been the chairperson of the Indonesian Conference on Religion for Peace, an NGO that promotes interfaith dialogues, pluralism, and democracy.

Author's collection

C.5 Benazir Bhutto was twice Prime Minister of Pakistan, the first female in the world elected to that position in a Muslim nation. This interior image shows her as artistic sophisticate, very unlike her campaign photos. *Google Images/patdollard.com*

C.6 Mukhtaran Mai sits inside her home in rural Punjab with her mother at her right and two undercover policewomen on her left. By taking to court the perpetrators of the gang rape against her, she became not only a Pakistani icon, but an example for all peasant women, and an inspiration to the oppressed in any condition.

Photo: Stephanie Sinclair, VII Photo Agency

C.7 Lubna S. Olayan of Saudi Arabia is depicted here in her persona as an international businesswoman, although she is naturally comfortable in *hijab* dress. She is a director of the Olayan Group as well as Deputy Chairperson and CEO of Olayan Financing Company, which oversees the group's investments and operating businesses in the Middle East. When named a director of the Saudi-Hollandi Bank in 2004, she was the first woman to join the board of any Saudi listed company. She has been active in the Women's Leadership Initiative of the World Economic Forum, and a trustee of the Arab Thought Foundation. She also serves on the boards of INSEAD, Cornell University, and the King Abdullah University for Science & Technology. Ms. Olayan topped *Forbes Arabia*'s first list (2006) of the fifty most powerful Arab businesswomen, and frequently appears on other media lists of influential people. *Photo: courtesy of Olayan America*

C.8 Nimah Nawwab is a multi-faceted humanitarian and activist. Her accomplishments in poetry, writing, editing, speaking, photography, and film have established her as an internationally recognized cultural leader, much sought as a mentor by young entrepreneurs as well as young artists. Her compassionate sense of justice for men, women, and children made her a major organizer of relief in the sudden Jeddah floods of 2009. She was a leader of petition to royalty in a famous case of forced divorce. And at least since her first volume of poetry in English, she has been a relentless public critic of male "guardianship of women" — perhaps the single most execrable flaw of Saudi society.

Photo: author's collection

C.9 Shirin Ebadi was the first woman in Iran to serve as a judge. When the revolution of 1979 reduced all female judges to clerks, she protested and chose early retirement. Finally winning back her license, she opened private practice in 1992 and took on a number of sensitive and controversial cases. For her work in human rights, most concretely in women's and children's rights, she was awarded the Nobel Prize for Peace in 2003. For her defense of critics of the elections of 2009, all of her assets were frozen by the government of Iran, and her Nobel Prize was confiscated, the first such punitive action in over a century of history of the prize. Here in 2009 she appears in front of the European Parliament in Brussels, leading a protest against the election and suppression of dissent in Iran that year. *Photo: Jim Buell*

C.10 Tamineh Milani has been for more than twenty years a productive film writer and director. Her confronting memories of the revolution in "Hidden Half" led to her arrest in 2001 under charges carrying the death penalty. Even without such direct challenge to the authorities, her films on middle-class women and families touch frontier consciousness in Iran and the wider Muslim world.

Photo: www.rozanehmagazine.com/NoveDec05/Tamineh_Milani

C.11 Vildan Yirmibesoglu, lawyer, prosecutor of
honor killings, and promoter of public consciousness
on that problem, has recently been head of the Human Rights Department of the Istanbul Governor's
Office. Her most sustained research, however, was as
a lawyer in Southeast Turkey, where she assembled
300 cases of honor killings — data that helped move
a parliamentary commission and a presidential circular, followed by changes in the criminal law.

Photo: author's collection

C.12 Zarah Khadim at age five carries a chalkboard. Learning opportunities for girls like
her were opened up by Muktharan Mai's rural school. Education is the simplest and most
secure hope for those Muslim women previously denied it.

Photo: Stephanie Sinclair/VII Photo Agency

Power, Culture, and Equality

Torsions of Gender Culture

The five nations of my study distributed themselves in a crude U-curve, in which the conditions for women roughly correlated with the degree of democracy present. Indonesia and Turkey were the highest, at either end of the curve, and Saudi Arabia was the nadir — where oil wealth does not liberate women, but stimulates puritan theological exports. Iran and Pakistan lie in between, not upon mirroring points but in multiple disanalogy. In Iran a millennium of heritage and a century of democracy provide women with resources to contend with the recent theocratic state, notably in protest of the election of 2009. In Pakistan, democracy is riddled with the furies of political Islam, but a variety of roles for women have been inherited from the British Empire.

Both nations at the peaks of the curve may be undergoing some attenuation of their position: Turkey from the electoral triumph of the AK Party and gingerly erosion of Kemalist absolutism by its leaders; and Indonesia by conservative Islamic resurgence and petro-gold stimuli from Saudi ideologues. Neither country seems likely to lose its comparative position; but Indonesia seems more able to secure it, if only because its largely bilateral family system is far older and much deeper than the liberating edicts for women uttered by Atatürk just three generations ago.

Impressions such as these may help synthesize my findings, but critical dialogues and statistical tables are indispensable. In such dialogue, Isobel Coleman's *Paradise Beneath Her Feet* is a great contribution. Her sympathies and instincts for productivity are unassailable. But her mind seems unresolved on the strength of basic forces at play. How can she state both that "secularism as a political force is on life support across the Middle East" and also say that "Islamic feminism, like other reform movements that preceded it, will end up unapologetically secular"?[1] Is Islam going to wipe out secularism, or is secularism going to flood out Islamic feminism? I don't know, and don't try to say. But Ms. Coleman should not go unchallenged in having it both ways.

A far finer interplay of forces is acknowledged in the works of Margot Badran across four decades, who is historically attuned to a century of secular feminism and Islamic feminism, each threading its way into the texture of the other. Also in the work of Durré Ahmed, gathering essayists from South and Southeast Asia.[2]

The recent appearance of Kecia Ali's *Sexual Ethics and Islam* carries women's reflections on Qur'an, hadith, and *fiqh* to new levels of cogency, in which male reason and revelation must find their balance with "historical context . . . and . . . critical principles of justice, kindness, and love."[3]

Other phenomena, other dynamics, are revealed in recent comparative studies, from whose global rankings I extract the data in the table on page 305. Three of the Muslim nations — Saudi Arabia, Turkey, and Iran — have rankings in gross domestic product per capita that significantly surpass their rankings in human development index (in which gross domestic product per capita is a significant component). In the cases of Indonesia and Pakistan, the reverse is true — although, depending on the observed values, their absolute deficiencies may outweigh that relative achievement. Certainly the case of the Philippines, with its high ranking in overcoming the gender gap, registers the importance of looking through a different lens than the standard "development" optics of the last half-century. The gender gap computations also show four of the nations in this study to be among the bottom seven in the world so ranked.

The circumstances of women in Indonesia are as diverse as the nation itself; but recent losses of standing in the gender gap index reflect a worldwide stiffening of Islam. Indonesian roles, however, were established far back in pre-modernity by a family structure that is most often bilateral,

1. Coleman, *Paradise Beneath Her Feet,* pp. xxiii, 275.

2. Badran, *Feminism in Islam, passim;* Durre S. Ahmed, ed., *Gendering the Spirit: Women, Religion, and the Post-Colonial Response* (London, Zed Books, 2002). See also Theodore Friend, ed., *Religion and Religiosity in the Philippines and Indonesia* (Washington, D.C., Johns Hopkins SAIS, 2006, distributed by the Brookings Institution).

3. Kecia Ali, *Sexual Ethics and Islam,* p. 133.

Human Development[a] and Gender Gap[b] Data, 2009

Five Muslim Nations plus the U.S. and Philippine Republic

	Life Expectancy (in years)	Adult literacy (percent)	GDP[c] per capita	HDI[d] rank (182)	GDP/cap rank minus HDI rank	GGGI[e] rank (134)
U.S.	79.1	92.4	$45,592	13	9-13 = -4	31[f]
Kingdom of Saudi Arabia	72.7	85.0	22,935	59	40-59 = -19	130
Turkey	71.7	88.7	12,965	79	63-79 = -16	129
Iran	71.2	82.3	10,955	88	71-88 = -17	128
Indonesia	70.5	92.0	3,712	111	121-111 = +10	92
Pakistan	66.2	54.2	2,496	141	150-141 = +9	132
Philippines	71.6	93.4	3,406	105	124-105 = +19	9[g]

a. United Nations Development Programme, Human Development Report, October 2009; based on data for 2007 in categories 1, 2, and 3, plus gross educational enrollment.

b. World Economic Forum, Global Gender Gap Index, October 2009; updated annually since initiation in 2006.

c. GDP = Gross Domestic Product

d. HDI = Human Development Index

e. GGGI = Global Gender Gap Index

f. The U.S. has declined steadily since being #23 in 2006.

g. The Philippines has led Asia in rank ever since the first report; but after three years at #6 globally, slipped to #9. Other 2009 regional leaders: Ecuador, #23; South Africa, #6; Iceland displaced Norway as #1 globally.

The Global Gender Gap Report examines four major areas of inequality (and fourteen variables) between men and women: health and survival; educational attainment; economic participation and opportunity; and political empowerment.

The Human Development Index has been criticized from many angles, such as measuring "how Scandinavian" one's country is. HDI lacks, for instance, an ecology factor. But the composite data have often been useful to policy makers.

reckoning one's relationships through both the father and the mother. Absolute patriarchalism is rare in such an environment, even though the dictator Suharto was able for a while to institute a relative masculinism, focused chiefly in Java. Even at the very height of his power, however, his parliament adopted the Convention to Eliminate all Forms of Discrimination Against Women (CEDAW). As a result, Indonesian women enjoy favorable legal presumptions. Still more basic, they are not pinioned by tight knotting of religion to family system. Islam is suspended over them like a mist net. They may fly under it. It only seizes them up as captives of shari'a where local demographic histories are intensely Muslim, and where a political lowering of the net aims to entangle deviants.

In Indonesian cities, among upper working class and lower middle class, Islam serves as a major defense against dissolutions of identity found in urban anomie. And in the province of Aceh, always more closely oriented to Mecca than to Jakarta, thirty years of modern rebellion against the central government (1976-2006) reawakened Islamic history and tradition. Spurred by the Indian Ocean tsunami disaster as a creative opportunity, however, both government and rebels moved toward compromise, and their eventual peace agreement has thus far withstood its tests.

On a totally different level, uncompromising forms of Islam that have awakened in the last thirty years have also been felt in Indonesia. Saudi money has attracted local attention to them, there as elsewhere; and American invasions of Muslim countries have intensified their appeal. Such "Arabisme" presents challenges to Indonesian women in their pursuit of education as autonomous creatures of God and their opportunities as free citizens, but their autonomy and freedom remain anchored in Indonesia at an anthropological depth. In contrast to Arab patriliny, the large Minangkabau tribe is matrilineal, having long ago integrated their Islam to protect customs focused on women. Indonesian diversity embraces family systems of every sort, but their prevailing organization is bilateral. That minimizes the possibilities for patriarchal dominance, which occurs in the other four countries — Turkey, Iran, Pakistan, and Saudi Arabia — where Islamic dicta, by ascending degrees, reinforce patrilineality and lead to a religio-anthropological repression of women. On this issue, the statistical difference between Shi'ite and Sunni is trifling. Iran is in the bottom cluster of Islamo-patriarchal nations, where family systems subjugate women. In contrast stands Indonesia — arguably more Sufi than the others, and certainly distinct from them in its overwhelmingly bilateral family system.

This interplay of factors is further dramatized by considering the Philippines, geographic neighbor of Indonesia, sharing with it an open bilateral family system — one even further extended by the ritual religious affinities known as *compadrazgo* ("godfatherhood"). Instead of Islam, observed by less than 10 percent of its population, most of the Philippines practices a Mary-focused Christianity. Christian elaboration of a bilaterally extended family system and Christian values regarding females help account for its always ranking close to the Nordic countries in minimizing the gender gap.

Indonesia, far below the Nordics, nevertheless manifests a big contrast with patrilineal Saudi Arabia. Presumably it arises chiefly from Indonesia's diversity of family systems, mostly nuclear and bilateral, with important matrilinear minorities. Argument and legislation cannot change basic familial groundings such as these — Arabian, anti-Arabian, indifferent or irrelevant to Arabia. The figures illuminate many social conditions that can be alleviated by awareness and intelligent action. To the utter tribal patriarch, nevertheless, especially one who is a dogmatic Islamist, such data will have no meaning. Where inherited custom and a memorized Qur'an converge, it is extremely difficult to entertain the critical thinking that might allow intellectual or social headway. But some other Muslims may see the whole human enterprise as a great evolving experiment, even one with open theological dimensions. For them, the gender gap findings will be helpful in reforming failed or fossilized modes of human organization, including those which repress womanhood.

Pakistan, as the most highly populated unstable state in the world, does not presently show the will or the means to transform itself. No president of Pakistan, balanced on a tightrope, has been able to change the rings of the circus beneath him, or the structure of the tent that holds the circus. Prevailing anarchy is an unpromising condition for women in which to seek advances of their rights and opportunities. If they are poor, tribalism compounds their affliction; if middle class, they may be subject to feudalism; if wealthy, they may not escape patriarchism. Whatever one's class, but more markedly the lower one's standing, the leverage of the state to work for the commonweal in Pakistan is minimal. At the top, power-wielders become edict-hurlers to consolidate personal power. The most extreme example, the Hudood Ordinances of 1979, promulgated by President Zia, were the most far-reaching retrogressive acts by any Islamic leader until the military victories of the Taliban under Mullah Omar and the ensuing repression of women in Afghanistan.

Pakistani women, however, at last obtained major amendments to the Hudood Ordinances in 2006. The Women's Protection Bill removed rape from shariʿa law, where it was impossible to prove, and put it under the Pakistan Penal Code, based on civil law. Islamist party members went absent from the vote so as not to defile themselves by considering such issues of moral pollution. Pakistani women had not achieved what could be considered progress on a global stage, but they undid much of Haq's gross retrogression and established ground for future gains.

The playing field, however, went from anarchic to disastrous in 2007, a year which the Human Rights Commission of Pakistan described as "one of the worst years in Pakistan's history, if not the worst." Not only was Benazir Bhutto assassinated, but the half-year state of emergency earlier declared by Musharraf left "the justice system . . . largely paralysed and the channels of redress . . . blocked." With grim understatement, the Commission remarked that "the traditional agents of human rights abuse were by no means inactive . . . [for] at least 636 women were killed for their lords' honour. . . ."[4]

Women cannot push reform legislation in Saudi Arabia. The Wahhabi dispensation there, interlinked for over two centuries with the sheikhdom of the family al-Saud, and royally privileged by it through its twentieth-century ascension and conquests, continues to define woman as the property of man. If slavery as late as the nineteenth century was technically chattel bondage, the relation of woman wedded to Saudi man in the twenty-first century is a chattel marriage. By law, she cannot study, work, marry, travel, testify, contract, or undergo medical treatment without permission of her closest male relation.

The *Arab Human Development Report 2005,* conceived and written by Arabs, and bringing to a plateau four years of articulation of intertwined issues, puts the matter with striking directness in its summary of the fam-

---

4. The Human Rights Commission of Pakistan, "Pakistan in a State of Emergency: State of Human Rights in 2007," introduction (http://www.hrcp-web.org/hrcpDetail_pub3 .cfm?proId=528).

ily and the status of women. Going beyond Saudi phenomena to pan-Arab conditions, it notes that patriarchal pressures, in crisis, are resolved to the detriment of women: "The man's right of disposal over her body, his watch over it, his use of it, his concealment, denial and punishment of it all become more blatant. This violence in turn comes into play to intensify the feminisation of poverty, political misery, dependency, domination, and alienation."[5]

These findings, of course, embrace a total of over 300 million Arabs from Morocco to Egypt to the Gulf states. They are embedded among many other discoveries, such as those which put female literacy and education rates and female economic activity rates in world perspective. In Arab states overall, female literacy is nearly three-quarters that of male, a percentage which surpasses South Asia while trailing that of sub-Saharan Africa, Latin America, and Europe. In rates of female economic activity, however, Arab states, at just over 30 percent, are collectively the lowest in the world.[6] As the study calmly notes, "Given women's superior achievements in education, their higher unemployment level goes against the grain of pure economic efficiency."[7]

The Beijing Declaration of 1995 stresses that to protect the human rights of women, reservations to the Convention on Elimination of all Forms of Discrimination Against Women must be avoided as far as possible. Nonetheless, since Egypt led the Arab world in signing CEDAW in 1980, reservations have been many and significant. Saudi Arabia signed at last in 2000, but with reservations on all that conflicts with shari'a. Throughout the Arab world, regardless of signing the convention, "legislators have leaned so heavily towards the principle of gender differences that they have codified gender discrimination, thereby violating the principle of equality, which is sanctified in religious canons and rendered an international obligation under international treaties."[8]

It would be hard to choose between the obtuse provinciality of the U.S. in not ratifying CEDAW, and the hypocrisies of Arab states in signing it, were not forms of violence against Arab women so pronounced. Those include honor crimes, domestic violence, and female circumcision. The

5. *Arab Human Development Report, 2005* (New York, UNDP, 2006), pp. 16-17. Hereafter, AHDR.

6. Data dramatizing these points may be found in AHDR, pp. 74 (fig. 2.4), 85 (fig. 301), and pp. 80, 85, 86, 117, and 180.

7. AHDR, p. 86.

8. AHDR, p. 182.

existence of honor crimes throughout the Arab world may dangerously mislead one to think that this is a specially Arabian aberration against human rights. But the practice of patriarchal murder also flourishes in Pakistan, Iran, and Turkey — distinctly non-Arab cultures. Can it then be called an Islamic practice? No, because honor killings of women do not exist in Indonesia and Malaysia, where bilateral family systems prevail, and cultural dynamics do not grossly magnify masculine "honor." One must limit any general statement about honor crimes to their existing chiefly in those parts of Southwest and South Asia where tribal patriarchy, poverty, and sub-literacy converge. They are neither caused nor cured by Islam. The killers often use Islam for justification, but misuse of creed to sanctify the unjustifiable is common to other religions.

Domestic violence is obviously global in extent, and nearly universal in its being condemned. That said, "the persistent denial in some Arab countries that it exists" is a disturbing phenomenon. Lack of data inhibits even estimates of the extent of such violence. In Saudi Arabia, no one is paid to protect women. But guardians of the propriety of women's clothing and conduct, whether state-employed or volunteer, can bring summary infliction of punishment "within full view of the State."[9]

The custom of female circumcision has come under international scrutiny only in recent years, despite the grave health risks and complications arising from all its varieties of practice, and the wide radius of psychological deprivations it may entail. Its extent in Egypt, for instance, persists at very high rates where it correlates with low levels of education, residence in rural areas, and above all, personal beliefs, culturally transmitted and impacted. The Council of State, Egypt's highest administrative court, nonetheless ruled late in 1997 that such circumcision was not inherent in the shariʿa, and it is therefore illegal even with consent of the girl or her parents. There is nothing, the Court ruled, in the Qurʾan or Sunna that sanctions it.[10]

In all of these ultrasensitive areas, it is difficult or impossible to obtain trans-Arab statistics. And in Saudi Arabia, despite its wealth and relatively high levels of education, there even appears to be some systemic inhibition against survey research, as likely to reveal discomfiting facts. The very idea of the empirical, indeed, is sometimes treated as an intrusion of Western imperialism, suspect and unholy.

9. AHDR, pp. 116, 117.
10. AHDR, p. 117, table 4:1; p. 118.

Just how far such defensive fear may run, and how deeply it may flare, is suggested by an official circular received at major Saudi hospitals in 2005, conveying a royal order. It banned the sending of Saudi blood products, or evidence of DNA, to any international source. One level of rationale might have been to protect for the Kingdom's own researchers the value of its inbred genetic pool, which like that of Iceland (one-eightieth as large, and also highly inbred) might yield major clues for the treatment of polygenetic diseases like diabetes. But that was not the prime rationale conveyed by the circular. The reason most seriously discussed among medical researchers affected was "to protect our DNA from the Jews."[11] That Israel might systematically use such information to devise stressors in a gene war appeared to me as a luridly fearful fantasy. In saying so, I may be chiefly revealing my own naiveté and ignorance of how rapidly politics catches up with science fiction. In any case, the document, and such discussion of it, exists as signs of Saudi hyper-nationalism and of a latent pan-Arab dementia.

The pride of Persians, like Turks, includes counter-definition as non-Arabs. Persians never prevailed over their neighbors in such a comprehensive military-imperial way as the Ottomans, but they readily see their culture as a rosebush surrounded by Arab brambles. What fact, they offer, could better illustrate the point than this: Iran alone publishes more books in a year than do all Arab nations together?

Culture, of course, includes matters difficult or impossible to compress into numbers. The condition of women is such a cultural phenomenon — a complex series of functions, not numerically reifiable, of female initiatives, of male prerogatives, and of ideas of divinity. When the numerous factors weighed in the Global Gender Gap Index are arrayed by nation, Iran is near the bottom of the cascade, barely surpassing Saudi Arabia and Yemen. But the observable or "discussable" status of Iranian women is much higher than such numbers convey. The tradition of feminine achievement there is pronounced, and may be illustrated by the 2003 Nobel Peace Prize winner, Shirin Ebadi. To be a human rights lawyer in Iran is itself a courageous choice. Ebadi's career as a female judge was amputated

---

11. Confidential interview, 27 Feb 06. Neither my informant nor I have a copy of this document.

by the theological revolution of 1979, which was dogmatically anti-feminine in matters judiciary. She dared to use her powers of advocacy in behalf of a Canadian journalist, a woman seized outside of Evin prison, incarcerated there, tortured, and killed. Ebadi herself suffered brief imprisonment, but was undeterred. Her persistence in the case led to a decision in the World Court, but no relief from Iran's government. Yet that judgment itself constituted moral victory.[12] Clarifying brute repression, exhibiting it, and embarrassing the guardians of the system is the only chastisement that can be cast upon the mullahs, self-protecting managers of the state. "International opinion" is a mercurial abstraction, but the clerico-judicial establishment continues to show fear of it by incarceration, interrogation, and harassment of both natives and visitors who are thought to cultivate it.

Iran's governance, in the quarter-century during which the lava of its revolution cooled, has been almost wholly male, excepting a few members of parliament. Although Reza Shah Pahlevi forbade the veil in 1935, and his son, Mohammed Shah Pahlevi, gave women the right to vote in 1963, these two reforms no longer march in tandem. The veil has a new revolutionary mandate. But the vote, even if manipulated, cannot be denied. Shahs are irretrievable; democracy is irreversible. It has percolated in Iran for a century now, and continues to be pressure-bubbled into the system. Women vote. But their clothing and conduct are monitored by religious police, backed by a Supreme Leader with every punitive inch of the power of the shahs.

The contrast with Saudi Arabia is revealing. Theological monarchy in the Kingdom means, thus far, that veils may only be lifted by millimeters, and that votes are legitimized by handfuls, and only in male municipal elections. One may wonder if the ruling family will have the collective wisdom over time to let its monarchy become a reserve wheel of government, as in Thailand since 1932, or a social symbol, as in Great Britain following Victoria. For the present, however, what may be called "full-face democracy" is clearly threatening to the Kingdom's leaders, both in voting and in unveiling.

Europe's encouragement to Turkey to route itself toward tests of membership in its expanded Union gave off an initial glow. Would this overcome

---

12. Shirin Ebadi, *Iran Awakening* (New York, Random House, 2006), *passim.*

ugly Crusade history and still-evident wreckage of the Ottoman Empire? No. European insincerity became palpable. The Union introduced more hurdles on the steeplechase required of Turkey, along with higher ratcheting of the obstacles. None of this was lost on the critic and poet Talat Halman, who has translated all of Shakespeare's sonnets into Turkish, and has been awarded the highest knighthood in the Most Excellent Order of the British Empire. "I suppose," he said to me in 2004, "the Europeans have noticed that we are smaller than they, and swarthier, and poorer. And," he twisted a smile, "that we are Muslim." Feeling this diplomatic distancing, in 2006 only three-eighths of Turks favored entry into the European Union, whereas three-quarters would have welcomed membership just a few years earlier. Down by half.

Turkey, at the westward end of my five-nation travels, shares with Indonesia, at the eastern end, the highest degrees of political democracy and social pliability, but with major differences. As a self-styled secular republic, Turkey is distinct from Indonesia's multi-confessional state. Occasional Islamist outbreaks against the heterodox Alevis[13] have marred Turkey's striving for even-handedness. Freedom of worship, nonetheless, largely distinguishes both Turkey and Indonesia from the Islamic republics of Pakistan (Sunni) and of Iran (Shi'a), with their persecutions, respectively, of Ahmadis and Bahais. The "secular" and the "multi-confessional" contrast still more sharply with the Islamic monarchy of Saudi Arabia, where even non-Wahhabi Sunnis may be considered heretical.

Religious freedom is an intrinsic good, and an essential blessing to women wherever it is found. In Turkey, however, it is complicated by social counter-reactiveness of various kinds. A resumption of veiling has accompanied the new successes of "green capitalism" in Anatolia (a green not ecological, but Islamic) and follows the immigrant flow from the East and South into Ankara, Istanbul, and other traditionally more European cities. When careful polls in 1999 revealed that nearly three-quarters of women used some form of head covering, the Kemalist orthodoxy and most of the military took anxious note. These tensions were coiled within overt politico-constitutional questions about what kind of man of faith

13. On this large, endogamous group who are considered *shi'a ghulat* ("exaggerators") by Sunni ulama, see David Zeidan, "The Alevi of Anatolia," www.angelfire.com/az/rescon/ALEVI.html. Indonesia's even-handedness, in turn, is weakened by its Constitutional Court decision (8 to 1; April 2010) upholding the Blasphemy Law of 1965 which imposes civil and criminal penalties on those, like the Ahmadis, who "deviate from" the six officially recognized religions.

— observantly Muslim or insistently secular — to elect to the presidency late in 2007.

After months of testing, the Turkish people seemed to find less wisdom in military statements than inflammatory bombast. They chose for leaders, as prime minister, president, and speaker of Parliament, men who were Muslim modernists, pragmatic, and successful in economic policies. What the people decided in 2007 they reconfirmed in 2011. Turkey was developing in a way that Atatürk could not have imagined seven dozen years before. The cultural and constitutional questions before the people seemed resolvable by social compromise, accompanied by a high degree of tight-lipped but nonviolent dissatisfaction.

In Indonesia surely, and Turkey less certainly, the veil is more definitive of a person than of a government, and far less of a whole society. In Indonesia as few as one-quarter of women cover themselves, and the proportion is surely less than half. In Turkey, remarkably, even as the reasons for retaining or adopting the veil become more avidly advanced, the numbers of wearers are somewhat declining. The Turkish and Indonesian conditions, different as they are, may both be described as socially positive in contrast to repressive laws and conditions prevailing in Saudi Arabia and Iran. In Indonesia and Turkey the choice is usually made by a woman to cover herself or not. If she chooses to do so, she also chooses degree — with scarf or *turban* only; with full *hijab;* rarely with entire body veil, eyes barely discernible behind mesh. This is a matter of choice, in which a husband or father may be an intimately important consultant, but it is not ordinarily a matter of family male dictate. "Our clothing, ourselves," as practiced by women in these republics, is a far shout from male ownership of the woman's body decried in the *Arab Human Development Report.*

The Prophet and Modern Social Terrain

The Prophet in his wisdom long ago observed that it is difficult to be just to one woman, even as his revelation allowed a man to marry four. That dispensation tried to alleviate the severe conditions of widowhood in Arab culture of his time; Muhammad himself, in all but his marriage to young Ayesha, wed widows.

In the Prophet's concern for justice and lifelong social security for women, perhaps an even more dramatic reversal he undertook was to end the practice of female infanticide. These moral achievements on behalf of the newborn and the bereft should earn him global appreciation as a compassionate social revolutionary.

Fifteen centuries later, however, conditions have vastly changed, along with ways of coping with them. Regressively: many who would model their lives on the era of the Prophet lack his social vision. Progressively: many of those who wish to modernize their Islam see life partnership as far healthier for both husbands and wives than the tribal conceit of ownership by a male of one or more women.

Whereas Arab conditions of the seventh century permitted or encouraged polygamy, now, even in the four Arab countries recently surveyed on the matter, a majority of males and females reject it. Where they support polygamy, they link approval to the agreement of the wives concerned. The rise of Arab women is also attested by 95 percent agreement on their right to choose their spouses on an equal footing with men, and 68 percent agreement on their right to initiate divorce.[14]

Freedom is only an absolute to sentimental minds. It exists in tension, in specific cultures and on various planes, with necessity, order, and design. Order is likewise a false absolute, likely to be exacted in extremes by rigidly limited mentalities. One might well ask, how ultimately *creative* are American freedoms? Do they outweigh mere affluent habits and unexamined indulgences? In a like spirit: how ultimately *necessary* are current Islamic orderings for women in its many cultures? To what degree are they merely repressive rather than sublimely instructive? These questions are best answered severally in the cultures where they arise.

Indonesia and Turkey manifest far less arbitrary unfreedom regarding women than do Pakistan, Iran, and Saudi Arabia. How well is progress for women truly rooted where it is already most evident? In Indonesia, securely: bilateral family systems are the most stable grounding against patriarchalism. In Turkey a basic but less secure foundation for women has lain in the vision of Kemal Atatürk and his vigorous execution of it. But not all Kemalism is pro-feminine. Turkish military masculinism tends to be obtuse in social matters. And, simultaneously counter-feminine from a different direction, the Islamic resurgence of the last thirty years carries with it capabilities of curbing or even sweeping back women's advances.

Salafi culture wherever it occurs tends to suppress women. This is true without regard to its violent *"jihadist"* extremes, which Muslim critics deem irrational and irreligious. Salafis include highly intelligent men who

14. AHDR, pp. 136, 190, 192.

may nevertheless be undersophisticated or just plain ignorant. They will not easily recognize the 8,000 women hadith scholars across the centuries identified by Muhammad Akram Nadwi. The numbers of those women dwindle after the sixteenth century, as part of "decline in every aspect of Islam."[15] But most of the Islamic hyper-puritans who reach back to model themselves on the seventh century are not likely to put in the forefront the social achievements of the Prophet in that era. Modern women have far more to fear than to gain from Salafism, especially as centered in Saudi Arabia and motivated and funded from the Kingdom.

Pakistan and Iran are also affected by their own puritan fundamentalisms in parts of their respective Sunni and Shi'ite domains. Indonesia and Turkey have had bombs go off, too, ignited by extremists, but neither country is yet dramatically affected by Salafism in cultural life. Their forms of Islam, for different reasons, incline to be more open — to personal growth, social development, and spiritual exploration.

Hypertextualism and Culturism

The two most significant misreadings which confound and block women in today's Muslim countries are those which presume to grasp the Qur'an with complete literal understanding and those which imprison Qur'anic texts in a limited cultural context. The first may be called "hypertextualism," and the second "culturism." Each of these linked errors limit understanding. Both distort growth.

One must accord to Arab culture its pride of achievement in reduction to agreed-on script the revelations that voiced themselves to the Prophet Muhammad. In comparison to that, the Christian Gospels appear wretchedly post facto and contradictory, whatever essential truths they may contain. But having a single text, one supreme narrative-instruction in writing, is not to have the complete, eternal, immutable, and unmistakable articulation of the Divine. The very existence and elaboration of Sunna, hadith, and shari'a prove the inescapability of interpretation. There is no incontestable fax from heaven to resolve dispute. There is no distinct CD which records the tones of Gabriel as heard in the brain of the Prophet. Human beings must study and discuss human understandings. That is *ijtihad:* interpretation.

15. Carla Power, "The Secret History of Feminist Islamic Scholars," *New York Times Magazine*, 25 Feb 07.

Monopoly of meaning, or hypertextualism, is at best comic, at worst dangerous and belligerent. To proclaim that one's own, or any one, culture presents the perfect filter for understanding the message of the Prophet, or Jesus, or Moses, compacts both temporal and provincial absolutisms into the farce of culturism. This is just as true, analogously, of the American Northeast and Southwest, in their many religious differences, as it may be true in Islam. To say so is not to undervalue backward-looking pietisms. One may respect the Amish without conceding that they should rule the Commonwealth of Pennsylvania.

Human societies will best improve themselves, and address the differences between themselves, by allowing a vigorous and open polylogue. That includes listening, among the contradictions, for the subtle harmonies that may intimate divine themes.

Religion, Culture, and Tribe

I am struck with critical wonder at the repeated conviction of the authors and sponsors of the *Arab Human Development Report, 2005:* "Religion has no connection with any of the mistaken practices that are carried out against women."[16] Can that be true? Or is it primarily an astute rhetorical tactic to slide a controversial report into Islamic consciousness — a cloaking of the text, as it were, to get it into Mecca? It is certainly plausible to say that Arabic societies give rise to their own traditions. And that they then "give precedence to custom over true worship and provide foundations for assumptions that have no grounding either in the Holy Qur'an or in the authenticated practices and sayings of the Prophet (the Hadith)."[17] This is no more than to argue that for the Arab, like other socio-religious histories, time and locality become the strongest authenticators. Development analysts treading on religious ground might also be moved to remark, upon finding bizarre or inhuman practices in Turkish, Farsi, Urdu, or Javanese cultures, "That is 'cultural,' not religious. That has nothing to do with Islam." The name of God, the ground of being, is nevertheless invoked by self-admiring purists to eternalize practices born in the quicksands of history.

Only twice in history has the Arab world been shaken up in such a way as to advance the status, inclusiveness, and productivity of women: early in

16. AHDR, p. vii.
17. AHDR, p. vii.

the Abbasid Caliphate (750-1258 C.E.), and in the era following penetration of European capitalism in the early nineteenth century. The potential of the latter, which includes our present time, is largely still underrealized. The authors of the Arab Human Development Report (AHDR) are unmistakably motivated to use modern historical momentum, and to lay out a strategic vision for human development in the broadest sense, with closer ties between men and women, and critical expansion of women's freedom and rights.

The best of visionary vehicles, however, must be on guard against the worst of continuing phenomena. In the tables that demonstrate the care and comprehensive sentience of the authors are thirteen survey categories of present protection of women and recent advancement of their condition in Morocco, Egypt, Lebanon, and Jordan. Overall the least protected area and the least improved is the banning of girls' circumcision (only 45 percent improved in the last five years, contrasted with over 80 percent in education and work).[18] The Prophet Muhammad, an immensely compassionate teacher, of course never said "Mutilate the reproductive organs of women to guarantee their virginity before, and faithfulness within, marriage." But some persons retreat to antique and invented religion to justify the unjustifiable, from which grotesque fortress they wage defense of the unjust — not only female genital mutilation, but honor killing, vendetta rape, and other horrors. Here the authors of the AHDR rightly take us back repeatedly to patriarchy, tribalism, and provincial twists of culture. They stress that "in the beginning was the agnate"[19] (commanding principle of descent from a specific male line) rather than the cognate (descent, without discrimination by gender, from a common ancestor). Still again, the report contains an undervoiced embarrassment that all this transpires within the religion of Islam. Mitigations lie in important exceptions from the periphery: Egyptian Copts, for instance, practice female genital mutilation, though not with such high incidence as do Egyptian Muslims. Malaysian and Indonesian Muslims do not practice it at all, which testifies to the huge power of a cognate starting point somewhere in pre-recorded times.

Salafis, going back to the roots to purify practices, would do well to campaign against honor killing and female genital mutilation wherever they are found, as practices extrinsic to the message of the Prophet and be-

18. AHDR, pp. 264-68.
19. "Agnate," p. 163.

smirching of his memory. That would do more for the Arab and other tribal worlds than violence against Western phenomena which purports to be cleansing. The West must clean up its own garbage, and will not be motivated to do so by seeing Westerners murdered.

The authors of the *Arab Human Development Report,* in any case, envision against "impending disaster" a "human renaissance in the Arab world." They lay out concrete steps in that regard, including redistribution of power and invigoration of civil society. Advancement of the condition and prospects of women is central to all such endeavors. They recommend ensuring the completion of twelve years of basic schooling for every Arab girl, and raising their required age of marriage to eighteen. Along with strides in freedom and knowledge, such vital steps in the empowerment of women are vital to an Arab human renaissance.[20]

Power, Culture, and the Feminine

Power — the appetite for it and the exercise of it — raises endless challenges in history, affecting religion, culture, and gender. The Prophet Muhammad and Jesus of Nazareth solved its problems in different ways. The Prophet became a field marshal and a lawgiver. He consented to the massacre of Jews who had betrayed his forces. He articulated a vision of fairness in a great variety of practical matters, such as divorce, inheritance, and usury, which continues in shari'a to this day with strictures for resolving disputes. Jesus abjured power as Satanic temptation. He killed nobody. He healed many. He allowed himself, arguably, to be sacrificed in expiation of the sins of others.

Neither the Prophet's social vision nor the Christ's moral example, however, ensures collective or individual goodness in those who follow. Schisms rend both religions. Social entropy afflicts both of their visions. The vortex of history sucks down their examples.

Lord Acton was surely right when he said — talking about popes, and particularly about issuance of the dogma of papal infallibility — "Power tends to corrupt; absolute power corrupts absolutely." In a like spirit one might say that power magnetizes culture and, unrestrained, destroys it.

To expect that women will redeem history is to expect far too much of the feminine. Golda Meir was Defense Minister before Prime Minister.

20. AHDR, pp. 178, 228-31.

Margaret Thatcher waged victorious war in the Falkland Islands. Benazir Bhutto was surrounded by untamed violence in her personal family and uncorrected corruption in her official family. Even if billions of women could be summoned to refuse their sons to war, hundreds of millions of them might still pursue vengeance for lost fathers and brothers. The appetite for retribution never ends, but chains itself to future potential. Contributions to culture, dazzling as they might be, are overwhelmed by new imperial ambitions. Great cats and small ones feast on zebras and giraffes, who are vegetarian. Gender does not correct appetite, or cure vulnerability.

Complementarity

In clashes of arms, power will triumph, if fully willed, rightly focused, and well timed. In clashes of culture, however, a wise endurance may prevail toward a subtle coherence. The Prophet knew this in distinguishing between the lesser *jihad* of military campaign and the greater *jihad* of moral struggle. The present moral struggle, in its global dimensions, is much more interesting than the level of American forces in Iraq, which arose from military power being applied in the wrong place for the wrong reasons. Moral struggle is much more important than the logistics of homeland defense, or the tactics and fulminations of al-Qaeda. In the Arab literary proverb, "A stone dropped on an egg will break the egg; and an egg dropped on a stone will also break the egg." The attack on the World Trade Center, ingenious and calamitous as it was, will represent in history a futile act: an egg dropped on a stone. The trading and market systems interrupted by the attack resumed within days. The international condition of Islamic nations, summarized five years later by President Yudhoyono of Indonesia, remained lesser in every dimension of standard national comparisons.[21]

What requires attention, beyond standard comparisons, and far beyond the forays of fanatics, is new measures of old verities. Here the gender gap index comes into play. However some might fault the methodology or dislike the findings, the end numbers confute nobody's intuitions. With respect to education, health, economic opportunity, and political leverage, women in Muslim countries lag behind most of the world, and in Arab countries have the very most to overcome. What comforteth it a man to

---

21. Yudhoyono speech in Riyadh, at the Islamic University of Imam Muhammad bin Sa'ud, 26 Apr 06. For full discussion, see Introduction, above, subsection on "Dialogues."

quote the Qur'an in the face of the facts, when such facts testify to neglect in observing the example of the Prophet? Woman undereducated is a social asset ignored and a human integer endangered. An educated woman in arbitrary constraint is creativity stifled and a blighted source of hope.

Without presuming to equate slavery and feminine subjection, I would observe that arguments from holy writ which suppress women in the current century are no more valid and no less anachronistic than those justifying the enslavement of African American men and women two centuries ago. Such legalized chattel slavery had to end, and was ended, even though millions in the modern world do work compelled through force or fraud, without pay beyond subsistence.[22] No less unholy now is gender bondage.

The suffocation of women cannot be guiltlessly ascribed to "systems," as if shari'a law were not of male manufacture and were beyond bi-gendered remedy, or as if excesses of patriarchal culture were inscribed by the finger of God. Men are actually co-sufferers in the unnatural diminution of roles for women. Having written the rules, men as enforcers pay an unseen price in their own unnatural exaltation. By diminishing their women, men only lessen themselves. Whatever their illusions of grandeur, they become tethered Gullivers, tied down by invisible threads. Unnaturally supine and expectant of service, they are tempted to grow plump and lax; and if they wake to their true condition, they may lurch through life with errant social energy, barely aware of their atrophies.

Yin/Yang is a useful complementarity — especially when complementarity is seen in function as fulfilling equality in principle, rather than being used to obstruct such equality. Even though the paired concept originated in still-largely patriarchal East Asian cultures, its long-recognized universality is agreeable to this argument. Yang, the male element, when separate and preoccupied with itself, becomes a military masculinism. When at work alone, and glorified theologically, it becomes a thundering Jove, or murderous Yahweh.[23] Yang needs Yin to make creative sense, and vice versa.

22. Kevin Bales's definition of modern slavery in *Disposable People* (1999) is fleshed out in narrative from five continents by E. Benjamin Skinner, *A Crime So Monstrous: Face to Face with Modern Day Slavery* (New York, Free Press, 2008).

23. Regina M. Schwartz, in *The Curse of Cain: The Violent Legacy of Monotheism* (Chicago, University of Chicago Press, 1997), is ready to discard Yahwism and its preoccupations with scarcity and violence for the vision of an alternative Bible which will stress plenitude and multiplicity. See also, for different perspectives, Rodney Stark, *For the Glory of God: How Monotheism Led to Reformation, Science, Witch-Hunts, and the End of Slavery* (Princeton,

Overdeveloped Yin also may occur, as in some young New York women who cast about lamenting the loss of the radical feminism of the 1970s.[24] Or possibly in the writings of Naomi Wolf, when she is looking for a parade under whose banner she can march in front. Her essay on travel in Morocco, Egypt, and Jordan was subject both to ridicule among Muslim female critics (for her "discovery" that behind modest dress Muslim women were motivated by allure and pleasure) and to rage among reactionary bloggers (who do not comprehend her intelligent appreciation of those modern Muslim women who are working for equality and democracy regardless of style of clothing).[25]

Fine counter to such thinking are some feminists of South Asia. They have taken cues from American, Australian, and European writers of the last four decades. Gathered by Durre Ahmed, they probe archetypes of feminine and masculine, and study paradoxes of divinity in fertile ways, where it is hard to be either original or profound, and extremely difficult to be both. Some of them study invented matri-centric religions of their areas; others re-inhabit old myths and clean them out for modern living; none of them appear to be in disproportionate fear of patriarchal men.

Such writers, as frontier feminists, know that unchecked Yin bores and vanishes (which may be why some Northern can-you-top-this? feminists go silent). They realize that the eternal complementarity of Yin/Yang can be framed with endless productivity. And they engage with spirituality in its many dimensions, without the fastidious embarrassment of some North Atlantic intellectuals. Those who disdain belief, ritual, and religious

Princeton University Press, 2003); Roxanne L. Euben's *Enemy in the Mirror: Islamic Fundamentalism and the Limits of Modern Rationalism* (Princeton, Princeton University Press, 1999); and Karen Armstrong's books on religion. In her autobiography, *The Spiral Staircase: My Climb out of Darkness* (New York, Anchor Books, 2004), Armstrong quotes Ibn al-Arabi: "God, the omnipresent and omnipotent, is not confined to any one creed, for, he says, 'Wheresoever you turn, there is the face of Allah'" (p. 289).

24. For instance, Elizabeth Isadora Gold's essay on "Ephron, French, Jong," *The Believer*, 5:6, Aug 07, pp. 44-50.

25. Naomi Wolf, *The Beauty Myth: How Images of Beauty are Used Against Women* (1st ed., New York, Morrow, 1991; 2nd ed., New York, HarperCollins, 2002); *Promiscuities: The Secret Struggle for Womanhood* (New York, Random House, 1997); *Misconceptions: Truth, Lies, and the Unexpected on the Journey to Motherhood* (New York, Anchor Books, 2001). For the veil tempest: Wolf in the *Sydney Morning Herald*, 30 Aug 09, and *Huffington Post*, 5 Oct 09; Muslim women's reaction, Yale Conference of Critical Islamic Reflections, 10 Apr 10, at which I was present; reactionary bloggers summarized in Tracy Clark-Flory, salon .com, 5 Sep 09.

meaning in all its agonistic varieties appear to such women of the South to be living in ivory apartment buildings — excessively secular and comfortable, and dangerously arid in apartness. The Southern feminists make friendly proclamations that point in totally different directions. They compare and they cross religious boundaries. They delight in heresy and humor. They offer insight, drive, creativity, and spiritual riches. They invite men to stop castrating each other with radical fundamentalisms. Because they are rooted in the underground, they can offer complementary dialogue with men, and creative polylogue among cultures and religions.[26]

Perhaps "God" and "Allah" should be treated as nicknames for the Divine, or as in ancient tradition, sobriquets for the Unnameable. But insofar as either "Allah" or "God" invokes an Abrahamic god of live sacrifice and vengeance, I would that we shun such altars. Thunder-and-slaughter gods must give way to light and mercy and compassionate justice. Not because anger is ungodly, but because murder is unholy. We need and seek the Divine as the ground of being. We do not find it on any of the innumerable battlegrounds where the blood of Abel stains the club of Cain and sinks into the soil, from the immemorial to the Somme — a million casualties in five months — to today. Not in the radioactive rubble of Hiroshima and Nagasaki. J. Robert Oppenheimer, upon the test explosion of the terrible toy, and with knowledge of the Bhagavad Gita, recalled to himself the words of Krishna, avatar of the God Vishnu, to Prince Arjuna: "Now I am become death, destroyer of worlds." Did Oppenheimer comfort himself that he, like Arjuna, was only a dutiful agent of the inevitable?[27] I don't know. But I believe we sin if we compliment ourselves on ability to destroy each other with microcomponents of the energy of the universe. Einstein knew that. Having urged research to win a war against Nazi Germany, he struggled thereafter for restraint in nuclear policy.

In certain acts, of course, heroism or patriotic courage may be undeniable. I simply say that God or Allah must not be confused with national identity or strategic planning, or battle flags, or allegedly holy pieces of real

26. Ahmed, in *Gendering the Spirit* (see note 2 above), connects five authors, including herself, in thirteen different original essays, rising from the piquant to the archetypal. Compatible with their thinking, but unconnected to it except in her distinctive Jungian Buddhist individualism, is Polly Young-Eisendrath's *Gender and Desire: Uncursing Pandora* (College Station, Texas A&M University Press, 2002).

27. A clear distillation of the vast literature radiating from the historic moment and the Hindu quotation is James A. Hijiya, "The *Gita* of J. Robert Oppenheimer," *Proceedings of the American Philosophical Society* 144:2.

estate; must not be conflated into thrilling advances in military technology any more than into bomb packs about one's own middle for the ecstasy of suicidal killing.

This universe, the only one we yet know, is more than shrapnel hurtling away from a Big Bang. In understanding it we must hold tight to the basic ideas of being and meaning. If we apply ourselves to understanding these ideas, not as evolved folly, but as our evolutionary capacity, we may begin to apprehend a god of *kenosis,* who cascades creativity into our reach; a god of emptying-into-being whose godhood never becomes vacant. As part of that divine provender which we are given to share, we may see male and female not in hierarchy, but as complementary in creativity and equal in principle.

Fulfillments

The communications storm of our times tends to rip roofs from traditional shelters. Even the poor have new aspirations provided them by the media; usually, however, without the means of satisfying hungers of the soul. But among their educated sisters, in every country, there exist extraordinary volunteer energies to help bring to the poor literacy, understanding, guidance, and means of coping. As demographic projections suggest that one-quarter of the world may be Muslim in an imaginable few decades, the pivotal roles of educated Muslim women will become even more pronounced. They will be conductors of the best changes, resistors to the worst; rememberers of the best ways of the past, visionaries of better ways in the future. How they themselves are fulfilled has been the major subject of this book. Considering the dimensions of their fulfillments allows me to voice an order of needs, which runs from the irreducibly basic to the hopefully optimal.

Identity

In the most extreme tribal conditions, woman's identity as a human being is not conceded, and dogmatic Islamic teachings are used to authenticate tribalism. In Saudi Arabia, pursuant to the rulings of Wahhabi jurists, woman is ancillary to man, auxiliary in function, subordinate in essence, and sometimes effectual slave in fact.

The work of the poet and activist Nimah Nawwab aims at assuring women of basic identity. For their education, choice of spouse, employment, and mobility, women must be relieved of male "guardianship," which is an onerous artifact of peculiar Saudi history and social conditions. Nimah's effort began in her youthful poem, "Life Imprisonment." It continues in her petitionary work on behalf of those socially maimed by assumptions that they are lesser in the eye of God.

Wherever repressive tribal conditions obtain, women are in danger of terrible diminishment, especially in conditions of poverty. That combination often prevails from Eastern Anatolia, eastward and southward through Arab countries to Pakistan, India, and Bangladesh. But oil wealth and hyper-masculine jurisprudence especially mark the social conditions of Saudi Arabia. Against male "guardianship" and the tendency of petro-theology to make women invisible, Nimah Nawwab contends with courageous others. Their greatest obstacle, perhaps, is a self-protective royal concern for social cohesion, embedded in judicial reliance on the Permanent Council for Scientific Research and Legal Opinions. That Council's ruling on employment registers its overall view that "God Almighty . . . commanded women to remain in their homes. Their presence in the public is the main contributing factor to the spread of *fitna* [strife]."[28] No statement could better illustrate a closed system, with dogmatic blockage of social circuits.

Choice

Above the level of raw existence, there need to be opportunities for women in which they themselves have an influential voice. The dismaying prevalence of clinical depression among rural Pakistani women is a sign of barren lack of options, and of grinding repetitive routine. Many of their educated sisters from major cities are working to help them form both group and individual consciousness, and to advance the education of their children while widening their personal horizons.

From the midst of illiterate peasantry itself has arisen that courageous

28. Human Rights Watch [after cooperative discussion with Saudi government officials coordinated by the Human Rights Commission of Saudi Arabia], "Perpetual Minors: Human Rights Abuses Stemming from Male Guardianship and Sex Segregation in Saudi Arabia" (New York, 20 Apr 08, 52 pp.), quotation, p. 8. http://www.hrw.org/doc?+-mideastLc =saudia-43k.

exemplar, Muchtaran Mai. She has shown that suffocating confines do not require surrender; life-defiling actions may be resisted; and frontiers of action and understanding can be advanced for all women by initiative from below. Where silent suffering, or worse, was the only option, an ingredient of choice may open up, essential for life itself, with continuing growth.

Individuality

Once women exist on a plane of history and morality equal with men, with choices for growth, it becomes easier to recognize their distinct ranges of sensibility and feeling. Revealing this realm, the cinema of Iran and Turkey thus far surpasses that of other Muslim nations. Clichés of the farm wife accepting misery and the migrant woman burdened with anomie in the city are still extant, but in exploratory films these stereotypes yield to real variety. Women digest vicariously understood experiences and take on new demands in communication. No more *kabuki*-like masks. No more lifeless ciphers of womanhood. Actresses may not merely have roles to play, but lives to imagine.

Tamineh Milani of Iran has written and produced several feature films in the last twenty years that illuminate the lives of middle-class women and men. She not only shows the way for younger filmmakers, but clears the day for those many women who feel better understood by her movies than by their own families.

Equality

The social standing of women, as measured by best practices in family law, is now encouragingly registered through reforms in Morocco, Tunisia, and Turkey. Even so, "the work on reclaiming our rights and equal status in Islam has only just begun."[29] However jurisprudence may be assessed, it is clear that the standing of women rests primarily, if unconsciously, on matters determined long before shariʿa existed. The Minangkabau of Indonesia, a tribe of eight million in modern number, so firmly established matrilineality with regard to property inheritance that it is now viewed as

---

29. Norani Othman, ed., *Muslim Women and the Challenge of Islamic Extremism* (Selangor, Malaysia, Sisters in Islam, 2005, funded by the Rockefeller Foundation), p. 207.

providing "social security" for women. While respecting shariʿa, they have not let it undermine their own customary law.

Without projecting for women elsewhere this unique solution, one may point to it as both tribal and humane, both traditional and enlightened. It guarantees respect and freedom for women in a tribe also noted for the initiative and creativity of its men. Matrilineality, however, is not required to protect women. Bilateral family structure, common in Indonesia and Malaysia, defines relationships through both female and male lines of descent. Such bilateral reckonings serve as a guard against patriarchalism, which is patrilineality exaggerated. On the tightrope of modern life, male privilege is a teetering weight, its balance not guaranteed by a strained balance pole of quotations from Qurʾan and hadith.

In Indonesia, the systematic arguments of Siti Musdah Mulia[30] have cleared away excesses and arbitrary readings caused by inherited prejudices. Her thorough review of shariʿa, although not adopted by the Indonesian parliament, remains an inspiring project for women throughout Islam. Also for those who would reexamine any religious culture in conditions of modern life — and for any who would free themselves from hyper-masculine principles adopted in a non-congruous era by an alien culture for antique reasons.

Variety

Turkey in the twenty-first century has continued to build on its major twentieth-century advances under the leadership of Atatürk. He followed his abolition of the Caliphate with edicts that emancipated women and gave them the vote. Secularism as managed by the Turkish military, however, has threatened in recent decades to become a strangling dogmatism of its own kind. Against it, in 2007, popular and parliamentary votes brought to power for the first time both a prime minister and a president of Muslim faith. The contest between secular and Muslim elites continues. A secularist attempt to ban the ruling party, AKP, and its leaders failed by one vote in the Constitutional Court. The long-term impact of the counter-case, labeled "Ergenekon," launched by the AKP in criminal court, is not yet clear. Will it, by digging into thirty years of ultranationalist mili-

30. Especially Siti Musdah Mulia, *Islam & Inspirasi Kesetaraan Gender* [Islam and Gender Equality] (Yogyakarta, Kibar Press, 2006).

tant action, clarify some of Turkey's impacted modern history? Or, by fuzzy radiation of charges against several varieties of critics, will it blur legal principles, weaken the judiciary, and dampen variety in Turkish public life?

Meanwhile, continuing arguments over head-covering are certainly noisy, but not as profound as the comprehensive revisions of Turkish civil law in 2004 on matters of family and sexuality.[31] That extraordinary achievement by Parliament was done in transparency, after open consultation with the public. This procedural sunlight, and ensuing regulatory liberations, have arguably transformed Turkey so basically as to make the headscarf issue ultimately marginal. For the present, however, tensions over its visual symbolism persist every day.

One could hope for a Turkey in which "alterity" was acceptable: a reversible option with regard to attire in which a woman might go scarved or unscarved without concern — a condition incomparably less restrictive than the policed head-coverings in the Kingdom of Saudi Arabia and in the Islamic Republic of Iran. But instead of being a matter of the wearer's conscience only, it remains too much a matter of the watcher's opinion as well. Alterity, or otherness with regard to dress, becomes an instant visual argument in the national political debate. So a more supple word is required to describe women's needs in Turkey, and elsewhere.

"Variety" might be the better term. The word suggests a culture in which contrasting others may flourish as Fatma Benli and Vildan Yirmibeşoğlu have done, but more easily. Fatma can express her religious tradition and her conviction that covering the head does not suffocate the brain. She will continue to struggle for the right of scarved women to attend universities, argue in courts of law, and otherwise express freely their talents and rights as citizens of the republic. Meanwhile Vildan, uncovered, has already accomplished a mighty project in compiling honor killings in Eastern Anatolia. She has gone further, in Istanbul, to focus the support of police and the public on the problems of migrant tribal males, forced into or threatened with complicity in such murders.

Fatma and Vildan, as lawyers, are women of articulate courage. It does Turkey honor that both may contribute to its modern social vitality. "Variety" may seem a pale word in reference to the vivid colors of their different

---

31. European Stability Initiative, *Sex and Power in Turkey: Feminism, Islam, and the Maturing of Turkish Democracy* (Berlin/Istanbul, 2 Jun 07), 41 pp.; full report at http://www.esiweb.org.

achievements. But in positing a train of language to analyze the conditions and needs of women across seven thousand miles of Islam, I see "variety" as a locomotive term to which the others — "identity," "choice," "individuality," and "equality" — may be coupled and pulled forward. Different tracks of national culture will suggest different sequences and speeds, but nowhere need progress go off indigenous rails.

What is true for different countries is further true for different women. Each one has constraints to observe and liberties to seek, neither of which need engender strife. The speed of world-circling phenomena may sometimes suggest a cyclone. But individual women, in consultation with their own integrity and in league with forces of their own choice, may determine what progress-in-Islam means for themselves, their families, their nations, and the *ummah* — the world community of their religion.

Toward an Open Islam

Equality for women is a compelling need, an innate catalyst, and a transformative energy toward an open Islam. An open Islam, indeed, in a democratic sense has always existed. Among the qualities that sent it roaring through Southwest Asia and North Africa a millennium and a half ago was its outreach to all souls, later called its universality. The same quality assisted its penetration of caste-structured South Asia and hierarchical societies of Southeast Asia.

If egalitarian energy accounts for much of the early spread of Islam, what then happened? Original zeal cooled. Convictions on equality crumpled into preferential convenience. And the local, with its vertically crenellated structure of interests, prevailed over the universal.

Woman was the early beneficiary of Islam. The social vision of the Prophet raised her standing in the world, appropriate to seeing her as a child of God rather than the powerless ward of a man, subject to all masculinity. But Islamic theologies introverted themselves, especially after the fourteenth century, and Muslim sociologies became involuted once more.

The Northern imperial powers that jolted Muslim societies in the nineteenth century lacked the purity in theology and the egalitarian liberation that had originally set the Southern worlds aflame with the Prophet's vision. Christian dogma now assumed subjacent the peoples conquered by Northern armies. The real status of women among the conquerors did not support lofty assumptions: they were voteless and undereducated, with only tenuous claims to property. But the Southerners tended to imitate their conquerors, if only to escape them.

The imperial shock was not a one-time event. Several generations of influences followed, from societies changing more rapidly than they understood or could control, transmitting new social, economic, and cultural influences to societies either receptive to change or defenseless against it.

By the time of the twentieth-century high-water mark of Northern sovereignties, advancing new rights and elaborating roles of women were major parts of the creative convulsions they interjected into Muslim societies. Imperial ebb after World War II and the 1960s left many of those social forces still running.

Then a worldwide movement, Western and Eastern, Northern and Southern, took hold in religions, strengthening conservatisms and fundamentalisms, as if to hold on to ideas of the holy and texts of revelation lest traditional understanding and all profounder value be washed away.

If 1979 is an apt date to mark the resurgence of reactive and hunkering-down religion, we have had more than three decades of it by this writing. Across that time the matter of an open Islam has taken on new dimensions. Some modes of its discussion are thin. Some are even pitiful, as in Northern political pleas for a "moderate Islam," which is irrelevant and debilitating to the essence of religion, and just as insulting as the label of a "moderate Christianity." The dialogues that matter have relatively little to do with states or with the non-state actors who have become more notable since 9/11. More penetrating and more enduring discussions concern how whole populations conceive of women and how they conceive of God.

The hopeful tilt of this discourse is against deprival, in women, of their nurture, or status, or growth, or life itself. Women deserve to be considered social and legal equals of men. This of course requires a growth in vision of certain kinds of text-bound, life-blind Christianity far beyond their present norms. And in Islam it requires reconsideration of the social revelation of the Prophet. To review the vision of the Prophet should have as an aim that the twenty-first century exceed the twentieth in fair and just treatment of women by the same enlightened, exuberant vastness that the seventh century surpassed the sixth.

A more open Islam, in the livable future, will think of God as Rumi and Hafez did eight and seven centuries ago — a universal, benevolent, and forgiving God, intimate to humans drunk or sober, wrong or right, errant or correct. This need not rule out a God that is passionately just and eternally accurate in justice; but it does exclude a vengeful, maiming, or murdering divinity. God may have three Christian persons, or thirteen Talmudic attributes, or ninety-nine Islamic names, or infinite Hindu avatars, or no Buddhist meaning. But God may be shared as our planet must be shared — and our universe, or pluriverse, if that it proves to be.

The Arab Uprisings of 2011:
Ibn Khaldûn, Civil Society, and Societies Uncivil

The journalistic notion of an "Arab Spring" is faulty on two counts. Climatologically, from Morocco to Yemen, it is absurd; there is no such season. It is also misleading, because analogy with the "Prague Spring" of 1968 runs into the unhappy fact that protests by Czech citizens against their imperial masters were crushed by Soviet tanks. The Cold War did not thaw out until two decades later.

The "Arab uprisings" of which I speak have a more penetrating focus than the Nasserite rumbles of fifty years ago, which were heavily laced with anticolonialism. Now it is clear to multitudes of Arabs that they are exploited by native elites. And even if some new poverty has been overcome by growth, that same growth illuminates gross inequalities. Those who feel relative deprivation and overt discrimination are prone to rage. So far the anger has tended to play out constructively in Tunisia and Egypt. Even where strangled by armed force (Syria) or suffocated by money (in Saudi Arabia, the $130 billion unloaded into the social economy was described to me by a Turk as a "royal bribe"), present time in the Arab world is unforgettable. Like the systemic surprises in the Soviet Empire and Union, 1989-91, those dynamics have come swiftly to seem inevitable. But we need to understand them further. What is being *risen against,* and to what end?

Arab Dynastic Cycles

Can Ibn Khaldûn be of help here? This fifteenth-century North African traveler, scholar, diplomat, and judge reflected on the troubles of his own times. Going far beyond customary chronicles, he attempted to show the dynamics of social organization and urbanization that underlay them. In so doing, he generated an Arab philosophy of history three and a half centuries before Vico and four centuries before Gibbon produced works in Europe of equal ambition. Key to the thinking of Ibn Khaldûn is the concept of *asabiyyah:* group solidarity or social cohesion. It was vital to overcome the savage pride of the Bedouins in order to generate cooperation, establish dynasties, and cultivate urban civilization, as distinct from the raw survival of desert life. Once the principle of group solidarity was established, Ibn Khaldûn saw dynasties going through predictable cycles of five phases: (1) successful overthrow of a royal predecessor; (2) gaining of complete control; (3) leisure and optimal expression of rule; (4) contentment succumbing to lassitude and luxury; (5) squandering that breeds hatred in the people and disloyalty among the soldiers, whereupon dynastic senility becomes an incurable disease.[1]

Ibn Khaldûn's cycle helps to describe the authoritarian continuities found in recent Arab history: three rulers across sixty years in Egypt; two across fifty years in Tunisia; one for more than forty in Libya; one for more than thirty in Yemen; father and son for more than forty years in Syria. The most continuous line of authority in the region of course is in Saudi Arabia, where the clan of Al-Saud has been preeminent for over a hundred years, testing the elasticity of Ibn Khaldûn's theory and buying the patience of the people with social subsidies.[2] In contention with royal modes of ruling are democratic recognitions that all leaders are flawed. Term limits minimize the chances of peculiar flaws becoming endemic and also maximize the chances of systemic flaws becoming identified and treated.

Egyptians grew alarmed when they recognized that Hosni Mubarak was attempting to create an actual bloodline dynasty. Now he must answer for ordering the shootings of protesters that marked his last days in power; and his sons in jail cells must also answer for the greedy amassing of wealth that characterized the last years of that regime. The Egyptian revolt will be

---

1. Ibn Khaldûn, *The Muqaddimah: An Introduction to History,* trans. Frank Rosenthal; ed. N. J. Dawood (Princeton University Press, 1967); *asabiyyah,* pp. xi; 152; stages, pp. 140-42 and *passim.*

2. Excellent articles: Peter Turchin, "Scientific Prediction in Historical Sociology: Ibn Khaldûn meets Al Saud," in Peter Turchin, Leonid Grinin, Andrae Korataev, and Victor C. de Munck, *History and Mathematics: Historical Development of Complex Societies* (Moscow, Kom Kniga, 2006), pp. 9-38; William R. Polk, "Encounters with Ibn Khaldûn," www .williampolk.com/pdf/2001/Encounters. . . .

the most important model for the rest of the Arab world, even though the Tunisian one, which preceded and inspired it, may reach a further point of development and stabilize at a more secure level of democracy.

But here we broach an idea that was unknown to Ibn Khaldûn. The sovereignty of the people would have struck him as a wondrous and dangerous extravagance. But precisely because that idea now exists, the Arab political dynamics in our own time do far more than replicate royal cycles. Beyond democracy they summon other modern concepts — human rights, rule of law, pluralism, transparency, and accountability. These define health and disease in the body politic, attention to which may allow continuous renewal rather than recurring declines into the senilities that Ibn Khaldûn predicted.

Tunisia and Egypt

Such multiple values came suddenly into play in Tunisia, which had been the first Arab nation to outlaw slavery (1846, a year before Sweden did so), and among the first to enact women's suffrage (1959). There, on December 17, 2010, a twenty-seven-year-old fruit vendor in the town of Sidi Bouzid had his wares confiscated. He was allegedly slapped in the face by a female inspector and beaten by her aides. After being denied interview by the town governor, Mohamed Bouazizi set himself on fire in the town square. He died in a coma, January 4, 2011. His dramatic suicide was picked up by Al Jazeera and became a national symbol — a furious expression of frustration with a regime going rapidly from Ibn Khaldûn's fourth stage (hateful luxury) into its fifth and final condition (incurable senility). Demonstrations mounted rapidly. Zine El Abidine Ben Ali, twenty-four years in power, fled his own country with his family on January 14, 2011, and took refuge in Saudi Arabia. Tunisia, backed by Interpol, issued a warrant for his arrest, and the arrest of his wife, on multiple and grand counts of illegal seizure of properties and dozens of other charges. Swift conviction in absentia led to thirty-five-year sentences for each and $66 million in fines.

The Tunisian example of revolt, despite its 300 deaths, gave courage to the young-and-fed-up as well as the under-fed and angry in several countries, most notably Egypt. Controlled as that great nation was, its media had some grasp of critical reality and were allowed occasional gasps of truth. A presidential election in 2005, although marred by low turnout and many irregularities, was won by Mubarak with 89 percent of the vote. Ayman Nour, runner-up, obtained only 7 percent and was then jailed for a

334

five-year term, apparently for the effrontery of opposing the autocrat. His example of daring nevertheless sank into popular consciousness.

For January 25, 2011, not long after Ben Ali fled Tunisia, a protest in Cairo was scheduled on National Police Day — intentionally targeting police abuse. The killing of Khaled Said had stirred thousands of people for many months, and now they could focus their feelings. Said was a twenty-eight-year-old who had filmed police in the act of profiting from the sale of drugs. In retribution, two policemen repeatedly slammed him against stone steps and an iron door just one block from his home, and dumped his body in front of an Internet café. The bloody visage of his corpse in the morgue with its fractured skull and broken bones, snapped by his brother on a mobile phone, went viral on Facebook.

Young leaders of many kinds brewed up revolt, such as Asmaa Mahfouz, a twenty-six-year-old female activist who, in eloquent videos, urged a turnout in Tahrir Square. As one Egyptian who responded emotionally observed, the protests gathered momentum, calling for dignity (the freedom *to be*), freedom (the opportunity *to do*), and social justice (things that *must be done*). Egyptians began to break through their fear and to end it with growing demands like "drumbeats . . . you start soft, then go louder."[3]

For eighteen consecutive days, they protested massively and nonviolently in Tahrir Square. In retrospect, a young activist summarized new lines of communication: "We use Facebook to schedule the protests, Twitter to coordinate, and YouTube to tell the world." A Google executive, Wael Ghonim, was critical to administration of the social links that expressed desires for a better life, while summoning righteous anger as a motivation. "We are all Khaled Said" became a powerful slogan.

The masses protesting in Tahrir Square and elsewhere — later estimates put their accumulated total at six to eight million — hit at unemployment, food prices, corruption, and insults to personal dignity. They were unappeasable, and further aroused by Mubarak himself in two condescending and rambling speeches on TV. On February 11 he resigned. During many of the days of protest Wael Ghonim himself was in jail. Abroad, however, he stood for the revolt to a degree captured in a remark by President Obama. In answering a question from a staff member, Obama said, "What I want is for the kids on the street to win and for the Google guy to become president."[4]

3. Heba Ramzy, e-mail correspondence with the author, 28-29 Jun 11.
4. *New York Times*, 12 May 11, p. A10.

In fact, the young crowds in Egypt found Obama's own posture indistinct and insufficiently supportive; and American public opinion influenced them little. When Obama sent his personal representative, retired Ambassador Frank Wisner, to talk Mubarak out of office, he came back instead urging continued support of the dictator. Thus Wisner clouded his own previous reputation by failure to understand what was going on in Egypt, and what had to happen there.

The eventual tally of the Egyptian dead went well over 800, mostly civilians. Those who died did not intend to pay a price for a Gandhian principle of nonviolence. It was common sense to see that a weaponed regime led by an ex-general could not be overthrown by ordinary demonstrations. The uncommon sense that made history was to maintain civil discipline in resistance to that regime, returning to the squares not in an idolatry of peace, but in determination to win major goals by unarmed struggle in solidarity. Resort to even minor acts of violence would have played into the hands of the regime, which seemed to entice such an error. Discipline prevailed.[5]

The real question for Egypt became what further goals could be achieved after Mubarak was gone, and his ominous subaltern, Lt. Gen. Omar Suleiman, was refused as a successor. The crowds achieved a civilian prime minister at last. But that still left the Supreme Council of the Armed Forces, nineteen generals, at the apex of power in Egypt. Accommodating in tone but paternal in determination, they accepted as national strategy that the constitution must be rewritten and elections held. But entrusting such matters to a council of generals is not the same as handing it over to Jeffersonian yeomen. The referendum submitted to the populace in March 2011 contained a necessary minimum of constitutional change. Article 41 stipulated that election procedures would begin within six months. That was not time enough, many protesters declared; not adequate to organize and educate the electorate. The military did not budge; they likely did not want and do not want an electorate overeducated.[6]

---

5. And prevailed despite enormous national frustration, already symbolized in 2010 by the performance artist Ahmed Basiony. He had publicly run in place an hour a day for thirty days, while sensors on his suit used his sweat to project a flush of colors on video screens around him. On January 30, 2011, in Tahrir Square he was shot dead. His artistic career subsequently became the centerpiece of the Egyptian exhibit at the Venice Biennale, breaking the tradition of previously academic submissions by Egypt. www.thenational.ae/arts-culture/art/egypt-displays-an-artful-legacy-at-the-venice-biennale.

6. Lally Weymouth interviewed generals for washingtonpost.com/world/middle-east/Egyptian-generals-speak. . . . 18 May 11. The evaluative language is mine. All 63 articles are

For upper-middle-class inhabitants of Cairo, longer deliberation appeared the better course, so that Egypt would lay down surer guidelines for the future. By one account, listening to his employer's family dinner table conversations against the referendum convinced their chief manservant, who had to return to his rural village to vote. He persuaded a great majority of the village to his views. Then the Salafis, hyper-traditionalists of the neighborhood, began to sound off. They said, "A 'no' vote is *atheism*." They threatened fines of thousands of Egyptian pounds to those who so voted. What regulation they pretended to did not matter. Nor did invasion of the secret ballot matter. "We will *know* if you vote 'no.'" The servant came back to Cairo and told his employers of pressures that could not be surmounted. He and his followers in the village had chosen to abstain.[7] Nationwide the result was 77 percent "yes."

Such powerful manifestation of Salafi opinion will affect the probabilities for the national election. [This is written in June-July 2011.] The neutered NPD, the tame majority party for Mubarak, will get new life and credibility from context alone, rather like ex-communists in post-1989 Eastern Europe.[8] The oft-penalized Muslim Brotherhood has declared that it will not seek the presidency, and will not offer candidates in more than half of the races for parliamentary seats. But this apparent forbearance is a careful calculation. In many constituencies they can make a deal *not* to run, and thereby affect the outcome. Their organization, developed since 1928, gives them power far beyond the impact of their social-service organizations. Under three authoritarian regimes they have aimed to Islamize society from the ground up. Now they are ready to reap their rewards.[9] They appear likely to win, or otherwise to "own," perhaps 40 percent of the seats. In coalition politics they can be imagined to ally with blocs of Salafis[10] (perhaps 10 percent of the electorate) and with progressive Mus-

---

available on http://egyptelections.carnegieendowment.org/2011/04/01/supreme-council-of-the-armed-forces-constitutional-announcement

7. Interview, Heba Ramzy, 19 May 11.

8. I am grateful to Ambassador (ret.) Adrian Basora, Director of the Project on Democratic Transitions at the Foreign Policy Research Institute, Philadelphia, for his essay, with Jean F. Boone, "A New U.S. Policy Towards Democracy in Post-Communist Europe/Eurasia," Jan 10; and for his personal notes, "Arab Revolutions of 2011 vs. Post-Communist Transitions of 1989-91."

9. Here I owe perspective to three scholars who presented a seminar on "Egypt, Regime Change, and the Muslim Brotherhood" at the Foreign Policy Research Institute, Philadelphia, 24 May 11: Samuel Helfont, Aaron Rock, and Eric Trager.

10. Whereas Salafis number in "the low millions," they are diverse and divided. The

lims (perhaps 5 percent). How many ideological leftists will win seats; and how many un-ideological businessmen? Working control of the national legislature cannot be predicted, but it will generate a new constitution, and a presidential election. Hassan Al-Banna's dream has a possibility of being realized seven dozen years after he founded the Muslim Brotherhood. The chance for an Obama option, some variant of a "Google guy" being elected president, is of course none at all.

The Military

We cannot yet see the outcome of the numerous and momentous movements in the Arab region, which are greater even than the Nasserite upheavals half a century ago. But some patterns are evident. One-party governments, despotic at their worst, feel threatened by localized protests. From tear gas to rhetorical kisses there is a great range of options, in which the military and police are critical, and not always coordinate. Armed forces may be deployed systematically and brutally with tanks and helicopter gunships (Syria), or may take sides with the people (Tunisia), or may shatter along tribal and geographic lines (in civil war, Libya; or in anti-establishment anarchy, Yemen).

There is no true or sustained neutrality possible for an army in such times. Egypt's military was not charmed into democratic solidarity with demonstrators by the popular chant, "The people and the army are one." No: a conscript army simply did not wish to fire into large crowds, because their own relatives could be there; and officers were unwilling to give such an order. The top senior generals finally judged Mubarak, one of their own, to have become unsupportable. They removed him to his villa at Sharm al-Sheikh and later put him under custody in a hospital nearby. Then they consented to a trial beginning in August 2011. Though it would mask their own complicity in previous oppression, it would promise to give the public symbolic satisfaction for long-felt injustices.

Comparison with Indonesia is highly interesting. There, too, in the crisis of 1998, the army finally tilted against its own three-decade autocrat, but afterward protected Suharto at home in Jakarta until he died ten years later. Even now, they guard his reputation, as part of a massive national

---

Muslim Brotherhood has only about 300,000 members, but eight decades of political experience have given it organizational discipline. Shadi Hamid to the author, 4 Aug 11.

syndrome of undigested history. Indonesia, nevertheless, would be an excellent standard were any Arab nation to care about Muslim Asia. After toppling their dictator, Indonesians proceeded to constitutional revisions, to administrative reorganization, and to two free, open, and direct presidential elections (2004, 2009). They also achieved some curbs on corruption, and between 2000 and 2010 increased per capita income from $500 to $3,000.

Civil Society

One of the most broadly informed American experts on Islam observes summarily that "Civil society in Egypt has never been — and I would argue, can never be — free from significant government interference, constraints, and outright oppression."[11] Although Islamist activists and secular intellectuals both have been allowed their latitudes in the last sixty years, there was always an implicit leash by which the authoritarian regime (whichever one — the characteristic in Egypt is by now innate) could yank them back or even, metaphorically, strangle them.

Nowhere in the region is civil society in the North Atlantic sense guaranteed. Tunisia may be the closest, but Ben Ali trimmed it back.[12] In fully flowered development, civil society is guaranteed by a constitution, unhindered by police, and defended by a military. With a constitution supplying the skeleton of national organization, and laws in continual play and counterplay more important to its protection than the muscle of weaponed forces, then civil society may complete the anatomy of an evolving nervous system. It must be free to inquire into whatever it chooses, and manifest whatever it legally can, so that the creativity of a people will count more than its capacity to be policed. At an opposite extreme, the nervous system barely matters at all, and the armed muscle of the organism can break its own bones.

With regard to civil society, social networking may be seen in proper perspective. Its prevalence in Egypt and elsewhere is important, and the late, failed effort of the Mubarak government to suppress it proves its

11. Bruce B. Lawrence, "Islam and Civil Society — Perspectives from Egypt before and after Mubarak," talk prepared for Philadelphia, 2 May 11 (but not formally given, displaced by news of the death of Osama bin Laden), p. 2.

12. Christopher Alexander, "Authoritarianism and Civil Society in Tunisia," *Middle East Report*, Oct-Dec 1997.

consequentiality. The grim successes of the Assad government of Syria in keeping out foreign reporters and shutting down the Internet demonstrate by absence the importance of such communication. Social networking may further become key to the nervous systems of civil societies; but talk of "Facebook revolutions" is exaggerated and misplaced. The motivations for what occurred in Tunisia and continues to happen in Egypt come from the gut — from humiliation and the desire to connect in fighting against it. Social networking then provides *speed* in connection, and in this year of tumult it has massively surprised some despots. But swiftness of communication does not transform the persons that for a while it brings together in common motivation and constructive action. The nodes of the network are still human beings. The long-term impact for peace of new techniques in communication may be judged by asking: Did invention of the telephone prevent World War I? Did invention of the radio prevent World War II?

The norm of North Atlantic societies is peculiar to itself and revealing in its origins. In the era of the Holy Roman Empire, perhaps, state and church and society could be said to have been inseparable. But Western Europe developed in a manner that made state and church distinct and contending entities. The Protestant Reformation then added another dimension of society in which individual conscience became preeminent.

Islam and the Muslim world, however, proceed from different premises. There is no "church." Regardless of the state to which one may pay taxes, the broadest entity to which one owes allegiance is the *umma,* or the global community of believers. Invoking "civil society" therefore does not have the muscle tone historically developed in France or the United States, nor does it have the same powerful claim on personal values. Nonetheless, educated persons in the Arab worlds, professionals and intellectuals, often proclaim "civil society" to justify and advance their vision.

As they do so, they may or may not be aware that the present currency of the term derives from its use before and after 1989, in the Eastern European countries throwing off Soviet imperial rule and internal exploitation by communist autocrats and elites. Its use was meant to signify votes that counted, consciences that mattered, and organizations — both for business and not-for-profit — that were allowed independent roles in creating a new national vitality. Not all the nations that redesigned themselves are stories of success; the best may not yet be exuberantly productive, and the worst still contain some police repression. But none would seek to return to the communist era, with its citizen-automatons, glorified bureaucrats, state-controlled media, and schools with dogmatic curricula. Something new has emerged: not error-free by any means, but in principle tolerant of error, and willing to proceed by the public contest of opinions.[13] Those are essential characteristics of society becoming civil. Whatever the historical background or the present circumstances of the Arabs desiring something new, they are not wrong to express their yearning as "civil society." But there may exist a point — a transformation point beyond Khaldûnian repetitions — that nations must reach before they have securely surpassed the condition of societies being predominantly *un*civil.

By being youthful and peaceful, the majority of those participating in present uprisings radiate more hope than Nasserite pan-Arab nationalism ever contained. Their peacefulness conveys promise to non-Arab nations, and their youthfulness supplies promise to their own cultures. What matter still more are the concepts of society they bring forward to their citizenry. The best of those are anti-dynastic, non-patriarchal, and democratic. They reflect Alexis de Tocqueville far more than Ibn Khaldûn. They may be based on neither, but instead arise from a twentieth-century vocabulary of hope. They ignore the elite lockjaw that shuts down argument. They plunge instead into a pluralistic discourse for engaging whole populations. Regrettably, however, in the mega-model of hoped-for change, Egypt, SCAF's resort to military tribunals for trying civilians (estimates range from 5,000 to 20,000 in this first half-year) has an astringent effect on new latitudes of freedom. Worse still are those places, Syria and Libya most notably, where using armed force to shut people up is a habitual substitute for dialogue.

Shi'ite Absolutism, Sunni Royalty

The societies of West Asia ("Middle East") most markedly averse in principle to civil society are Iran and Saudi Arabia. Iran, of course, projects Persian values, and is therefore unlikely to adopt Arabian trendlines. More basically still: the ideology of its revolution against the Shah in 1979 has replaced a hereditary secular autocrat with his ecclesial equivalent, a Grand Ayatollah. Jurist-theologians are ascribed a Shi'ite infallibility, elevated in faith, practice, and policy. Their Supreme Leaders have con-

---

13. My outlook here was informed by numerous trips, as President of Eisenhower Fellowships, to Poland, Hungary, Czechoslovakia, Romania, and Bulgaria, 1985-92.

signed thousands to death in the 1980s (Khomeini) and treat articulate liberal democrats today to prison and torture (Khamenei).

Faith and the state are also interlocked, but differently, in the richest kingdom of the region. Saudi royalty and Wahhabi theocracy linked up a quarter of a millennium ago. No parliament threatens to contest the king; consultative councils are royally appointed; petitions come less from subjects than from those who might be called "abjects"; and women, half the population, have no legal standing at all. King Abdullah and his government pumped the equivalent of $5,000 per person into the social economy, and then revived a counter-terrorism law that effectually criminalized political dissent and would mandate ten years in jail for certain criticisms of the king or crown prince. While upheavals proceed elsewhere, the Saudi people appear lulled or even stupefied. When adventurous women proclaimed June 17, 2011, a day for themselves to drive in defiance of custom and police, only thirty or forty were estimated to have done so across the country. Twenty years previous, more women — forty-seven — had gone briefly to jail in Riyadh for taking the wheels of their cars.[14]

These two neighboring absolutisms, Iran and Saudi Arabia, loathe and fear each other. Upon the Persian/Arab divide is built Shi'ite/Sunni antipathy; and upon both is loaded national competition for regional influence. Their tensions recently came to a head in Bahrain, when the majority Shi'ite population arose to protest felt discrimination by King Isa Al-Khalifa and his Sunni elite advisors. Fearing that the meager freedoms already allowed would become the basis for further agitation, the government shut down the media, closed off the social networks, and physically obliterated the Pearl Square monument, so that no symbol or place might remain for the dissidents who camped there. Twenty-eight Shi'ite mosques were completely leveled, of which ten had been counted as historic structures.[15] Saudi troops and forces from the Gulf Cooperation Council were invited in as reinforcements where an estimated 100,000 people — one-seventh of the native population — had demonstrated. Even though organizers like Munira Fakhro, with decades of feminist experience, stressed national unity, many of Bahrain's Sunnis and neighboring Saudis want no

14. The figure "47" comes from my own interviews in Riyadh with two female drivers of 1991. Other information: //www.guardian.co.uk/world/2011/jun/17/Saudi-arabia-women-drivers-protest. . . .' //English.aljazeera.net/indepth/opinion/2011/06/201161694746333674.html.

15. On mosques: www.mcclatchydc.com/2011/05/30/114980/bahrain's-official-tally-shows.

event like Tahrir Square in the Gulf, fearing it would play to the advantage of Iran.

In the vortex of the Arab uprisings, royalty itself began to project its concerns. The Gulf Cooperation Council, a nest of rich familial kingdoms, extended invitations to membership far beyond its region, to Morocco and to Jordan. This hope of turning the affinities of monarchy into a wider political solidarity may be reckoned as one of the effects of the uprisings of 2011. But it might have less potential as a decisive trend than piquancy as a defining moment in the endangered history of Arab royalties. The most effective monarchical coping comes from King Mohammed VI of Morocco, who from the beginning of his reign in 1999 has tried to anticipate the people's needs and to preempt their demands. He has liberalized the family code and rights for women. He shrank demonstrations in 2011 by offering a constitutional referendum on July 1 that gave over several of his powers to a prime minister selected from the largest party in parliament. The populace, in a turnout of three-quarters of the electorate, overwhelmingly approved.[16]

Libya, Yemen, Syria

Libya, Yemen, and Syria complete the list of major national actors in the Arab convulsions. Their civil war, anarchy, and extreme repression respectively do not foster the creative discourse from which modern societies are built. Libya, even though its population of six million is less than a third of the other two countries, has long attracted attention because of the antics of its dictator, Muhammar Qaddafi. His ruthless killing of protesters triggered an intervention by NATO forces, which remained conflicted in motive and mission. To what degree was the intervention humanitarian (as Obama pictured it) and to what degree anti-immigrant (by fearful European countries)? To what degree protective of Libyan civilians, and in what measure protective of oil flow to the West? After a half-year of Arab uprisings, there was no sure answer to such questions, nor a clear outcome of the struggle. All the elements of civil war were present, including geographic split between status-quo government in Tripoli and rebel government in Benghazi.

16. Shadi Hamid, "The Monarchy Model," 1 July 2011, www.slate.com/id/2298194/; Ahmed Charai and Joseph Braude, "All Hail the (Democratic) King." *New York Times,* 12 July 2011, p. A21.

Yemen's troubles were embodied in its autocrat of three decades, Ali Abdullah Saleh. When he seemed an obstacle, agreements were brokered by the Gulf Council and encouraged by the United States that he withdraw from power in return for immunity from prosecution. Three different times on the verge of accepting them, he publicly reneged. He finally departed for Saudi Arabia for treatment of wounds received in an attack on his palace mosque. His country was in the grips of urban battle in Sana, Taiz, and elsewhere, colored by tribal divisions between his followers and the allies of the clan Ahmar. Blood feuds persist in Yemen, and are not conducive to solving its problems. At the bottom of the Arab League in GDP per capita, its 22 million people were "awash in weapons" while its oil reserves were emptying out and its water supplies were drying up. "Water stress" has been growing intense as annual demand exceeds renewable supply, with ground water seriously declining. Some urban housewives cannot wash dishes or flush toilets. Here human dignity was challenged in a fundamental way: compromised personal cleanliness. Could a new national culture emerge from the protests? After five months of campout, marches, lectures, and demonstrations focused in University Square, a detectible fusion was emerging of hip, academic, feminist, and liberal oppositionist values. But a similar long-term cultivation of solidarity was going on among nearby pro-government forces, making continued conflict certain.[17]

Syria's government has its uncompromising style in suppressing protest. When Iran does so by clubbing and jailing those who demonstrate, it is employing recent historical leverage from its revolution of 1979, by which it can brand any dissident as a counter-revolutionary. This charge benefits from the theological undertone conveyed by being the world's leading Shi'ite power, and the political overtone of having deposed the corrupt Westernizing Shah. The Syrian government has no such psychic resources. It is held together in its presidential family and its top military echelons by Alawites — a religious minority that may be characterized as Shi'ite or syncretist, depending on who is articulating its beliefs. And those Alawite leaders have, instead of a revolutionary heritage to draw on, the ugly memory of the father and uncle of the current leaders stomping down revolt of Muslim Brotherhood members in 1982 with many thousands of deaths.

The family clique of Al-Assad, involved in many businesses and en-

17. For an eloquent on-the-ground article regarding tribes and weaponed men, Robert F. Worth, "Yemen on the Brink of Hell," *New York Times Magazine,* 24 July 2011, pp. 26-31, 46-47.

twined in the apex of government, wield power for the interests of the military, intelligence, arms trade, and repression of protest.[18] As a family corporate conglomerate, their form of security-obsessed power replaces the old idea of dynasty. The regime of the Al-Assads does not believe in freedom of information. An American journalist friend of mine, in Damascus during the regime of the father, Hafez, witnessed a failed attempt to assassinate that president, and he accordingly filed a report to his wire service. He was then arrested, interrogated, and told he was disseminating lies. "But I *saw* it," he said. "No, you didn't," was the reply. With rubber hoses they beat the naked soles of his feet until he recanted; then let him crawl into a prison cell with dozens of other men and two buckets, one for drinking water and one for excrement.

Foreign correspondents in Syria have been disallowed since first demonstrations in March 2011. Social networking is severely truncated. Under those conditions, nonetheless, crowds gathered in Dera'a to protest the imprisonment of boys eight to fifteen years old who had scrawled anti-regime graffiti on the walls of their schoolhouse. When a thirteen-year-old youth, Hamza Al-Khateeb, was allegedly tortured to death and his penis cut off, photos of his corpse further stoked the fires of civil rage.

The regime replied through a careful account by the president of the Medical Examiners of Syria, who nervously testified on video that three bullets ("life-wounds, not torture") caused Hamza's death, that there were no signs of torture, and that his penis was undamaged, although the body had decomposed in the weeks that it had remained unidentified.[19] This death has nonetheless been made into a symbol of Syrian protest in the pattern set by the case of Khaled Said in Egypt: "We are all Hamza Al-Khateeb."

To this the regime's reply is more tanks, helicopter gunships, and loyal troops with machine guns. Elite brigades have gone to rebellious cities west and east along the northern border with Turkey and "pacified" them with violence or preemptive presence. These heavily Sunni tribal areas mutter darkly against the Alawite leaders of the country, and their own Alawite neighbors.

In Hama, 1982, government forces under President Hafez Al-Assad's brother, Rifat, killed 10,000 (some say 20,000). As struggle resumes and in-

18. bbc.co.uk/news/world/middle-east-13216195-"Bashar Al-Assad's Inner Circle," 18 May 11.

19. This video appears on YouTube as "Hamza Al Khatib-Truth of his Death." I cite it despite its unpersuasive tone and its unpopularity. Several other videos on Hamza are dramatically sympathetic to him, highly political, and much more often visited.

tensifies a generation later, another pair of brothers, Bashar and Maher, are poised to do the same, against demonstrators lightly armed or weaponless but willing to look death in the eye. Blood feuds run deep — still deeper when fueled by religion.[20]

Bashar Assad's speech of June 28 seemed less that of a determined dictator than that of a nerdy ophthalmologist, fingers dancing in front of his face, with forced laughter and nervous self-interruption. The response in Hama was a mass-energizing rap-chant with percussion: "*Get out, Bashar! . . . You're a wanted man in Hama! Get out Bashar! . . . Syria wants freedom!*" The rapper, Ibrahim Qashoush, was reported killed on July 3, throat cut to stop his chanting.[21]

Will crack Alawite divisions of the military become overextended, and sectarian fractures weaken the army? Those who think so see a regime that will "collapse in ultra slow-motion." Others observe, however, that until the opposition, toughened by battle, can hold together more securely than the state-military elites, the regime cannot be brought down.[22] All prospects are ugly. Relentless cruelty makes a society resolutely uncivil.

Gender Justice and Justice in General

For over a century, feminisms in the Arab regions and across the Muslim world have been produced by women, for whom stakes are higher than men in rethinking gender, religion, and culture.[23] In the uprisings of 2011, women are even more intensely than before registering those dynamics and seeking new definitions. It is far too early for conclusive summary, but not premature to look at specifics.

Tunisia, which abolished slavery more than a century before Saudi Arabia, remains a social leader among Arab nations. For their national election in late October 2011 all participating parties are required to list as

20. For historical ideology and emotion on this subject, see talismangate.blogspot.com/2007/05/new-syrian-group-delivers-anti-alawite-calling-card.

21. Sources: for Assad, YouTube.com/watch?v=xcs83sFOBAI; for Ibrahim Qashoush, chant, and throat cutting, see Ibrahim Qashoush.flv." by Abojibrih.

22. For the first view, Michael S. Doran and Salmen Sheileh, "Getting Serious in Syria," www.the-american-interest.com/article.cfm?piece=1001. For the second view, Joshua Landis to the author, 1 August 2011, and Syria Comment, passim on www.joshualandis.com/blog.

23. Margot Badran, *Feminism in Islam: Secular and Religious Convergences* (Oxford, Oneworld, 2009), p. 310 and *passim.*

many women as men candidates, and to alternate them on the ballots. The liberal Progressive Democratic Party, with co-leaders, male and female, says it had already planned to field gender in equal numbers. Al Nadha, which is a liberal Islamist party by regional standards even if conservative in the Tunisian value spectrum, supports the requirement, declaring that it had already developed a strong cadre of women to pursue its work when Ben Ali put many of its party's men in jail.[24]

Egypt, with over eighty million people, is by size and length of tradition closely watched, even if the phenomena permitted by the supreme military council are neither supple nor subtle. Young women such as the Coptic physician, Dr. Sally Tooma Moore, were leaders of the youth groups who took over Tahrir Square and made all the world hold its breath. Even a near-octogenarian slept out there, the aged and tested feminist Nawal al-Saadawi, whose novels and books had been banned. As a physician herself, psychiatrist, and long-time leader (first a victim at age six) in the campaign against female genital mutilation, her eminence had won her international notice. Then by the Sadat regime she was dismissed from her fourteen-year job in the Ministry of Health. When she wrote a memoir about her time in jail, she began it using a prostitute's eyebrow pencil and toilet paper. In Tahrir she knew she belonged. Her American friend, Islamicist Bruce Lawrence, managed to reach her there by cell phone. "Bruce, Bruce," she exclaimed in delight at the young people all around her, "they are *reading my books!*"

There were notable reversals as well. The male mob groping of American reporter Lara Logan was a frightening spontaneous incident. Systematically ugly, however, was the post-Mubarak incident of "virginity tests," as demonstrations continued for diverse causes. Young women were taken in by the military and, as alleged defense against false charges of rape, were stripped, photographed, and required to submit to medical proof (or disproof) of their virginity, restrained by female soldiers while a man in a white coat examined them. Widespread outrage in Egypt moved the military to disown this illogical and humiliating practice.[25] Rotten masculine intimidation arose again when a "Million Women March" was planned for March 8, International Women's Day, especially to protest non-inclusion of any women on the constitution reform panel then at work. Fewer than a thousand women appeared, and they were taunted and quickly disrupted by aggressive men.

24. *New York Times*, 9 Jun 11, p. A10.
25. Isobel Coleman, cnn.com/2011/OPINION/06/01/coleman.egypt.women/index.

Libya, in its civil war, has women far more prominent as victims than as leaders. Iman al-Obeidi, who complained of gang rape by Qaddafi soldiers, was then forcibly abducted by agents of the government from a hotel lobby where she was meeting with journalists.[26] After release from imprisonment, she left the country. A human rights group says that Hillary Clinton has helped arrange a flight to the United States for her and her father. Will the National Transition Council in Benghazi focus on countering such barbarities against women? The Council has only one female member.

A timeline of opposition in Syria bulges with religious contention and brutal repression, but not with female heroes. The government uses Bouthaina Shaaban, a British-educated scholar of Arab women and literature, to reach out to old oppositionists while young ones are disinclined to talk. Who will preserve the "canopy" of religious and cultural variety that has survived, even flourished, in Syria under minority sectarian power?[27] Gunships are not good for canopies. Fifteen hundred have already died, activists say, and over 10,000 have been arrested. Perhaps a lost provincial event will have to stand for female courage in Syria. When hundreds of men were rounded up in the villages of Bayda and Beir Jnad to crush dissent, two thousand women and children the following day blocked the coastal highway, demanding their release. "We will not be humiliated," they cried. And the authorities freed about a hundred men, some bruised and with apparently broken bones, to cheers and cries of triumph from the protesters.[28]

Yemen has been absolute last in the world in the Global Gender Gap Report ever since it was first published in 2006. It is likely to remain there, significantly below Chad and Pakistan. Sixty-seven percent of its women are illiterate. Of its 301 parliamentarians, just one is female. Above this data, a mother of three stands out. Tawakkul Karman is chair of Women Journalists without Chains, which addresses national issues not just of women, but of unemployment and corruption.[29] She has also orated to

26. The abduction appears on yahoo.com/video/play?p+iman%20%20obeidi&tnr. . . . More offensive detail is conveyed, compellingly, on YouTube, "Eman Al-Obeidi to Anderson Cooper (complete)."

27. Quotation from Malise Ruthven, "Storm over Syria," *New York Review of Books,* 9 Jun 11, pp. 16-20. "Women and the Rise of Religious Consciousness," by Anonymous, is a brave attempt, necessarily controversial, to open up the subject for Syria and the region: Joshua Landis, Syria Comment, 28 Sep 10.

28. huffingtonpost.com/2011/04/13/Syria-protest-women-block-highway+n_848475.

29. Alice Hackman, mideastposts.com/2011/03/03/tawakkul-karman-the-woman

crowds for four years, in weekly protests against the rule of Ali Abdullah Saleh; and she astonishes men that they are not only spoken to by a woman, but roused by her remarks. One woman does not make a political revolution, nor can one alone spark a gender transformation. Where there is one such as Karman, however, there are many others hoping for change and willing to do something about it. But does Yemen have sufficient cohesion in its makeup to prevail over its combustibility? The prospect of Saleh coming back as president touches in Tawakkul Karman a self-destructive anger: "If [he] returns and is president, people will blow themselves up. We will not care about our lives."[30]

Margot Badran has been surveying feminisms in Egypt and throughout Islam across four decades. The eighteen days of protest in Tahrir Square, getting millions beyond fear, have given her "jet fuel" of renewed optimism. Exclusion of women from the drafting committee of the interim constitution was a blow, but female lawyers and judges were freshly energized. She sees senior women as having the networks, standing, and skills for new achievement; middle-generation women as experienced and sensitized in development and human rights; and young women as "hellbent" on getting things done, working together with young men.

The sequence ahead on the Nile appears to be: elections late in 2011; constitutional matters percolating forward into 2012; revisions of the Muslim Personal Status Code and family law reform only possible after changes in the constitution, but likely to be deferred. Everything is up for grabs. But not everything will be transformed. Politically, Badran realizes, idealists will lose to hard religious forces and stiff patriarchalism if they insist too fiercely on gender justice. But this is the time to determine what is critical and to press for it. "Women . . . [like] citizens of all classes and religions . . . have plunged into the light of a free day . . . and cannot be deenlightened [from] . . . the revolutionary experience powered up in the first 18 days. . . . Part and parcel of this revolution [still] in the making is a transformational gender revolution, and with this the passage from patriarch[al] religion to egalitarian religion."[31]

-leading-yemens-protests/. Further on Karman, Asmaa Mahfouz, and Munira Fakhro is found in Natana DeLong-Bas, "Women of the Arab Spring. . . ." *Common Ground News Service*, 20 Jun 11.

30. *New York Times*, 11 Jun 11, p. A6.

31. Margot Badran to the author, 7, 8 Jun; 30, 31 Jul 11; extended quotation, 30 July. In addition to Ms. Badran, I am grateful for communications helping this essay from Mary French, Shadi Hamid, Joshua Landis, Bruce Lawrence, and Heba Ramzy.

Such views, I believe, do not require a miracle to be realized. They require work, today, tomorrow, and the next day. Time has shown that Ibn Khaldûn's philosophy of history is far from adequate to the present Arab era. *Asabiyyah* may explain how cities and civilization arose from Bedouin savagery. But cities are now a given, and civilization emerges variously in new dimensions. To evolve in the Arab regions, a new and greater cohesion is necessary beyond desert tribalism and between genders; and there must also be a new civil sensibility, accessible to minorities. Accompanying both, to ensure against Ibn Khaldûn's tedious cycles, probity is required in management of resources and in delivery of benefits to whole populations, not just to narrow elites and self-indulgent princelings.

Interviews

Religious, military, cabinet, academic, professional, and royal titles are generally omitted.
In a few cases where personal contact was not possible, dialogue was by telephone; in extremely rare cases, exchange was by e-mail only.

Indonesia

Ulil Abshar Abdalla
Amin Abdullah
Irwan Abdullah
Tanya Alwi
Dewi Fortuna Anwar
Rosihan Anwar
Sri Artaria
Azyumardi Azra
Zainal Abidin Bargir
Chatib Basri
Shukri Bay
Titot Soedjono Bay
Theophilus Bela
Harry Darsono
Herawati Diah
Juni Djamaluddin
Jetti Hadi

Wardah Hafidz
Meutia Hatta
Komaruddin Hidayat
Dana Iswara
Fuad Jabali
Nuraini Jatim
A. D. Kusumaningtyas
Amani Burahuddin Lubis
Musdah Mulia
Arief Mulyadi
Achmad Munjid
Thang D. Nguyen
Saparinah Sadli
Emil Salim
Ina Samadikun
Din Sjamsuddin
Hasan Soedjono

Rini Soewandi
Ahmad Suaedy
Juwono Sudarsono
Franz Magnis Suseno

Hidayat Nur Wahid
Yenny Zannuba Wahid
Galuh Wandita
Renée Zecha

Pakistan

Anis Ahmad
Nuzhat Ahmad
Durre S. Ajmed
Shahnaz Wazir Ali
Shagufta Alizai
Salman Ansari
Sultan Ul-Arfeen
Raja Ehsan Aziz
Farzana Bari
Mahmud Ali Durrani
Mohammad Al-Ghazali
Riazul Haq
Shahid Haq
Sufia Shahid Haq
Alia Hyder
Fahad Hyder
Maleeha Hyder
Muhammad Islam
Ahmed Raza Kasuri

Fehmeeda Kasuri
Abdul Khaliq Kazi
Tanwar Khalid
Abdul Bari Khan
Jamshad Ayaz Khan
Sahabzada Yakub Khan
Zaigham Khan
Shahid Mahmoud
Agha Masood
Zafar Ullah Mirza
Ashad Munir
Mufti Muzammil
Hafiz Aziz ur-Rahman
Amina Sajjad
Aliya Salahuddin
Sadiqa Salahuddin
Kazi Zulkader Siddiqui
Muhammad Taqi Usmani

Saudi Arabia

Abdulaziz M. Al-Abdulkader
Madeha al-Ajroush
Hamadi Ahmad Al-Aslani
Awwad S. Al-Awwad
Khalid I. Al-Awwad
Sara Al-Ayad
Majedah Bessar

Nadia Bukhardji
Fatin Bundagji
Laura Collins
Soad Al-Dabbagh
Abdullah Sadek Dahlan
Razi Ghazi
Jim and Lisa Greenberg

Saleh bin Hamid
Suaad al-Harthi
Mishael Al-Hegelan
Tanya Cariina Hsu
Seema Khan
Haifa Al-Lail
Saleh Al-Malik
Khaled A. Al-Maeena
Rashid al-Mubarak
Monera Al-Nahedh
Nimah Ismail Nawwab

Saad Abdulaziz Al-Rashid
Abdulwahab A. Al-Sadoun
Fahad M. Al-Safh
Muhammad Al-Saggaf
Nayef bin Sultan bin Fawwaz
    Al-Sha'lan
Asma Siddiki
Abdullah al-Salih al-Uthaymin
Faten Al-Yaffe
Yahya Al-Yahya

Kuwait

Badriya Al-Awadi
Rola Dashti
Mona Al-Saleh

Safia Al-Sharah
Asmahan Al-Shubaili

Iran

S. A. Abhari
Sudabei Agah
A. Alizamoni
Dr. Assidipour
Mehdi Golshani
Shiva Khalili
Soraya Maknoon
Farshid Mesghal
Tamineh Milani

Mohammad Reza Mohammadi
Mahnaz Nobari
Farhad Rahimi
Isa Saharkhiz
Daryush Shayegan
Nahid Tavassoli
Ebrahim Yazdi
Makan Zahrai

Turkey

Pelin Akat
Rengin Akillioğlu
Ayşe Gül Altınay

Kemas Aran
Zeynep Atikkan
Aydin Ayan

353

Can Ayan
Ali Bardakoglu
Fatma Benli
Figen Çeltekli
Ipek Nur Cem
Selehattin Çimen
Turhan Çomez
Suleyman Demirel
Tansel Demirel
Ali Doğramaçi
Sibel Eraslan
Bülent Gultekin
Dilavel Gürer
Talat Halman
Martin Heper
Aysil Karadesoğlu
Süle Kiliçarslan
Nezir Kirdar

Nezhoun Kirdar
Fehmi Koru
Hülya Kücük
Selin Kylycoğlu
Nilüfer Narli
Ahmet Önkal
Nicole Pope
Sami Selçuk
Farouk Seyrek
Zühtü Sezer
Nukhet Sirman
Hirşit Tolon
Semsettin Ulusal
Murat Yetkin
Yurdakul Yiğitguden
Vildan Yirmibesoğlu
Ahmet Turan Yüksel

U.S. and Global

Aziz El-Aguizy
Roger Allen
Mahmoud Ayoub
Margot Badran
Maarten Brands
Soheil Bushrui
Craig Charney
Katherine Clerides
Cathy Collins
Marcia Grant
Shadi Hamid
Claude Henrion
Rachid Kaci
Thomas Kessinger
Daisy Khan

Hala Al-Kholy
Joshua Landis
Bruce Lawrence
Luis Lugo
Neyson Mahboubi
Omar Mustafa
Syed Hossein Nasr
Kian Nobari
Valentina Qussisiya
Kavita Ramdas
Heba Ramzy
S. Abdallah Schliefer
Suzanne Siskel
Gisela Webb
John Wolf

Acknowledgments

I must begin with special thanks to those who gave me major networking help in obtaining interviews: Siti Nuraini Jatim in Indonesia, Sufia Shahid in Pakistan, Seema Khan in Saudi Arabia, Faézé Woodville in Iran, and Nezir Kirdar in Turkey. I am also particularly grateful to those who have commented critically on chapters in draft: on Indonesia, Siti Nuraini Jatim and Dr. Dewi Fortuna Anwar; on Pakistan, Dr. Durre S. Ahmed; on Saudi Arabia, Professor Roger S. Allen and Dr. Rula Jurdi Abisaab; and on Turkey, Nicole Pope and Zeynep Attikan. The chapter on Iran is more expressly personal, and perhaps because of that my critic never fulfilled her promise of comment.

I am warmly indebted to M. Claude Henrion, Paris, and to Professor Maarten Brands, Amsterdam, for discussions on the dynamics of Europe and Islam, which are beyond the focus of my work but are contributory to it. Likewise to Mrs. Daisy Khan for the privilege of allowing me to be the only male presenter and commentator to the July 2007 conference at the Pocantico Center, Tarrytown, New York, of WISE (Women's Islamic Initiative for Spirituality and Equality) of the American Society for Muslim Advancement. And in October 2008, to the extraordinary assembly of the Liberal Islamic network, Indonesian feminists, and various others gathered by Guntur Ramly at Utan Kayu, the intellectual center founded by Goenawan Mohammad in working-class Jakarta. Other gatherings which have helpfully tested my thinking include CREA-Studium Generale of the University of Amsterdam; the History Honors Seminar of Dr. Patrick Dassen, University of Leiden; the graduate seminar of Prof. Leonard Swidler, Temple University, in Interreligious Dialogue; the Philadelphia

Committee on Foreign Relations; and the Foreign Policy Research Institute (FPRI, Philadelphia), where I am a Senior Fellow without stipend. FPRI has steadily maintained a focus on the importance of religion in foreign affairs.

I am proud to be published by the Eerdmans Company in its hundredth year; and am grateful for the special interest taken in the book by William B. Eerdmans Jr., the publisher, and by Norman Hjelm, his advisor. David Bratt, as editor, gave the work his steady and disciplined discernment. Willem Mineur's art team coped creatively with design. Erica Vinskie consulted independently on graphics. Gillian Grassie provided the index.

In William B. Goodman I have been lucky to have as agent and friend a man who loves books. For tender interest in this project from conception through production, I owe inexpressible thanks to Mary French.

THEODORE FRIEND
Villanova, Pennsylvania
July 2011

Glossary

Allah Arabic word for God.

dawa Activities directed toward educating non-Muslims about Islam, or converting them to that faith.

fatwa (Sunni) non-binding legal opinion of a jurist (illustrated in presumptive extravagance by Osama bin Laden's issuing *fatawa* [pl.] in his own name, despite his lack of legal standing in Saudi society).

fiqh Jurisprudence (most literally, "understanding"). A jurist may be called a *faqih,* or expert in understanding. Shi'ites venerate such scholars, most dramatically in the modern instance of the Grand Ayatollah Khomeini, whose concept of *velayat-e-faqih,* "guardianship of the jurist," was a precipitate of the Iranian revolution of 1979, and a premise of organizing the subsequent state.

fitna Chaos; particularly in Saudi Arabia and Iran, the moral and psychological disorder that accompanies or produces irregular sexual behavior.

hadith Recordings of the actions of the Prophet Muhammad, and his evaluative statements on practices of his time.

hajj Pilgrimage to Mecca as one of the "pillars" of Islam — for those physically and financially able. Undertaken in the twelfth month of the lunar calendar. *Umra* is a pilgrimage in any other month.

halal (permissible) and

haram (prohibited)
  Describe acts allowed or proscribed under Islamic law, especially with regard to consuming food and drink.

Hijra The name given to the migration of Muhammad and his followers

357

from Mecca to Medina, 622 c.e., which event determines the first month of the Islamic calendar.

hudud In shariʿa, a class of punishments for violations of the laws of Allah, as distinct from human law. Major offenses include theft, fornication, drinking alcohol, and (arguably) apostasy. Amputation of limbs for the first and stoning to death for the second have overfocused Western attention on these penalties, which are rarely invoked. The Hudood Ordinance of Pakistan (1979), however, so dramatically affected the social landscape there as to lead to partial repeal in the Women's Protection Bill of 2006.

Id al-Fitr (Indonesian: Idul Fitri) Feast of fast-breaking on the first day of the month following Ramadan. A major social and family event, including children.

ihsan Excellence in work and social interactions. This cultivation of inner virtue, with the guidance of Allah, is complementary to shariʿa, which is regulation of the outer dimensions of faith. *Ihsan* is a particular focus of Sufism.

ijtihad Independent interpretation; legal reasoning by a jurist; or in modern conditions, by an individual believer.

imam For Sunnis, a prayer leader; for Shiʾites, spiritual successors to Muhammad, or especially high-ranking clerics.

insan (Arabic) soul, human; (Indonesian) mankind; (Turkish) man, people, humankind.

jahiliyyah Ignorance of divine guidance; the condition of the Arabs before the coming of Islam.

jihad Spiritual struggle (the greater struggle, as defined by the Prophet). Also: armed struggle (the lesser struggle, according to Muhammad).

madrasa In medieval times, a residential college for the training of jurists. Today (particularly in Pakistan with the failure of public education), a secondary school as a seminary, a small percentage of which give instruction in militant ideology. In Indonesia, ordinary Islamic day schools *(madrasah)* are distinguished from religious boarding schools for advanced Islamic studies *(pesantrén)*.

Mahdi The messianic figure who will come in the end-time to establish just society on earth in preparation for the Last Judgment. For Shiʾites, the Mahdi is expressly the Twelfth Imam, who has been in occultation since the year 874 c.e.

masjid Mosque; place of daily congregational prayer.

namus (Arabic) "Virtue"; now a modern gender-specific concept, with meanings clustered around virginity and modest behavior of woman, as reflecting upon man, family, and tribe.

(Farsi) Man's honor derived from conduct of his womenfolk.

(Turkish) Honor, good name.

"pillars" The five essential observances required of Muslims: profession of faith *(shahadah);* five prayers daily; almsgiving *(zakat);* fasting during Ramadan; and a pilgrimage to Mecca for all who are physically or financially able *(hajj).*

Qur'an Sacred scriptures of Islam, believed by Muslims to have been revealed to Muhammad by Allah in Arabic, through the archangel Gabriel.

Ramadan The ninth month of the Islamic lunar calendar, in which Muslims are expected to be especially obedient and focused on self-discipline and charity. The most notable overt practice of Ramadan is fasting from dawn to dusk.

salafi Term of historic reference to the companions of the Prophet and their immediate successors as morally superior to later generations. In modern parlance, the term is applied to several kinds of conservative to hyper-conservative Muslims. Some of those may be *jihadists*, but the terms are *not* synonymous.

shari'a Islamic religious law derived in principle from the Qur'an and Hadith, regulating the lives of Muslims. Shari'a may vary considerably from one culture to another.

Shi'ite From *shi'at* Ali (the party of Ali [ibn-Abi-Talib]), cousin of Muhammad, his son-in-law, and the fourth caliph. For Sunnis he is the last of the four "rightly-guided caliphs" of Muhammad's inner circle. For Shi'ites, Ali is the direct spiritual successor to Muhammad, and the first Imam of the Twelve they historically recognize.

shirk (Indonesian: *syirik*) The sin of "associationism," or in the belief of the Wahhabis, the dilution of devotion to a unitary Allah by reverence for others; or, ipso facto, "polytheism."

Sufi Loosely, a mystic. Originally an ascetic regarding worldly things. Later, anyone adopting practices of mystical piety, some of which, such as veneration of saints in Pakistan and Indonesia, are considered *shirk* by Wahhabi.

Sunna The "way" of following the exemplary teaching and practice of the Prophet Muhammad.

tariqa Sufi social groupings institutionalized as orders with spiritual lineages. Of especial note in Turkey, where their modern political appetites are a cause of government surveillance.

tawhid (Indonesian: *tauhid*) The absolute oneness and indivisibility of Allah, the breaching of which is the sin of *shirk*.

ulama (Arabic singular: *alim*). Scholars of religion. In the Indonesian language, where context must supply number, *ulama* is both singular and plural.

umma The global community of Muslims.

velayat-e-faqih "Guardianship of the jurist," a theory of governance based on Islamic theology and law, particularly that of Ayatollah Ruhollah Khomeini, who gave lectures under this heading and published a book on it in 1970. It became a theoretical basis of the Iranian revolution of 1979, and of the constitution that followed.

Women's Apparel Because of the importance of modesty in Islam, both for women and for men, I group these female articles of clothing together for the reader's composite sense of their function as outer garments. The list proceeds roughly from greater to lesser covering. A foreign vocabulary cannot do descriptive justice to items worn for religious, stylistic, class, and/or personal reasons, and which manifest many regional variations.

> *burqa* All-body veil. The most complete have only tightly meshed openings for vision.
>
> *çarşaf* Turkish body-veil.
>
> *abaya* In Arab regions, a long shapeless robe or caftan, usually black, generally worn with headscarf or veil. The *abaya* exposes only face, hands, and feet, and some women take extra precaution to cover those. Full and subdued covering is mandatory in Saudi Arabia, and is policed there.
>
> *chador* Iranian equivalent of *abaya;* also policed.
>
> *niqab* Face veil to accompany the *abaya* (esp. Arabic and Pakistani worlds). Covers all but the eyes, and sometimes the bridge of the nose.
>
> *hijab* Simply means "covering." The word generally means covering head, hair, and neck; but is sometimes used to mean a "regulation outfit," as in being *"hijabbed."*
>
> *jilbab* Indonesian term for a head covering that exposes only the face.
>
> *manteau* Iranian term for long, loose overcoat for women, or informal over-garment for those who choose not to wear *chador.* Must be accompanied by scarf or head-covering.

turban Turkish headscarf, often large and colorful, draping over shoulders and pinned under the chin. Tends to be worn by younger, educated women.

başörtüsü The more common Turkish headscarf, resembling the Slavic babushka. Mostly worn by older, Eastern, and/or lower-class women; but also marketed in high-fashion varieties.

selendang In Indonesia, a shawl or over-the-shoulder stole that can also be wrapped around head and neck in a mosque or other situation that requires covering. Sometimes used to carry a baby. The *selendang* may also be used by men: on the head for protection against the elements; as a sash for binding at the waist; or as a sling over the shoulder to carry food and water.

zakat Obligatory annual religious tax of one-fortieth of accumulated wealth; one of the pillars of Islam.

zina Fornication, adultery, or rape; an act of premarital or extramarital sex transgressing *hudud* laws.

Index